Justin McCarthy

Ireland Since the Union

Sketches of Irish History from 1798 to 1886

Justin McCarthy

Ireland Since the Union
Sketches of Irish History from 1798 to 1886

ISBN/EAN: 9783744679206

Printed in Europe, USA, Canada, Australia, Japan

Cover: Foto ©ninafisch / pixelio.de

More available books at **www.hansebooks.com**

IRELAND
SINCE THE UNION

SKETCHES OF IRISH HISTORY

FROM 1798 TO 1886

BY

JUSTIN H. M'CARTHY, M.P.

WITH COPIOUS INDEX.

Chicago and New York
BELFORD, CLARKE, AND CO.
1887

TO

THE RIGHT HONOURABLE

WILLIAM EWART GLADSTONE, M.P.

I DEDICATE THIS BRIEF RECORD
OF
A WRONG HE HAS DONE SO MUCH TO RIGHT AND

AN ENMITY HE HAS RECONCILED

PREFACE.

HOME RULE is the question of the hour. Every one is talking of it, thinking about it, writing upon it. The newspapers daily devote leading articles to the consideration of every phase of the subject, couched in the most contrasting terms of approval and disapproval. Most of them allot a portion of their columns to the reception of outside opinion of the most varied kind upon the problem. Statesmen of every school seem eager to express their views, on the platform and in print, upon the question whether Ireland is entitled to any form of self-government or not. Mr. Morley, Mr. Labouchere, Mr. Stead, and others write and speak upon the subject with the same cool, keen good sense, and the same steadfast adhesion to Radical principles, which make them the true representatives of a Radical Party in and outside the House of Commons. The so-called 'Unionist,' on the other hand, fumes and flares. He is consumed by fiery indignation. He is all for an appeal to the god of battles. The good old principle of might meaning right animates and sustains him, and his attitude towards the Irish people appears to be the old-fashioned 'Squelch them, by God!' one.

It is a relief to turn from letters and from speeches which, if uttered to express the other side of the case, and printed in the *Freeman's Journal* or *United Ireland*, or spoken on National League platforms by any prominent Nationalist, would have been denounced for their shameless attempt to sow dissension between the two races. It is pleasant to turn from such utterances to the letter from Mr. Ruskin which appeared in the *Pall Mall Gazette* on Tuesday, January 5, 1886. I am glad to be able here to express my gratitude to a great man, to a great Englishman, for having cared to remember just now, first, that the Irish 'are an artistic people, and can design beautiful things, and execute them with indefatigable industry;' secondly, that 'they are a witty people, and can by no means be governed by witless ones;' and, thirdly, that 'they are an affectionate people, and can by no means be governed on scientific principles by heartless persons.' If English statesmen had more often cared to recognise or to remember the truths which Mr. Ruskin so opportunely enforces, the question which is called Home Rule would not have so long and so profoundly troubled the minds of politicians and the time of Ministries.

At last, after a period of infinite pain and infinite patience, that proud patience which the gods are said to love, the Irish people have found their reward. The question of Home Rule has been at last admitted into the charmed circle—as unstable in its circumscription as the enchanted tent of the Eastern Pari Banou—the region of practical politics. It is some years since the words Home Rule became the watchwords of a political party; it is some years since they became the recognised war-cry of a devoted and determined minority in the House of Commons. Those years have been years of more than Egyptian trial to the Irish people. During their first days, in the age of what our opponents are now pleased to call the moderate Home Rulers, the English Press and the members of all English parties were well-nigh unanimous in their assurances that the question of Home Rule was inadmissible and undebatable, and that if we pleaded till the crack of doom no English statesmen would ever condescend to entertain any scheme whatever for the restoration of an Irish Parliament. Hearing, indeed, was not refused to us—occasionally. In that Saturnian epoch of amiable inactivity when Butt and Shaw swayed the destinies of an almost absolutely unimportant section of the House of Commons, the Government was wont, every session, to allow the Home Rulers a field-night for the exposition of their hateful but harmless doctrines: hateful because they were the expression of any discontent with the perfection of existing rule in Ireland; harmless because they were but the birth of a midsummer madness working on the brains of a few idle or eloquent politicians, and were about as serious a contribution to statesmanship as the desire of the moth for the star and the night for the morrow. So these field-nights came and went, and Mr. Butt made his speech and Mr. P. J. Smyth gave a well-prepared entertainment, in which the ideas of 1848 and the perorations of Henry Grattan formed an ingenious and not unattractive medley, and Mr. Butt's other followers said their permitted say, and were decorously listened to. Then the leaders of the Treasury Bench would make elaborate replies, in which the Irish demands were quietly puffed out of sight in a cloud of compliments to the sincerity and the ability of Mr. Butt, or Mr. Shaw, or Mr. P. J. Smyth. At this rate of progress any recognition of the Irish claim would have been accorded at the time when, according to Rabelais, the Coqcigrues come home—that is to say, never.

But towards the end of the last Parliament which Lord Beaconsfield presided over, the Home Rule party in the House of Commons began to display signs of unusual animation, of commotion, of agitation. Their languid ranks had been recruited by some new men, and the new men carried on the fight after new methods. This heralds the opening of the second period of Home Rule, the period of Parnell.

When the Liberal Government entered into office in the early spring of 1880, Mr. Parnell was the chosen leader of the Irish Parliamentary party. That party, in obedience to the wishes of the Irish people, sat in opposition to the new Government, and announced their intention of sitting in opposition to any Government that refused to recognise the right of Ireland to regulate her own local affairs after her own fashion. That resolve, apparently a slight thing in itself, had a deeper significance in it than many politicians at that time were keen enough to perceive. Up to that hour every Irish party in Parliament had been made the victim of a spurious tradition which forced them into an alliance with the Whigs, and dragged them helpless and hopeless at the tail of every successive Whig Administration or Whig Opposition. The recent elections, which have for the first time severed the connection between the Whigs and the Radicals by creating the amazing Whig-Tory alliance, were the fitting sequel to and the fitting justification of the attitude of the followers of Mr. Parnell in 1880. A few fossil members of the old sham Home Rule school persisted for some time in sitting below the gangway on the Government side of the House, but these have all vanished from the field of Irish politics, and their place knows them no more.

I am not going to tell over again here the history of the past six years as it affected Ireland in and out of Parliament. The Liberal Government, face to face with a small but solid group of Irishmen, who boldly avowed that they placed their own country's interest before the temporary interests of either of the two great parties, lost for a time its temper and its head. In defiance of the principles which are most dear to the Liberal mind, the Government determined at once to grapple with this defiant minority and crush them out of existence. Then began one of the most marvellous constitutional struggles which the world has ever witnessed. On the one hand was the most powerful Ministry of modern times, numbering in its ranks all the talent of its party, supported by a swollen and certain majority; on the other, a band of men, all unknown, almost all young, led by a young man who had only been a short time in the House of Commons, but to whom Ascendency already paid the compliments of a cordial dislike. The Irish nation at home, in England, in America, and in Australia, watched the contest with burning eyes and throbbing hearts. They saw their representatives expelled again and again, for fighting against coercive measures of new and miraculous strictness. They saw their country bound by successive Coercion Acts which recalled, by their ingenious ferocity, the pleasant days of the Penal Laws. They saw their leaders imprisoned for failing to admit that the administration of Mr. Forster was the greatest blessing that heaven could offer them. They saw the degradation of Dublin defended by what it seemed not unfair to term executive conspiracy. They saw themselves reproached for crimes and outrages which were the direct fruit of the administrative folly of Mr. Forster. They saw, day by day, how the most influential voices of the English Press kept taunting the party which followed Mr. Parnell with representing in no sense either the Irish people or their wishes, and assuring them that, come what might, they should never, never have Home Rule.

Well, they saw all this, but they saw other sights which made their spirits more of comfort. They saw their leaders come out of prison as determined to carry on the struggle as when they went into prison. They saw victim after victim of the coercive laws sent as delegate of the Irish people to take a place by Mr. Parnell, and help him to fight for the cause in the House of Commons. They saw the fall of Mr. Forster.

They witnessed the resignation of Mr. Trevelyan. They saw the defeat of the great Ministry. They rejoiced at last in the adoption by England's greatest statesman of the principles for which they had so long struggled.

The bitter taunt which has been so often levelled at the Irish Parliamentary party, that they do not represent the Irish people, has been satisfactorily answered once for all. The principles which Mr. Parnell advocates have swept Ireland from the centre to the sea, and he returns to Parliament the unquestioned leader of a following of nearly ninety men, of whom no inconsiderable portion are recruited from that province of Ulster which was for so long the hope, the prop, and the garrison of 'Ascendency' in Ireland. With Derry and the west division of Belfast represented by Irish Nationalists, arguments based on the hostility of Ulster to Home Rule do not count for much. Lord Hartington finds some cheer in still repeating the old parrot cry. When once Lord Hartington gets an idea into his head, it is not very easy to dislodge it, and accordingly Lord Hartington still finds a strange delight in declaring that Ireland cordially detests Mr. Parnell and all his works and pomps, and is only coerced by the terrible National League into returning his lieutenants by enormous majorities. Horror of coercion in the mind of the upholder and the approver of coercive laws for Ireland seems to me as incongruous as the name of honour in the mouth of Joseph Surface seemed to Lady Teazle, or as the name of God seemed on the lips of Margaret to the dying Valentine. If, however, Lord Hartington can really delude himself into the belief that Ireland sends eighty-five men to support Mr. Parnell in Parliament because Ireland distrusts and detests Mr. Parnell, I can only express my sympathy for those who see in Lord Hartington the future leader of the Liberal party.

The question that is before the English public just now is

simply this: 'Are you prepared to listen at all to the voice of Ireland, speaking as it does in strict accordance with constitutional tradition and usage through the mouths of a vast preponderance of Irish members, duly and constitutionally elected, and supported as it is by so large a proportion of the English people? or are you determined to deny to Ireland that expression of a national desire and that freedom of national government of which you are so proud to have been the champions in almost every other country in Europe?'

What, after all, is the meaning of this demand for Home Rule, of which in one way or another we have heard so much for the last decade? What is the demand which for so many years the leaders of the two great English parties have agreed in ignoring, and which now the real leader of the Tory party would be willing to satisfy, if by so doing he could deprive the leader of the Liberal party of the honour of carrying out the great work he has begun?

The opponents of Home Rule are, roughly speaking, of two kinds: those who refuse even to consider the question at all; and those who temporise with it, who do their best to dyke it back for the time being, for the hour, even for the minute, and who feel a curious gratification in the most temporary postponement of a puzzling problem. The first of these two classes of opponents of Home Rule has at least the merit of simplicity in its arguments. It boldly asseverates that Home Rule means dismemberment of the Empire, and it stubbornly refuses to listen to any argument which would interfere with that assumption. 'Dismemberment of the Empire' is its catchword, its counter sign; it has even become its war-cry. It repeats it, as the credulous might repeat some wizard's spell, in the hope of dissipating the danger which it believes to menace it.

In certain of his speeches, most notably that ever-memorable utterance at Newport, Lord Salisbury invoked Home Rule. When the invocation was answered, he seems to have shrunk from the consequences of his own temerity, and to be now nursing a baffled indignation because a stronger statesman than he has stepped boldly forward and prepared to deal righteously with the spirit of Irish discontent.

Mr. Gladstone lost a great opportunity when, after his visit to Ireland some years back, he failed to perceive the strength of the national demand, the keenness of the national desire for some form of home government. He lost some precious years in the effort to suppress the Irish party in Parliament, and in shutting his senses to the fact that they were strong because they spoke with the voice and acted with the strength of a people. But Mr. Gladstone was too great a statesman to let one lost opportunity prove the precedent for another, or to excuse loss of time in the past by losing more time in the present. The result of the two recent elections proves the strength of Irish Nationalism. That political map of Ireland which the *Pall Mall Gazette* published the other day, with its vast surface of white representing the constituencies which have returned Mr. Parnell's followers, and its pitiful patch of black in the far north to distinguish all that is left of Ireland which is not national, is the eloquent symbol of a more remarkable change than has ever been represented in any atlas of maps of Europe by treaty. If the voice of a nation is ever to count for anything, the voice of a nation has spoken in Ireland, and Mr. Gladstone has been too ardent an advocate of the rights of nationalities abroad to deny their existence at home.

If, however, any explanation of what Home Rule means is really needed—and I am compelled, to my surprise, to believe that it is, from hearing the question still so often asked, in all honesty, 'What do you Home Rulers really want?'

—I can explain what I mean by Home Rule easily enough. I should like to see, I hope soon to see, Ireland placed in much the same relationship to the Imperial Parliament as that in which a State of the American Union stands to the central governing body at Washington. That I consider to be, roughly speaking, the length and breadth of the Home Rule demand. It may perhaps, however, be well further to set down a few of the things that Home Rule does not mean.

It does not mean dismemberment of the Empire, or disintegration of the Empire, or any injury whatever to the Empire. It does not mean separation or anything like separation. It does not include any control of an army or a navy, or any power of levying what may be called Imperial taxation, or of negotiation with foreign Powers. It does not propose to abrogate in any way the Imperial functions of the English Parliament. It no more proposes to do any of these things than the State of Massachusetts proposes to do them.

What is there, then, so alarming in the suggestion of Home Rule for Ireland? Englishmen see with composure some form of Home Rule or other existing in all the dependencies of the Crown, from the great Antipodean colonies to the little Isle of Man, within almost a stone's throw of these shores. If Canadians and Australasians and Manx have Home Rule, and having it are happy and contented, and the solidarity of the Empire is in no way injured, but rather greatly strengthened thereby, why should it be denied to Ireland?

But if Home Rule for Ireland, some of our opponents argue, why not Home Rule for Scotland? why not Home Rule for Wales? To which I answer, question for question, 'Why not, indeed?' If Scotland and Wales desire Home Rule, I can conceive no just or even sane reason for denying it. If the Scotch people were to demand Home Rule to-morrow, with anything like the unanimity of the Irish people, we all know perfectly well that it would be conceded to them immediately, and almost without discussion. The reason why Scotland does not demand Home Rule as yet is because, up to this time, she has practically enjoyed the bulk of its benefits. Scotland has had her own way all along. She has worshipped in freedom at her own shrines; she has lived beneath the shelter of her own laws. When she wishes for greater freedom than she now enjoys, all she has to do is to ask for it and she will get it immediately. But because Scotland and Wales do not ask for Home Rule, and presumably do not want it, is no reason why Ireland, who does ask for it, and does want it, should be denied her petition.

Some writers and speakers have expressed a fear that, in the event of any system of self-government being granted to Ireland, the Protestant minority would suffer, in one way or another, from oppression at the hands of the Catholic majority. Such an apprehension is curiously unfounded. It is scarcely likely that a people, many, indeed most, of whose best beloved heroes were Protestants, and whose present leader is himself a Protestant, would be likely to prove in any sense or degree hostile to their Protestant fellow-countrymen. I may remind my readers that while Protestants have been returned, again and again, as representatives of Catholic constituencies in Ireland, that while Irish Catholics have, again and again, entrusted the representation of their grievances to Protestant delegates, it was until within the last few months practically impossible for any Catholic to find a seat in any English constituency. The present Parliament, upon its new and extended franchise, does contain a few Catholic representatives of English constituencies, but in the Parliament of 1880-1885 there was, I think, only one, and he was regarded as remarkable for having gained that rare and almost unattainable distinction. It is not long ago since the English

Press and English public opinion generally seemed unanimous in agreeing that the career of Lord Ripon as a statesman and politician was closed in England because he had become converted to the Catholic faith. On the other hand, I have heard that Catholic voters in Ireland have expressed regret that some Nationalist candidate was not a Protestant, in order that they might show their tolerance of a creed which was not their own, and in the present Nationalist party several Protestants are enrolled among its most prominent members. It is a matter of statistics, too, that a vast number of Protestant votes were recorded for the Nationalist and Catholic candidates at the just-passed general elections, a fact which serves to show that a very great number of the Irish Protestants do not share the apprehensions expressed for their safety by some writers and thinkers on this side of the Channel. The tolerance which English Protestantism has not always extended to Catholics, the Irish Catholics have always extended, and always will extend, towards their Protestant fellow-countrymen.

In the following pages I propose to sketch briefly the more salient features of Irish history since the Union, including, of course, certain of the events which heralded the Union. I do not propose in this volume to give a minute and exhaustive presentment of the history of eighty-six troubled years. Some parts will be dwelt upon at greater length than others. My aim is to present a sketch, not a complete picture; a sketch, however, that may be of service to the student of the Home Rule question.

I hope and believe that the time of Home Rule for Ireland has arrived. I am convinced that it will bring peace and welfare and content to my country. Her manufactures will again rise and flourish; commerce will once more visit the grass-grown wharves of her sea-cities, and fill the vacant spaces of those deserted buildings which now stand in ruined desolation, more melancholy than Karnak or Corinth. A people trained at last to patience and self-reliance will take a just pride in the fulfilment of those duties as citizens of which they have been so long deprived. The Church that has for so long guided the nation through darkness and the valley of the shadow of death will exercise its loftiest duty as the guide and guardian of a regenerated race. The Irish nation has been taking shape under our eyes; her children need now only the privileges of freedom to exercise those privileges worthily. The activity of the country will be directed into its proper channels. National occupation, and the responsibilities of administration, will bring with them those virtues of statesmanship which the Irish race have always shown in lands more happily ruled than their own. That national strength which now is spent, and rightly spent, in agitation for a great end, will be then employed in the fulfilment of those civic duties which the new conditions of political existence will create and establish.

Not to Ireland alone, however, will the advantages be limited. All that is to be gained from friendship instead of enmity, from trust instead of distrust, from loving fellowship and the heart's alliance instead of suspicion and the heirloom hate, all these may yet be England's if England choose. In God's name, is it not better to have, across that strip of stormy water, a nation of free men who are friends, fellow-workers for the Empire's welfare, firm allies in danger, than to be the most unhappy masters of an island of unconquered and insurgent bondsmen?

JUSTIN HUNTLY McCARTHY.

CONTENTS.

CHAPTER		PAGE
I.	THE PENAL LAWS	1
II.	THE PARLIAMENT	14
III.	THE VOLUNTEERS	29
IV.	NINETY-EIGHT	38
V.	THE UNION	56
VI.	CATHOLIC EMANCIPATION	75
VII.	DANIEL O'CONNELL	85
VIII.	THE TITHE WAR	102
IX.	REPEAL	109
X.	THE 'NATION'	117
XI.	YOUNG IRELAND	125
XII.	YOUNGEST IRELAND	133
XIII.	THE IRISH BRIGADE	141
XIV.	THE PHŒNIX CONSPIRACY	148
XV.	JOHN DILLON AND JOHN BRIGHT	156
XVI.	THE LAND QUESTION	168
XVII.	FENIANISM	177
XVIII.	DISESTABLISHMENT AND EDUCATION	194
XIX.	THE HOME RULE MOVEMENT	211
XX.	THE LAND LEAGUE	239
XXI.	COERCION	290
XXII.	ORANGE AND GREEN	311
XXIII.	HOME RULE	344
	INDEX	355

IRELAND SINCE THE UNION.

CHAPTER I.

THE PENAL LAWS.

IN Limerick city there stands a statue of one of the greatest of Irish patriots and one of the most gallant of Irish soldiers. It is the statue of Patrick Sarsfield, Earl of Lucan, and seldom was statue more appropriately situated than that of the heroic soldier within the compass of the city of the violated treaty. All that a man could do to secure the rights of his country, and the civil and religious liberties of his countrymen, was done by Sarsfield. His conduct of the immortal defence has been told a thousand times, but every fresh repetition of the familiar tale only serves to lend a brighter lustre to the genius and the courage of Sarsfield, and to add a darker stain to the faithlessness of those in whom Sarsfield, with the generous simplicity of a soldier and a gentleman, had been induced to place a mistaken confidence.

The siege of Limerick is one of the most famous events in history. Seldom have the fortunes of two countries and of two kingly causes depended more definitely upon the result of one single episode in a great campaign. The fight by the Boyne water, the capture of Athlone, the rout of Aughrim—all these defeats and disasters might yet have been repaired if only the siege of Limerick had ended otherwise, or, ending as it did, had been followed by faith from the victors. The cause of King James looked gloomy enough, but the cause of Ireland was hopeful. The Stuart prince had promised much, had performed somewhat. Poynings' Act had been repealed. A measure had been passed restoring the dispossessed Irish to their property. But the king lost heart and head in the hour of adversity, and, abandoning the Irish and the French who had served him so well, he fled with more than royal rapidity to France, and left the last act of the great drama to be played out without him by the Shannon River and behind the walls of Limerick. The Stuart princes, with all their faults, were not wanting in personal courage, although actual heroism was not included among their virtues then or thereafter. But James lives in the Irish ballad literature, which has preserved so well and so truly the salient features of her story at a time when any other kind of chronicling was wellnigh impossible, as 'Craven Shemus,' and under the burden of yet more uncomplimentary epithets.

James had fled and St. Ruth was dead, and the last hopes of Ireland were hidden behind the walls of Limerick, where Talbot of Tirconnel and Patrick Sarsfield were making the last stand. The two men were widely different. Richard Talbot, Duke of Tirconnel, witnessed as a youth the Cromwellian massacres in Drogheda. The memory of those horrors never left him, we are told. We may easily imagine that the lighthearted Irish nobleman, who plays so considerable a part in the De Grammont 'Memoirs' of the court of the second Charles, could not easily banish from his memory the fearful political baptism of his boyhood. Even in merriest and maddest hours, at Whitehall, while conversing with the 'languishing Boynton,' whom he afterwards wedded, or jesting with Killegrew and Hamilton and Buckingham, or losing money to his Merry Majesty, we can readily believe that often and often thoughts came across his brain which turned the lustre of the flambeaux to the glare of burning houses, the chatter of the courtiers to the cries of Cromwell's Ironsides, the soft speech of Lely's painted beauties to the groans of murdered women, and the shining Thames beyond to the Boyne, rushing fearful of its bloody foam to the sea.

Talbot of Tirconnel had always been faithful to the Stuart

cause. He had followed the young prince of the house to exile over seas; the historical 'twenty-ninth of May,' when 'the king did enjoy his own again,' was a glorious day in his eyes, as in the eyes of hundreds of other Cavalier gentlemen. Under the restored Stuarts he had been appointed to the Governorship of Ireland, the first Roman Catholic who had held the post since the introduction of the Protestant faith into the country. His rule was characterised by his strenuous efforts to undo the anti-Catholic legislation of the Ormond administration. The fact that he, a Catholic and an Irishman, should wish to see justice and religious liberty allowed to his countrymen and the companions of his faith, has made his name too often the object of the obloquy and the scorn of historians, who are unwilling to see liberty, either political or religious, enjoyed by any but themselves and their own people or party.

When the war between James and William broke out the Stuart king found his fastest and best ally in the Duke of Tirconnel. Talbot had been the Duke of York's closest friend and confidant; he was now, in the hour of stress, for a time the prop of his hopes and the buttress of his tottering throne. The Catholics in Ireland fought for the Stuart monarch less for that monarch's sake than for love of Talbot of Tirconnel and the name he bore. But victory went with William; and so, in course of time, Talbot of Tirconnel found himself shut up in Limerick to make the last stand for a lost cause, with only one man to help him in the inevitable hour. But that one man was worth a hundred, for his name was Sarsfield.

Sarsfield's courage and daring, his military genius, his ready enterprise and unfailing resource, had kept the flag of Limerick flying in the face of disaster after disaster. His famous midnight raid, which resulted in the destruction of the Williamite siege-train, is one of the most gallant, as it is one of the most desperate, deeds recorded in the history of the war. Perhaps, however, the qualities which most especially deserve our admiration in Sarsfield are the patient dignity and soldierly composure with which he consented again and again to take a secondary place to men of abilities and capacities infinitely below his own. The young Duke of Berwick, indeed, might complain that Sarsfield's imperial tongue, like that of Shakespeare's Suffolk, was sometimes 'rough and stern, used to command, untaught to plead for favour;' but the marvel rather is, that a man of the military genius of Sarsfield should have played so long and so patiently a secondary part to commanders so much his inferiors—and a man might be a very able soldier indeed, and yet remain inferior to Patrick Sarsfield—with no further display of impatience than an occasional rough word to a royal or semi-royal duke.

But a little while and Sarsfield was practically alone in Limerick. Tirconnel, whose body had long been wasted by disease, died suddenly of apoplexy. Death behind the walls of Limerick was a not unfitting close to a career that had practically begun behind the walls of Drogheda. Between those two fatal sieges how much that strange, brilliant, fitful life had experienced! Exile in Flanders, faithful adherence to what seemed a ruined cause, triumphant return, flight from Popish Plot phantasm and Titus Oates' accusations, the glitter and riot of an evil court, rule in Ireland, once again a struggle for the Stuart cause, this time going out for ever, and then the end. A month and a half after Tirconnel's death the treaty was signed, the city was surrendered, and Sarsfield marched out with all the honours of war.

All the world knows the eventful scene which followed. The standards of England and France, set up outside the city, wooed the Irish soldiery with a choice of foreign service. Out of fifteen thousand men only one thousand turned to the banner of the Boyne. The great bulk of the Irish army, with the exception of a few who chose neither service and sought their homes, rallied beneath the flag of France.

On the October morning of 1691 when the lilies of France and the standard of St. George floated opposite to each other outside the walls of Limerick, one Irish gentleman believed that he had secured for his countrymen something like due recognition of their political rights and their religious liberties. Patrick Sarsfield, as he watched the flower of the Jacobite army rallying beneath the French banner, must have rejoiced in his heart to think that his countrymen, who were thus marching with all the honours of war into foreign service, had left their country under the shame of no inglorious defeat and no humiliating subjugation. The Treaty of Limerick was signed and sealed. The first article of that Treaty promised solemnly that the Roman Catholics in Ireland should enjoy all the privileges in the exercise of their religion which were consistent with the laws of Ireland, or which they had enjoyed in the reign of King Charles II. As this was not precise enough, the article went on to say that, as soon as a Parliament could be summoned, the English sovereigns pledged themselves to procure for the Roman Catholics such further security in that particular as would preserve them from any disturbance upon the account of their religion. The thought of this article must have soothed the mind of Sarsfield on his way to exile. He may well have believed, in the fine words of John Mitchel, that he was leaving behind him as a barrier against oppression of the Catholics at least the honour of a king.

The honour of a king was as worthless as a dicer's oath. At lovers' perjuries Jove, according to Juliet, is said to laugh, but no poet has ever yet dared to fancy the Power of Heaven smiling upon the treachery of monarchs and the repudiation of solemn covenants entered into between State and State. There is a beautiful Irish ballad, with music melancholy as a caoine, which asks, ' Ah, why, Patrick Sarsfield, did we let your ships sail away to French Flanders from Green Innisfail?' If Sarsfield could have dreamed that the Magna Charta of his faith was but to prove the perjured preface to the Penal Laws, we may well be sure that the twelve thousand men who marched out of Limerick town, with colours flying and drums beating, to take service under Louis of France, would have whitened with their bones no 'far foreign fields from Dunkirk to Belgrade,' and that the blood of Landen would, indeed, have been shed for Ireland. But the hope of Ireland was across the seas; her leaders had kissed James's hand at Brest; the rank and file of the defenders of Limerick had become French citizens, when the monstrous perfidy of the English Government, in horrible travail, gave birth to the Penal Laws.

Sarsfield was dead before this. At the great overthrow, in July 1693, of the allies under William by Luxembourg, at the battle of Landen, he received his death-wound. Everyone knows the sad and lovely legend, according to which the dying soldier, putting his hand to his wound and drawing it back wet and red with his best blood, sighed out the heroic aspiration that that blood had been shed for Ireland. He died of his wounds a few days after the battle. His wife, Lord Clanricarde's daughter, married, some two years after his death, that very Duke of Berwick whose hot youth had protested against Sarsfield's superior judgment. It is one of the curiosities of history that almost all the women who were loved by the great heroes of Ireland married after the deaths of their lovers—Lady Lucan, Lady Edward Fitzgerald, the wife of Wolfe Tone, and Sarah Curran.

Historians of all schools agree in praise of Patrick Sarsfield. Macaulay, who had little love for Ireland and for any champion of the house of Stuart, admits that he was a 'gentleman of eminent merit, brave, upright, honourable, careful of his men in quarters, and certain to be always found at their head in the day of battle.' A Williamite historian, quoted by Mr. O'Callaghan, says: 'Arminius was never more popular among the Germans than Sarsfield among the Irish. To this day his name is venerated—*canitur adhuc*. No man was ever more attached to his country, or more devoted to his king and his religion.' It may, indeed, be declared that all Irish history does not boast a nobler gentleman than the gallant soldier, great of mind as he was gigantic of body, whose brave heart ceased to beat in the little town of Huy in 1693.

There were, indeed, penal laws existing before ever seal had been set to the Treaty of Limerick. Catholics were debarred from belonging to corporations; certain civil offices were closed against them; they were subject to fine for non-attendance at the places of worship at the Established Church on Sundays; and the Chancellor had the power of appointing a guardian to the child of a Catholic parent. But these penal laws were not very oppressively enforced in the days of Charles II. Catholic lawyers and Catholic doctors practised their callings comparatively freely. The very least, therefore, that the stipulations of the Treaty of Limerick could be tortured into meaning, guaranteed to the Irish Catholics the degree of toleration accorded to them under Charles II. But the Williamite Government soon showed that they preferred to act with a treachery unparalleled in Occidental history rather than continue to extend to the Catholics of Ireland even this miserable measure of toleration.

The Dutch general Ginkel, who had been most eager to swell the ranks of William with the heroic defenders of Limerick, was bitterly disappointed at the failure of his hopes. He endeavoured in vain to induce Sarsfield to remain in Ireland. Promises of all kinds were plentifully proffered, but Sarsfield was not to be tempted. He crossed the sea and laid his bright sword at the feet of King Louis. The French monarch, who thoroughly appreciated the value of his Irish adherents, welcomed the hero of Limerick, and immediately appointed him to the command of the second troop of the Irish Guards, the first troop being under the command of the impetuous young Duke of Berwick.

Up to this time Catholics had sat among the Lords and Commons of the Irish Parliaments. But on the assembly in 1692 of the first Irish Parliament held after the surrender of Limerick, an oath was framed by the Protestant majority and presented to all the members of both Houses. It must be remembered that the oath to be administered to Catholics had been specially provided for in the Treaty of Limerick. It called upon the Catholic subjects of William and Mary to swear allegiance to the sovereigns, and it was specially laid down by the famous ninth article of the Treaty that the oath to be administered to Catholics who submitted to the English Government should be this oath and no other.

This ninth article was the first part of the Treaty to be broken. The new Parliamentary oath was fashioned with horrible ingenuity to insult and outrage every Catholic. The Catholic Peers and Commons who had attended the Parliament of 1692 quitted the two Houses in indignation. From that hour, for more than a century, till the Parliament itself ceased to exist, no Catholic Irishman sat in his country's Senate. When a National Parliament again meets in Dublin it will be undoing by its presence not merely the evil work of the Act of Union, but the evil work of the Parliament of 1692.

All obstacles being thus removed from the National Assembly by this flagrant violation of the Treaty, the 'Ascendency' party were free to pursue unimpeded their process of repression. In 1695 the Viceroy, Lord Capel, summoned a Parliament, whose business it was to repudiate, one after another, the pledges and stipulations of the Treaty of Limerick, and to persecute the Catholics of Ireland with a ferocity which is without a parallel in the records of Oriental fanaticism. The wild multitudes who followed the conquering generals of Omar and Othman, and who offered the alternative of the Koran or death to the proud and populous cities of Syria, Persia, and Egypt, never attempted to impose upon their subordinated empires any code of laws so ingeniously intolerant, so fantastically cruel, as those which the Ascendency party in Ireland now levelled at a Catholic people and the Catholic creed.

In shameless defiance of the obligations of the Treaty of Limerick, and insolent disregard of the pitiful degree of tolerance towards Catholics which had been observed during the reign of the second Charles, the Parliament of Capel deprived the Catholics of Ireland at one blow of education, of arms, and of their priesthood. Sarsfield was in his soldier's grave when that 'honour of a king' to which he had trusted was thus perfidiously set aside. Certain historians have found some excuse for William of Orange and the part he played in this treachery. The Treaty, we are told, was violated against his will, and in spite of his own strongly-expressed resolution to keep faith with his Catholic subjects in Ireland.

In these arguments there is no excuse for William. In those days the kingly office was invested with more personal power than belongs to it now. A king still had some of the influence and incurred some of the obligations of his position. If the king's supporters had prized their master's honour at anything more than contempt, they would not have forced him to break his word. Nay, they could not force him. The whole point of the argument against William lies in this: they could but urge him to be untrue; they could not compel him. If William were unable to make his Ministers respect the royal honour he could have respected it himself and resigned his sceptre. He was not obliged to wear a dishonoured crown. But if, under no matter what pressure, he consented to be a party to the breaking of the Treaty and the persecution of the Catholics, the ignominy is as much his as if his were the tongue which first prompted the treachery and his the hand which first desecrated the Treaty.

Yet even Capel's Parliament, with all its hatred of the Catholics, and all the malignant ingenuity which turned that hatred into legal engines of oppression, was not comprehensive enough or thorough enough in its work to satisfy the Government. Capel and his creatures had done their best, but their work appeared clumsy and half-hearted to the statesmen of Queen Anne. It needed supplementing in the eyes of the politicians of St. James's, and supplemented it accordingly was. The perverted intelligence of Capel's colleagues had not made the life of the Irish Catholic so hopelessly unbearable as to afford any reasonable hope of his disappearing as completely from the valleys of Ireland as the wolf had been made to disappear from English forests. Fresh work was done under the viceroyalty of the last Duke of Ormond—he who died years after an exile, who owed his safety to one Catholic country, and a beggar, who owed his daily bread to the bounty of another Catholic country. What was begun under Capel and well-nigh perfected under Ormond, received some further additions under the first and even under the third George. But it is to the ten years which embrace the last lustre of the seventeenth century and the first lustre of the eighteenth century that the Penal Laws practically belong.

It is not necessary now—it is terrible to think that it ever could have been necessary—to waste any words in condemnation of these measures. Eloquence itself cannot add one stain to the shame or one sting to the horror of the bare recital of what these laws sought to do. Not even the genius of Burke, not even the eloquence of him ' on whose burning tongue truth, peace, and freedom hung,' can move the soul with a fiercer indignation than the mere enumeration in all their naked iniquity of what the Penal Laws were and what they were framed to accomplish.

Under the Penal Laws the Catholic population of a Catholic country were deprived of almost every right that makes life precious. Dopping, Bishop of Meath, had proclaimed from the pulpit that Protestants were not bound to keep faith with Papists, and the violation of the Treaty of Limerick had justified his utterance. Lord Chancellor Bowes and Chief Justice Robinson had proclaimed from the bench that the law did not suppose any such person to exist as an Irish Catholic. The Penal Laws certainly did their best to insure that no such person should exist as an Irish Catholic. In their own country Irish Catholics were shut out from every civil or military profession; from every Government office, from the highest to the lowest; from almost every duty and every privilege that can be obeyed or enjoyed by citizens. A Catholic could not sit upon the benches of the Lords or Commons of the Irish Parliament. He could not record his vote for the election of a member of Parliament; he could not serve in the army or the navy; he could not plead at the bar or give judgment from the bench; he could not become a magistrate or a member of a corporation, or serve on grand juries or in vestries; he could not be a sheriff, gamekeeper or a constable; he could not give education; he could not receive education; he could not send his children abroad to be educated. If in defiance of the law he, a Catholic, did send his child to receive in Continental colleges that knowledge which was refused at home, he was subjected to a fine of 100*l.*, and the child so educated was excluded from inheriting any property in Ireland or England.

Not only was the Catholic denied the practice of his own religion, but conformity to the Protestant faith was enforced by statute. Every Catholic was liable to a fine of 60*l.* a month for not attending a place of Protestant worship, and at any time any two justices of the peace could call a Catholic over sixteen years of age before them and bestow what property he possessed upon his next of kin if he refused to turn from his faith. Any four justices of the peace could, without the formalities of a trial, send any Catholic refusing to attend Protestant service into banishment for life. Every Catholic priest in the country pursued his sacred calling under a penalty of death. Deprived alike of his civil and religious rights, the Catholic was further plundered of his property. No Catholic might buy land, or inherit it, or receive it as a gift from Protestants, or hold life annuities or leases for more than thirty-one years, or any lease on such terms as that the profits of the land exceeded one-third the value of the land. Any Protestant discovering that a farm held by a Papist produced a profit greater than one-third of the rent could, immediately upon announcing this discovery, dispossess the Catholic owner, and seize the farm for himself. The estate of any Catholic not having a Protestant heir was gavelled, or divided in equal parts, between all his children. As cases occurred in which Protestants helped their Catholic fellow-citizens or relations by holding property in trust for them, it was made legal for any Protestant who suspected another Protestant of holding property in trust for a Catholic to file a bill against the suspected trustee, and, if he proved the case, to take the property away from him. A Protestant might at any time compel a Catholic to sell him his horse, however valuable, for 5*l.*, and the horses of Catholics could always be seized without payment for the use of the militia.

In order to guard against the consequences of any exasperation into which these laws might goad their victims, they were rigidly prohibited from possessing arms. Any two justices or sheriffs might at any time issue a search warrant for arms against any Catholic household. Any Catholic who was discovered with any kind of weapon in his possession was liable to fines, imprisonment, whipping, and the pillory. Not content, however, with depriving the Irish Catholic of all the rights of a free man, the Penal Laws aimed insidiously at his destruction by endeavouring to turn his own kin, his flesh and blood, his children, and his very wife against him. The eldest son of a Catholic upon apostatising became heir-at-law to the whole estate of his father, and reduced his father to the position of a mere life-tenant. An apostate wife was immediately freed from her husband's control, and assigned a certain proportion of her husband's property. Any child, however young, who professed the Protestant faith was immediately removed from its parents' care, and a portion of the parental property assigned to it. Furthermore, no marriage between a Catholic and a Protestant was recognised by the law. The fact that the husband and wife were of opposite faiths in itself rendered the marriage null and void, without any process of law whatever. A man might leave his wife or a woman her husband, after any period, no matter how long, of wedlock, free to marry again and bring a legalised illegitimacy upon all the offspring of the former marriage. Such is the catalogue of the provisions of the Penal Code.

The Code was well calculated to destroy for ever the Catholic population of Ireland. But it is the glory of the Irish people that they conquered, and were not conquered by, the Code. That proud patience which, according to the poet, the gods are said to love, was never more loftily displayed under circumstances of more heart-breaking oppression than by the Irish Catholics during the long horror of the eighteenth century. Of course there were some cases in which the tyranny of the law fostered a kind of servile homage to Protestant ascendency. 'I knew,' says Mr. O'Neill Daunt, 'one most respectable and very wealthy Catholic merchant who declared that, when a boy at school about the year 1780, he felt overwhelmed and bewildered at the honour of being permitted to play marbles with a Protestant schoolfellow.' But these were exceptional cases. To the majority persecution only stimulated the ardour of their devotion to their faith. The same persecution only lent a fresh courage and heroism to the ministers of that faith. Many and many a time were secret congregations fallen upon by the soldiers; many and many a time was the Mass-stone, the 'Corrig-an-Aifrion,' reddened with the blood of a martyred priest.

The ministers of religion were no less active in offering to their scattered flocks that education which the harsh laws denied them. On the highway and on the hillside, in ditches and behind hedges, in the precarious shelter of the ruined walls of some ancient abbey or under the roof of a peasant's cabin, the priests set up schools and taught the children of their race. With death as the penalty of their daring—a penalty too often paid—they gave to the people of their persecuted faith that precious mental food which triumphantly thwarted the efforts of the Government to brutalise and degrade the Irish Catholic off the face of the earth. In those ' hedge-schools,' as they were called in scorn, the principles of religion, of morality, and of patriotism were kept alive, and those elements of education which are the very life-blood of national existence freely dispensed. Eagerly as it was given, it was no less eagerly sought for. The readiness of the priests to teach was only equalled by the readiness of the people to be taught. The proudest place of honour in Irish history belongs to those hedge-schools and their heroic teachers. But for them the national cause and the national existence would have withered away under the blighting curse of the Penal Laws. From those hedge-schools came some of the brightest ornaments of modern Irish history. That great churchman who died a few years ago passed his childhood under the shadow of the Penal Laws. John M'Hale, Archbishop of Tuam, received at a hedge-school those early lessons which developed into that ecclesiastical scholarship and profound piety which would have done honour to the proudest epoch in the history of the Church of the West.

But though the 'unparalleled oppression,' as Burke called it, of the Penal Code might and did outrage and oppress, hang and scourge, fine and imprison, it could not succeed in degrading its victims. With all the bribes that it offered to apostasy, to family feud, and to infidelity in wedlock, it wholly failed to shake the loyalty of the Irish people to their faith and their affections. Few, indeed, were the renegades from their creed, few the unfilial sons, few the faithless husbands or the unworthy wives. The law might sanction and encourage the basest treachery and set a premium upon shame, but there was one thing it could not do—it could not make its victims treacherous or shake the unalterable firmness of their honour.

CHAPTER II.

THE PARLIAMENT.

It has been happily said that Ireland has no history during the greater part of the eighteenth century. What Burke called 'the ferocious legislation of Queen Anne' had done its work of humiliation to the full. For a hundred years the country was crushed into quiescent misery. Against the tyranny which made war at once upon their creed, their intellect, and their trade, the Irish had no strength to struggle; neither in 1715 nor in 1745 did the Irish Catholics raise a hand for the Pretenders. The evidence of Arthur Young shows how terribly the condition of the peasantry had sunk, when he is able to state that 'Landlords of consequence have assured me that many of their cottars would think themselves honoured by having their wives and daughters sent for to the bed of their masters; a mark of slavery which proves the oppression under which such people must live.'

To add to the wretchedness of the people, a terrible famine ravaged the country in 1741, the horrors of which almost rival in ghastliness those of the famine of 1847. Great numbers died; great numbers fled from the seemingly accursed country to recruit the armies of the Continent, and found death less dreadful on many well-fought fields than in the shape of plague or famine in their own land. Such elements of degradation and despair naturally begot all sorts of secret societies amongst the peasantry from north to south. Whiteboys, Oakboys, and Hearts of Steel banded against the land tyranny, and held together for long enough in spite of the strenuous efforts of the Government to put them down. If the military force,' said Lord Chesterfield, 'had killed half as many landlords as it had Whiteboys, it would have contributed more effectually to restore quiet; for the poor people in Ireland are worse used than negroes by their masters, and deputies of deputies of deputies.'

Bad as the condition of Ireland was, the English in Ireland proposed to make it worse by depriving it of what poor remains of legislative independence it still possessed. So early as 1703 a petition in favour of Union with England, and the abolition of the Irish Parliament, was presented to Queen Anne; its prayer was rejected for the time, but the idea was working in the minds of those—and they were many—who wished to see Ireland stripped of all pretence at independence afforded by the existence of a separate Parliament, even though that Parliament were entirely Protestant. Seventeen years later, in the sixth year of George I., a vigorous blow was dealt at the independence of the Irish Parliament by an Act which not only deprived the Irish House of Lords of any appellate jurisdiction, but declared that the English Parliament had the right to make laws to bind the people of the kingdom of Ireland. The 'heads of a Bill' might indeed be brought in in either House. If agreed to, they were carried to the Viceroy, who gave them to his Privy Council to alter if they chose, and send to England. They were subject to alteration by the English Attorney-General, and, when approved by the English Privy Council, sent back to Ireland, where the Irish Houses could either accept or reject them *in toto*, but had no power to change them.

The condition of the Irish Parliament all through the eighteenth century is truly pitiable. Its existence as a legislative body is a huge sham, a ghastly simulacrum. The Parliament was one of the most eccentrically composed, most circumscribed, most corrupt legislative assemblies that the ingenuity of man has ever devised. To begin with: no Catholic could sit in Parliament; no Catholic could even record his vote for a Protestant member. The Catholics were as absolutely unrepresented as if they did not exist; and yet they made up the vast majority of the population which the Irish Parliament tried to govern or misgovern, and by an amazing fiction was supposed to represent. 'The borough system,' says Mr. Lecky, 'which had been chiefly the work of the Stuarts—no less than forty boroughs have been created by James I. alone—had been developed to such an extent that out of the 300 members who composed the Parliament '—Mr. Lecky is, of course, speaking of the Lower House—' 216 were returned for boroughs or manors. Of these borough members 200 were elected by 100 individuals, and nearly 50 by 10. According to a secret report drawn up by the Irish Government for Pitt in 1784, Lord Shannon at that time returned no less than 16 members, the Ponsonby family 14, Lord Hillsborough 9, and the Duke of Leinster 7.'

That borough system was the successful means of corrupting both Houses. James I. had been earnestly remonstrated with for calling forty boroughs into existence at one blow, and we have it on the authority of Hely Hutchinson that the king replied: 'I have made forty boroughs, suppose I had made 400—the more the merrier.' A pleasant, statesmanlike, truly Stuart way of looking at all things, which was destined to prove fatal to the Stuarts and to nobler hearts and heads than theirs. Borough-owners who returned supple lieges to the Irish Parliament generally found their reward in a peerage. Thus, with a simplicity of corruption, the two Houses were undermined at once, for it is said that some half a hundred peers nominated no less than one hundred and twenty-three members of the Lower House.

The Irish Parliament was like one of those buried cities dear to Irish legend which lie beneath the waters of some legend-haunted lake. The dark waters of corruption covered it; there came a moment when those waters fell away and revealed an ancient institution, defaced, indeed, but still honourable and imposing; then the engulfing waves closed over it again, and it vanished—but not for ever.

Mr. Gladstone has summed up very happily the nature of Grattan's Parliament in words which apply appropriately enough to the condition of the Parliament which Grattan entered.

'I know,' says Mr. Gladstone, 'that it is exceedingly difficult to arrive at a clear and also a simple view of the state of Ireland under Grattan's Parliament. Ireland was at that time sharply and variously divided. Just let us consider the multitude of various and powerful interests that worked upon her destinies and fortunes. First of all there was a small section of the population who conducted the Government mainly with a view to jobbing and to personal interests—a very important section, on account of the power which they not uniformly, but frequently, exercised upon the English Government with regard to its policy in Ireland. Then there was the Presbyterian party. Though they were not less Protestant than the other, they had little or nothing to do with the Government. They, on the contrary, had at that period a strong inclination to Republicanism. Then there was the Executive Government and the British interest concentrated in Dublin Castle, which has ever since, and certainly recently, become a proverbial expression, conveying but little to the minds of Englishmen, but conveying a great deal to the minds of Irishmen. It exercised a great and powerful influence. Then I look at the Roman Catholic majority, but I cannot treat the Roman Catholic majority of that period as being entirely one. It is quite clear that both the Roman

Catholic aristocracy and prelates stood in a position distinct from the mass of the Roman Catholic people, and were liable to act on inducements held out to them from this side of the water. Then there was the great interest of the landlords. The Irish landlord of that time was a character not entirely devoid of certain attractive features. He was hospitable, he was high-spirited, he was bold; but still he had his interests as a landlord, and he worked for them pretty generally, although not with that rigour and severity in all cases towards the tenant of which I am inclined to believe that the nineteenth century in a measure has seen more than the eighteenth century. Then there was a body of Irish represented by Grattan and Ponsonby in Parliament, and by the greatest of Irishmen, Edmund Burke, on this side of the water. It is very difficult to get at the truth of Irish history with regard to this Irish Parliament. It was lamentably corrupt; it was liable beyond anything to influence, and to sinister influence; but there are certain things to be said in its favour. It made great and beneficial changes in the laws of your country. The distinction is to be drawn between the Irish Parliament before 1795 and the Irish Parliament after 1795, when a spirit of what may be called ferocious alarmism, instilled by the British Government and by the jobbing clique who called themselves Protestants, that is the Episcopalians in Ireland, took possession in the main of that Parliament. Before that time it had done many good things. Another good thing that may be said of it, I believe with truth, is this—I am not aware that upon any occasion it refused to do any good act for Ireland which the British Government and which the Executive of the country were willing and desirous that it should do. But I have to give it one other credit. Whatever vices it had, and whatever defects it had, it had a true and genuine sentiment of nationality; and, gentlemen, the loss of the spirit of nationality is the heaviest and the most deplorable and the most degrading loss that any country can undergo. In the Irish Parliament, with all its faults, the spirit of nationality subsisted, and I say with grief and shame that it is my own conclusion and my own conviction that the main object of the Irish Legislative Union on the part of those who planned it and brought it about was to depress and weaken, and if possible to extinguish, that spirit of Irish nationality. So much for Grattan's Parliament.'

It slowly drifted into the custom of sitting but once in every two years to vote the Money Bills for the next two twelvemonths. The Irish Exchequer derived half its receipts from the Restoration grant of the Excise and Customs; and the greater part of this money was wasted upon royal mistresses, upon royal bastards, and upon royal nominees. In the Upper House many of the temporal peers were Scotchmen or Englishmen, some of whom had never even set foot in Ireland. The actual Irishmen on its roll were mostly the corrupt purchasers of degraded titles. Its Spiritual Peers, foreign to the country by religion and by race, were so obnoxious even to men of that religion and that race, as to wring from Swift the satirical declaration that all the Irish bishops appointed in England must have been murdered on their way by highwaymen who stole their garments, and filled their offices in Dublin. The Lower House was torn by factions, which the English Government ingeniously played off against each other; it was crowded with the supple placemen of the Government, who were well rewarded for their obedient votes; the bulk of the House was made up of nominees of the Protestant landlords. The Opposition could never turn out the Administration, for the Administration was composed of the irremovable and irresponsible Lords Justices of the Privy Council and certain officers of State. The Opposition, such as it was, was composed mainly of more or less ardent Jacobites, and of a few men animated by a patriotic belief in their country's rights. These men were imbued with the principles which had been set forth in the end of the seventeenth century by William Molyneux, the friend of Locke, who, in his 'Case of Ireland,' was the first to formulate Ireland's constitutional claim to independent existence. His **book was burnt by the** English Parliament, but the doctrines it set forth were in themselves a living fire, and unquenchable.

During the reigns of the first two Georges, the Patriot party had the support of the gloomy genius and the fierce indignation of the man whose name is coupled with that of Molyneux in the opening sentences of Grattan's famous speech on the triumph of Irish independence. Swift, weary of English parties, full of melancholy memories of St. John and Harley and the scattered Tory chiefs, had come back to Ireland to try his fighting soul in the troublous confusion of Irish politics. It has been asserted over and over again that Swift had very little real love for the country of his birth. Whether he loved Ireland or no is little to the purpose, for he did her very sterling service. He was the first to exhort Ireland to use her own manufactures, and he was unsuccessfully prosecuted by the State for the pamphlet in which he gave this advice. When Wood received the authority of the English Parliament to deluge Ireland with copper money of his own making, it was Swift's 'Drapier's Letters' which made Wood and his friends the laughing-stock of the world and averted the evil. In Swift's 'Modest Proposal,' we have the most valuable evidence of the misery of the country. He suggests, with savage earnestness, that the children of the Irish peasant should be reared for food; and urges that the best of these should be reserved for the landlords, who, as they had already devoured the substance of the people, had the best right to devour the flesh of their children.

The year that Swift died, 1745, was the first year of the viceroyalty of Lord Chesterfield, one of the few bright spots in the dark account of Ireland in the eighteenth century. If all viceroys had been as calm, as reasonable, and as considerate as the author of the famous 'Letters' showed himself to be in his dealings with the people over whom he was placed, the history of the succeeding century and a half might have been very different. But when Chesterfield's viceroyalty passed away, the temperate policy he pursued passed away as well, and if we except Lord Fitzwilliam in 1795 and Lord Aberdeen in 1886, has seldom been resumed by the long succession of viceroys who have governed and misgoverned the country since.

In the meanwhile a new spirit was gradually coming over the country. Lucas, the first Irishman, in the words of the younger Grattan, 'who, after Swift, dared to write freedom,' had founded the *Freeman's Journal*, a journal which ventured in dangerous times to advocate the cause of the Irish people, and to defy the anger of the English 'interest.' In the first number, which appeared on Saturday, September 10, 1763, and which bore an engraving of Hibernia with a wreath in her right hand and a rod in her left, Lucas loudly advocated the duty and dignity of a free press, and denounced under the guise of 'Turkish Tyranny,' 'The Tyranny of French Despotism,' and 'The Ten Tyrants of Rome,' the Ministries and the creature whom his unsparing eloquence assailed. The Patriot party, too, was rapidly increasing its following and its influence in the country. The Patriotic party in Parliament had found a brilliant leader in Henry Flood, a gifted politician, who thought himself a poet, and who was certainly an orator.

Henry Flood was born near Kilkenny in the year 1732, an uneventful year which his birth makes eventful. Like Grattan he shone for a season within the walls of Trinity, but he chose to complete his education by the Isis instead of by the Liffey, and coming to England he passed some time in that scholastic region where 'the warm, green-muffled Cumnor hills' behold the towers of Oxford, and Bagley Wood, and Hinksey Ridge, and distant Wychwood, and 'the forest ground called Thessaly.' While Flood was at Trinity, a wealthy young man, of good family and influential connections, with a future opening easily and attractively out before him, there was a young sizar on the books of the college of whom he probably knew nothing and of whom the world was destined to hear much. There could hardly be two careers more widely separated by destiny than that of the son of the Chief Justice of the King's Bench in Ireland, rich, well-favoured, surrounded by friends and admirers, and the poor, wild, reckless, good-humoured lad from the pleasant plain of Longford, who was always penniless and always merry and always idle, and whose face, so grimly seamed with smallpox, was always bright with humour and tender with pathos.

While Henry Flood was enriching his mind and ennobling his style in the classic shades of Oxford or the learned retirement of the Temple, Oliver Goldsmith was enjoying that 'thirty shilling' revel which was so disastrously interrupted, or dreaming of American emigration, or listening with an author's pride in his heart and an author's very scant remuneration in his pocket to his own songs sung by itinerant balladmongers at the college gates. Fortune was all smiles and roses for the one, all frowns for the other. Their lots were unlike in all particulars; but the goal of both was the same, and both attained it, for both alike had, if nothing else in common, the common privilege of genius. The rich young gentleman and the poor young sizar had no connection within the confines of Trinity, but they were destined alike to attain in widely-differing ways to fame and honour and an abiding-place in the memory of their country. Destiny has reversed their two positions, and the poor sizar is more famous than the colleague who seemed so high above him.

In 1759, while Goldsmith was struggling in London, writing 'The Life of Voltaire' and bringing out the *Bee* in miserable lodgings, Flood entered Parliament as member for Kilkenny. He was then but twenty-seven years of age, singularly good-looking, well-trained in mind and body for the political life on which he was launched. His Oxford hours had been devoted chiefly to the study of oratory, varied by the somewhat ineffectual pursuit of poetry.

He wrote an ode to 'Fame,' which was perhaps as unlucky in reaching its address as that poem to posterity of which poor Jean Baptiste Rousseau was so proud. But his oratory was a genuine gift, which he carefully cultivated. We hear of his learning speeches of Cicero by heart, and writing out long passages of Demosthenes and Æschines. His character was kindly, sweet-tempered, and truthful. He was ambitious because he was a man of genius, but his ambition was for his country rather than for himself, and he served her with a daring spirit, which only the profoundly statesmanlike qualities of his intellect prevented from becoming reckless. Two years after his election he married Lady Frances Maria Beresford, a wealthy match, which secured to him absolute independence to follow out his political career.

Flood soon found himself the most conspicuous man in the Parliament and the head of what may be called the Opposition in the Irish Parliament. The Parliament, thanks in a great degree to his genius and his labours, was destined to rise for a time out of its slough, and shine for a while resplendent in the eyes of all men. The Opposition hardly existed as a serious Opposition until Flood's genius and capacity for leadership welded it together into something like a homogeneous whole. Before Flood's time the nominal Opposition was made up chiefly of Jacobite adherents still dreaming in a dim kind of purposeless way dreams of a possible Stuart restoration, which the lessons of 1715 and 1745 had not quite cured them of, and of a small number of disinterested and patriotic men who struggled as best they might against the overwhelming injustice and corruption which they faced These men Flood rallied. These men, proudly accepting the title which their enemies scornfully gave them of the 'Patriots,' followed Flood zealously, and some of the oldest and basest privileges of the Parliament began to reel under the sturdy blows of the newly-inspired Opposition. Flood's best ally in his efforts was the man whose addresses a few years before had been burnt by the common hangman, who had been obliged to fly for safety into England, whom Johnson had hailed as 'the confessor of liberty,' and who now by Flood's side in Parliament was about to render the cause of Irish liberty sterling service by the publication of the *Freeman's Journal*, Samuel Lucas.

The first person against whom Hercules Flood flung himself in his effort with the Augean stable of the Legion Club was that strange ecclesiastic, famous among the infamous, Primate Stone.

Even as the most conspicuous supporter of the Irish interest during the first half of the century was the Dean of St. Patrick's, the two most remarkable supporters of the English 'interest' in Ireland in the eighteenth century were both Churchmen, the Primate Boulter and the Primate Stone. Compared to Stone, Boulter appears an honest and an honourable man. He was only shallow, arrogant, and capricious, quite incapable of the slightest sympathy with any people or party but his own—a man of some statesmanship, which was entirely at the service of the Government, and which never allowed him to make any consideration for the wants, the wishes, or the sufferings of the Irish people. Perhaps the best that can be said of him is that, while belonging to the English Church, he did not wholly neglect its teachings and its duties, or live a life in direct defiance of its commands— which is saying a good deal for such a man in such a time. So much cannot be said of his successor in the headship of the Irish ecclesiastical system, Primate Stone. The grandson of a jailer, he might have deserved admiration for his rise, if he had not carried with him into the high places of the Church a spirit stained by most of the crimes over which his ancestor was appointed warder. In an age of corrupt politics he was conspicuous as a corrupt politician; in a profligate epoch he was eminent for profligacy. In the basest days of the Roman Empire he would have been remarkable for the variety of his sins; and the grace of his person, which caused him to be styled in savage mockery the 'Beauty of Holiness,' coupled with his ingenuity in pandering to the passions of his friends, would have made him a serious rival to Petronius at the court of Nero.

Some ten years of persistent but unsuccessful struggling against the evils of the Irish Parliament resulted at last under the viceroyalty of Lord Townshend in a distinct triumph for the Patriotic party. Up to that time the Irish Parliament, unless specially dissolved by the sovereign, lasted for the whole reign, and George II.'s Parliament was in existence for no less than three-and-thirty years—more than a generation of men. In 1768, however, the duration of Parliament was limited to eight years, and the enthusiasm which the measure provoked lent a temporary lustre to Lord Townshend's administration. Lord Townshend—he was the brother of that Townshend who made the celebrated 'champagne' speech—had an important mission to fulfil, and a measure of popularity was of great importance to aid him in fulfilling it. The Irish nobility, with all their faults—and they had many and grievous—formed what was in a measure an independent Irish party. They might be hungry of gain, avaricious of place and profit, corrupt, but they in a measure held together and maintained the independence of the Irish Parliament. That independence Lord Townshend was commissioned to break up and destroy, but his efforts only broke up his own administration and destroyed his short popularity. 'Baratariana' literally blew him out of the island. Flood's ready pen counted for much in the merits of 'Baratariana.' His style was so much admired that his name has been included amongst the many candidates for the honour of having written the 'Letters of Junius.' It is certain that Flood did not write the 'Letters of Junius,' but he rendered his country a far greater service in writing the 'Letters of Syndercombe' in the 'Baratariana Papers,' which pulverised Lord Townshend.

In the construction of 'Baratariana' Flood had two colleagues: one, Sir Hercules Langrishe, a man of much merit, chiefly remembered as the recipient of Burke's famous letter; the other, the greatest Irish statesman of his age, Henry Grattan. Grattan and Flood were at the 'Baratariana' epoch the closest friends. In spite of the disparity between their ages, for Flood was some fourteen years older than Grattan, they had formed a warm attachment, based upon the similarity of their tastes, the kinship of their genius, their common political ambition, and their common love for their country. But what might have been one of the most famous friendships in the world became shortly after the 'Baratariana' epoch one of the most famous enmities in the world.

Mr. Lecky tells in his essay upon Grattan an affecting anecdote. After the death of Swift a paper was found in his desk containing a list of the Dean's friends, a list which Swift, with the melancholy irony of his nature, had classified as grateful, ungrateful, and indifferent. It is gratifying, though it is not surprising, to learn that the name of Henry Grattan occurs three times, and on each occasion it is marked as grateful. The verdict of history and the sentiments of his country endorse the judgment of the Dean of St. Patrick's. There is no man whose name is more truly 'grateful' to the Irish people, and if we cared to pursue the fanciful parallel further, we might even assume that there are three special episodes in Grattan's life, corresponding with the three entries in the list of Swift, which especially endear him to his nation —his connection with the Volunteers, his advocacy of the claims of his disabled fellow-citizens, and his heroic battle against the Act of Union.

Henry Grattan was born in Dublin, on July 3, 1746. His father, who was Recorder of Dublin, and member of the Irish Parliament, was a fierce-tempered, narrow-minded man, of a temperament always ready to entertain violent animosities, and to adhere stubbornly to them. Such an animosity he displayed towards Lucas; such an animosity he displayed towards his own son, Henry Grattan, for venturing to entertain opinions whose Liberal tendency was highly distasteful to the stern Recorder. When Grattan's father died, his animosity towards his son survived him, and manifested itself in his will, in which the family mansion was bequeathed to another. A small provision was, however, secured for Grattan through the influence of his mother, which enabled him to devote himself to the career he had marked out for himself. From his very boyhood he had distinguished himself by a passionate devotion to letters, and of all branches of human art that of oratory appeared at an early age to have the most attractions for him. After a shining record at Trinity he was called to the Bar, and crossed St. George's Channel to devote himself in London, in the Temple, to the profession which in the eighteenth century offered the most prizes to its disciples, the legal profession. But it seems certain that his rooms echoed more often to the sound of lofty passages of ancient and modern eloquence than to the dry repetition of leading cases. Oratory was the young man's passion, and in London he was able to gratify his passion to the full. London, in the middle of the eighteenth century, was a pleasant place enough for the stranger—even a dangerously pleasant place for the imprudent and unwary. But to Grattan the chief charm of London lay in its suburb of Westminster. He preferred the debates in the House of Lords to the attractions of the playhouse, the ambitions of the great man's levée, or the intrigues of the masquerade. The genius of Chatham taught him that oratory was as powerful as it had been on the Bema or the Rostra, and he listened with a breathless fascination to the majestic periods and glowing language of the foremost statesman of his time.

What he heard at Westminster Grattan studied, imitated, exercised himself upon in all manner of likely and unlikely places. We hear of an alarmed landlady imploring Grattan's friends to look after the wild young man who paced his room of nights when decent folk were abed, muttering to himself and apostrophising some mysterious individual whom he hailed as Mr. Speaker. Another even more fantastic story is recorded of him. Wandering one day in Windsor Forest he came upon an abandoned gibbet. His moody imagination—at that time his mind was strangely moody—fired by the strange scene, inspired him, and he was declaiming to himself energetically before the deserted gallows when his eloquence was interrupted by someone touching him on the shoulder, and on looking round he was addressed by a passer-by, whom the strange spectacle had attracted, with the whimsical query: 'Pray, sir, how did you get down?' a query significantly pointed by a gesture in the direction of the tenantless gibbet.

In 1768 he returned to Ireland to become the close friend

of Henry Flood, and, more gradually, of all the eminent men of the day. Charlemont, scholarly, travelled, urbane; Hercules Langrishe, whose services, says Burke, ' will never be forgotten by a grateful country '; Hussey Burgh, eloquent and eager; these and many others were in the nearest circle of Grattan's friendships. In such company his political zeal could not fail to flourish and his political ambition to increase. His rare talents were well known; his friends were influential; a Parliamentary career was essential. In 1775 he entered Parliament as member for the borough of Charlemont, to which he had been nominated by Lord Charlemont. He entered Parliament at a peculiar time—a time which afforded him an opportunity of immediately distinguishing himself, and his enemies of accusing him of acting ungenerously towards a friend.

Flood, most unfortunately for his fame, had gratified the natural desire of Lord Harcourt by accepting a lucrative office. As Vice-Treasurer he was practically muzzled, and the indignant Patriots found themselves without a leader. Grattan, by natural right stepped into the vacant leadership. It is probable that, even if Flood had not accepted office and alienated his party, Grattan's superior genius would have given him the leadership; but with Flood swathed and silenced by office, Grattan's only possible course and duty was to take the lead of the Patriot party, and he can in no sense be said to have acted unfairly towards Flood. Flood lost the confidence of his followers and his friends by his own fault; he could no longer lead his party, nor would the party longer submit to be led by him. Grattan came upon the scene in a timely hour to rally the Patriots and carry on the important work of opposition.

It is indeed deeply to be regretted that one result of Flood's action was the quarrel which followed between Grattan and him. Undoubtedly Flood's action in accepting the Vice-Treasurership seemed to Grattan an act of base political apostasy. On the other hand, Flood, striving eagerly to justify to his own mind his action, smarted at the swift success with which Grattan took his place as leader of the Patriots. The alliance between the two orators was definitely broken off. They had been the closest friends; they had worked jointly on that marvellous 'Baratariana' which upset Lord Townshend. They had seemed destined by their common genius and their common aims to be comrades for life. But the hot friendship cooled after Flood's acceptance of office; it was finally severed in the fierce discussion that took place between them some years later in the House of Commons, when Flood tauntingly described Grattan as a mendicant patriot, and Grattan retorted by painting Flood as a traitor in one of the most crushing and pitiless pieces of invective that have ever belonged to oratory.

CHAPTER III.

THE VOLUNTEERS.

ENGLAND's difficulty was Ireland's opportunity. Over in the American colonies Mr. Washington and his rebels were pressing hard upon the troops of King George. More than one garrison had been compelled to surrender, more than one general had given up his bright sword to a revolutionary leader. On the hither side of the Atlantic the American flag was scarcely less dreaded than at Yorktown and Saratoga. Paul Jones had found his world beyond the sapphire promontory of St. Bees, and the *Bon Homme Richard* was a name of terror still by Flamborough and elsewhere. Ireland, drained of troops, lay open to invasion. The terrible Paul Jones was drifting about the seas; descents upon Ireland were dreaded; if such descents had been made the island was practically defenceless. An alarmed Mayor of Belfast, appealing to the Government for military aid, was informed that no more serious and more formidable assistance could be rendered to the chief city of the North than might be given by half a troop of dismounted cavalry and half a troop of invalids. If the

French-American enemy would consent to be scared by such a muster, well and good ; if not Belfast, and for the matter of that, all Ireland, must look to itself. Thereupon Ireland, very promptly and decisively, did look to itself. A Militia Act was passed empowering the formation of volunteer corps—consisting, of course, solely of Protestants—for the defence of the island. A fever of military enthusiasm swept over the country; north and south and east and west men caught up arms, nominally to resist the French, really, though they knew it not, to effect one of the greatest constitutional revolutions in history. Before a startled Government could realise what was occurring sixty thousand men were under arms. For the first time since the surrender of Limerick there was an armed force in Ireland able and willing to support a national cause.

Suddenly, almost in the twinkling of an eye, Ireland found herself for the first time for generations in the possession of a well-armed, well-disciplined, and well-generalled military force. The armament that was organised to insure the safety of England was destined to achieve the liberties of Ireland. England, in the fine words of Hussey Burgh, had sown her laws like dragons' teeth, and they had sprung up as armed men. All talk of organisation to resist foreign invasion was silenced; in its place the voice of the nation was heard loudly calling for the redress of its domestic grievances. Their leader was Charlemont; Grattan and Flood were their principal colonels; one of their chief patrons was Frederick Hervey, Earl of Bristol and Bishop of Derry.

James Caulfield, Earl of Charlemont, whose name will be for ever associated with the struggle of the Volunteers for liberty, was a high-minded and accomplished gentleman, scholar and statesman. His grave, handsome face, in which the air of sternness imparted by the intensely dark eyebrows, is softened by the kindly grace of the mouth, is as familiar to students of Irish history as the countenance of a friend. At the time when the volunteer movement gave him his prominent place in Irish history he was fifty-four years old. He had travelled much in his youth—much, that is, for an age in which the traditions of the Grand Tour still taught men to regard the circle of a few Continental towns as extended travel. He had been in Sicily; he had been in Greece, then almost an *ultima Thule* to travellers; he had been in Constantinople, and had formed a more favourable notion of the 'unspeakable Turk' than was then fashionable; he had been in Egypt—'that land of wonders,' as he called it—at a time when the 'Mille et Une Nuits' of the ingenious Galland was still almost a new book. He numbered among his close personal friends in London all that was cultivated, all that was brilliant and attractive of that strangely brilliant society. To read some of his correspondence is to live over again the age of Johnson, and to join fellowship with the famous shades of Boswell's biography. Querulous Italian Baretti, dashing Topham Beauclerk, Horace Walpole, Dr. Johnson, Goldsmith, Burke, Sir Joshua Reynolds—in a word, all that matchless world of men of letters, wits, statesmen, and artists were his closest personal friends. He was himself well fitted to take his place amongst them as a scholar and an author. His favourite study was Italian literature, of which he had a profound knowledge, and his translations of Petrarch may be found pleasing by the most enthusiastic admirer of the lover of Laura. 'One of the most accomplished persons of the time,' his biographer, Mr. Francis Hardy, calls him, 'and certainly as amiable, as patriotic, and truly honest man as ever yet existed in any age or in any country.' Such was the man whom destiny now called upon to take the lead in one of the most remarkable military movements in history, and to write his name indelibly in the roll of those who have laboured for Irish liberty.

Seldom, perhaps, has a more eccentric figure strutted upon the stage of history than the Earl of Bristol, who was also Bishop of Derry. The Bishop was a son of the famous Lord Hervey, who wrote those memoirs of the reign of George II. which give us so living a picture of the stupidity and brutality of the Hanoverian king, and the corruption of his court. The memoir-writing Lord Hervey was not a very admirable specimen of the last century gentleman. Pope has gibbeted him for ever under the nickname of 'Sporus,' and there is little that is either honourable or attractive in the whole of his record. His marriage with the beautiful Molly Lepell, for whom Chesterfield wrote some famous verses, his absurd duel with Pulteney, his quarrel with Pope, his sickly effeminacy, which would have better fitted him for some place in the court of Heliogabalus than in last century London, which, with all its faults, was not unmanly—all these facts are familiar to us from the memoirs and the scandals of the Georgian age.

The son was worthy of the father. As unprincipled, as eccentric, as ridiculous as his sire, the Lord Bishop of Derry affected to be, on the one hand, a consummate dandy, and, on the other, to be not merely a profoundly cultured scholar but a great statesman. He had not, however, the physical feebleness, nor did he affect the contemptible effeminacy of his father. He seemed rather a combination of the typical Parisian *abbé* of the last century and the conventional soldier of fortune. If there were something in him of De Choisy, there was something in him also of Dougall Dalgetty, or Sir John Hawkswood. He loved splendour of all kinds; he loved gorgeous dresses; he loved to make himself conspicuous by any means and in any manner. He fancied himself to be the type of man who can dash off an epigram to a lady's lap-dog at one moment and direct the movement of an army at the next; who can sit up all night in a revel with boon companions and reel from the supper-table to dictate the terms of a treaty, or lay down the principles for some new scheme of mental or moral philosophy. He thought himself the Cæsar of the English peerage and the English Church; he was, in fact, a sort of vulgar caricature of Bolingbroke, with all Bolingbroke's most besetting weaknesses, and none whatever of Bolingbroke's ability. Such was the man who saw in the volunteer movement the opportunity for making himself especially prominent—who is said to have seen in it the opportunity for exchanging the mitre of a bishop for the crown of a king.

On a day early in the October of 1779 three men walked by the seashore at Bray, and talked of the strange fortune of their country while the autumn haze hung over the grey slopes of 'the year grown old.' There are few fairer sea-views within the compass of the world than that which presents itself to the wanderer along the Wicklow coast. Not where Parthenope sleeps in the blue embrace of the tideless sea, not where the rock of Palamedes overlooks the town of Nauplia, nor where the citadel of the Byzantine emperors frowns over the smooth waters of Smyrna Bay can a fairer prospect be found, or a nobler theatre for a scene in the arenas of freedom. The three men who trod that enchanted ground were Grattan, Hussey Burgh, and Daly, and their talk was of the Volunteers and the new power they gave to the Patriots, and of the coming session of Parliament. That morning gave birth to the resolve to demand free trade for Ireland, which found its realisation a little later when the Irish Parliament accorded its thanks to the volunteers for their exertions in 'defence of their country.' From that same morning's walk by the sea may be traced the steady progress of events which culminated at last in the Convention at Dungannon on February 15, 1782, when the Volunteers formed themselves into an organised convention for the purpose of agitating the national wrongs. Grattan was not, indeed, a member of this Convention, but he was heart and soul in sympathy with it. With statesmanlike sagacity he saw that with the existence of the Volunteers had come the hour to heal the hurts of the Irish Parliament, and he seized upon the opportunity. He had an army at his back; the Government was still striving with Mr. Washington and his rebels; it was out-manœuvred and had to give way, and to the formal national demand for liberty formulated by Grattan in his immortal appeal to the spirit of Swift and the spirit of Molyneux. All that Grattan asked for was granted; the hateful sixth Act of George I. was repealed. Grattan had, indeed, traced the progress of his country from injury to arms and from arms to liberty, and it was with no faltering voice that he wished her as a nation a perpetual existence.

Unfortunately for Ireland, the history of her Volunteers comes to an end with the opening of the brief chapter of her national existence. Unfortunately for Ireland, the genius of Grattan was not able to perfect the work it had so nearly accomplished. Grattan, backed by the Volunteers, had obtained the repeal of the famous Declaratory Act asserting the dependence of the Irish Parliament upon the English Parliament. In the accomplishment of this repeal Grattan and his friends saw the completion of their task; while Flood and his allies saw in it only the preface to a fresh and greater task. Repeal of the Declaratory Act was not enough, Flood urged; they must seek to win, while they still had the power to dictate terms, a full and formal renunciation of the usurped authority over the Irish Parliament. Flood, therefore, was eager for the retention of the Volunteers in armed existence to force the hand of England's tardy and reluctant justice. Grattan, who maintained that England had conceded all that could rightly be demanded of her, was no less eager for the immediate disbandment and dispersal of the Volunteers. He believed that their duty was done, and he saw in their further existence a Prætorian menace to the newly-acquired liberties which they had been so powerful in obtaining. Grattan carried his point; the full and complete renunciation which Flood desired was not won. Flood failed, too, in carrying the Volunteer Reform Bill for enlarging the franchise, and the Volunteers disbanded and dispersed. Wonderful as was the way in which they had come into existence, their dispersal was almost as wonderful. That vast body of men who yesterday were in arms to achieve their country's freedom, to-day had vanished, and left 'not a wrack behind.' The citizen army had been absorbed into civil life. 'The earth has bubbles as the water has, and these are of them,' we may imagine some English statesman saying, as the formidable array that had proved so threatening for a season melted out of existence at the bidding of Grattan.

The rise of the Volunteers and the repeal of the sixth Act of George I. had given triumph into Grattan's hands. But at the moment when the desires of the Patriot party had been apparently fulfilled the popularity of Grattan, by a curious example of the law of historical reaction, began to wane, and that of Flood, which had clouded over ever since his acceptance of office from Lord Harcourt's hands, began to wax anew. The difference of opinion between the two great leaders is eminently characteristic of their respective natures. Grattan maintained that by the repeal of the Declaratory Act England had sufficiently and practically abandoned her supremacy over the Irish Parliament. Flood maintained that the mere repeal of the Declaratory Act was not enough without a formal renunciation of the principle upon which that Declaratory Act had been based. Here Grattan showed a certain generous confidence in his opponents which Flood believed to be misplaced. Grattan, too, was convinced of the imperative necessity of immediately dissolving and dispersing the Volunteers. Their work, he contended, had been happily accomplished; their further existence would be a standing peril to the independence of Parliament and the liberties of the people. Flood, on the other hand, urged that Ireland had not yet accomplished much, that her independent Parliament was in sore need of reform, and that a nation in arms was in the only position in which it could reasonably hope to accomplish that reform in the face of so many and so powerful antagonists. Here, again, Grattan's was the more generous, Flood's the shrewder view of the situation.

Reviewing the opinions of the two men, it is difficult to avoid the impression that it would have been happier for Ireland if Flood had carried his point, while it is scarcely less difficult not to feel greater admiration for the loftier theories of Grattan. If the world had been all Grattans, then Grattan's pure and high-minded principles would have been best for the welfare of the country. But, as the world contained only one Grattan, it is ten thousand pities that the advice of Flood was not followed, and that the Volunteers were not kept in existence, at least until some of the most crying needs of reform were satisfied. It is one of those cases in which, while the event proved Flood to have been in the right, we could wish for the honour of humanity that time should have justified Grattan.

Mr. Lecky thoroughly supports Flood. 'Had he succeeded,' he says, ' he would have placed the independence of Ireland on the broad basis of the people's will; he would have fortified and completed the glorious work that he had himself begun, and he would have averted a series of calamities which have not even yet spent their force. We should never have known the long night of corruption that overcast the splendour of Irish liberty. The blood of 1798 might never have flowed. The Legislative Union would never have been consummated, or, if there had been a Union, it would have been effected by the will of the people, and not by the treachery of their representatives, and it would have been remembered only with gratitude or with content.'

After the failure of his Reform Bill and the disbandment of the Volunteers, Flood retired from the Irish Parliament in despair, and, crossing the sea, sought and found a seat in the English Parliament. But, as Grattan said, 'he was an oak of the forest too great and too old to be transplanted at fifty.' The prematurely-aged man, with his countenance disfigured by disease, and his temperament embittered by long years of unpopularity, misunderstanding, and strife, was a very different being from the handsome, easy-tempered, happy-minded young man who, a quarter of a century before, had entered the Irish Parliament under such favourable auspices. His first speech in the English House of Commons was, unhappily, made in an Indian debate upon a theme of which he knew little, and though the House soon crowded to hear the renowned orator, the effect was disappointing, and Flood's discomfiture was rendered more painful by a fierce and contemptuous attack which was made upon him by another member the moment he sat down. After that Flood spoke seldom in Parliament, and after a while he retired from political life altogether, a disappointed, broken man. He died at his estate at Farmley, near Kilkenny, on December 2, 1791. He may be considered happy in escaping, even by this too early death, from the horrors of ninety-eight and the degradation of the Union, horrors and degradation which his shrewdness foresaw, and which his policy would have avoided.

When Grattan lay upon his death-bed, after his last heroic attempt to plead the cause of the Catholics at Westminster, some of his latest words were uttered in generous praise of the man who had been his closest friend and fiercest enemy; who had been for long his rival in oratory and in the affections of the Irish people; who was almost his peer in genius—Henry Flood. Grattan had outlived Flood by the length of nearly a generation of men; unlike too many statesmen, he had outlived also the passions and animosities of his hot manhood, and could afford, in his ultimate hour, to speak with decorous admiration of the man whom he had once confronted pistol in hand, whom he had more than once believed it his duty to denounce with all the vehemence and all the vigour of which he was capable.

The wild Bishop of Derry was very indignant at the dispersal of the Volunteers. His occupation was gone. He had little or no influence with the Volunteers, but it delighted him to believe that he was all-potent in the councils that directed them. He saw in himself the chosen leader of a great rebellion, holding in the hollow of his hand the destinies of nations, arbitrating between peace and war, and settling the Parliamentary independence of Ireland as easily as the appointment to a living. He drifted in disgust out of Dublin and out of history. He lived for a while in Naples a mad, foolish life, and died in Rome in 1803. Wiser heads and better hearts than the Bishop of Derry regretted the disbandment of the Volunteers. Flood was more far-seeing than Grattan in his policy. Englishmen and Irishmen, who are learning to agree upon so many great questions, may very well be agreed upon this point, that it would have been well to keep the Volunteers in existence yet a while. Had Flood's advice been followed it is possible that Ireland and England might at this moment be proud of the reformed Parliament; that Irishmen and Englishmen would have had no need to speak of ninety-eight.

Certain English statesmen are fond of asserting in the present day that Ireland is in reality devotedly attached to the English connection in its present form; that it is only the harsh voices of a discontented few which make themselves heard with the greater distinctness because of the general peace and contentment of the country. Yet the statesmen who deceive their followers, if not themselves, by such pitiful pretences, would be horrified at the bare idea of allowing Irishmen again to organise a volunteer force, to publicly arm and drill, to unite in vast bodies at great military conventions. Luckily for Ireland, she no longer needs such volunteers to accomplish her purpose of a restored Parliament. In the unconquerable nationality of her children, in her friendship with true English Liberalism, in the determination and fidelity of her delegates to the English Parliament, in the wisdom of her leader, in the genius of the great English statesman who has eclipsed the fame of Fox and made himself the founder of a true union between the two divided countries, in the sympathy and the honest desire for justice of the English people, lie Ireland's hope and Ireland's certainty of perfecting the work of constitutional freedom which was begun by the Volunteers of 1782.

CHAPTER IV.

NINETY-EIGHT.

THE Parliament which Grattan and the Volunteers had created did much that was worthy of its founders, but the difficulties against which it had to struggle were too severe to allow the liberty-tree which had been planted to come to anything like a full maturity. Viceroy after viceroy was sent over to counteract by all the means in his power—and a viceroy in those days had many means—the gradual revival of Irish independence. The vast system of corruption which then existed rendered such efforts on the part of the viceroy comparatively easy, and practically placed the majority in the House of Commons in the hollow of his hand. Discontent and distress reigned over the greater part of the country. Religious feuds had broken out in the North, owing to the continued oppression of the supporters of the Ascendency party, who could not be induced to recognise the new spirit of toleration for the Catholic majority, which was gradually making its way into the political creed of the day. The feud, which gradually spread, was augmented and intensified by the existing system of tithes. The unpopular clergy of the Established Church paid little heed to their benefices. They left their very scanty congregations to be looked after by some unhappy curate, and followed themselves the majority of the landlord party in becoming absentees, and leaving to the middlemen and tithe-proctors the odious task of extorting from the suffering and reluctant Catholic population the heavy tithes enforced for the maintenance of the dominant Church.

It is small wonder that under circumstances like these there were disturbances in various parts of the country, and that secret and mysterious organisations came into existence under the guidance of an occult and potent Captain Rock, to protect the peasant against the tithe-proctor and the absentee clergyman. The Government, as usual, met the discontent and disaffection, which was engendered by misery, with coercion, and not with redress. Savage restrictive enactments were called into existence to curb the agitation which want and oppression had created. Under such circumstances, those Irish politicians who loved their country may well have thought that the work accomplished by the Volunteers was not sufficient, and it was time again to make an effort to protect the threatened rights and liberties of their country.

There was much to encourage a hopeful belief in the

success of any cause which had Right and Liberty for its watchwords. Just then France was giving, as she gave half a century later, the signal to Ireland to make an effort for self-redress. The French Revolution had just broken out. Its brilliant success had fascinated the minds of ardent politicians, whose better natures had not yet been revolted by the atrocities which later on disgraced and degraded it. When politicians of no very advanced temper, like Lord Charlemont and the members of the Whig Club, were celebrating with triumphant banquets the anniversary of the fall of the Bastille, and sending round such toasts as 'The Revolution' and 'The Rights of Man,' it is scarcely matter for marvel that younger and more impetuous spirits should have been fired by the example of democratic Paris, and thought that what the revolutionary clubs had accomplished across the Channel could be accomplished equally well in Dublin.

Grattan's first dream had been to obtain a free Parliament; his second was to make that Parliament worthy of its own freedom by recognising the right to liberty of the Catholics of Ireland. Catholic Emancipation was now the object of Grattan's ambition. The horrors of the Penal Code were no longer, indeed, enforced in all their naked brutality against the majority of the people of Ireland. In the words of Mr. Lecky, 'the Code perished at last by its own atrocity.' Its malignant ingenuity in the end defeated itself; to carry out with perfection and persistence the full clauses of that Code would have required the strength of a whole community as perverted as the original framers of the laws. Happily for human nature, no such corrupt community was to be found. The Irish Protestants sickened of the provisions of the Penal Code. Through the strength of public opinion most of its provisions fell into disuse, and only lingered in nominal existence on the pages of the statute-book. Even from the statute-book the clauses of the Penal Code were one by one being slowly effaced. In 1768 a Bill to modify the provisions of the Penal Code was passed in the Irish House of Commons and defeated in the English House. Relief Bills of various kinds were passed in 1774, 1778, 1782, and 1792. The effect of these measures was to restore to the Irish Catholics a large number of those rights and privileges of citizenship of which they had been so ruthlessly deprived. Most—but not all, nor the most important. The right to vote for representatives in Parliament, the right to enter Parliament, and the right to advancement in law or in arms were still sternly denied to them.

There was at this time a young barrister in Ireland who was looked upon by his family and by his friends as rather a hopeless kind of person. He had not employed his time at the University with that diligence which leads to the capture of academic honours, he had not devoted himself to his profession of the Bar with that patience and endurance which afforded any prospects of a Lord Chancellorship. He seemed to the sensible, prudent people with whom he came in contact to be a hopelessly lazy, impracticable young man, a dreamer of absurd dreams, with his head stuffed with fantastic political notions which no right-minded person could tolerate, or, indeed, understand ; the sort of young man, in fact, who never would come to anything, or bring credit upon his people. His name was Theobald Wolfe Tone. To Theobald Wolfe Tone, discontented with his lot, conscious, no doubt, of the waste of his fine genius in the narrow pursuits and possibilities of his daily life, and indignant at the oppression and injustice endured by his countrymen, the new ideas that were in the air very naturally commended themselves. It occurred to him that a union effected between the rising democracy in the North of Ireland with the long down-trodden and ignored Catholic interest might result in the creation of a formidable political party. He sketched out this idea in a pamphlet, and then went to Belfast and founded there a small association— destined to become one of the most famous organisations for political purposes ever founded—called the Society of United Irishmen.

Tone's pamphlet and Tone's organisation were the beginning of a new era. A branch society was immediately formed in Dublin, and joined by many conspicuous politicians.

Branches, too, were established in various parts of Ulster, and adherents came in with great rapidity. The objects of the Society would not seem to us of to-day to be very revolutionary, although they sounded horridly in the ears of the Ascendency. Every member of the United Irishmen pledged himself to use all his abilities to obtain an impartial and adequate representation of the Irish nation in Parliament, and to do all that lay in his power to forward a union of affection and of interest among Irishmen of all religious persuasions.

It must not be supposed, though it is too often imagined, that Wolfe Tone started with the desire of severing his country from all connection with England. Mr. Gladstone, in a recent remarkable speech, said very truly : ' If there is an Irish name associated with the idea of separation more than any other name, it is the name of Wolfe Tone ; but in the year 1791 Wolfe Tone declared that he was not favourable to separation from the British Crown. He declared then, what O'Connell declared afterwards in very clear terms, that the two countries were in his view to be united by the golden link of the Crown.'

It was at once resolved to hold a convention in Dublin after the fashion of the Volunteer Convention. On December 2, 1792, the convention met in Taylor's Hall, Back Lane, Dublin, and five delegates were chosen to present a petition to the king, praying for the restoration of his Roman Catholic subjects to the rights and privileges of the constitution. A month later the five delegates gave their petition into the hands of his Majesty, and the result was the Roman Catholic Relief Bill of 1793. So much the Government conceded to the new organisation, and to the feeling of alarm and insecurity caused by the rapid strides of the Revolution in France. But if the Government conceded something to the Back Lane Parliament, as it was called, with one hand, it struck at the existence of that body with the other.

A relief measure of any kind is always accompanied in the history of Ireland with a coercion measure ; and on this occasion the Catholic Relief Bill came into the world accompanied by three coercive measures, one of which—the Convention Act—was specially framed to prevent the possibility of any further Back Lane Parliaments dictating terms to the Government. As usual, coercive measures increased the disturbances in the country. United Irishmen became more active than ever in spreading their propaganda. And then the Government struck a decided blow at the new and dangerous body. Mr. Simon Butler, a brother of Lord Mountgarret and chairman of the United Irishmen, and Oliver Bond, were arrested, imprisoned, and fined. Hamilton Rowan, the secretary of the body, was arrested, imprisoned, and fined, but succeeded in escaping from prison to America. Wolfe Tone was to have been prosecuted, but, through the influence of powerful friends, he was allowed to go to America with his wife and family. Taylor's Hall, the Back Lane Parliament, was broken into by the police, and all the papers and United Irishmen were seized. An English clergyman named Jackson, who had joined the United Irishmen, was tried for treason in attempting to bring about an alliance with France. He would have been convicted on the evidence of the usual, and, indeed, inevitable informer, but he anticipated his judgment by committing suicide. The Government was under the fond impression that it had stamped out United Irishmen for good and all.

The very effort to suppress the United Irishmen, however, only gave it a newer and more dangerous existence. It had hitherto been a legal and constitutional body, acting, in accordance with the rights of every citizen, for the amelioration of the constitution; it was now to become a great secret society, spreading its influence into every part of Ireland, and having for its object the definite destruction of English dominion in Ireland, and the establishment of an Irish republic. Wolfe Tone, indeed, had gone away, in temporary exile, into the United States; but other and no less important leaders had joined the movement and filled his place. Wolfe Tone's absence was only temporary. He had said to a friend, as he was leaving Ireland, that he was going to France by way of

America. To Richard Lalor Sheil, it seems surprising that Tone should have cherished in the security and prosperity of his American home the revolutionary doctrines which drove him into exile. 'There,' says Sheil, 'in the bosom of his family, with a wife whom he adored, and children who shared in his idolatry for their incomparable mother, he might have had a long and prosperous life, if he knew how to form a just estimate of felicity, and could have appreciated the opportunities of happiness with which he was encompassed.' Sheil was a great orator, but he was not capable of understanding the principles which animated the nature of a man like Wolfe Tone. It evidently surprised him that an Irishman, with the opportunity of a comfortable and peaceful home in a foreign country, should really risk his welfare and his life for such a dream as patriotism—'perverted patriotism,' he calls the generous heroism which sent Wolfe Tone back from America to France, to Ireland and to his death.

Tone might well, however, have found encouragement for his action in the treatment received by Irish statesmanship of the most constitutional type. Grattan made himself the mouthpiece of a movement organised by the Irish Catholics in 1793, and having for its object the removal of these final disabilities. One of them Grattan succeeded in abolishing. In 1793, thanks to his efforts and his eloquence, the Catholics were admitted to the elective franchise. But in his second effort to allow Catholics to be elected to Parliament, Grattan failed. That failure and the recall of Lord Fitzwilliam precipitated the rebellion of ninety-eight. Despairing of the condition of his country, unable to sympathise either with the party of rebellion or the party of repression, Grattan retired from political life.

The United Irishmen had found other leaders during Wolfe Tone's absence. Of these the most conspicuous and the most famous was 'the gallant and seditious Geraldine,' who is dear to so many Irish national songs as 'Lord Edward.' Lord Edward Fitzgerald came of an ancient family, which on one side traced its descent from a proud Italian house, and on the other was linked with the line of the Stuarts. The courtly poet, Surrey, who had the misfortune to live under a monarch like Henry VIII., had loved a daughter of the house of Geraldine, and has devoted to her praise sonnets almost as sweet as those that were written in the native Tuscan of her race. It was of the Irish Geraldines that the phrase had come into existence that they were 'more Irish than the Irish themselves;' and more than one member of that brave and illustrious household had borne testimony to the truth of the saying with his blood. Latterly, however, the Geraldines had fallen away from their fame, and had ceased to play a conspicuous part in history. It was reserved for a young man, a soldier in the service of England, who had fought and bled in the American war, to revive the old glories of his race, and to lend them a brighter lustre.

Lord Edward Fitzgerald was almost the ideal hero of romance: young, handsome, brilliant, gallant, he shines in the darkness of the darkest pages in Irish history like the creation of a poet. It is easy to understand how Lord Byron was captivated by his story and by his untimely fate, and saw in him a magnificent subject for some future historical novel. There is a story, but we do not believe it, that Lord Edward Fitzgerald's beauty, bravery, and genius, were the means of inflicting a pang upon one of the most charming women of her time, and of causing a wrong to one of the greatest and most gifted of Irishmen. The legend is that Sheridan's beautiful and devoted wife fell hopelessly in love with Lord Edward Fitzgerald, and that her ill-fated passion hastened her death. Moore, however, denies the story strongly, and there is no reason for us to believe that the woman who was fortunate enough to have secured the homage and affection of Richard Brinsley Sheridan should have ever turned her heart towards another object, even were that another Irishman so handsome, so heroic, so accomplished as Edward Fitzgerald. Lord Edward Fitzgerald himself fell deeply in love with and married the fair and mysterious Pamela, who, in spite of the statements of Madame de Genlis, there is no reason now to doubt was indeed the daughter of Philippe Égalité. Fitzgerald adored his young and beautiful wife, who was, perhaps, hardly worthy of the devotion of that noble heart. It is curious to reflect that the three women whose names are associated with the three greatest figures of that revolutionary movement—the wife of Lord Edward Fitzgerald, the wife of Wolfe Tone, and the affianced bride of Robert Emmet—should each have injured the memory of the great men with whose lives they were associated by consenting to accept the love and names of others. The widow of Fitzgerald, the widow of Tone, and the betrothed of Emmet might well have been proud to have carried to their graves the names by which they were known to their patriot lovers.

The French Revolution had captivated Fitzgerald as it attracted Wolfe Tone. One small fact illustrates in a curious way the difference in the character of the two revolutionary leaders. When the United Irishmen in their early days insisted upon addressing one another after the fashion of republican Paris as 'citizen,' Wolfe Tone protested strongly against the innovation, very much as Mirabeau had himself protested against it. 'With your citizen, Riquetti,' said Mirabeau, 'you have perplexed all Europe.' Wolfe Tone protested scarcely less vehemently against the use of a title which did not really alter the relative positions of those who used it. But the imagination of Fitzgerald, on the other hand, was seized by the picturesque and poetic notions of equality, and he insisted at once upon dropping his own courtesy title and being greeted and addressed merely as Citizen Edward Fitzgerald. Fitzgerald's republicanism, his admiration of the Revolution, and his alliance with the daughter of Philippe Égalité earned for him the anger of his kinsmen and of his class, and the removal of his name from the roll of the British army. He threw himself with enthusiasm into the cause of the United Irishmen, worked vigorously with Oliver Bond and Thomas Addis Emmet and MacNevin and the other leaders of the movement, and went over to France on a mission to the Republican Directory.

Once again his alliance with the House of Orleans was injurious to him. The French Directory prohibited him from entering France, and he remained at Hamburg while other emissaries went to point out to the Republican Government the possibility of a French invasion of Ireland. Wolfe Tone, true to his promise of going to France by America, had now once more made his appearance in Europe. The eloquence and the arguments of the United Irishmen impressed the French Directory, and an army of invasion was organised under the command of General Hoche. But disaster attended upon all the attempts to land a French army in Ireland. The winds and waves, which had protected England against the Invincible Armada, protected her now against two successive expeditions. A third expedition was destined to be turned, not against England, but against Egypt.

In Ireland, in the meantime, things were going from bad to worse; the country was being administered by a system of savage repression which recalled the worst atrocities of the Cromwellian occupation. Martial law was made the excuse for every system of lawlessness, and the Catholic population were subjected to every species of outrage, of insult, and of injury. The actions of the United Irishmen were perfectly familiar to the Government. The organisation was literally infested with spies. Every needy placeman, every broken-down officer, every desperate adventurer, every scoundrel who could find no other occupation, joined the association, and made himself a hateful livelihood by selling its secrets to the Government. The Government could at any time have seized upon the principal leaders of the organisation; but the Government was playing a deeper game. It was determined to force the movement into open insurrection, in order that it might be justified in crushing it out more completely. Other Governments since that time have pursued the same policy, in days much nearer to our own. The policy was completely successful in the case of the United Irishmen.

Visitors to Dublin to-day, who wander within Trinity, may often have pointed out to them by their friends an elderly

man of scholastic appearance and academic garb, author of
'Who Fears to Speak of Ninety-eight?' There is something
very curious about the cloistered life of a man who gave to a
national movement one of its most powerful inspirations,
who enriched the literature of Irish discontent with one of
the most famous of rebellious ballads. For more than forty
years 'The Memory of the Dead' has been dear to the
hearts of Irishmen in every part of the world. When it was
written, when it first appeared in the pages of the *Nation*,
some of the 'brave, the faithful, and the few' still lived and
looked upon the sun. In foreign exile the hearts of Arthur
O'Connor, and Miles Byrne, of Wexford, still beat responsive
to the aspirations of Irish liberty. In the long interval two
fresh revolutionary efforts have been made. Through all this
great gap of time the author of the seditious ballad which has
'played so brave a part' has lived his quiet, studious life, in
self-chosen exile from the great world of politics, oblivious of
the fierce emotions and strong passions which he did so much
to stimulate. A Tyrtæus for ten minutes, he gave Ireland
an anthem, and then retired for ever into scholastic obscurity.
Rouget de Lisle, singing his one wild war song, which was
destined to become the voice not of one, but of a hundred
revolutions, and straightway sliding back again into nothing-
ness, an idle writer of foolish verses, known now only to the
curious, finds his historical parallel in this professor of
Trinity who was once the poet of rebellion. 'The Memory
of the Dead' was only a *tour de force* to him; it was destined
to become the hymn, the anthem, and the dirge of millions
of his countrymen.

Certainly the Government did everything in its power to
make 'Ninety-eight' an abiding memory with the Irish people.
It had bided its time patiently until it thought the moment had
come for swooping upon the United Irishmen and forcing a
futile insurrection. It nursed revolution with the cruel care
of the step-mother of a fairy tale. The country was ripe for
revolt. The infamies of Major Sirr's gang had roused the
anger and the indignation of others than revolutionary leaders.

The words, 'Remember Orr!' lingered on the lips of men who had never taken a secret oath. Men who might have been supposed to be friendly to the English Government were forced into horrified protestations against the atrocities which were being committed in the Government's name. Lord Moira, an Irish nobleman, who afterwards rose to high distinction in the English colonial service, spoke vehemently and earnestly against the way in which Ireland was being goaded into revolution. But his protest was met and answered by Black Jack Fitzgibbon, the hated Lord Clare, perhaps the basest of the many base tools that Pitt chose to employ against the Irish people. Sir Ralph Abercrombie was sent over to take command of the troops in Ireland, and was so disgusted with the disorder, the riot, and the undisciplined ruffianism of the soldiers placed under him, that he made a strong effort to curb their brutality; and when his action was not supported by the Home Government, he promptly resigned his command. The Government found a readier instrument in his successor, General Lake; and the picketing, the flogging, the torturing, and the bloodshed went on merrily as before. A recipe to make a rebel, which was popular in those days among Nationalists, ran thus: 'Take a loyal subject, uninfluenced by title, place, or pension: burn his house over his head; let the soldiery exercise every species of insult and barbarity towards his helpless family, and march away with the plunder of every part of his property they choose to save from the flames.' The recipe was excellent, and effected the purpose of the Government in enforcing the rebellion.

The Government now prepared to strike their final blow. Their favourite spy at the time was Thomas Reynolds, of Kilkea, the brother-in-law of Tone's wife, a man deep in the secrets of the United Irishmen. On March 12, 1798, the Dublin authorities, acting on the information of Reynolds, made a descent upon Oliver Bond's house, got in by means of the password supplied by the traitor, and seized Bond and thirteen delegates, with the most important papers of the United Irishmen. Lord Edward Fitzgerald was on his way to Bond's house when he received warning, and hid himself until he could head the general rising which was now resolved upon. But the Government spies were more than a match for the United Irishmen. Captain Armstrong, of the King's County Militia, who afterwards sent the brothers Sheares to the gallows, was, like Reynolds, deep in the councils of the United Irishmen, and faithfully transmitted to the Government all the plans of the proposed rising. Another traitor, Francis Higgins, the owner of the *Freeman's Journal*, sent word to the Castle that Fitzgerald was hiding in a house in Thomas Street. Major Sirr and a body of soldiers surrounded the house, and forced their way into the bedroom where Lord Edward was waiting unsuspicious of danger. Lord Edward knew well enough that there was small hope for a revolutionary leader who fell into the hands of the Government, and he offered a desperate resistance. In the narrow room he struggled with his assailants till the walls and the floor were splashed with his blood, and the blood of his enemies; and it was not until he had wounded one of his adversaries to the death, and was himself wounded in many places, that the soldiers were enabled to overpower him, and carry him to prison. In the prison Lord Edward Fitzgerald died of his wounds, and the revolutionary movement lost in him one of the bravest, the noblest, and the ablest of its leaders. To this day strangers in Dublin seek eagerly for the place where he met his death. Thomas Francis Meagher, in one of the finest of his speeches, speaks of 'the ducal palace in this city, where the memory of the gallant and seditious Geraldine enhances more than royal favour the splendour of his race.' The memory of Edward Fitzgerald, however, is more closely associated with that small, dismal room in Thomas Street, in which the last Geraldine who played any part in Irish history met his death.

The great insurrection which had been schemed out in the brain of Fitzgerald and his friends was destined to be dissipated in a series of untimely and unsuccessful local risings, the chief of which took place in Wexford. The rebels fought bravely, and in some parts, for a time, with something like success; but the odds against them were too heavy, and the revolution was crushed out with pitiless severity. The Catholic clergy played a conspicuous part in the rising. Many of them entered the rebel ranks, and led the rebel bands to action. Father John Murphy, Father Philip Roche, and Father Michael Murphy, were conspicuous among the revolutionary priesthood. The men who followed Father Michael Murphy believed him to be invulnerable; but he was killed at last by a cannon-ball at the fight of Arklow. Father Philip Roche also fell in battle. Father John Murphy, more famous perhaps than either of the others, and less fortunate in his fate, was captured and hanged. The assistance which the revolutionary party had hoped for from France came to nothing. A few troops, indeed, under General Humbert, did land in Killala Bay; but they were surrounded by the English at Ballynamuck, and compelled to surrender at discretion. The French soldiers were made prisoners of war; the unhappy peasants who were with them were slaughtered without mercy. The rebellion of ninety-eight was over. Many of its leaders died on the gallows. Bagenal Harvey, of Bargy Castle, and Anthony Perry, both Protestant gentlemen of fortune and position, who had been forced into the rebellion by the persecution of Government, were hanged. The two brothers Sheares were hanged. M'Cann was hanged. Of the other leaders, Oliver Bond died in Newgate; Arthur O'Connor, Thomas Addis Emmet, and MacNevin were banished. Arthur O'Connor entered the French service, and lived long enough to send, nearly half a century later, kindly messages of sympathy and encouragement to a subsequent body of revolutionaries—the Young Irelanders.

Great and unjust use has been made by the enemies of Ireland of some unhappy episodes in the history of the rising. It has surprised certain English historians beyond measure that a people goaded into frenzy by outrage, torture, insult, and oppression of every kind, should when their hour came have attempted some reprisals. The marvel rather is that so few reprisals have to be recorded. The Irish historian would be, indeed, happy who could say that rebel cause was unstained by other than the inevitable bloodshed of war. Unfortunately this cannot be said. 'Blood will have blood,' says Macbeth. It is not surprising that some fierce revenge was taken for the men who had been flogged, tortured, and murdered; for the women who had been outraged by a licentious and brutal soldiery.

Mr. Froude, who is at once the most famous and the most unfair of anti-Irish historians, seems almost paralysed with amazement because ignorant and unhappy men treated with merciless cruelty should have been cruel in their turn to their oppressors. Another historian of a very different temper from Mr. Froude has criticised Mr. Froude in language which it will be well to borrow. He sternly and justly condemns the atrocities that were committed by some of the rebels, but he goes on: 'An impartial historian would not have forgotten that they were perpetrated by undisciplined men, driven to madness by a long course of savage cruelties, and in most cases without the knowledge or approval of their leaders; and from the beginning of the struggle the yeomen rarely gave quarter to the rebels; that with the one horrible exception of Scullabogue, the rebels in their treatment of women contrasted most favourably and most remarkably with the troops, and that one of the earliest episodes of the struggle was the butchery, near Kildare, of 350 insurgents who had surrendered on the express promise that their lives should be spared.'

Even of Scullabogue itself another writer, the Honourable Lewis Wingfield, has written in his powerful novel, 'My Lords of Strogue,' after a fashion and with a temperance rare in those who write for an English audience—' the three hundred innocent women and children had been consumed as a holocaust on the altar of his Majesty King George, who, large-minded man, was consistently without mercy for the Isle which God had given to his keeping; who was pitiless for the professors of a faith which did not agree with his own fancy;

who, by reason of his policy regarding Ireland, must be held accountable for the tragedy which took place on June 5 within the barn of Scullabogue.'

If there had been during the last eighty-five years more thinkers and writers in England like Mr. Lewis Wingfield and like Mr. Lecky, in the temper in which he wrote 'Leaders of Public Opinion in Ireland,' and less like Mr. Froude, the quarrel between the two nations would not be where it is to-day.

It must never be forgotten by the serious student of ninety-eight that the rising was in no sense a religious war. The United Irishmen were organised openly first, and secretly afterwards, by Protestants; the most conspicuous leaders of the revolution were Protestants; some of its most famous martyrs were Protestants. Not only was the struggle not one of creed against creed, of Catholic against Protestant, but large numbers of Catholics were strongly opposed to the rebellion, and in many cases took active measures against it. Something of the character of a religious war was lent to the struggle in Wexford by the efforts of the Orangemen, but the movement as a whole was never of this complexion. The Irish Catholic race have never shown the slightest intolerance for the professors of the creed under whose special sanction the Penal Laws were promulgated. They have welcomed Protestant leaders in successive struggles, from the days of Grattan to the days of Parnell. The liberty of conscience which they asked for themselves, they have never sought to deny others. Ninety-eight, like the movements which succeeded it, was a national movement, an uprising against burdens too bitter to bear, and it was sympathised with and supported by Irishmen of all religious denominations, bound together by common injuries and a common desire to redress them.

There was still one more scene to be played out in the melancholy drama of ninety-eight. Some French ships were sent to Ireland, but were attacked by an English squadron before a landing could be effected. After a long and desperate battle the French were hopelessly defeated. A large number of French officers who were taken prisoners were brought to Lord Cavan's house on Lough Swilly. Among the guests there was Sir George Hill. Looking into the faces of the French officers Sir George Hill discerned one face very familiar to him—the face of an old college friend; the face of England's most dangerous enemy; of the most prominent of the Irish rebels—the face of Theobald Wolfe Tone. No one else had recognised Wolfe Tone. He was habited as a French officer, he spoke French easily, and everyone present assumed him to be a Frenchman—everyone with the exception of Sir George Hill. An honourable man would scarcely have cared to betray even his bitterest enemy under such circumstances; but Sir George Hill chose to play the Judas part. He went up to Wolfe Tone and addressed him openly by his name. Tone was too proud to affect further concealment. 'I am Theobald Wolfe Tone,' he answered to the greeting of his treacherous friend. He was immediately seized, and sent heavily ironed to Dublin. In Dublin he was tried by court-martial, and sentenced to death. As an officer in the French Republic he claimed his right to a soldier's death; he asked to be shot by a platoon of grenadiers. The members of the court-martial were inexorable. They had got their rebel, and they meant to show him no mercy. He was sentenced to be hanged.

On the morning fixed for the execution Wolfe Tone was found in his cell with his throat cut. There is some mystery hanging over these later hours of Wolfe Tone's life. It is said, and generally believed, that he strove to commit suicide in order to escape the indignity of being hanged like a dog, and to preserve the uniform of which he was so proud from disgrace. On the other hand, there are not wanting voices to maintain that Wolfe Tone was murdered in prison by those who feared that even yet he might escape the vengeance of the law. Indeed there was a chance of escape. Curran, heroically fighting his desperate fight single-handed for the men of ninety-eight, moved in the King's Bench for a writ of *habeas corpus*, on the ground that the civil law was still in force in Dublin, and that as Wolfe Tone held no commission in the English army, the court-martial had no jurisdiction. The point was an important one, and Curran carried, and obtained his writ. It came too late to save Wolfe Tone's life, but it saved him from a shameful death. His wound had not proved mortal, and he would have been hanged but for the arrival of the writ. He died of his wound in prison.

Some eighteen miles from Dublin, not far from the little village of Sallins, there is a little churchyard, the churchyard of Bodenstown. In that churchyard there is a little grave to which Irishmen make pilgrimages from all parts of the world. It is the grave of Theobald Wolfe Tone. Thomas Davis has devoted one of the noblest of his lyrics to the green grave in Bodenstown churchyard, with the winter wind raving about it, and the storm sweeping down on the plains of Kildare. Those see Wolfe Tone's grave best who see it under such aspects of earth, and air, and sky as Davis has immortalised in his poem. The desolate and deserted grass-grown graveyard of the little lonely church, ruined and roofless, the crumbling walls thickly grown with ivy, the mouldering tombs, are seen in their most fitting aspect on a sombre day, and under weeping heavens. When Davis wrote the poem no stone marked the grave. Since then the patriotic spirit of neighbouring Clongowes has railed it in with iron rails, wrought at the top into the shape of shamrocks; and the stone slab bears an inscription setting forth the name and the deeds of the man who lies beneath, and ending with 'God save Ireland!'

The rebellion of the United Irishmen had drawn into its eddies none of the leaders of the constitutional agitation. Neither Grattan nor Flood had ever belonged to the body, even in the days when it was an open organisation; and neither of them had any sympathy with its efforts, or had believed in its possible success. While the desperate struggle to which it gave rise was raging, they stood aside, dropped for the moment from the page of history, and their places were taken by a man no less gifted, no less eloquent, no less patriotic than either of them—John Philpot Curran. Curran, like Grattan and like Flood, had begun his career by trying to play on the double pipes of poetry and oratory, and like Grattan and Flood he soon discovered the superiority of his prose to his verse, and abandoned rhymes for rhetoric. Unlike Grattan, however, and unlike Flood, Curran might perhaps have been a poet. He has at least left behind him some verse which deserves to be, and will be remembered, while nothing of Flood or Grattan can seriously be said to have remained in literature. Curran's poem of 'The Deserter' is one of the most pathetic, and one of the most beautiful pieces of work in Irish literature.

Curran rose from very humble origin, by the sheer strength of his genius, to a high position in Parliament and at the Bar; and his patriotism was never sullied by the slightest political subservience. He had been remarkable before the rebellion broke out for his courageous defence of men unpopular with the Government. He had been threatened, like a new Cicero, with armed menaces, in his defence of Hamilton Rowan, but unlike Cicero he had faced the menaces undismayed. After the rebellion had broken out and been crushed, he made himself the mouthpiece of freedom, and championed one after another the causes of all the leading political prisoners with an eloquence, a courage, and an ability which have earned him immortal honour. It is one of the proudest features in the struggle of ninety-eight that it produced men of the robe who were worthy of its men of the sword.

CHAPTER V.

THE UNION.

'How did they pass the Union?' asked an indignant poet in the pages of the *Nation* more than thirty years ago; and he answered his own question very eloquently:

> By perjury and fraud;
>   By slaves who sold their land for gold,
> As Judas sold his God;
>   By all the savage acts that yet
> Have followed England's track—
>   The pitchcap and the bayonet,
> The gibbet and the rack,
>   And thus was passed the Union,
> By Pitt and Castlereagh;
>   Could Satan send for such an end
> More worthy tools than they?

The poet who penned that denunciation of the Union, of its agents and its accomplices, is now an eminent land commissioner and a graceful and cultivated man of letters, whose translation of the 'Chanson de Roland' has almost made that fine old epic a possession of the English language. Only the other day, in the House of Commons, England was reminded that Mr. O'Hagan, when this century was in its forties, uttered flaming treason under the signature of 'Sliabh Cuilinn,' and assured the supporters of foreign rule in Ireland that—

> We conquered once before, and now
> We'll conquer once again,
> And rend the cursed Union,
>   And fling it to the wind—
> And Ireland's laws in Ireland's cause
>   Alone our hearts shall bind!

The description of the Union, fiery, impetuous, and youthful though it be, is a sufficiently accurate presentment of the feeling which the Union inspired, and still inspires, in the minds of most Irishmen, which the Union now inspires in the minds of most Englishmen.

Bloodshed and bribery were the means by which the English Government accomplished the legislative ruin of Ireland. They had forced on a futile revolution in order that by crushing it out they might remove from their paths all the more dangerous obstacles to their scheme of destruction of Irish independence. The crimson year of ninety-eight had extinguished all possibility of active opposition to anything the Government might choose to attempt. The leaders of the national party were gone. Edward Fitzgerald was dead, the Sheares were dead, Wolfe Tone was dead, Bagenal Harvey was dead, Oliver Bond was dead. Some still lived, like Arthur O'Connor and Addis Emmet, but exiled for ever from Ireland. The spirit of the people, goaded for a moment into mad insurrection, was crushed by merciless retaliation. Blood had done one-half of the Government's work; it was now left for bribery to accomplish the other. All that was necessary was to obtain a Government majority in the Irish Parliament. That majority was to be obtained, like any other useful commodity, by purchase.

All the resources of the Treasury were employed to corrupt the corruptible. The flood-gates of the Exchequer were opened, and a very Pactolus drowned with its golden current the few dying sparks of patriotism and honour which may have lingered somewhere in the hearts of the majority of Ireland's representatives. The Parliament was a Danaë and Cornwallis a new Jupiter, dissolving himself into gold in order to work her ruin.

It must be recognised that Cornwallis, who, with all his faults, was a soldier and a gentleman, took no great delight in his part of Jove the Corrupter. Destiny was a little hard upon Cornwallis. Not many years before he had been compelled to strike his flag and surrender his bright sword to those hated American revolutionaries, who were driving out their masters in the name of the Continental Congress and the great Jehovah. Surrender was bad enough; but surely the part that Cornwallis was now called upon to play was infinitely worse. Better to surrender as a soldier than to succeed as the profligate buyer of a nation's liberty, 'I am kept here,' he complains in 1799, ' to manage matters of most disgusting nature to my feelings.' . . . 'My occupation is now of the most unpleasant nature, negotiating and jobbing with the most corrupt people under heaven. I despise and hate myself every hour,' he declares, 'for engaging in such dirty work.' And again the soldier spirit gets the better of him, and he cries out : 'I trust I shall live to get out of this most accursed of all situations, and most repugnant to my feelings. How I long to kick those whom my public duties oblige me to court.'

Cornwallis could not, however, afford to gratify his desire to kick the supple and servile majority whom he was employed to manipulate. With Lord Clare at his right hand and Castlereagh at his left, he went his way against the Irish Parliament, and won her as the Sabines won Tarpeia—with gold. It is said that when Castlereagh offered direct bribes to Shapland Carew, member for Wexford county, Carew threatened to expose Castlereagh's corruption in the House of Commons. Castlereagh answered the threat as Wilkes answered a similar threat of Luttrell's, by declaring that he should in that case promptly deny the charge. The story is characteristic of the man; Carew did not make his accusation.

When the Irish Parliament met in the January of 1799, the first hint at the desirability of Union was to be found in the speech from the throne. It was immediately and earnestly opposed by a man whose name was destined to become famous well-nigh a century later in the same struggle against the Union, Sir John Parnell. He held high office in the Irish Government when the attempt to effect the Union was first tentatively made. Sir John Parnell was resolute in his opposition. His determination immediately cost him his office. The Government was determined to strike, whenever they safely could, at all who resisted their overtures; and as Parnell was not to be influenced by the highest allurements that Cornwallis could hold out, he was promptly removed from his position as Chancellor of the Exchequer.

But, though the Government could deprive Parnell of his place, they could not silence him. The debate which he had inaugurated was carried on for two-and-twenty hours, and ended at last by giving the Government a majority of one. Such a majority was in reality a victory for Parnell and the Opposition; and on report, a fresh motion against the paragraph approving of Union was carried against the Government by a majority of five. For the moment it seemed as if the scheme of Union was defeated. But, though the Government was alarmed and annoyed by its failure, it was not seriously dismayed. It had evidently not been generous enough in its offers. It had not scattered its largesse with sufficiently comprehensive discretion and liberality. Heavy pressure was put upon all the placemen who seemed inclined to prove recalcitrant. Obedience to the Government, or immediate dismissal were the alternatives laid before them. For those who were not already in the Government pay, and in the Government power, no price was deemed too heavy. Place and office were lavishly distributed. Peerages secured the highest, and secret-service money won the lowest of those who were to be bought. Vast sums changed hands in the enormous bribery which, in the end, conquered the Parliament. The whole sum amounted to much more than a million; and in many cases the fortunate masters of many seats in the House of Commons received no less than 50,000l. as their share of the booty.

I have seen a very interesting letter from James Fitzgerald, dated Dublin, January 5, 1799, and addressed to 'Edward Malone, Esq., Queen Anne Street East, London.' It is endorsed by its recipient with a certain dry humour with these words : ' Overcharged, as almost every letter coming through the Irish Post Office is. E. M.' This letter was given to Mr. Parnell by a distinguished Irishman, an author and colonial official, on account of an allusion it contains to his ancestor Sir John Parnell's place being given to James Corry. It is sealed in red wax with an altar and a fiery heart. It begins: 'My dear Malone,—I am sure no circumstances within human foresight can prevent the alarming proposition of an Union. It is, I believe, determined to recur to every instrument short of the bayonet to carry it.' This sentence might be taken as the text for the history of the Union. The Government were prepared to use every instrument to carry their point. They might very well except the bayonet. It had been used to such bloody purpose already that there was little apparent chance of their being immediately called upon to resume it.

In the January of 1800 an Irish Parliament met for the last time for nearly a century. Its assembling found the Government party confident of victory, the Opposition desperate and despairing. It would seem that for a moment the Opposition dreamed of making that appeal to arms which they had regarded with such horror when it was made by the United Irishmen. But they made no such attempt. The Government was far too well prepared, and any effort of the kind would have been hopeless. Nothing was to be done but to discuss the merits of the Bill which was to deprive Ireland of her representative assembly, and to hope against hope that they might be able to defeat it. The tactics of the Government were ingenious. The address from the Crown contained no allusion to the threatened and dreaded Union. The very omission alarmed the Opposition, and a debate immediately sprang up upon a motion directly asserting the independence which had been obtained for the Parliament by the Volunteers in 1782.

It was curiously appropriate that in the very middle of this debate the man who had done more than any other to obtain the independence of the Irish Parliament should make his appearance, coming from his sick bed to fight once more for the liberties which were themselves in the throes of death. Grattan had faded for some time out of public view. He had no sympathy for the movement which Wolfe Tone had begun, and which ended with Wolfe Tone's death in a Dublin prison. But when the independence of that Parliament of which he was the parent was threatened, he came out of his self-chosen obscurity to fight one last fight in its favour. He came too late. The silver voice which had so proudly hailed the regenerated assembly, and wished it a perpetual existence, had no power to touch the hardened hearts or charm the deafened ears of the purchased Senate of Cornwallis and Castlereagh. Grattan himself was in some degree the cause of the disaster which was now about to fall upon his country. Animated by a too generous belief in the fidelity of his opponents' pledges, he had counselled the disarmament of the Volunteers, and his counsels had conquered the more prudent advice and the more far-seeing statesmanship of Flood. It was too late now to redress the mischief caused by this misplaced confidence.

Hussey Burgh's fine simile, taken from the legend of Jason, in which he compared the laws of England to the dragon's teeth which brought forth armed men, had, unfortunately, been completed into a more perfect parallel with the antique story. The armed men who sprang from the crop sown by Jason were compelled by subtle enchantments to turn their arms against themselves, and to destroy each other. The enchantments of Grattan's persuasive eloquence had destroyed the armed strength of Ireland, and had dissipated the legions which might have preserved her independence, and left her helpless and defenceless to the menaces of a triumphant Government.

Secure although the Government believed themselves to be, and confident as they were of victory, Grattan's appearance was none the less disquieting, and even alarming. The Castle turned Corry, one of the ablest of their tools, and one of the bitterest enemies of Grattan, against the returned Tribune. Corry had once played the part of a patriot, and had afterwards transferred himself and his services to the Government, for which he had been but lately rewarded by the Chancellorship of the Exchequer, from which Parnell had been driven. Corry might have believed that advancing years and ill-health had weakened the powers of Grattan's mind. He might for the moment have fondly imagined that he was a match for the great orator, and that the fierceness and the brutality of his attack would discredit and possibly discomfit his adversary. Corry was grievously mistaken. Grattan had once before assailed Flood in terms of almost unsurpassable bitterness. That speech against Flood might have been regarded as almost the high-water mark of triumphant Parliamentary vituperation ; but if no one save Grattan could have surpassed that effort, it was in Grattan's own power to sur-

pass Grattan. The savage vehemence of the assault upon
Flood pales almost into compliment and courtesy when contrasted with the merciless invective which he now launched
against Corry. Even through the thick skin and deadened
conscience of the Castle placeman the insults of Grattan's
speech burned and eat like a corrosive acid. The speech is
short, but it is a masterpiece of its kind. Every blow stings
like the blow of a whip ; every sentence draws blood.

'The limited talents of some men,' said Grattan, in
fierce scorn of his antagonist's clumsy attack, 'render it impossible for them to be severe without being unparliamentary.'
But Grattan promised Corry, and he kept his word, that
he would show him how to be severe and parliamentary at
the same time. The charge of treason which Corry had
levelled against Grattan he treated with defiant scorn. It
would have been in no sense dishonourable but only honourable for Grattan to have been guilty of treason in the sense
that Wolfe Tone, Lord Edward Fitzgerald, and Arthur O'Connor were guilty of treason. The sting of the accusation lay
in the suggestion that Grattan was a traitor who had saved
himself discreetly from the consequences of his treachery. It
was perfectly well known that Grattan never had any sympathy
whatever with the movement of the United Irishmen, and it
was perfectly easy for him to disprove the clumsy falsehoods
of Corry. 'I despise the falsehood,' said Grattan. 'If such
a charge were made by an honest man I should answer it in
the manner I shall do before I sit down; but I shall first
reply to it when not made by an honest man.' Then came a
succession of sentences glowing like living lava. The fool
had awakened the sleeping volcano, and it answered him with
annihilation.

The speech is familiar to every student of Irish history,
and yet there are sentences of it which bear incessant quotation. When he declared that he scorns ' to answer any wizard
of the Castle, throwing himself into fantastical airs ;' when
he described him as 'deserting the occupation of a barrister
for that of a parasite and pander ; ' when he said, 'I will not

call him villain, because it would be unparliamentary, and he is a Privy Councillor; I will not call him fool, because he happens to be the Chancellor of the Exchequer;' when he asserted ' that the treason of the Minister against the liberties of the people was infinitely worse than the rebellion of the people against the Minister,' he conferred on Corry a kind of infamous immortality.

The Castle parasite sent a challenge to Grattan. The opponents met next morning in the Phœnix Park. Grattan was as ready with his pistol as with his tongue, and he wounded Corry in the arm. The physical injury to Corry was slight; morally he was pulverised. Grattan had not taken his life, but he had ruined his reputation. No further attempt was made by any of the creatures of the Government to draw upon themselves the destruction of Grattan's eloquence.

But the eloquence of Grattan could not save the constitution or the country. The resolutions in favour of the Union of the two kingdoms were carried by successive majorities, and on May 21, Lord Castlereagh's Bill, based on the resolutions, was carried on its first reading by the majority which the Government had calculated upon—a majority of sixty. On May 26, the second reading of the Bill was carried, after the House had listened to the last of Grattan's anti-Union speeches. There need be no apology for quoting here again the immortal peroration of that final speech. Like the passage from Shakespeare which it enshrines, as a relic is enshrined in a frame scarcely less precious than the sacred inclosure, it is eternally fresh and eternally beautiful.

' Yet I do not give up the country: I see her in a swoon, but she is not dead; though in her tomb she lies helpless and motionless, still there is on her lips a spirit of life, and on her cheek a glow of beauty—

> Thou art not conquered, beauty's ensign yet
> Is crimson in thy lips, and in thy cheeks,
> And death's pale flag is not advanced there.

While a plank of the vessel sticks together, I will not leave her. Let the courtier present his flimsy sail, and carry the light bark of his faith with every new breath of wind; I will remain anchored here with fidelity to my country, faithful to her freedom, faithful to her fall.'

It was fitting that Grattan should pronounce the funeral elegy for the liberties whose birth he had hailed. That liberty which he had hoped might be perpetual endured exactly eighteen years. Grattan had traced the career in Ireland from injuries to arms, and from arms to liberty. He had now in his old age to witness the reverse process—to watch the progress from liberty to arms, and from arms to injuries. Sir Jonah Barrington has described with an eloquence beyond his wont, and worthy of the solemn occasion, the scene inside the House of Commons when the fatal moment came which deprived Ireland for nearly a century of her constitutional liberty. The scene outside the House when all was over was even more impressive. The Speaker of the House, followed by a small body of the faithful and honourable Opposition, passed out into the crowded streets. The people uncovered as people uncover in the presence of the dead, and followed in august silence the Speaker and his companions to the Speaker's house in Molesworth Street. There the Speaker faced for a moment the still silent people, the death of whose liberty he had so unwillingly witnessed, and passed without a word into his dwelling.

So ended the Parliament of the Volunteers. As a legislative body it was not an ideal assembly. It had many faults, many weaknesses, and it perished in the end through its own unworthiness. But it still was, however insufficiently, the representative body of the nation. In time it would have grown more liberal; in time Catholics would have been admitted to its deliberations; in time it would have proved the true head of a free state. Such as it was, with all its imperfections, it preserved for Ireland that proud privilege of legislative independence which now, for eighty-six years, she has mourned without cessation. The Parliament which is destined speedily to take the place of the lost Parliament will

F

be a very different body from that which Grattan welcomed into existence, and lamented over in its fall. It will be a body worthy of the Irish nation, which, in the long lapse of years since the beginning of this century, has been steadily forming itself and training itself for the restoration of its liberties. It will be a free Parliament in the sense that Grattan's never was; for in it for the first time the representatives of the national faith will find their rightful place. It is to be hoped, it is to be believed, that the orator who hails the inauguration of this Parliament may say, addressing it with a greater confidence even than that of Grattan—*Esto perpetua*.

But though the Union was accomplished it was not acquiesced in by the Irish people without one final struggle. At the time when the plans of the United Irishmen were slowly ripening towards revolution, and when Wolfe Tone and Edward Fitzgerald still believed in the immediate regeneration of their country, there were two young men in Dublin University—close personal friends—who were watching with peculiar interest the progress of events. Both were exceptionally gifted young men, and both were destined to leave behind them names that will live for ever in the history of the Irish nation. One was Thomas Moore; the other, his junior by a year and his senior by one class in the University, was Robert Emmet. It is especially natural that two such young men should take the keenest interest in the national movement that was going on about them. It was a movement calculated to attract all the generous and impassioned impulses of youth. Both Moore and Emmet were profoundly ambitious for their nation's welfare; both of them, we may well assume, felt conscious of the possession of abilities beyond the average; and both were animated by a desire to be of active service to their people. The desire, however, which merely led Moore to become the poetical voice of Ireland's aspirations and regrets, urged Emmet into directer and more decided action. Robert Emmet was a brother of Thomas Addis Emmet. He was, therefore, closely in connection with the revolutionary movement, and did all that lay in his power to advance it by his speeches in the Debating Society and in the Historical Society of the College. Political speeches were, of course, forbidden in such bodies as these two societies; but Emmet always contrived to introduce into his utterances upon any of the themes set down for debate some burning words, which those who listened to him, and loved him, could readily interpret into justification of the United Irishmen, and encouragement of their efforts.

Between the young orator and the young poet the closest friendship and affection existed. The genius of Moore was naturally captivated by the pure and lofty enthusiasm of Robert Emmet, and it is almost surprising that under the circumstances Moore did not become more deeply involved in the conspiracy that spread all round him. Moore had not, however, the nature of the conspirator, or of the very active politician. He was called upon to do other work in this world, and he did that work so worthily that he may well be forgiven for having been so little of a rebel at a time when rebellion seemed the duty of every Irishman. Moore tells a touching little story of himself and of his friend, which in itself illustrates the different natures of the two young men. Moore had become possessed of that precious volume in which the labours of Mr. Bunting had collected so much of the national music of Ireland; and he delighted in passing long hours in playing over to himself the airs which he was destined later on to make so famous by his verses. Emmet often sat by him while he played, and Moore records how, one evening, just as he had finished playing the spirited tune called 'The Red Fox,' Emmet sprang up as from a reverie, and exclaimed, 'Oh, that I were at the head of twenty thousand men marching to that air!' The air which awakened in Emmet the gallant hope, which he was never destined to see realised, had probably started in the brain of Moore dim memories of the lost glories of Ireland; of the Knights of the Red Branch of Malachi with the gold torque, and of the buried city of Lough Neagh. The music which Emmet had desired to hear as the marching song of victory is familiar to every Irishman as, 'Let Erin remember the days of old.' 'How little did I think,' said the poet, 'that in one of the most touching of the sweet airs I used to play to him, his own dying words would find an interpreter so worthy of their sad but proud feeling; or that another of those mournful strains would long be associated in the hearts of his countrymen with the memory of her who shared with Ireland his last blessing and prayer.'

Ninety-eight had come and gone like a dream. The leaders of the United Irishmen were dead, in exile, or hiding from the law. The Irish Parliament had passed from existence, and the hated Union had become an accomplished fact. The promises of the British Minister, which had done so much to facilitate the passing of the Act of Union, had been shamefully violated. One of the most important factors in securing the Union was the pledge entered into by Pitt, and promulgated all over Ireland in the form of a printed speech, that legislation upon Catholic Emancipation and the Tithe question would immediately follow the legal union of the two countries. It cannot be denied that such a promise, made in so solemn a manner, and by so responsible a Minister, must have had the greatest effect in winning support to the Union; and in many cases where it did not win actual support, at least it must have prevented energetic opposition.

To the vast bulk of the Irish people the question of Catholic Emancipation was so immediately important, on so large a number the grievous burden of the Tithe question pressed heavily, that it can scarcely be a matter of surprise if many men were ready, or, at least, not unwilling, to welcome any measure which offered to grant the one and relieve the other. But Pitt had pledged himself to more than he could perform. The bigoted and incapable monarch, whose peculiar privilege it was to cause more injuries to his own country—that is, to his own kingdom—than any other English monarch, and who had always consistently and steadily hated the Irish people because of their religious belief, obstinately refused to give his consent to any measure for the relief of Catholics. Pitt immediately resigned his office, just eleven days after the Union had become law. The stubborn folly of the Third George does not excuse the Minister who had done his best to delude Ireland by raising hopes which he was not certain of gratifying, and making pledges which he was unable to fulfil.

The Union brought with it nothing whatever that bettered the condition of Ireland. The system of political corruption, which had engendered the Union, continued in full force after the Union had come into existence. Every place of profit, every post of importance, was held by Englishmen. Lord Clare, the hated Fitzgibbon, had died, indeed, soon after the Union—died it was said of disappointment at discovering that his own power and influence had vanished with the political change of which he had been one of the most active causes. Castlereagh had gone back to England, to end some years later his dishonourable life by a desperate death. But the removal of one enemy only left room for the admission of another. The places of Castlereagh and Fitzgibbon were filled by politicians no less devoted to Ascendency, no less inimical to anything approaching to patriotism or to nationalism.

Although the prospect of Catholic Emancipation seemed as far off as ever, there was, however, a change in the attitude of the Castle circle towards the Irish Catholics, at least towards the rich and influential among them. A policy of conciliation was the order of the day, and conciliation meant treating the more eminent among the Catholics with something approaching to the ordinary courtesy of civilised existence. The vast bulk of the Catholic population was, however, as badly off as ever. Ireland was labouring under heavy coercive legislation, and the policy of coercion which began with the Union has existed almost without intermission ever since. It could be said almost without exaggeration in 1885 that Ireland had not been governed by ordinary law for a single year of all the eighty-five years that had elapsed since the two islands were linked together in unholy and unreal union. Coercion, as it always did, begot disturbance and outrage. There were desperate riots in Limerick, Waterford, and Tipperary in the year of the Union—smouldering embers of the revolution of ninety-eight, which were destined still to break out into one final, fitful conflagration.

Robert Emmet saw the sufferings of his country with indignation, but not with despair. He conceived the possibility of reviving the spirit of ninety-eight. In his eyes revolution was not dead, but only asleep; and he proudly fancied that his might be the voice to wake rebellion from its trance, and lead it to its triumph. He had some personal fortune of his own, which he unselfishly devoted to the purpose he had in view. Gradually he began to gather around him a cluster of the disaffected—survivors of ninety-eight who had escaped the grave, the gibbet, or exile—men like the heroic Myles Byrne, of Wexford, who had evaded the clutch of the law, and was lying hidden in Dublin, as assistant in a timber-yard, and waiting upon fortune. In Myles Byrne Emmet found a ready and a daring colleague, and each found others no less ready, no less daring, and no less devoted to their country, to aid in the new revolutionary movement. Like the United Irishmen, Emmet was willing to avail himself of French arms; but he trusted France less than the United Irishmen had done. He had been in Paris; he had had interviews with Napoleon; he had distrusted the First Consul, and, as we know from his dying speech, he never for a moment entertained the slightest idea of exchanging the dominion of England for the dominion of France. His scheme was desperate, but it was by no means hopeless. Large stores of arms and gunpowder were accumulated in the various depôts in Dublin. Thousands of men were pledged to the cause, and were prepared to risk their lives for it. The means of establishing a provisional Government had been carefully thought out, and had been given effect to in an elaborate document, of which a vast quantity was printed, ready to be sown broadcast through the city and the country as soon as the green flag floated over Dublin Castle.

That was Emmet's chief purpose. Once master of the Castle, and Dublin would be practically in his power; and Dublin once in the hands of revolution, why, then rebellion would spread through the country like fire in a jungle, and Ireland might indeed be free. The plot was daring; but the brain that conceived it was keen and bold; the hands and hearts that were pledged to it were true and gallant. Everything seemed to promise, if not a successful revolution, at least a rising which should come so near success as to shake the power of the Government, and practically compel great concessions, if not the Repeal of the Union. It all ended in a street scuffle, and a small and abortive provincial rising. Treachery, which has always been at the right hand of Authority in Ireland, was, as usual, at work: and although the Executive appear to have made light at first of the information that was daily conveyed to them of Emmet's purposes, it is certain that the carefully-matured plot failed disastrously at the moment of execution.

It is scarcely necessary to recapitulate the events of that memorable evening of July 23, 1803. At ten o'clock a rocket sent up from Thomas Street blazed for a moment, the meteor of insurrection, in the unwonted darkness of that summer night. But the signal that was to have been the herald of freedom was only the herald of failure. A small mob of men hastened to the depôt in Marshalsea Lane, which was the principal store of arms. There pikes were hurriedly handed out to the crowd, and there Emmet, who had hoped to head an army, found himself the centre of an undisciplined rabble. His hopes must have sunk low as he stood there in the dim and dismal street, in his glittering uniform of green and gold; but his heart did not fail him for a moment. He turned towards the Castle at the head of his turbulent horde as composedly as if he had been marshalling the largest army in Europe. But the crowd lacked cohesion, lacked purpose, lacked determination. It fell away from its leader loosely, even aimlessly. Some rushed wildly towards the Castle; others, at the moment when unity and concentration were of the utmost importance, hurried off in another direction to sack a debtor's prison and set the inmates free.

While the disorganised crowd was still in Thomas Street, while Emmet was vainly trying to rally his forces and accomplish something, a carriage came slowly down the street—the carriage of Lord Kilwarden, Lord Chief Justice of the King's Bench. Inside the carriage were Lord Kilwarden, his daughter, and his nephew, the Rev. Mr. Wolfe. The mob surrounded the carriage; Lord Kilwarden and his nephew were dragged from the carriage, and killed with innumerable thrusts. The girl was left untouched, was, it is said, carried out of danger by Robert Emmet himself, who had vainly attempted to stop the purposeless slaughter. Before the Chief Justice was quite dead Major Sirr and a large body of his soldiers made their appearance, and the mob vanished almost without resistance, leaving several prisoners in the hands of the military. The stores of arms were seized, the prisoners safely put under lock and key, and in a few hours Dublin was as quiet as if no effort at insurrection had ever disturbed the tranquillity of its streets. Emmet had disappeared, no one knew where. Upon the following day a small insurrection took place in Ulster under Thomas Russell, which came to nothing. Russell made his escape, but was captured a few months later, tried, and hanged. Two of his co-revolutionists, Andrew Hunter and David Porter, shared his fate.

Emmet had disappeared, no one knew where—no one, that is, except some dozen of his followers and some farmers in the Wicklow mountains, whose hospitality and protection were extended to the fugitive patriot. Emmet might easily have escaped to France if he had chosen, but he delayed till too late. Emmet was a young man, and Emmet was in love. ' The idol of his heart,' as he calls her in his dying speech, was Sarah Curran, the daughter of John Philpot Curran, the great orator who had played so important a part in defending the State prisoners of ninety-eight. Emmet was determined to see her before he went. He placed his life upon the cast, and lost it. He returned to Dublin, and was hiding at

Harold's Cross when his place of refuge was betrayed, and he was arrested by Major Sirr, the same who had brought Fitzgerald to his death, and who now, strangely enough, occupies a corner of the same graveyard with the 'gallant and seditious Geraldine.'

Curran very bitterly opposed Emmet's love for Sarah, and the voice which had been raised so often and so eloquently in defence of the other heroes and martyrs of Irish revolution was not lifted up in defence of Emmet. Curran has been often and severely censured for not undertaking Emmet's defence, and he has been accused, in consequence, of being at least indirectly the cause of his death. But we may safely assume that no advocacy either of men or of angels could by any possibility have stirred the hearts of those in authority, and saved the life of the man who was presumptuous enough to rebel against the Union. The trial was hurried through. Every Irish schoolboy knows the impassioned and eloquent address which Emmet delivered—an address which even the tragic circumstances could not save from the brutal interruptions of Judge Norbury. On the altar of truth and liberty, Emmet had extinguished the torch of friendship, had offered up the idol of his soul and the object of his affections. With the shadow of death upon him, the doomed patriot addressed his country in words of well-nigh prophetic import, forbidding them to write his epitaph until his country had taken her place among the nations of the earth. The words did not pass his lips long before his death. He was found guilty late in the night of September 19, and he was hanged the next morning in Thomas Street, on the spot where the gloomy church of St. Catherine looks down Bridgefoot Street, where his principal stores of arms had been found.

Just before his death he wrote a letter to Richard, Curran's son, full of melancholy tenderness, regret for his lost love, and resignation for his untimely death.

'If there was anyone in the world in whose breast my death might be supposed not to stifle every spark of resentment, it might be you. I have deeply injured you—I have deeply injured the happiness of a sister that you love, and who was formed to give happiness to everyone about her, instead of having her own mind a prey to affliction. Oh, Richard! I have no excuse to offer, but that I meant the reverse; I intended as much happiness for Sarah as the most ardent love could have given her. I never did tell you how I idolised her; it was not with a wild or unfounded passion, but it was an attachment increasing every hour, from an admiration of the purity of her mind and respect for her talents. I did dwell in secret upon the prospect of our union. I did hope that success, while it afforded the opportunity of our union, might be the means of confirming an attachment which misfortune had called forth. I did not look to honours for myself—praise I would have asked from the lips of no man; but I could have wished to read in the glow of Sarah's countenance that her husband was respected. My love, Sarah! It was not thus that I thought to have requited your affection. I had hoped to be a prop round which your affections might have clung, and which would never have been shaken: but a rude blast has snapped it, and they have fallen over a grave!'

Such was the fate of Robert Emmet. His dying request has been faithfully obeyed by his countrymen; no tombstone bears his name, no statue typifies his memory. His old friend, the companion of his youth, the poet who had loved him, has honoured his memory with two of his noblest lyrics, and has devoted a third to the girl whom Emmet's love has made immortal. Curran never forgave his daughter for having given her affections to Emmet; he practically disowned her, and did not, it is said, even extend his forgiveness to her at the hour of her death some years later. It is melancholy to have to record the fact that the betrothed wife of Robert Emmet was not entirely faithful to his memory. She married, at the instance, it is said, of her friends, and did not long survive her marriage.

CHAPTER VI.

CATHOLIC EMANCIPATION.

THE White Terror which followed upon the failure of Emmet's rising was accompanied by almost all the horrors which marked the hours of repression after the rebellion of ninety-eight. As soon as the news of Emmet's daring attempt reached London, a royal message was sent to Parliament, imploring fresh powers to deal with the mutinous island. The two Houses displayed all the alacrity usual with them when their business is coercion for Ireland. There was not then, nor for more than two generations later, an Irish party in the English House of Commons, to warn an indifferent majority that coercion could only be won with bitter travail and by yet further violation of constitutional rights. The measures which the king demanded were rattled through the two Houses at breakneck speed. A *Habeas Corpus* Act Suspension Bill and a Bill enforcing military law in Ireland were passed through all their stages in the Lower House before ten o'clock of the evening on which they were introduced. By eleven o'clock the same night they had received the assent of the Lords and become part of the law of the land. Then the old brutal business began again; the old devil's dance of spies and informers went merrily forward; the prisons were choked with prisoners. The spies and informers received liberal rewards for each arrest, and took good care to keep the prison market well stocked with victims.

It is simply horrible to read of the treatment endured by these unhappy prisoners. The Russian Nihilist, Stepniak, has lately given, in his grim record of 'Russia under the Tzars,' ghastly accounts of the way in which political prisoners were treated in the dominions of the Tzar. All that Russian political prisoners are said to have suffered, Irish political prisoners suffered under the gentle rule of the Third George in the early part of the present century. Men who were arrested immediately after Emmet's rising were in many cases kept in prison for no less than three years, and subjected to inhuman indignities without any kind of trial or any kind of investigation into their guilt or innocence. 'If anything,' says an English writer who cannot be accused of undue sympathy with Irish aspirations, 'if anything could extend a show of reason, or the colour of an excuse, to the insurrectionary movements of Emmet and Russell, it was the subsequent barbarity of the Government to every person accused or suspected of sympathy with their designs or the will to aid them.'

The Government acted in blind panic. The fear of a French invasion was eternally before their eyes, and they could conceive of no better means of linking the sympathies of the Irish people to the English Crown than the jail and the gallows. They guarded themselves against further insurrections with ferocious ingenuity, but they took not a single step towards allaying the discontent which animated and kept alive the spirit of revolution. The juggle of the Union had been successfully accomplished by deluding the Catholics with pledges of emancipation, but the moment that the Union was passed the covenant with the Catholics was broken. Pitt retired from office eleven days after the passing of the Act of Union, because the king would make no concessions to the Catholic claims; he returned to office in 1804 on the distinct understanding that he was no longer to weary his intolerant monarch with suggestions of relief for the Irish Catholics. The Minister accepted the terms and kept the engagement. The royal ears were unvexed by any importunities from his obedient Cabinet about the wrongs of Irish Catholics.

The supporters of Pitt's policy urge that there is the clearest proof of his anxiety to legislate upon three great questions—Catholic Emancipation, the Tithes of the Established Church, and the support of the Roman Catholic clergy. They rest mainly upon Pitt's speech, which was showered like autumn leaves all over Ireland—which by its promises, indeed by its pledges, did so much to facilitate the Union. A former secretary to the Chancellor of the Irish Exchequer has declared that Pitt had actually prepared a Bill for the commutation of tithes. This may be; the certainty is that nothing was done. The stolid and bigoted king was obstinate in his refusal to sanction any measures of Catholic toleration, and Pitt, exculpating himself by ingenious distinctions between expediency and right, gave way, after a comparatively brief interval of absence from office.

Outraged by the law, detested by the Sovereign, abandoned by the Minister, the position of Irish Catholicity was bad enough, but it had not merely to contend with the harshness of the law, the hatred of the king, and the treason of the statesman. A fresh enemy swelled the ranks against it—an enemy growing more powerful and more hostile with the failure of every fresh effort for Catholic relief—the enemy that was known by the name of the Orange Society. 'The Orange Society,' says an English author, 'grew out of the violent spirit into which the selfishness of Protestant monopoly now precipitated its animosity. Lured by the lust of power and the avarice of self-interest, the Protestants began to band themselves together by secret oaths; and in many places committed themselves with the blind fury of zealots to the trammels of their leaders.' The Orange Society first came into existence immediately after what is known as the 'Battle of the Diamond.'

On September 21, 1795, a violent conflict took place between the Protestant 'Peep-o'-day Boys' and the Catholic 'Defenders' at the Diamond, a place where four roads meet in Loughall, not far from Armagh. After a desperate struggle the 'Defenders' were defeated, and many of their number killed. In commemoration of this event the first Orange lodge was formed in Armagh on the same date, on September 21, 1795, at Timaekell; and soon after another lodge was established in Dublin.

It has been said, however, that the first Orange lodge was founded in the camp of William of Orange at Exeter, early in November 1688. There is no evidence to support this claim, which is not alluded to by Sir Richard Musgrave. Musgrave, the dedication of whose work on the Rebellion of 1798 was coldly and decisively declined by the nobleman to whom it was proffered, says : ' In commemoration of that victory ' (the battle of the Diamond) ' the first Orange lodge was formed in the county of Armagh, though the name of Orangemen existed some time before.' Furthermore, in 1835 Lieutenant-Colonel Vernon, M.P., said before a Select Committee of the House of Commons, that there was no Orange institution in any other form in existence before 1795. In the January of 1798 a solemn manifesto was issued by the members of the Dublin lodge, declaring that the principles of their existence were the maintenance of Church and State—that is to say, the maintenance of the Protestant faith, and the imposition of the Protestant faith upon Catholic Ireland. For some time the society made but little progress, and it was not until after the passing of the Act of Union that it began to make sensible advances in number and in influence. According to Francis Plowden its purpose was to uphold the Crown so long as the Crown upheld Protestant ascendency—and no longer. He even goes further and declares: ' It has been asserted by well-informed though anonymous authors that the original obligation or oath of Orangemen was to the following effect : I, A. B., do swear that I will be true to king and Government, and that I will exterminate the Catholics of Ireland so far as in my power lies.' This oath, it must be admitted, has been denied by the Orange lodges, but it is not apparently denied that their oath of allegiance was only conditional on the Crown supporting Protestant ascendency.

The Orange Society gained from its very earliest days much support and encouragement from the ostentatious patronage of the Duke of York. The Duke of York was not an estimable person. In a family that was rarely remarkable for the moral qualities of its members, he was conspicuous for his indifference to all the restraints that religion and civilisation impose upon humanity. But it pleased him to come forward on all possible occasions as the patron and champion of the Church of England, whenever that patronage and championship might be calculated to inflict an injury upon the professors of some other creed. In the Orange Society he saw an excellent opportunity for striking a blow at the Catholics of Ireland, whose claims, as he and the fiercer fanatics of Ascendency began to dread, were upon the eve of obtaining some recognition from the English Government. In the year 1797 he became a prominent patron of the Orange lodges in Ireland, and he seems to have made use of his power as Commander-in-Chief to encourage the formation of Orange lodges in the regiments stationed in Ireland, in direct defiance of military regulations. So bitter was his animosity to the Irish Catholics that more than a generation after the formation of the Orange lodges he called upon God to witness that he would never assent to the enfranchisement of the Irish people. This saying inspired Sheil with a fierce attack upon the Duke of York when the Duke's health was proposed at a public dinner at Mullingar. Naturally incensed by the proposal of such a toast in a Catholic assembly, the orator inveighed against the ducal patron of the Orange lodges with a vehemence which, for long enough, was prejudicial to his own career.

When the Duke lay dying, a little later, Sheil, in a public speech, gave utterance to what has been called an apology for his attack upon the Duke of York. He did, indeed, express some regret at the terms he had employed, but the manner in which he expressed that regret was scarcely likely to win his pardon in high quarters.

'It is right,' exclaimed Sheil, 'that the offence which the Duke of York committed against our country should be committed to forgetfulness. Indeed, it is almost unnecessary to express a desire which the natural oblivion that must befall the greatest as well as the humblest of mankind cannot fail to accomplish. In a month hence the Duke of York will be forgotten. The pomp of death will for a few nights fill the gilded apartments in which his body will lie in state. The artist will endeavour to avert the decay to which even princes are doomed, and embalm him with odours which may resist the cadaverous scent for a while. He will be laid in a winding-sheet fringed with silver and with gold; he will be enclosed in spicy wood, and his illustrious descent and withered hopes will be inscribed upon his glittering coffin. The bell of St. Paul's will toll, and London—rich, luxurious, Babylonic London—will start at the recollection that even kings must die. . . . The coffin will go sadly and slowly down: its ponderous mass will strike on the remains of its regal kindred; the chant will be resumed, a moment's awful pause will take place—the marble vault, of which none but the Archangel shall disturb the slumbers, will be closed—the songs of death will cease—the procession will wind through the aisles again and restore them to their loneliness. The torches will fade again in the open daylight—the multitude of the great will gradually disperse; they will roll back in their gilded chariots into the din and tumult of the great metropolis; the business and the pursuits and the frivolities of life will be resumed, and the heir to the Three Kingdoms will be in a week forgotten. We, too, shall forget; but let us before we forget forgive him!'

Such a speech, animated with all the scorn and all the passion of Hebrew prophecy, and spoken as it was while the object of its scorn was still lingering in life, will serve to show the hatred which the fanatic and vindictive bigotry of a foreign prince could inspire in the mind of a statesman and an orator like Sheil.

While, however, the Duke of York had still more than twenty years to live, and the Orange Society was yet in its infancy, the position of the Catholics was pitiable in the extreme. The statesmen of the Union who had promised much had performed nothing; the law still held nothing but terrors, the Government had nothing but hostility for Roman Catholics. Under the benign Lord Lieutenantship of Lord Hardwicke all the judicial offences which had darkened the close of the eighteenth century and compelled insurrection were in full force. The vile old policy of shameless corruption on the one hand and shameless oppression on the other was followed out with stubborn persistence. A purchased Press and a place-hunting minority strengthened the hands of the Executive and gave it full force and sanction for the hangings, the floggings, the transportations, and imprisonment which were so lavishly employed in order to make the Irish appreciate the blessings of the Act of Union.

It is one of the most remarkable features of Ireland's history, however, that no oppression has ever retarded her steady and persistent advance towards freedom. The desire for liberty, like the torch in the old Greek game, is handed over from hand to hand. One runner may fail, grow faint and fall off, but there are always others ready to snatch the torch from his loosening grasp and carry it a further stage nearer to the goal. Emmet's insurrection had been only just crushed out; the blood of the young leader was scarcely dry; his body scarcely cold in the nameless grave which his dying bequest had left without an epitaph, when the new movement began which was destined to gratify one of the greatest and justest of Irish ambitions in a quarter of a century, and to culminate in unavailing revolution nearly half a century later.

Pitt, the Prime Minister who had promised the Catholics their emancipation, was Prime Minister again, on the distinct understanding that he should make no concessions to the Catholics. The Irish Catholics resolved to combat this understanding. The old Catholic Committee met in Dublin, drew up a petition and entrusted it to Lord Fingall and some other Catholic noblemen and gentlemen to place in the hands of Mr. Pitt. Pitt received the deputation with courtesy, and listened to their appeal with that unalterable composure which had produced so irritating an effect upon Edward Gibbon many a long year before when Pitt was little more than a lad, and had ventured to traverse some opinion of the historian of Rome. He absolutely refused to support the Catholic claims in any way. Previous promises, early pledges he graciously admitted; he was still, it seemed, an ardent advocate of Catholic relief; but just then Catholic relief was inexpedient, in fact, impossible. The deputation wasted its

G

words and its wits upon the Minister. He was civil, smooth-spoken, and immovable. Pitt had in his hands the greatest chance ever offered to a statesman of ameliorating the condition of Ireland, and of damming a sea of troubles from many generations of men. But he had come into office on the condition that he was to be deaf to the voice of the Irish Catholics, and he preferred office to honour. Other ministers since Pitt have pursued a like policy, and with a like disastrous result.

The disappointed deputation then turned from the Minister to the Opposition, and placed their petition in the hands of Lord Grenville and Mr. Fox. The question was the cause of long and eloquent debates in both houses, which ended in recording the vote of a small minority in favour of the Catholic claims and of an overwhelming majority against them. The debate is memorable especially because it was the occasion of Grattan's first appearance in the English House of Commons. In spite of all the disadvantages of his voice and manner, in spite of the still greater disadvantage of a great reputation gained in another country and another assembly, Grattan's oratory earned an unqualified triumph. It was applauded by the Minister against whom it was levelled, and whose secret opinions it, no doubt, expressed while it censured his public action. In vain, however, Grattan contended that the principle of religious liberty was equally sound whether applied ' to constitution where it is freedom, or to empire where it is strength, or to religion where it is light.' In vain he condemned the proscription which ' made in Ireland not only war but peace calamities.' In vain he told the attentive senate that ' what the best men in Ireland wished to do but could not do, the patriot courtier and the patriot oppositionist, you may accomplish.' Neither the genius of Grattan nor the genius of Fox could move or reduce the anti-Catholic majority, and the hopes of the Catholics were lowered to be raised again unexpectedly by an unforeseen accident, only to be dashed to earth again by another accident yet more unforeseen.

On the 2nd of December, 1805, Napoleon defeated the armies of the allies at Austerlitz. On the 26th of January, in the following year, Pitt had ceased to live. Not for a moment before his death, it is said, did the 'Austerlitz look' leave his face. His fears foresaw the unrestrained triumph of Napoleon and the ruin of England; his genius could not predict Moscow and Waterloo. The death of Pitt was immediately followed by the fall of the Pitt Administration and by the accession of the Opposition to power, nominally under Lord Grenville, but actually under the commanding influence of Fox. The hopes of the Catholics rose high. Pitt had been their most dangerous enemy; Fox had promised to be, and seemed like to prove himself, their fastest friend.

But the ingenious combination of the followers of Grenville, the followers of Fox, and the friends of Lord Sidmouth, which its friends proudly and its foes contemptuously styled the Ministry 'of all the talents,' was not destined to do much for the Irish Catholics or for Ireland. Lord Hardwicke, indeed, freed Ireland from his obnoxious presence, and a Duke of Bedford held sway at the Castle in his stead—the same Duke who has earned a dishonourable immortality by his attack upon Burke, and by the magnificent reply with which Burke held his name up for ever to the contempt of posterity.

But a change of viceroys meant little in Ireland. It was simply an Amurath succeeding to an Amurath. To this Duke the Catholics of Dublin presented an address expressing the hope that the new Government was prepared to accomplish Catholic relief. The Duke gave a guarded answer, but let it be noised abroad that as soon as Fox could convert his king the Catholics should reap the reward of their patience. Whether even Fox could ever have converted such a king must remain one of the most unanswerable speculations of history. At least, he did not convert him. We may well believe in the integrity of Fox's intentions, and in his loyalty to his convictions and his promises, but he was not allowed the time to ratify his pledges or to verify the hopes of those who depended upon him. In the September of that same year, 1806, which had opened with the death of Pitt, Fox himself was carried to Westminster Abbey. The two great rivals slept in neigh-hour graves, and the hopes of the Irish Catholics seemed to be buried in Fox's monument.

The prophetic wisdom of Fox had warned the Catholics, on his accession to power, that the unpopularity of their cause might mean the ruin of the Ministry that advocated it, and the accession of a Ministry formed on the avowed principle of defeating the Catholic claims, and so put all hope further off than ever. What he expected came to pass. The Ministry ' of all the talents ' showed some signs of sympathy with the Roman Catholics. The grant to Maynooth was increased by 5,000*l*. An effort was made to pass a Bill admitting Catholics to hold commissions in the army and the navy. Even this small concession to justice roused the passions of the bigot king. After it had passed the Commons he declared himself against it, and attempted to extort from his new Ministers the pledge he had successfully imposed upon Pitt, never again to importune his kingly ears with proposals to relieve the Catholics. The Ministers refused to make this humiliating concession, pushed their Bill through the Lords, and placed their resignation in the hands of the monarch. George immediately sent for Mr. Spencer Perceval, a man more after his own heart than Grey or Grenville, and entrusted him with the task of forming the Ministry which, from its supple acceptance of the royal bigotry, came to be known by the nickname of the ' No-Popery Ministry.' Catholic relief was postponed for twenty years.

The new Ministry began its work in no spirit of compromise or conciliation. It had come into office on the strength of its anti-Catholic pledges, and it was determined to retain its power by a thorough-going fulfilment of those pledges. New measures of coercion signalised their entrance into office, and the new measures of coercion were as usual followed by fresh outbreaks. In 1807 we hear for the first time of two desperate local factions, the Shanavests and Caravats, who seem to have agitated for a time very fiercely before they disappeared under the pressure of the law. Patronage, corruption, and coercion held their familiar carnival. The grant to

Maynooth was reduced, and in every possible way the Catholics were made to feel the enmity of the king and of his Ministers. But, though the hopes of the Catholics seemed to be dashed to the ground, they did not despair. They still agitated, still petitioned, still united. It was their darkest hour, but it heralded the dawn. The hour which had come had brought the man with it. The leader for whom Ireland was waiting was at hand. There was a young man in Dublin taking an active part in the work of the Catholic Committee whose name Ireland, England, and the world were destined to hear a great deal of. That name was Daniel O'Connell.

CHAPTER VII.

DANIEL O'CONNELL.

THE new leader in Irish politics was one of the strangest and most remarkable figures that had ever moved across its stormy scene. Unlike most of the later leaders of Irish national movements, Daniel O'Connell was a Catholic. The men of ninety-eight, Fitzgerald, O'Connor, Wolfe Tone, and Emmet, had all been members of the Protestant faith. Daniel O'Connell came of an old Catholic Kerry family. As Catholics, the O'Connells experienced the pressure of the Penal Laws. Morris O'Connell, the eldest son of the liberator's grandfather, held an estate that was not 'discoverable'—that is to say, was not liable to be seized by any Protestant that chose to claim it, because it was held by leases conveyed prior to the enactment of the Penal Laws. Morgan O'Connell, Daniel O'Connell's father, though he was a rather large landowner, ruled his estate at his own risk, and through the forbearance of his Protestant neighbours. He held his lands through a trustee, who was, of course, a Protestant, and who would have been perfectly within his legal rights in violating his trust and seizing Morgan O'Connell's property. Nor was the mere fidelity of the trustee in itself a safeguard. Any other Protestant who chose to file a Bill of Discovery could compel the trust to be disclosed, and could seize the estate without making any payment or compensation whatever to its Catholic proprietor.

The O'Connell family was, in many ways, a remarkable one. Daniel O'Connell, the liberator's namesake and uncle, had himself a story which reads like some of the most brilliant pages from the romance of adventure. The two-and-twentieth child, he entered the French service at an age when most boys are at school, and raised himself to high rank by his own merit. He served with signal distinction in many parts of the world. He was in command of a large number of foreign troops in Paris in 1789, and used often to declare, in his later years, that, if Louis XVI. had allowed him to act, the revolution might have been crushed almost at its inception. After a long life of battle and adventure, he died as colonel in the British army in 1834, in his ninety-first year.

The more famous Daniel O'Connell appears to have inherited the courageous spirit and magnificent constitution of his warlike uncle, as well as his name. All his early years belonged to a time of great European excitement. While he was still but a child, his youthful ears were filled with the fame and fear of Paul Jones's name, and with the desperate doings of the *Bon Homme Richard*. Later on, he was at school in France at the very time when the Reign of Terror began, and it was only with considerable danger that he and his brother were able to make their way back from France to Ireland. The packet-boat that conveyed them from Calais conveyed to England the tidings of the death of Louis XVI., and it also carried among its passengers two men whose names are famous in Irish history, two men who were destined to play a prominent part in the insurrectionary movement of ninety-eight—the brothers John and Henry Sheares. It is said that John Sheares declared to those on board that he and his brother had been actually present at the execution of Louis XVI., having bribed two soldiers of the national guard to let them wear their uniforms, and take their places. That was surely an ominous and fateful vessel which left France with such strange tidings and such a strange company.

The tidings that France, in the words of Danton, 'had answered Europe's challenge with the head of a king,' were but the bloody preface to a long series of terrible events which were destined at last to end in empire, after the revolution, like Saturn, had consumed its own children. The company was one of the strangest that chance had ever brought together on shipboard, for it included two men who were yet to stir up desperate rebellion against the foreign dominion, and who were doomed to die for the attempt, and included, too, the lad just fresh from college, who was fated to accomplish one portion of the freedom of his country, and to be himself the cause of another unsuccessful revolution.

Daniel O'Connell's young manhood was passed chiefly in Dublin, at first studying for, and afterwards gradually working his way to eminence at, the Bar. It is possible that his eager and active patriotism might have included him, too, in the struggle and ruin of ninety-eight but for an accident in a street scuffle. The injuries received therein kept him in confinement during some of the most critical days in the history of the rebellion, and during this confinement he received sure and trusty warning of the Government's intimate knowledge with every detail of the conspiracy. Whatever sympathy O'Connell might have felt for the United Irishmen then, he certainly felt none in his later days. He could not, we are told, forgive them for helping Pitt to pass the Union; and in his eyes and in his words the heroes of the Irish people—Fitzgerald, Emmet, Tone—were only 'a gang of scoundrels.' When 1803 arrived, O'Connell had nothing to do with the revolutionary movement of Emmet. He was a prominent member of the lawyers' corps, and seems to have played an honourable part in attempting to defend the lives of unoffending citizens against the panic-stricken excesses of the citizen soldiery.

One of the chief characteristics of O'Connell's early life was courage. It needed no small courage for a young man, and a Catholic, to lift up his voice loudly and eloquently against the Union at a meeting well-nigh overawed by the presence of an armed soldiery, under the command of the detested Major Sirr. At a time when the insurrection of Emmet was but an event of yesterday, and when the savage repression of obnoxious political opinions was the creed and the principle of the Irish Executive, the unknown young lawyer, who had at one time, according to his own words, ' been almost a Tory,' dared to express himself as an eloquent and indignant opponent of the Union. It needed no small courage, too, for such a man to take upon himself, as he did a little later, the part of the champion of the Catholics of Ireland. At the time when O'Connell was rapidly making his way into the front rank of his profession, the Irish Catholics were reduced by oppression, by privation, and the Penal Laws to a condition of almost despairing apathy. They had no ambitions which they could hope to gratify; they had no privileges as citizens; they had almost no rights as human beings.

Their attitude in most cases was not unnaturally that of the oppressed towards the oppressor, of the subjected to the conqueror, of the slave to the master. To be a Protestant meant, then, to belong to a dominant, privileged, and powerful minority; to be a Catholic meant to belong to a degraded and outraged and an insulted majority. The liberties, the possessions, the very life of the Irish Catholic could hardly be called his own, and he had fallen in many cases into that listless torpor which is one of the most fatal symbols of vassalage. The intolerable cruelties of the Orange Society had here and there aroused a certain spirit of retaliation. The Ribbonmen sometimes met and met successfully the attacks upon their kin and their creed. But in the majority of cases Orangeism was all powerful. If a Lord-Lieutenant administered the law after a fashion displeasing to them, as Wellesley did, he was made the victim of an organised attack for which the offenders were never brought to book. Conviction of an Orangeman was practically impossible, as he was sure to be tried before an Orange jury; conviction of a Catholic was certain, for the same reason. No wonder if the Irish Catholics as a class were broken-spirited and apathetic. It was for this class, which had for so long been silent, that a young man of their own faith now dared to come forward, not merely as their defender, but as their vindicator and justifier. The tone of plaintive apology which had been so familiar in the mouths of some advocates of the Catholic cause was never adopted by O'Connell. From the first he held his head high, and cared for no man. From the first he adopted an attitude of defiance, and a tone of even aggressive scorn of his opponents. He fought the Catholic cause in all places and in all seasons, on the public platform and in the crowded court-room, with an eloquence which was not less remarkable for its power than for its passion, for its beauty than for its bitterness, for its admirable arguments in favour of its cause, than for its merciless attacks upon his powerful adversaries.

It was a new thing for the Irish Catholics to see a man of their own creed rising up from their midst to assail the Ascendency with all the weapons of wit, and scorn, and satire, and invective of which O'Connell was then and always so complete a master. Fearless and serene, he assailed the dominant class after a fashion to which they were indeed unaccustomed, and the surprise of the Catholics, on discovering such a defender, can scarcely have been greater than that of the Ascendency in finding that the despised Catholics had found at last a tongue that was more terrible to them than the sword. A Spartan gentleman of some twenty centuries since, or a Virginian gentleman of one century ago, would scarcely have been more amazed if Helot or Blackamoor had risen up to agitate against them, and to hold them up to contempt and derision, than the Castle clique must have been when they gradually awoke to the growing influence of O'Connell.

Sometimes when Irishmen are disposed, and not unnaturally, to deal somewhat hardly with various passages in

O'Connell's life, when they think of his more than servile homage to royalty, when they remember how he waded into the waters of Kingstown Harbour to greet with servile welcome the basest of the Georges, when they reflect upon his unjust denunciation of the United Irishmen, and his unbridled and unhappy animosity to Young Ireland, when they think of him as the patron of a little army of placemen, they would do well to season their indignation by dwelling upon the great things he did accomplish for Ireland. The strength of a chain may lie in its weakest part; but the career of a great man must be tested not where it has failed but where it has succeeded. We should not, in the words of the dying Antony, lament nor sorrow too much over some passages in O'Connell's life, but please our thoughts by feeding them on those of his former fortunes, wherein he lived the greatest of Irishmen, the noblest. He dared the hatred of England. He courted poverty, he abandoned all the highways of personal success for the sake of the cause he honoured, and the country from which he sprang. He could not have foreseen that the cause would carry him to greatness, and give him an immortal memory.

It was a favourite taunt of his English opponents in later years to call him 'the big beggarman,' and to point the finger of scorn at him because he accepted a tribute from the nation he redeemed. If such a taunt needed any answer at all, it was answered by O'Connell himself in the pathetic words in which he speaks of his early toils and hardships, of his laborious youth and its incessant studies, and of the promising and lucrative career from which he always found time, when time was as precious as gold, to labour for the Catholic cause, and which in the end he gave up altogether, in order to devote himself with greater singleness of purpose to the service of his country.

In the Conservative press of to-day, O'Connell is exalted at the expense of Mr. Parnell. Eloquent tributes are paid to the genius, the integrity, and the honour of the great orator; melancholy regrets expressed for the leader of the past who contrasts so worthily with the leader of the present. Irishmen are assured that if only Ireland had such a man as O'Connell at her head, her demands would be more readily listened to by her appreciative rulers. Yet if Irishmen took the trouble to refer back to the dusty files of the newspapers of O'Connell's time, they would not find there any evidence of this latter-day admiration. Then no epithet was strong enough, no adjective sufficiently offensive to fling at O'Connell's name. It is an undoubted reputable fact that a hostile press raved itself into sheer hysterics of hatred against him. Writers who would have been sane and sensible enough in treating of the political life of old Rome or modern Paris, lost their heads completely when they came to speak of O'Connell, and could do nothing better than to bellow at him in blind fury of abuse. The coarsest vituperation was daily poured upon O'Connell by a generation certain of whose children to-day point to him in admiration, and appeal to his memory as to a holy spell, with which to conjure hence the modern spirit of Irish patriotism.

Upon O'Connell this whirlwind of objurgations had little or no effect. Those who assailed him he could assail again; those who abused him he could abuse yet more roundly. He could meet the ferocity of his opponents with a ferocity of his own, far more acrid and far more galling. His marvellous eloquence made him more than a match for the ablest of his opponents. It is not easy for us of to-day to judge of the effects of that eloquence. O'Connell's speeches are not such delightful reading as the speeches of Grattan, or of Sheil, or of Meagher. We, as we read, can hear no echo of that marvellous voice which all who ever heard it agree in pronouncing well-nigh unsurpassable in its beauty. Other speakers, far greater than O'Connell in their mastery of words, in the fulness of their thoughts, in the splendours of their literary form, seemed to dwindle into insignificance as orators beside him, when their feeble voices, harsh delivery, and uncouth gestures were contrasted with the magnificence of his voice and the majesty of his presence.

Men of the most varied types, and of the most differing political opinions, agreed in a common admiration of O'Connell's oratorical powers. Lord Jeffrey, Mr. Roebuck, Lord Beaconsfield, Lord Lytton, and Charles Dickens, have all borne impressive testimony to the spell of O'Connell's eloquence. Charles Dickens tells how, when he was once reporting a speech of O'Connell's in the House of Commons on one of the tithe-riots, he was so touched and moved by its exquisite pathos, that he was compelled to hold his hand, to lay down his pencil, and to listen motionless. The late Lord Lytton, in his poem, 'St. Stephen's,' has given a very poetic description of the impression produced on him by hearing O'Connell speak at a great public meeting in Ireland. 'Then,' says Lord Lytton, 'did I know what spells of infinite choice

> To rouse or lull, has the sweet human voice;
> Then did I seem to seize the sudden clue
> To the grand troublous life antique—to view
> Under the rock-stand of Demosthenes,
> Mutable Athens heave her noisy seas.'

Such was the man who had now come forward to take the lead in Irish politics, and to press upon the English Government the twin national demand for Catholic Emancipation and for the repeal of the Union. The repeal of the Union had been one of the earliest themes of O'Connell's eloquence; but it was to Catholic Emancipation that he devoted himself actively in the earlier period of his career, and it was over Catholic Emancipation that he achieved his greatest triumph, and rendered the greatest service to his country.

He was not unnaturally hated—and feared as well as hated—by the Ascendency. They suddenly saw their rule, which had been preserved so successfully from the dangers of more than one revolution, now threatened by a danger more deadly to their privileges than revolution itself. The power of eloquence, which has upset thrones and exiled princes in all the cities and empires of the world, the eloquence that appeals to and animates and unites a vast body of the people in one common purpose, was now levelled against them.

O'Connell's was no mere eloquence of the senate or of the school; it was as much at home on the hillside as in the council-chamber, upon the hustings as in the hall. It did not need for its audience a chosen group of cultivated, educated men. It stirred the blood and fired the mind of the humblest peasant with the same national pulsations and aspirations that it gave to the statesman and to the scholar.

His opponents had no eloquence of their own to pit against that of this people's tribune; but there still existed a tradition of another means of silencing a too eloquent opponent. The duel was still one of the cherished institutions of political life in the early part of the present century. A duel was forced upon O'Connell. His opponent, Mr. D'Esterre, appears to have been an unconscious tool of party faction. O'Connell and he met, and exchanged shots; and O'Connell wounded his adversary so severely that he died a few days after. That practically ended any idea of silencing O'Connell by wager of battle. It left, however, a profoundly-lasting, melancholy impression upon the mind of O'Connell himself. He bitterly regretted the death of his adversary; and that life-long regret must be taken very largely into account in considering the strong and unchanged opposition always offered by O'Connell to any struggle for freedom which could possibly involve the shedding of human blood or the loss of human life.

In the May of 1829 the English House of Commons was the theatre of the last act in a great religious and political movement. A man had made his appearance on the floor of the House as the chosen representative of an Irish county, who was the object of the keenest curiosity to an assembly crowded beyond its custom. The galleries and the avenues of the House were filled with individuals anxious to learn as soon as possible the result of a certain event. Every eye in the Chamber was riveted on the stranger who waited with grave unmoved countenance for the moment when Mr. Speaker rising from his seat should desire new members to come to the table; the name of the stranger and the name of

the constituency which he came there to represent were on
every lip. The name of the constituency was the County
Clare, and of its representative Daniel O'Connell. Well
might the members of that thronged Senate gaze with eager
interest on the stranger within their gates. He stood there
as the champion of a cause and of a creed which had long
been championless; he came as a conqueror in the name of
those who had been conquered. Centuries of pain and
passion, of injustice and of degradation worse than death, had
found in this man their apostle and their vindicator. The
Catholics of Ireland, so long the last among the nations, so
long the outcasts of the law, the scorn of power and the sport
of princes, were entering at last into the dearest of all human
inheritances, and they owed their disenthralment to the man
of genius who waited in Westminster on that afternoon of
early summer with the eyes of the world upon him.

How much this man had accomplished! Against the
hostility of the Ascendency; against the apathy of his own
people steeped in the Lethe of long oppression; against the
soldiers of Sirr and the pistol of D'Esterre; against Veto and
the friends of Veto; against Quarantotti advocating concession over in Rome, and Fingall counselling compromise at
home in Dublin; against Canning and Castlereagh resolutions; against Government prosecutions and State proscrip-
tions, this man had fought his way. A new Titan, he had
scaled Olympus and demanded admission into the councils of
the Immortals. A Catholic, he came to the British House of
Commons to champion the rights of his co-religionists, which
at that very moment the Government had granted, owing in
no small degree to his labours, toils, and energy.

When O'Connell stood below the bar of the House, the
House was but fresh from the discussions on the Catholic
Emancipation Bill, which had been introduced in order to
avoid civil war. That Ireland was raised from the stagnation
of slavery to a mood in which she was ready to fight for her
faith and freedom of conscience was in a great degree due to
O'Connell. It is, of course, certain that in course of time

Catholic Emancipation must have been conceded if there had been no O'Connell—if O'Connell had died of that fever which threatened his young manhood. But it would not have been conceded so soon. His indomitable energy, his unwearying patience, his marvellous eloquence had stimulated his friends, had formed a following, had frightened his foes, and now in this mid-May of 1829, Catholic Emancipation was an accomplished fact of some few days old. The Clare election was the immediate cause of Emancipation, and it was as the chosen of that struggle that O'Connell now waited to take his place in the House of Commons.

The Clare election was the great event of the day. The Duke of Wellington was at the head of the Tory Ministry which had just succeeded to the temporary and trumpery Goderich Administration. Lord John Russell had carried the Repeal of the Test Act and the Corporation Act, and this moderate measure of reform had offended Sir Robert Peel's supporters, and there were several secessions from the Cabinet. The vacant place of President of the Board of Trade was offered to Mr. Vesey Fitzgerald, member for the county of Clare. Mr. Fitzgerald accepted the offer, and as the assumption of office necessitated re-election, he immediately issued his address to his constituents. It is possible that he did not expect opposition; it is practically certain that the idea of his not being returned never occurred either to himself or to his friends. He considered his seat for Clare County to be as much his personal property as his hat.

The Catholics, it is true, had passed a resolution pledging themselves to oppose every candidate who was not sworn to oppose the Duke of Wellington's Government. Even this pledge did not at first appear very inimical to Mr. Fitzgerald's peaceful return. The Whigs as well as the Tories were desirous to see him re-elected. Lord John Russell had the audacity to suggest to O'Connell that Mr. Fitzgerald should be allowed to be returned unopposed, and for a short time O'Connell had the weakness to hesitate as to his line of conduct. But if the leader for a moment faltered or paltered the country was in no compromising temper. O'Connell soon saw that Clare must be contested, and the only question left to answer was, 'By whom?' A Major M'Namara was suggested, but Major M'Namara declined to trouble the peace of Mr. Fitzgerald. There was a brief period of suspense, and then the three kingdoms were startled by the intelligence that O'Connell himself was coming forward to contest Clare.

At that time it was impossible for a Catholic to enter Parliament. The law did not indeed prohibit him from standing, from being returned, from crossing the seas to Westminster; but on the threshold of St. Stephen's he was called upon to take an infamous oath, and by a shameful shibboleth he was excluded from his rights. O'Connell could not take this oath, but he saw that the hour had come when the appearance of an Irish Catholic at the bar of the English House of Commons, demanding to be sworn according to his conscience and his creed, and supported in his demand by millions of fellow-countrymen and fellow-believers, would have an effect well-nigh irresistible upon the Government. He was making a bold stroke, and he knew it. The Government knew it too, and both sides strained every nerve for victory.

O'Connell, like Toussaint L'Ouverture in Wordsworth's poem, had great allies—with him were exaltations, agonies, and love; and man's unconquerable mind. The sympathies of the people, newly awakened to a sense of their power, were with him. He had aroused a nation and made himself its leader. The whole story of the fight in the County Clare is one of the most exciting, as it is one of the most important, in the record of contested elections in Ireland. O'Connell was aided in his campaign by able and remarkable lieutenants, two of them especially remarkable. The Clare election seems a thing of the past, seems to belong to ancient history. More than half a century has since gone by, a half century big with importance to the Irish people. Well-nigh two generations of men have come and gone since O'Connell came forward on the Clare hustings, and no generation of Irishmen has ever witnessed or taken part in events more fateful to their country-

It is a half-century which has witnessed two armed risings in Ireland, a half-century of incessant coercive laws, a half-century that has seen the Irish race dwindle by millions through famine and emigration, a half-century that has seen a new Irish race grow up on the other side of the Atlantic, no less patriotic, no less determined than their kindred in the parent island; a half-century that has seen extorted from reluctant Ministers concession after concession, and piecemeal measures of reform. Such a half-century lies between us of to-day and the men of the Clare election. The big events of such an interval in themselves seem well-nigh to double the actual length of time, and O'Connell and his compeers appear almost as far from us, almost as much the mighty ghosts of heroes as Emmet, or Grattan, or the men of ninety-eight.

Yet there is a man now living, a man lately sitting in the English Parliament for that same county of Clare, a follower of Mr. Parnell to-day, who, more than fifty years ago, was most conspicuous among the champions and supporters of O'Connell during the stormy days of the Clare election. Colonel The O'Gorman Mahon was one of the most remarkable figures in the Parliament of 1880-1885. The historic muse, observing with admiration his stalwart form, his stately presence and youthful carriage, holds her breath, and refuses to whisper the age of the veteran politician. The wildest rumours circulate as to the years and the adventures of a man who played a prominent part in Irish politics long before most of his recent colleagues were born; who brought O'Connell forward for Clare and who was in Parliament some fifty years before his connection with Mr. Parnell's party. The intervening half-century he spent in all parts of the world, soldiering, sailoring, travelling, enjoying adventure for its own sake. He took a considerable share in making the history of one of the South American republics. Rumour says of him that at one time he was not merely Lord High Admiral of its fleet, but Generalissimo of its army as well, a divided duty which may, however, be regarded as savouring of exaggeration. He was in Parliament again from 1847 to 1852; he came in for the third time in 1879. In 1885 he did not present himself for re-election. His parliamentary friends were fond of rallying him for his supposed antiquity, but there was no young man in the Irish party, or, indeed, in the House of Commons, who carried his head more erect, walked with a firmer step, or showed less evidence of the weight of years than The O'Gorman Mahon.

Such is The O'Gorman Mahon to-day; here is what The O'Gorman Mahon was more than fifty years ago : ' He would deserve to stand apart in a portrait. Nature has been peculiarly favourable to him. He has a very striking physiognomy, of the Corsair character, which the Protestant Gulnares and the Catholic Medoras find it equally difficult to resist. His figure is tall, and he is particularly free and *dégagé* in all his attitudes and movements. In any other his attire would appear singularly fantastical. His manners are exceedingly frank and natural, and have a character of kindliness as well as of self-reliance imprinted upon them. He is wholly free from embarrassment, and carries a well-founded consciousness of his personal merit; which is, however, so well united with urbanity, that it is not in the slightest degree offensive. His talents as a popular speaker are considerable. He derives from external qualifications an influence over the multitude, which men of diminutive stature are somewhat slow in obtaining. A small man is at first regarded by the great body of spectators with disrelish; and it is only by force of phrase, and by the charm of speech, that he can at length succeed in inducing his auditors to overlook any infelicity of configuration; but when O'Gorman Mahon throws himself out before the people, and touching his whiskers with one hand brandishes the other, an enthusiasm is at once produced to which the fair portion of the spectators lend their tender contribution. Such a man was exactly adapted to the excitement of the people of Clare, and it must be admitted that, by his indefatigable exertions, his unremitting activity, and his devoted zeal, he most materially assisted in the election of Mr. O'Connell.'

The words which we have quoted are the words of another

of the lieutenants of O'Connell, of Richard Lalor Sheil. The name and the fame of Sheil have been too much suffered to fade into obscurity of late. Ireland has produced a long and illustrious succession of famous orators. The names of Grattan, of Plunket, of Meagher—not to mention the names of living men—shine like stars, but in the splendid galaxy no name is more luminous than the name of Sheil. His oratory deserves something of the careful study which is given to Cicero or to Mirabeau. Few public speakers have been masters of a more glowing style, have shown such a rich command of words, have made such gorgeous use of ornament which never became trivial because it never ceased to be majestic.

English statesmen of both parties have combined to pay striking tribute to the eloquence and to the genius of Sheil. Lord Beaconsfield, in one of the most famous of his novels, awards to Sheil enthusiastic praise, and contrasts him favourably with the great English orator Canning. Mr. Gladstone described Sheil not very long ago as one of the three great speakers who had come to success in spite of conspicuous personal defects of manner and of voice. Dr. Chalmers and Dr. Newman were the two examples chosen by Mr. Gladstone. Of Sheil he wrote that 'his voice resembled the sound produced by a tin-kettle battered about from place to place.' 'In anybody else,' Mr. Gladstone went on to say, 'I would not, if it had been my choice, like to have listened to that voice; but in him I would not have changed it, for it was part of a most remarkable whole, and nobody ever felt it painful while listening to it. He was a great orator, and an orator of much preparation, I believe, carried even to words, with a very vivid imagination, and an enormous power of language and of strong feeling. There was a peculiar character, a sort of half-wildness in his aspect and delivery; his whole figure, and his delivery, and his voice, and his matter were all in such perfect keeping with one another that they formed a great Parliamentary picture; and, although it is now thirty-five years since I heard Mr. Sheil, my recollection of him is just as vivid as if I had been listening to him to-day.' Such was the man and such the eloquence which was enabled to render O'Connell sterling service in the fight of Clare, a fight of which the most brilliant and fascinating picture has been left us by the pen of Sheil himself.

These events and this man were in the minds of that crowded assembly as they watched O'Connell standing below the bar of the House between Lord Ebrington and Lord Duncannon. Presently, the Speaker rose, and called upon new members desirous of taking the oath to come to the table. O'Connell advanced between his introducers to take the oath. It had been O'Connell's intention, when originally he stood for Clare, to come to the House of Commons and to refuse to take the shameful oath then tendered to Catholics. He believed that the result of such a daring step would be to advance materially the cause of Catholic Emancipation. But the cause of Catholic Emancipation had not to wait for that. The Clare election settled the matter, and between the time when O'Connell came forward to contest the county and the time when he stood at the bar of the House waiting to be sworn, Catholic Emancipation had become the law of the land.

With petty ingenuity, however, Sir Robert Peel had provided that only those who should be returned as members to the House of Commons 'after the commencement of that Act' should be allowed to take their seats under the new oaths. O'Connell had been returned before the Bill became law, and against him this retrospective clause was levelled. He, of course, refused to take the infamous form of oath which, except to him, was never again to be offered to a Catholic. He was directed to withdraw, and he did so. An animated discussion at once sprang up as to whether or not he should be heard at the bar of the House in his own defence. The debate was continued upon another day, and for three days in all this matter occupied the attention of the House. O'Connell was finally allowed to speak in his own defence at the bar. He made a long and eloquent speech. The old offensive oath was again tendered to him, and again he refused to take it in words which are now historic. He declined to take the oath because ' one part of it he knew to be false, and another he did not believe to be true.' A new writ was issued for the County Clare. But the action of Sir Robert Peel had no further effect than of allowing O'Connell a further triumph. He was, of course, immediately re-elected.

If the party that opposed O'Connell then are inclined to laud him now they are not alone. The Whigs, who feared or hated him in his life, who reviled him in their press and in their speeches, who alternately cajoled and calumniated him, as their fear or their hate rose uppermost; the fossil Whigs, the ruined remnant of a great party whose power is gone, and whose principles are as extinct as the dodo or the dynasties of the Shepherd-Kings; the Whigs whom O'Connell himself bitterly satirized are not now unwilling to pay O'Connell some empty honours, and to offer to his memory the respect which they denied him in the flesh. It is no commendation to O'Connell in the eyes of his sincere admirers that his merits are extolled at the expense of his political successors; it is to the supporter of the Melbourne Government, it is to O'Connell the enemy of Young Ireland, it is to the O'Connell of his later and failing years that his latter-day enthusiasts offer their unneeded tribute.

The Irish people owe much to O'Connell. They owe to him the privilege of professing in freedom the faith of their fathers; they owe to him the long agitation against the Union which kept alive the spirit of patriotism, and obeyed the commands of Grattan to keep knocking at the Union. They can forgive him for his falling off, for his unwise alliance with the Whigs; they can forgive him for the praise with which Tory politicians now load his memory, in consideration of the contumely which Tory politicians heaped upon the living man. As they think of O'Connell they hear rather the echoing crash of the sword which fell from the hands of the effigy of Walker on the day when the Act of Catholic Emancipation received the royal signature, than the voice of Young

Ireland protesting against the inaction that was betraying them.

The Clare election was the last act of the long struggle for Catholic Emancipation. It may be regarded as the preface or prelude to a struggle equally great, equally arduous, but not equally successful—the struggle for Repeal.

CHAPTER VIII.

THE TITHE WAR.

IT has already been mentioned that on one occasion, when Daniel O'Connell was speaking in the English House of Commons, his eloquence was so touching that Charles Dickens, who was reporting in the gallery of the House, laid down his pen, and was unable from very emotion to proceed with his work. The speech which so powerfully affected the great English novelist was one of the many speeches uttered by O'Connell with regard to what is now known in history as the Tithe War. O'Connell was giving an account of a tithe riot. He described how, during the struggle between the people on the one side and the police who were collecting parsons' tithes on the other, a blind man was led near to the scene of strife by his little daughter. A policeman's bullet, recklessly discharged, found its billet in the body of the child and killed her; and the blind man suddenly discovered that his little guide and companion had fallen lifeless in his arms, with her warm blood running over him. It is not surprising that the picture of such a scene, told as O'Connell could tell it, should have compelled one who was destined himself to be one of the greatest masters of pathos in the English language to stay his hand and drop his pen, and find himself unable to proceed with his task.

Such scenes as that described by O'Connell were only too common, only too frequent, during that terrible Tithe War. Such events have been neither uncommon nor unfrequent since, whenever the people have come into conflict with the ministers of oppressive laws. But, during the fearful years of the Tithe War, scenes of bloodshed and of death were of such ordinary occurrence that their recital in the end became part of the commonplaces of parliamentary debate, and Ministerialists listened at last almost with indifference to details that must have shocked them deeply when they were first recounted. I know of hardly any more melancholy reading in the world than to take down the volumes of Hansard for these early years of the decade of 1830, and to read in them the debates on the question of tithes. O'Connell's genius never reached loftier heights of eloquence, and was never devoted to a nobler purpose than in those burning words with which, again and again, he sought to impress upon a hostile assembly and an inimical Ministry the terrible injuries and injustice under which the Irish peasant was suffering.

The Tithe question was the natural—or rather the unnatural—offspring of the system of the Penal Laws. The rulers of Ireland had done their best for generations to crush out the national faith of the country by a code of which it has been well said that it could never have been practised in hell, or it would have overturned the kingdom of Beelzebub. When, at length, after generations of patient agony, the Penal Code became a thing of the past, and its obnoxious principles were dissipated to the free air; when at last the common rights of humanity and citizenship were granted to Catholics, and Irish Catholics sat and spoke and voted in the English House of Commons, even then Ascendency did its best to oppress and outrage the national creed. The Catholic Church was no longer directly persecuted, but the English Protestant Church was still the State Church of Ireland, supported by contributions exacted at the point of the bayonet from a people who did not believe the tenets of their Church, and to whom that Church had been for centuries the symbol of a relentless oppression.

It is scarcely surprising that the Irish people should have protested against being compelled to pay tithes to the professors of a creed which was not their creed, and for the support of churches over whose thresholds their feet never passed. Against this extraordinary imposition, justifiable by no principle whatever beyond the old blunt, brutal principle of the might that maketh right, the Irish peasant protested bitterly. Sometimes he carried his protest farther than mere words, and refused to pay the hateful tribute. Then the followers of the foreign Church called in the aid of arms. The tithes demanded in the name of religion were enforced by soldiers, and by police. If the peasant resisted, he was shot down.

A great English writer, Sydney Smith, had the courage to protest against the infamous exactions of the so-called Irish Church. 'There is no cruelty like it in all Europe, in all Asia, in all the discovered parts of Africa, and in all we have ever heard of Timbuctoo.' Sydney Smith draws a powerful and vigorous contrast between the influence of the Established Church and the National Church on the Irish peasantry. 'On the Irish Sabbath, the bell of a neat parish church often summons to church only the parson and an occasionally conforming clerk; while, a hundred yards off, a thousand Catholics are huddled together in a miserable hovel, and pelted by all the storms of heaven.' To support that parson and his 'occasionally conforming clerk,' the bayonets and the bullets of a military force were employed against the impoverished Catholic peasantry. The stones of that 'neat parish church' were too often cemented by the blood of its victims. The Tithe question was the cause of a kind of perpetually-smouldering civil war. To the collection of tithes in Ireland Sydney Smith concluded that in all probability a million of lives may have been sacrificed.

The Tithe question practically came to a head in consequence of a controversy in the county of Kildare. A Protestant curate of a Kildare parish obtained a rate for the purpose of rebuilding the parish church, by packing the vestry with Protestants. The example thus afforded, Protestant curates in other parts of the country were not slow to follow. The vast body of Catholic parishioners, justly incensed by this unfair additional levy, bound themselves into a solemn league and covenant against the payment of tithes and church cess. They resolved never again to meet these impositions with a voluntary money payment. The anti-tithe feeling ran high in Kildare. For many reasons the Catholic clergy—though, no doubt, as legally liable to pay tithes as any other parishioners—were usually, by a kind of half-hearted courtesy, exempted from the imposition. One of the Protestant clergymen in Kildare broke through this rule, and called upon a Catholic priest to pay his tithes, and, in default, seized upon the priest's horse. From the pulpit the priest condemned the whole disgraceful tithe system. The people began to offer more and more opposition to the imposition. The Protestant clergymen attempted to seize the cattle of Catholic farmers who refused to pay tithes. They called the police to their aid, and turned them, for the time being, into a force of cattle-lifters, or rather of would-be cattle lifters, for in most cases the police were unable to seize the beasts of the rebellious farmers.

As soon as it became noised abroad that a Protestant clergyman had appealed to the police, and that the police were going to make a descent upon the fields of some farmer, the cattle were locked up; and the law did not allow the police to break an entrance into barn or stable in order to seize upon them. In the rare cases in which the police were quick enough to lay hands upon the cattle in the fields, their triumph was merely nominal. When the beasts were put up for public sale no one thought of bidding for them except the owner, who, in consequence, got his beasts back again at a merely nominal price.

The organised opposition to the paying of tithes began to spread rapidly from county to county over the whole of Ireland. Under the amiable legislative system then in force, it was not legal for the Irish people to hold public meetings in their own country. But the law, which was clumsy as well as cruel, could be evaded. It was illegal to summon public meetings, and so no public meeting was summoned. But it was not illegal for the people of a particular town or parish to announce that on a certain day they were going to have a hurling match, and it was not illegal for the people of other counties and towns and parishes to come and take part in the national sport. It was perfectly plain, however, that the large assemblages that thus came together met not for the purpose of ball-playing, but for the purpose of opposing a strong front to the hated tithe system. Men came to these hurling matches to talk of other topics than balls and sticks. These hurling matches became the recognised medium of public opinion, and the public opinion of Ireland was dead against the payment of tithes. That public opinion hinted pretty plainly to those who were willing, for peace and quietness, to pay tithes to their Protestant masters, that such payment would not necessarily secure to them peace and quietness.

The organised opposition spread and flourished. The Government, with all its strength, was powerless against it. When a man was put into prison for refusing to pay his tithes, or for refusing to pay his rent—for the agitation against tithes was beginning to grow into an agitation against rent as well—the Government were unable to obtain a conviction against him. At last even the Government began to see that further struggle was futile, and that concession and compromise were inevitable. Not all the king's horses nor all the king's men could enforce an unwilling and united people to pay the detested tribute. The loss of life in exacting the tribute was terrible. That in itself was beginning to have a great effect upon the public mind. But the loss of money was also very heavy indeed. More money was spent in some petty parish in the attempt to enforce payment, and in the military movement consequent upon that attempt, than perhaps the tithes for a whole generation were worth. The Protestant clergymen, too, were growing heartily sick of the whole business. Many of them—indeed, most of them—came to hate the system which extorted, or tried to extort, their tithes with such a waste of blood and loss of life.

Moreover, their own interests were suffering severely. The tithes were not paid; and they took care to let the Government know that they would offer no opposition to some other method which would make them more securely masters of their means of livelihood. Then the Government set its usual machinery to work. Committees of Lords and Commons met and reported; and their reports were submitted to Parliament, and Parliament read them, and debated over them, and wrangled over them; and did little or nothing for long enough to settle the question satisfactorily. Temporary measures were brought in, which relieved the wants of the Protestant clergymen, and which left the task of collecting the tithes sometimes to compounding landlords, and sometimes to the Irish Executive.

But the Executive found it no easier to obtain the tithes than the parsons had found it. The arrears of tithes grew and grew till, in 1833, they amounted to considerably over a million of money. Ministries came and went, year succeeded year, and still found the English Parliament perplexed by the Tithe question, the Irish Executive helplessly attempting to enforce tithes, and the Irish people stubbornly resolved not to pay them. The country was growing more and more disturbed. The cost of the quarrel was growing heavier and heavier to the Government, and it was made plain in one of the debates in Parliament in 1834, that for some eight years England was compelled to maintain in Ireland an army well-nigh as strong as that which they thought to be necessary to support their will in India. In the year 1833 this military force had cost more than a million of money: 26,000*l.* had been spent in collecting 12,000*l.* worth of tithes. It was clear that the tithe system was too costly a luxury even for so wealthy a kingdom as England. But they indulged in the luxury for some years, still losing large sums annually, and striving by fierce coercive enactments to break the popular spirit, and to mould the popular will.

But the tithe agitation in Ireland had begun to rouse a tithe agitation in England as well. England had its Tithe question, too, and the action of the Irish people had awakened the English people to an appreciation of that fact; and an agitation was at once set on foot against it. This brought the matter nearer home. In 1836 Lord John Russell introduced a Tithe Bill that settled the question for England. Two years later, in 1838, he introduced a Bill that settled the question for Ireland. The advances made to the tithe-owners were considered in the nature of a gift, and a quarter of a million of money was voted for the extinction of the remainder of the arrears. Such was, for the moment, the end of the great and pressing difficulty.

Like most English measures passed for Ireland under the false and unnatural system of government which then existed and which still exists, it was only of a temporary nature, only a reform introductory of a far greater and more sweeping one which had to be accomplished in later years. Ever since the passing of the Act of Union the efforts of Irish politicians have been directed to extorting from unwilling Governments reforms which would have come naturally, simply, and far sooner, if the country had been left free to govern itself. The Tithe War struck a blow at the ascendency of the Established Church from which it never recovered. From the day when Lord John Russell's Bill was passed—nay more, from the day when the first Catholic priest denounced tithes from the pulpit, and the first Catholic farmer refused to pay his tribute—the fate of the Established Church was sealed. The long and bitter struggle, the years of agitation, the incessant debates in Parliament, and the many Ministerial attempts to arrive at some kind of compromise, by solving the difficulty after some fashion which should be most pleasing to Ascendency and least pleasing to the Irish people, all these, as they are now regarded after the lapse of more than a generation, may be seen to have been but the prelude to a greater agitation, and a greater reform, which had for its result the disestablishment of the Protestant Church in Ireland.

CHAPTER IX.

REPEAL.

THE Government acted on its usual give-and-take principle in passing the Catholic Emancipation Act—that is to say, it gave with one hand and took away with the other. It had been forced by O'Connell, and the gigantic movement which O'Connell had created and fostered, to concede to its Catholic subjects the rights of which they had been so long and unjustly deprived. It endeavoured to obtain some small set-off to the concession which was thus wrung from it.

Between O'Connell's first and second election a change had been made in the composition of the electors. By an Act of Henry VIII., which had been confirmed in 1795, freeholders to the value of forty shillings, over and above all charges, were entitled to vote, a system which naturally created a large number of small land-owners, who were expected to vote in obedience to the landlords who created them. O'Connell's election showed that the landlords would not always command the forty-shilling voters. It was clear that they might be won over to any popular movement, and it was decided to abolish them, which was accordingly done by an Act passed on the same day with the Catholic Emancipation Act. The new Act raised the county franchise to 10l.; and freeholders of 10l., but under 20l., were subjected to a complicated system of registration, well calculated to bewilder the unhappy tenant, and render his chance of voting more difficult. But all these precautions did not prevent the return of O'Connell the second time he appealed to the electors of Clare, nor did it even prove of much service in hindering the tenants from voting with the leaders of the popular movements.

The disfranchisement produced intense discontent throughout the whole country, and disorder followed close upon discontent. O'Connell now began to remind Ireland of his promise that Catholic Emancipation was a means towards an end—and that end, the Repeal of the Union. He started a society called the 'Friends of Ireland,' which the Government at once put down. He started another, 'The Anti-Union Association.' It was put down, too, and O'Connell was arrested for sedition, tried, and found guilty. Judgment was deferred, and never pronounced, and O'Connell was released to carry on his agitation more vigorously than ever.

With Ireland torn by disorders against which the Insurrection Acts found it hard to cope, with the country aflame with anger at the extinction of the forty-shilling vote, the Government judged it wise and prudent to bring in a Bill for Ireland in January 1832, effecting still further disfranchisement. The new Bill abolished the forty-shilling vote in boroughs as well as in counties, and the lowest rate for boroughs and counties was 10*l*. But for the next few years all recollection of Emancipation on the one hand, and Disfranchisement on the other, was to be swallowed up in the struggle which has passed into history as the Irish Tithe War. What the Tithe War was, and how it ended, has been already told. While it was going on, during the long years in which it alternately blazed and smouldered, there was little time for Irish politicians to think of Repeal.

But O'Connell still kept the great purpose in his mind, still agitated, still planned, still schemed. It did not seem to him and to his followers that the difficulties in the way of Repeal were in reality any greater than those which had menaced the movements in favour of Catholic Emancipation. The advocates of Catholic Emancipation had boldly faced all the obstacles that were brought against them, had overcome them all in turn, and Catholic Emancipation was now an accomplished fact.

To O'Connell, and O'Connell's allies, it seemed as if the difficulties which were in the way of Repeal might be as successfully struggled with, and as triumphantly overthrown. There was a great deal against the agitation. To begin with, the country was very poor. 'Every class of the community, says Sir Charles Gavan Duffy, 'was poorer than the corresponding class in any country in Europe.' The merchants, who had played a prominent part in political life since the Union, were now wearied and despairing of all agitation, and held aloof; the Protestant gentry were, for the most part, devoted to the Union; many of the Catholic gentry disliked O'Connell himself, and his rough, wild ways; many of O'Connell's old associates in the Catholic Emancipation movement had withdrawn from him to join the Whigs.

In England the most active dislike of O'Connell prevailed. The Pericles or the Socrates of Aristophanes, the Royalists drawn by Camille Desmoulins, were not grotesquer caricatures than the representation of O'Connell by English opinion and the English press. O'Connell himself was not so powerful with the people as he had been immediately after the triumph of the Emancipation struggle. He had paid the inevitable price of power in making many enemies. He used his power with an absolute indifference to appearances or public opinion, and that indifference made him many more enemies, who might well have been kept as friends, and alienated friends whose friendship was of value. The Catholic clergy, too, who had been his strongest allies in the Emancipation movement, were by no means to be counted on as supporters in the new Repeal movement. Many of them regarded the so-called settlement of the Tithe War, not as a victory, but as a pitiable compromise; and they held O'Connell responsible for having yielded to the compromise and for sacrificing the interests of Ireland to the convenience of the Whigs.

Under such conditions it must be admitted that the prospects of O'Connell's new movement were scarcely promising. But O'Connell was never a man to be frightened by stormy weather. He opened an Association on Burgh Quay, and he held meetings there regularly every week, at which he addressed exceedingly small audiences with as much impassioned enthusiasm as though he were swaying by his eloquence the gigantic gatherings of the Clare election. At Burgh Quay he taught the doctrines of the Association. The Association proposed, first of all, to dissolve the Union; but the dissolution of the Union was not its only object. It further proposed to abolish tithes, to give fixity of tenure to land-holders, and it called for extension of the suffrage, for shorter Parliaments, for the abolition of the property qualification for members of Parliament, and for equal electoral districts. These latter points were taken from the great Chartist movement in England, to which O'Connell had given its name, and to which he had given such earnest support.

The proud patience which the gods are said to love stood O'Connell in good stead now. For more than a year he laboured patiently at the hall on Burgh Quay, telling his scanty audiences again and again the shameful story of the Union, and appealing to all that was best and noblest in the national spirit to unite in breaking the hard bondage. But the audience did not increase. 'Conciliation Hall,' as O'Connell named his place of meeting on Burgh Quay, was sparsely filled with audiences which did not readily take fire at his glowing periods and passionate appeals. But O'Connell never for a moment lost heart, or appeared dismayed. He went on as if he had the whole country with him. The movement gradually spread. The Repeal agitation, which had first languished, suddenly began to swell up and assume large proportions.

O'Connell was always remarkable for the manner in which he contrived to utilise every national force for the great purposes to which he was devoted. While the Repeal movement was going on, another movement of a different kind was started in Ireland, and met with remarkable success. A good, pure-hearted Franciscan friar began a great crusade against intemperance, which proved strangely and unexpectedly successful, and which made the name of Father Mathew, the inaugurator of the temperance movement, very famous. O'Connell immediately saw what a strength such a movement would have if it were incorporated with his own movement, and he immediately gave all the support of his great authority and of his great name to the new crusade. He praised it enthusiastically: he influenced many of his followers to join it, and he always spoke with the greatest pride of his noble army of teetotallers.

Father Mathew himself was not an active politician. His duty in life was to wrestle with and to overthrow one of the greatest evils that can afflict humanity, and with the actual workings of political agitation he had little or no concern. His own personal opinions were, if anything, of a Conservative type, and he certainly had no kind of sympathy with any violent or demonstrative agitation of any sort. But he could not afford to decline the enormous assistance to the temperance movement which O'Connell's support and O'Connell's encouragement gave. So it came about that the temperance movement became, as it were, amalgamated with and absorbed into the Repeal movement, and Father Mathew's temperance recruits swelled the ranks of the army that O'Connell was levying to wage war against the Union. No, not to wage war against the Union. Nothing was further from O'Connell's thoughts than any kind of active demonstration against oppression. By peace, and peace only—by orderly, quiet, constitutional measures—was the Repeal of the Union to be obtained. O'Connell had a most cordial hatred of the revolutionaries of 1798 and 1803, and he was destined a little later to express the bitterest animosity to the revolutionaries of the Young Ireland movement.

'The year 1843,' said O'Connell, 'is, and shall be, the great Repeal year.' At the time when O'Connell uttered that prophecy, which was destined not to be fulfilled, it did indeed seem as if the Repeal of the Union was one of the contingencies—indeed one of the probabilities—of the immediate future. O'Connell had worked up his organisation and made it immensely powerful. Over in England he had established in the House of Commons an elaborate parliamentary system of his own. By his own influence he had secured seats in Parliament for his sons and for a great many of his relatives, and for a large number of his followers and supporters. The Repeal party in the House of Commons was yearly growing stronger and more numerous. O'Connell's influence was

I

almost all-powerful with the Irish constituencies; and whenever a vacancy occurred O'Connell sent down a Repeal candidate to contest the seat, and the Repeal candidate was in most cases successfully returned.

But what O'Connell chiefly relied on for effecting his purpose were the now historic monster meetings. Nothing showed O'Connell's strength as much as these monster meetings. They were held usually on a Sunday, and they were attended by thousands of people who came to the place of meeting, not merely from the immediate vicinity, but often from other localities miles and miles away. The roads leading to the fields or hall where the meeting was to take place would be choked for hours and hours previously, with the streams of people all making for a common centre. These vast meetings were addressed by O'Connell with the ever-ready eloquence which endeared him to the popular mind. His marvellous voice would carry to the farthest end of these great assemblies; and the peasant on the farthest verge of the crowd was as much stirred and swayed by O'Connell's fiery moods of passion, patriotism, and humour, as those who stood by his side on the platform.

O'Connell had another and most important ally in the *Nation* newspaper, which was destined, however, to turn against him in later years. But at the time of the monster meetings, the brilliant young men who wrote for the *Nation* were in complete accord with O'Connell, and gave him all the support of their varied gifts, genius, and eloquence. For a man who had no intention of ever attempting to attain his ends by any other than the most strictly constitutional means, O'Connell's actions and utterances had sometimes a very curious appearance. The vast crowds who assembled to listen to O'Connell's eloquence began to attend the meetings in something like military order, and with a decided appearance of military discipline. They listened to language from O'Connell which certainly did not always sound like the language of peace. O'Connell addressed these vast bodies of men—at one meeting, held at Tara, a quarter of a million persons are said to have been present—in terms of the bitterest denunciation of England, and made the most glowing appeals to the most painful memories of Irish history.

O'Connell had never any intention of making any attempt to repeal the Union by force; but English statesmen, witnessing these vast meetings, and reading the fiery words with which O'Connell addressed them, may well have thought that O'Connell was not prepared to keep his agitation strictly inside the limits of peace and order. There were others besides English statesmen who thought so, too. The young men who wrote for the *Nation* found it hard to believe that such great meetings were to be convened, and such inflammatory harangues to be delivered, if the whole thing were simply to be regarded as an imposing pageant, no more serious in its purpose, nor more dangerous to British rule in Ireland, than a Lord Mayor's show.

The Government thought that O'Connell meant rebellion. Many of O'Connell's immediate followers and supporters thought, too, that he meant rebellion in the last instance, if nothing could be done without it. O'Connell, it is clear, never for a moment dreamt of rebellion; but he was not unwilling to let the English Government see what forces he had at his command; he was not even unwilling that they should imagine that if they were deaf to his demands he might answer by an armed rising. But he was so convinced that the Government would give way, that Repeal would be conceded as Catholic Emancipation had been conceded, that he seems to have believed himself justified in making menaces which were meaningless, and in holding up to the English Government the symbols of danger, where no danger existed.

O'Connell's plan was, of course, a failure. The Government did not grant Repeal. They struck, instead, very sharply and decisively at O'Connell's movement. A great meeting was summoned by O'Connell, to be held at Clontarf, on Sunday, October 8, 1843. The meeting was proclaimed by the Lord-Lieutenant on the very morning before it was announced to take place. For the moment it seemed as if a collision between authority and agitation was inevitable. Masses of people were coming into Clontarf from all directions at the very time when the proclamation was issued. The Government, it was clear, were determined to prevent the meeting, if necessary by force of arms; and large bodies of police and soldiery were massed in readiness. It was said that the Government wished to provoke a collision; and a collision would have meant much bloodshed, and consequences which it was impossible to foresee. But no collision took place. O'Connell immediately issued a proclamation of his own declaring that the orders of the Irish Executive must be obeyed; that no meeting would be held; and that the people were to return to their homes at once. The order was implicitly obeyed. The people, who would have resisted the authority of the Lord-Lieutenant, did not dream of resisting the voice of their leader. The meeting was not held, and the people went to their homes in peace.

But with the dispersal of that meeting ended all the strength that the Repeal movement had; and ended too, practically, O'Connell's power in Ireland. Once it was clear that, under no circumstances, he had any intention of resorting to force, it was equally clear that his agitation offered no serious danger to the English Government. The Government immediately prosecuted O'Connell, and put him in prison. O'Connell issued another proclamation to the people, calling upon them to remain perfectly quiet; and the people again obeyed him. There was an appeal to the House of Lords, and the House of Lords gave the appeal in O'Connell's favour, and he was let out of prison. But he came out of prison practically a broken man. His agitation had failed hopelessly. All his young allies who had long believed in him were falling away from him, combining themselves into an alliance having far other objects than those dreamt of by O'Connell.

Other causes, too, combined to tell against O'Connell. He was an old man now, and his old age was, it is said, tortured by a hopeless passion for a young girl whom he was eager to make his wife. It is melancholy to think of the great

Tribune, the leader of a nation, the man whose words were listened to with reverence and almost with adoration by the vast body of his fellow-countrymen; who had occupied a position almost unique in modern history, being vexed in his latest years, and in the time of his sorest trial, by the pangs of misprised love. O'Connell may have been the uncrowned king of Ireland; the adored of his countrymen, and the dread of the English Government; but he could not succeed in winning the affections of one young girl, or in shaking himself free from his unhappy passion.

The last years of O'Connell's life are profoundly touching. The broken-down old man who had done so much for Ireland lingered for a few years after his imprisonment in fitful struggles with the Young Ireland Party, and in fitful appearances in the House of Commons, where the dying giant was listened to with a silent respect, which was in itself the most melancholy of homages. At last he resolved to go away to Italy. The one wish now left to him was to end his days in the sacred circle of the Eternal City; but that wish, like so many others that he had so fondly cherished, was not destined to be gratified. He died at Genoa, on his way to Rome, on May 15, 1847. This long, stormy, brilliant career ended in the saddest of shadows. Failure is the most melancholy epitaph for a great man, and the end of O'Connell's life was, indeed, failure; but he remains one of the greatest figures in Irish history. He has done great things for his country: what he failed to do he left as an inheritance to his countrymen to be accomplished by his successors.

CHAPTER X.

THE 'NATION.'

ONE autumn afternoon in 1842, three men were walking together in the Phœnix Park, in Dublin. They sat on a seat and proceeded to discuss together a project which was destined to prove one of the most remarkable events in Irish history, and to leave a lasting impression upon the country. The three men were Thomas Davis, John Dillon, and Charles Gavan Duffy. The project they were discussing was the founding of a newspaper to represent properly the national feeling of Ireland, and to be the organ and the mouthpiece of the new ideas, hopes, and ambitions that were coming into being under the influence of O'Connell's movement. The three young men were themselves sufficiently characteristic types of the party which was soon destined to be known as Young Ireland. All three were young; all three were gifted; all three were profoundly imbued with the loftiest spirit of patriotism, and all three were convinced to their hearts' cores that the hour for the regeneration of their country was at hand.

Physically there was not much resemblance between the men. Thomas Davis, then the best known of the three, and the man whom the only living member of that triple brotherhood would be the first to salute as the most remarkably gifted, was not remarkable in his personal appearance. He was described once by a brutal opponent, who at one time had promisings of a fair career, which came to a close disastrously a few years ago—the late Dr. Kenealy—as the 'dog-faced demagogue.' He looked, it is said, more like a young English man than a young Irishman; but he had what an English poet has called 'the brave Irish eyes,' and they were lit by the fire of genius. 'Davis,' says Sir Charles Gavan Duffy, 'was a man of middle stature, strongly but not coarsely built —a broad brow and a strong jaw stamped his face with a character of power; but except when it was lighted by thought or feeling it was plain, and even rugged.' In his boyhood he was 'shy, retiring, unready, and self-absorbed,' and was even described as 'a dull child' by unappreciative kinsfolk. At Trinity College he was a wide and steady reader, who was chiefly noted by his fellow-students for his indifference to rhetorical display. He was auditor of the Dublin Historical Society, had made some name for himself by his contributions to a magazine called the *Citizen*, and was a member of the Repeal Association.

John Dillon was a man of a very different appearance. Every Irishman or Englishman who knows his son, the present John Dillon, knows how singularly impressive his appearance is. That dark, melancholy, handsome face, with its deep, Spanish eyes, its olive complexion, and the midnight darkness of its hair, might have smiled in stately gravity from one of those canvases of Velasquez which are the glory of Madrid. Yet those who knew the father assure a later generation that he was even handsomer than his son. 'In person,' says Gavan Duffy, 'he was tall and strikingly handsome, with eyes like a thoughtful woman's, and the clear, olive complexion and stately bearing of a Spanish noble.' He had been designed for the priesthood, but had decided to adopt the Bar. Like Davis, he loved intellectual pursuits, and was a man of wide and varied learning. 'Under a stately and somewhat reserved demeanour lay latent the simplicity and joyfulness of a boy; no one was readier to laugh with frank cordiality, or to give and take the pleasant banter which lends a relish to the friendship of young men.' Long years after, Thackeray said of him to Gavan Duffy, that the modest and wholesome sweetness of John Dillon gave him a foremost place among the half-dozen men in the United States whom he loved to remember. Dillon was at no time what we should call a very extreme politician. He never had much belief in the benefits to be gained by the warlike spirit which was so soon to animate Young Ireland; and that fact should be borne in mind as one additional mark of honour in a career that was all honourable; for when the end did come, and the die was cast, Dillon, without a moment's hesitation, flung himself into the struggle, prepared to stand or fall with the comrades whose actions he did not believe to be opportune or well advised.

Of those three young men who walked in the Phœnix Park that day, and schemed out the starting of the *Nation* newspaper, one is still alive among us, and has lived to be the brilliant and eloquent historian of the movement in which he took part, of the paper which he edited, and of the allies of his youth. Sir Charles Gavan Duffy and Kevin Izod O'Doherty are almost the last of the conspicuous Young Irelanders who now live and look upon the earth. At the time when he walked with Davis and Dillon in the Phœnix Park, Duffy was only twenty-six years of age; Dillon was a year older, and Davis was twenty-eight. The first number of the *Nation* was published on October 15, 1842. It took for its motto the words of an answer made by Stephen Woulfe to Peel's contemptuous inquiry in Parliament as to what good corporations would do a country so poor as Ireland. 'I will tell the honourable gentleman,' said Woulfe; 'they will go far to create and foster public opinion, and make it racy of the soil.' The motto of the *Nation* was to 'create and foster public opinion, and to make it racy of the soil.' It succeeded probably beyond the fondest expectations of its founders. The first number was sold out almost as soon as it was printed, and a copy of that first number to-day is one of the treasures of the Irish bibliophile.

The success of the *Nation* was extraordinary. Its political teachings, its inspiring and vigorous songs and ballads, the new lessons of courage and hope that it taught, the wide knowledge of history possessed by its writers—all combined to make it welcome to thousands. The tradesmen in towns, and the country peasants, read it, and were animated with the story of their old historic island into the belief that she had a future, and that the future was close at hand, and that they were to help to make it. It was denounced by the Tory press as the organ of a hidden 'French party.' From France itself came words of praise worth having from the Irish officers in the French service. One was Arthur O'Connor, the Arthur O'Connor of 1798; the other was Miles Byrne, who had fought at Wexford.

O'Connell became alarmed at the growing popularity of the *Nation*. At first it had strongly supported him; he had even written a Repeal Catechism in its pages; but its young men had the courage to think for themselves, and to criticise even the deeds and the words of the Liberator. More and more young men clustered round the writers of the *Nation*, brilliant young essayists, politicians, poets. Gifted women wrote for the *Nation*, too—Lady Wilde, ' Speranza,' chief among them. The songs published in a volume called ' The Spirit of the Nation ' became immediately very popular. As the agitation grew, Peel's Government became more threatening. O'Connell, in most of his defiant declarations, evidently thought that Peel did not dare to put down the organisation for Repeal, or he would never have challenged him as he did; for O'Connell never really meant to resort to force at any time.

But the few young men who wrote for the *Nation*, and the many young men who read the *Nation*, were really prepared to fight if need be for their liberties. Nor did they want foreign sympathy to encourage them. In the United States vast meetings, organised and directed by men like Seward and Horace Greeley, threatened England with ' the assured loss of Canada by American arms ' if she suppressed the Repeal agitation by force; and later Horace Greeley was one of a Directory in New York for sending officers and arms to Ireland. In France the Republican party were loud in their sympathy for the Irish and Ledru Rollin had declared that France was ready to lend her strength to the support of an oppressed nation. No wonder the leaders of the national party were encouraged in the belief that their cause was pleasing to the Fates.

The establishment of the *Nation* newspaper marked a new stage in the resurrection of Irish nationalism. With O'Connel's name the emancipation of a nation of Catholics from the Penal Laws will always be triumphantly associated; and his name lends a lustre to the agitation in favour of the Repeal of the Union. But the warm breath of patriotism which in 1842 inspired the Irish nation with a new purpose and a new hope, and which with its afflatus has given a quicker vitality to every national movement since, is due, not to O'Connell, but to the young men who founded the *Nation*, who wrote for the *Nation*, and who made a nation.

Critics—even friendly critics—are accustomed to say, too lightly, that the Young Ireland movement failed in its object. If, because it did not add a successful revolution to the year of revolutions; if, because it did not overthrow British rule in Ireland and set up the green flag on Dublin Castle, it deserves to be called a failure, then, of course, it did fail, for it accomplished none of these things. It was not a revolution; it was hardly a rival rising. Its leaders were exiled almost without a struggle; its flag never showed upon a single field. But it gave a new impulse to the Irish cause; it gave the Irish new martyrs and a new tradition; it carried to Irishmen in every corner of the earth a stronger hope and a firmer conviction of the duty of nationality.

The *Nation* filled a great want in Ireland at the time that it appeared. The position of literature in the country was low indeed. The newspapers were few, and represented no national spirit. Literature was scantily cultivated in these newspapers; and any knowledge of foreign literature and foreign politics was only to be obtained through the medium of the English Press. Books were few and dear. There was not at that time in existence any of those many cheap libraries which now make the masterpieces of Irish literature so easily accessible even to the poorest. Such literature as came readily in the way of the vast bulk of the Irish people was pitiful in the extreme, only stuff of the worst cheap-book style, or anti-national bombast, like the 'Battle of Aughrim.' Irish history was nowhere taught. English history alone was recognised in the schools. It is probable that the national spirit has seldom been at so low an ebb as when the *Nation* first came out. The *Nation* promptly remedied this state of things. In its columns week after week the Irish people began to be made acquainted with glowing articles on their own history, with thrilling ballads devoted to the deeds and to the memory of Irish heroes, with animated appeals to the Irishmen of the present to be worthy of the Irishmen of that past which was now almost for the first time revealed to them.

The young men who wrote for the *Nation* were well qualified to make their organ powerful and impressive. It would have been difficult to find anywhere a more brilliant or more gifted company. Thomas Davis was the leader and master of them all. The most genuine poet Ireland had seen since Thomas Moore, he was inspired by a far more national spirit than Moore's, and the songs of Davis were adored by Young Ireland. None of the Young Irelanders adored Davis more than did John Pigot, the dark-haired, dark-eyed boy, whose winning sweetness and chivalrous bearing made him, according to Duffy, 'the woman's ideal of a patriot,' and also made him, not unnaturally, the appropriate hero for the novel of a satirical novelist who took Young Ireland for his theme. His closest friend was John O'Hagan, whom Davis declared to have been 'the safest in council, the most moderate in opinion, the most considerate in temper, of the young men.' His moderation of opinion did not prevent him, however, from writing some of the most impassioned anti-English poems that appeared in the *Nation*; but it preserved him from the later schemes of Young Ireland to take service years after under the English Government, and to translate 'The Song of Roland.'

Amongst the other men who wrote for the *Nation* in its early days, some of the most conspicuous were Denis Florence MacCarthy, MacNevin, and Clarence Mangan. Of these three, Clarence Mangan was blest with the most brilliant and the most unhappy genius. With a lyric power and fanciful imagination which have only been rivalled by Edgar Allan Poe, he was cursed by a fate as melancholy as that which pursued the author of 'The Raven.' To each, too—the Irishman and the American—might be applied those lines of Poe's masterpiece, which speak of some

<blockquote>
Unhappy master,
Whom unmerciful disaster
Followed fast and followed faster.
</blockquote>

Gavan Duffy gives a picture of him which reads like the fragment from one of the weird stories of Hoffmann—some description, it might be, of the student Anselmus in the enchanting 'Golden Jar'—'He lived a secluded, unwholesome life, and when he emerged into daylight he was dressed in a blue cloak, midsummer or midwinter, and a hat of fantastic shape, under which golden hair as fine and silky as a woman's hung in unkempt tangles, and deep blue eyes lighted a face as colourless as parchment. He looked like the spectre of some German romance rather than a living creature.'

Mangan's career ended like that of Edgar Allan Poe, and of another brilliant man of genius, Henri Murgen, in the hospital. A fatal and unfortunate taste gradually sapped and shattered his fine intellect and fantastic genius; but he has left behind him an imperishable monument in the songs which bear his name. It was one of Mangan's quaint humours to assume himself to be an Oriental scholar; and among his verses are many pieces claiming to be taken from the Turkish, the Arabic, or Persian. As a matter of fact, it seems that Mangan had no acquaintance whatever with the strange languages of the East. But he had what was far better—a mind that was perfectly able to appreciate the Oriental spirit, and his Eastern poems have in them that power of making the reader appreciate the gorgeous colouring of fancy and splendour of the East, which is worth the most intimate acquaintance with the lexicons of Richardson and Redhouse. The poem, which is called 'The Time of the Barmecides,' I have, for my own part, no hesitation in pronouncing to be one of the most stirring and beautiful ballads of our time; and the melancholy, dirge-like music of 'Karaman,' and the poem on the Bosphorus, with all its marvellous ingenuity of rhyming power, are two other proofs of the way in which Mangan was imbued, or appeared to be imbued, with the Oriental spirit. He might not read a line of Persian, but he was a poet worthy to have set up his tent in the company of Hafiz, near the pleasant waters of Rocknabad, and under the groves of Mosella.

Denis Florence MacCarthy long outlived his poetic colleagues of the *Nation*, but he, too, has now passed away, after enriching Irish literature with many beautiful poems and some admirable translations. The prose of MacNevin and the poetry of Williams are as familiar to-day to Irishmen as they were in the years when the *Nation* first became famous.

Seldom in the history of any nation has a more remarkable body of young men been banded together. Like O'Connell, they have experienced that curious Conservative canonisation which is represented by the exaltation and laudation of any body of Irishmen who are passed away, at the expense of any body of living Irishmen who are working heart and soul for the cause of the country. The Young Irelanders, who were the abomination of all Toryism at the time when they were trying to educate their countrymen, have suddenly become something like heroes in the eyes of Conservatism. They are held up to the men of to-day as honourable models, as a glaring and conspicuous contrast. The men of to-day are told that if they were as the Young Irelanders, they would be regarded with very different eyes, and so on. All of which is of no concern to Irish or English Liberalism, and can in nowise injure the memories of the young men who founded the *Nation*.

CHAPTER XI.

YOUNG IRELAND.

WHILE O'Connell was still the recognised head of the Irish national movement, a young man came forward as a prominent figure in Irish politics, Mr. William Smith O'Brien, member of Parliament for Limerick County. He was a country gentleman, of stately descent, a direct descendant of Brian Boroimhe, a brother of Lord Inchiquin. He was a high-minded and honourable gentleman, with his country's cause deeply at heart. Davis described him as 'the most extravagant admirer of the *Nation* I have ever met.' Smith O'Brien made his first appearance in Conciliation Hall on June 2, 1844, and for some time he was a constant attendant at its meetings. His views, however, were by no means entirely in accordance with those of O'Connell's. O'Connell was emphatically and definitely opposed to any appeal at any time or under any consideration to physical force. Smith O'Brien was of opinion that, under certain circumstances, it was the duty of the nation to defend its rights in arms.

O'Connell at first welcomed O'Brien cordially. 'I find it impossible,' he said, 'to give a proper expression to the feelings of delight I have in hailing Mr. William Smith O'Brien to the ranks of the Association. He now is in his true position—the position which was occupied centuries ago by his ancestor, Brian Boroimhe. Whatever may become of *me*, it is a consolation and a pleasure to remember that Ireland will have a true friend in William Smith O'Brien – a man who has a well cultivated mind, with intellectual endowments of the very highest order, powerful eloquence, untiring energy, constant love for his country, and every other true qualification of a popular leader; and I delight to hail him to his right place among his friends, at the post at which every true Irishman would wish to see him—at the head of the Irish people.'

But the alliance between O'Connell and O'Brien, between Old Ireland and Young Ireland, could not be, and was not, of long duration. The great majority of the Young Irelanders entertained a scarcely concealed contempt for the policy of O'Connell's old age. The great majority of the Young Irelanders talked, read, and thought revolution. In passionate poems and eloquent speeches they expressed their hatred of tyranny and their stern resolve to free their country by brave deeds rather than by arguments. They had now a brilliant orator among them, Thomas Francis Meagher, 'a young man,' says Mr. Lecky, 'whose eloquence was beyond comparison superior to that of any other rising speaker in the country, and who, had he been placed in circumstances favourable to the development of his talent, might, perhaps, at length have taken his place among the great orators of Ireland.'

Meagher had early endeared himself to the impetuous and gifted young men with whom he was allied, by a brilliant speech against O'Connell's doctrine of passive resistance. This speech of Meagher's, like all Meagher's speeches, is—or, at least, ought to be—familiar to every Irish nationalist; but its rare beauty and eloquence not merely justify, but prescribe its quotation here again. ' I am not one of those tame moralists,' the young man exclaimed, ' who say that liberty is not worth one drop of blood. . . . Against this miserable maxim the noble virtue that has saved and sanctified humanity appears in judgment. From the blue waters of the Bay of Salamis; from the valley over which the sun stood still and lit the Israelites to victory; from the cathedral in which the sword of Poland has been sheathed in the shroud of Kosciusko; from the Convent of St. Isidore, where the fiery hand that rent the standard of St. George upon the plains of Ulster has mouldered into dust; from the sands of the desert, where the wild genius of the Algerine so long has scared the eagle of the Pyrenees; from the ducal palace in this kingdom where the memory of the gallant and seditious Geraldine enhances more than royal favour the splendour of his race; from the solitary grave within this mute city, which a dying bequest has left without an epitaph—oh! from every spot where heroism has had a sacrifice or a triumph, a voice breaks in upon the cringing crowd that cherishes this maxim, crying, " Away with it! —away with it!" '

There are few passages in the ornate oratory of the world, in the glowing prose of some of the earlier Greek orators or in the stately magnificence of Cicero, in the richly-coloured periods of Burke, or in the shining sentences of Mirabeau or Vergniaud, which can be unhesitatingly declared superior to the brilliant utterances of the young Waterford gentleman of three-and-twenty. There is reason to believe, and to regret in believing, that Meagher's speeches are not studied in Ireland to-day with the attention and with the devotion which they deserve. Some few months ago a student made repeated and unsuccessful attempts, in Dublin, to obtain a copy of Meagher's speeches; but he searched in vain the bookshops of the quays, and searched in vain in the bookshops elsewhere, for a copy of the speeches of one of the greatest orators and truest patriots that Ireland has yet produced. He could not come across an example of the Lives and Speeches published in Ireland in the days when the memory of Young Ireland was the memory of yesterday, he could not obtain an example of the American edition of 1853. The shilling volume published by Cameron & Ferguson, which gives the life of Meagher, with selections from his speeches and writings, confines these selections almost entirely to his American speeches, which, however valuable in themselves, are not the speeches that made his name famous.

Luckily, many of his best speeches are preserved in the admirable series of Penny Readings which are issued from the *Nation* office. But it is hard to avoid feeling deep regret that it should not be possible for any patriotic Irishman to become at any time the possessor of the speeches of one of the most gifted of his countrymen. Speeches such as the one which has been quoted were not calculated to cement the alliance between Old and Young Ireland. Another speech of Meagher's was the direct cause of severing the alliance. In a speech at Conciliation Hall Meagher declared that 'the King of Heaven—the Lord of Hosts! the God of Battles!—bestows His benediction upon those who unsheath the sword in the hour of a nation's peril. From that evening on which, in the valley of Bethulia, He nerved the arm of the Jewish girl to smite the drunken tyrant in his tent, down to this our day, in which He has blessed the insurgent cavalry of the Belgian priest, His Almighty hand has ever been stretched forth from His throne of light to consecrate the flag of freedom —to bless the patriot's sword.' The speech was interrupted by John O'Connell, Daniel O'Connell's son. Smith O'Brien rose to defend Meagher. The quarrel was complete; the severance inevitable.

The Young Irelanders seceded from O'Connell. A second secession was yet to be made from the ranks of the Young Irelanders themselves. One of the most prominent men in the movement was John Mitchel, the son of an Ulster Unitarian minister. Thomas Davis, the sweet chief singer of the movement, died suddenly before the movement which he had done so much for had taken up revolution in any shape. Mitchel came on the *Nation* in his place, and advocated revolution and republicanism. He followed the traditions of Emmet and the men of ninety-eight; he was in favour of independence. His doctrines attracted the more ardent of the Young Irelanders, and what was known as a war party was formed.

There were now three sections of Irish agitators. There were the Repealers, who were opposed to all physical force; there were the moderate Young Irelanders, only recognising physical force when all else had failed in the last instance; and there was now this new party, who saw in revolution the only remedy for Ireland. Smith O'Brien was bitterly opposed to Mitchel's doctrines. Mitchel withdrew from the *Nation* and started a paper of his own, the *United Irishman*, in which he advocated them more fiercely than ever. Mitchel was a powerful writer. He had, perhaps, the strongest mind of all the men of his time. He almost alone, perhaps, saw clearly his way before him. He devoted himself and his paper to preaching 'the holy hatred of foreign dominion.' 'To educate,' he said, ' that holy hatred; to make it know itself, and avow itself, and at last fill itself full, I hereby devote the columns of the *United Irishman*.' His vehement genius overshadowed the name of a man to whom he owed much, Fintan Lalor.

The Young Irelanders and the Mitchelites were at least agreed in recognising revolution. Some regarded it as a possibility; more held it to be inevitable; all openly advocated it. Unfortunately for the success of the movement, most of the time and genius of the party was spent in advocating revolution; little or no time was devoted to preparation for it. The year 1848, the year of unfulfilled revolutions, when crowns were falling and kings flying about in all directions, might well have seemed a year of happy omen for a new Irish rebellion. But the Young Irelanders were not ready for rebellion when their plans were made known to Government; and the Government struck at them before they could do anything. Mitchel was arrested, tried, and transported to Bermuda. That was the turning-point of the revolution. The Mitchelites wished to rise in rescue. They urged, and rightly urged, that if revolution was meant at all, then was the time. But the less extreme men held back. An autumnal rising had been decided upon, and they were unwilling to anticipate the struggle. They carried their point.

Mitchel was sentenced to fourteen years' transportation. When the verdict was delivered he declared that, like the Roman Scævola, he could promise hundreds who would follow his example, and as he spoke he pointed to Meagher, John Martin, and others of the associates who were thronging the galleries of the court. A wild cry came up from all his friends, ' Promise for me, Mitchel—promise for me ! ' With that cry ringing in his ears, he was hurried from the court, heavily ironed and encircled by a little army of dragoons, to the war-sloop ' Shearwater,' that had been waiting for the verdict and the man. As the war-sloop steamed out of Dublin Harbour, the hopes of the Young Irelanders went with her, vain and evanescent, from that hour forth, as the smoke that floated in the steamer's wake. There is a pathetic little story which records Mitchel's looking out of the prison-van that drove him from the court, and seeing a great crowd, and asking where they were going, and being told that they were going to a flower show. There were plenty of men in the movement who would have gladly risked everything to try and rescue Mitchel. But nothing could have been done without unanimity, and the too great caution of the leaders prevented the effort at the moment when it could have had the faintest hope of success.

From that moment the movement was doomed. Men who

had gone into the revolution heart and soul might have said of Smith O'Brien as Menas, in 'Antony and Cleopatra,' says to Pompey: 'For this I'll never follow thy pall'd fortunes more. Who seeks and will not take when once 'tis offered, shall never find it more.' The supreme moment of danger thus passed over, the Government lost no time in crushing out all that was left of the insurrection. Smith O'Brien, Meagher, and Dillon went down into the country, and tried to raise an armed rebellion. There was a small scuffle with the police at Ballingarry, in Tipperary; the rebels were dispersed, and the rebellion was over.

Smith O'Brien, Meagher, and others were arrested, and condemned to death. Meagher's speech from the dock was worthy of his rhetorical genius: 'I am not here to crave with faltering lip the life I have consecrated to the independence of my country. . . . I offer to my country, as some proof of the sincerity with which I have thought and spoken and struggled for her, the life of a young heart. . . . The history of Ireland explains my crime, and justifies it. . . . Even here, where the shadows of death surround me, and from which I see my early grave opening for me in no consecrated soil, the hope which beckoned me forth on that perilous sea, whereon I have been wrecked, animates, consoles, enraptures me. No, I do not despair of my poor old country, her peace, her liberty, her glory!'

The death-sentence was commuted to transportation for life, and, in a little while, John Martin, Thomas Francis Meagher, Smith O'Brien, Kevin Izod O'Doherty and Terence Bellew M'Manus found themselves in Van Diemen's Land with John Mitchel. In 1853 a scheme was organised by the Irishmen in America to effect the release of the political prisoners, and the attempt was entrusted to Mr. P. J. Smyth. Mr. P. J. Smyth was, at that time, an earnest and active Nationalist, inspired by a passionate admiration for the greater abilities of his colleagues in Young Ireland. It was so much to his credit that he attempted and succeeded in effecting the rescue of his imprisoned brethren, that it must be a matter of regret to every

Irish Nationalist that his career did not end on the day after he had accomplished his purpose. His later life is only melancholy. He never outgrew the traditions of his youth. He lived and breathed in the air of 1848 at a time when the principles of 1848 were further removed from the immediate needs of the national cause than the old Brehon laws. He hated the young men because they were not content to be limited in the circle of an earlier generation, and he died a placeman.

The rescue of Mitchel was the first effected. The question of Mitchel's conduct in making his escape under the conditions in which it was made has often been debated. It is certain that he effected his escape while he was a prisoner on parole. The terms of parole would certainly imply that the prisoner who intends to effect his escape should put himself in the same position as he was in before the parole was granted to him. This undoubtedly Mitchel did not do.

It may be urged, it has been urged, that it is not necessary to keep faith with a hostile Government. To such an argument it is impossible to agree. It is the duty of a patriot to keep his faith and his word unsullied, and to make his rule of life an example to his country and the world. Undoubtedly, no leniency of parole would have been shown to the Irish political prisoners if it had become an understood thing that the parole so granted was to be made use of to facilitate the prisoners' escape. However, Mitchel, who was certainly an l onourable man, believed himself justified in making his escape; and the method of his escape was approved of by Smith O'Brien, who, however, did not avail himself of the same means of effecting his release, as he knew that by so doing he would prevent his returning to Ireland.

Meagher and some of the other exiles succeeded in getting away later on, and most of them followed Mitchel to America. In the great American civil war, Mitchel and Meagher were found on opposite sides. Mitchel became a tremendous advocate of the South ; and two of his sons fell in battle in the Confederate uniform. Meagher fought bravely at the head of his historic Irish Brigade. His end was a curiously and grimly inappropriate conclusion to that brilliant and varied career. He fell one night from the deck of a steamer, and the dark waters of the Missouri stifled one of the bravest and purest spirits that have ever been devoted to the cause of Irish independence.

Smith O'Brien received his pardon in the course of time, and he died in Wales in 1864. Mitchel came back to Ireland years and years after, and was put forward for Parliament and elected. The House of Commons refused to recognise the right of the Irish patriot, whom English law condemned a felon, to sit in the House of Commons. A new writ was issued; Mitchel's name was brought forward again, and he would undoubtedly have been re-elected, but in the midst of all the excitement and turmoil the grim Sergeant Death came and ended Mitchel's troubled life. He was followed to the grave soon after by his friend, John Martin, who had long occupied a seat in the British Parliament.

Most of the other Young Ireland leaders and exiles died abroad. Kevin Izod O'Doherty is still alive; he sat as a Nationalist member in the Parliament of 1885–1886. Gavan Duffy was tried three times, but could not be convicted. He afterwards sat some time in Parliament, and then went into voluntary exile, to find title and fortune in Victoria.

CHAPTER XII.

YOUNGEST IRELAND.

'YOUNGEST IRELAND' might well be the title of a little known chapter in Irish history—the story of an episode which had one city for its theatre, and which had its fellows and its rivals in other parts of Ireland. One day, in the summer of 1848, a group of young men waited about the post-house in Cork for the arrival of the coach which was to bring the news from Dublin. At that time the railway did not run all the way from Dublin to Cork. It broke off, if we remember rightly, at Tipperary, and from that point the mail and the passengers were conveyed by public coach. Presently the coach came in, and was surrounded by the waiting group, eager for news. One amongst them was especially eager. He hurriedly questioned as to all that had happened in the Viceregal city within the last few days, and he was told that John Mitchel had been tried, sentenced, and transported.

'Was there no attempt at rescue?' asked the young Corkman, impulsively. 'No,' was the answer, 'none whatever.' The young Corkman shrugged his shoulders. 'Bravo, my country! you will be a nation by-and-by,' he said, and so walked off. And from that hour he could never be induced to play any part or evince the slightest interest in Irish politics. To his mind, the fact that John Mitchel was allowed to go into exile without a hand being lifted to save him, was in itself sufficient proof of the hopelessness of the national cause. Happily for Ireland, this pessimistic mood was not generally shared. There were young men in that city by the Lee who did not think that even because the men of forty-eight had made no attempt to rescue John Mitchel from his sentence, that therefore the fires of patriotism were necessarily extinguished upon the altars of liberty. Forty-eight had failed; but there was no reason why forty-nine should fail.

In this very year, when the Queen was in Dublin listening to the fervid protests of loyal citizens, and while she was being assured by Ascendency that the Young Ireland movement meant nothing, and that Ireland was heart and soul devoted to Ascendency and its works, in that year a young man came down on a special visit from Dublin to Cork. The young man bore a name which is deservedly dear to Irishmen —Joseph Brenan, better known to his friends and better known to us to-day as Joe Brenan. Those who knew Joe Brenan are not likely to forget his wonderful dark eyes, his brilliant talk, and, what was better than either, one of the most national hearts that ever beat for Ireland. Joe Brenan was a young Corkman who had gone to Dublin and became a writer on Mitchel's paper, and who, when Mitchel was exiled, had started a paper of his own. He came down to Cork with the deliberate purpose of trying if he could not do something to stir into blaze again the revolutionary fires which seemed to have been extinguished when Meagher, and O'Doherty, and Smith O'Brien, and the others were sentenced to transportation.

Brenan was a man of many and varied gifts. If he was a brilliant talker, he was also a brilliant writer in prose and in verse. There is one of his early compositions, well remembered by all those who knew him, written on his eighteenth birthday, in which the young Irishman expresses his bitter regret that he has as yet accomplished nothing that is likely to make his name immortal :

> Eighteen ! why Chatterton was mighty then,
> And Keats had glimpses into fairyland !

And the young poet was almost inclined to regard himself as utterly worthless because he, too, was eighteen, and was not mighty, and had had no glimpses into fairyland which the world at large cared anything about. He had, however, no reason to complain. His youth was destined to be better spent than in peering into fairyland, or in writing verses like those of Rowley. He was inspirited by an unconquerable devotion to his country ; by an unswerving ambition to serve her ; and he did serve her, not ineffectively. One of the most romantic passages in his romantic life is that he was loved by a gentle poetess who is dear to all Irishmen as 'Mary of the *Nation*.'

Brenan came down to Cork, and entered into negotiations with two men, both young men, and about his own age. One of them is a member of the present Irish parliamentary party, and his name is not altogether unknown in literature. The other is now the editor of the most influential paper in the South of Ireland. There was, at this time, a kind of eating-house at Cork, in a street off Patrick Street, kept by a Mrs. Heron, which was an establishment distinguished for its sanded floors, the simplicity of its appointments, and for the excellence of its cookery. It was a great place for suppers of a simple kind, and it was very popular with the young men of Cork. At Mrs. Heron's Joe Brenan and his two friends often met in conclave. Joe Brenan's plan was simple and not unpractical; and, of course, his purpose was revolutionary. He had no great hope of a successful revolution. His idea was that a number of small risings should take place on the very same day, hour, and minute, in different parts of Ireland; that their suddenness and unanimity might serve to distract authority; that at least there would be a struggle; that some brave men would die for Ireland; and that something good for the country must happen out of that.

' Who knows but the world may end to-night ? ' says the lover in Browning's poem. Something of the same desperate mood seemed to possess Joe Brenan's men at that time. Let it at least be shown to Ascendency that there were young men in Ireland ready to die for their country, and then—— ? Well, the world might end; or Ascendency might grow humane; or any other strange and exceedingly unlikely thing might come to pass. It was the dream of a young man; and Joe Brenan was a young man, and his friends were all young men—many of them very young men. For the little group of three had soon increased, had spread in many directions, and had drawn into its charmed orbit many allies and comrades, and was widening and extending like the circles of a pool where a stone has fallen.

Soon in Cork alone there were a very large number of generous, high-souled, pure-hearted young men, whose one dream, hope, and ambition was to give their lives for the sake of their country. To do them justice, their scheme was not unpractical, and was by no means without sense or hope. They had plenty of arms, to begin with. There were few young men in Cork in 1848 who could not boast the possession of a rifle, or a sabre, or a pike; and when '48 failed, these rifles, and sabres, and pikes were hidden away in all sorts of unlikely places—buried in back gardens, or stored away in unsuspicious-looking barrels, or put out of sight, if not out of mind, somehow.

The young men who gathered about Joe Brenan, and who looked up to him as the prophet of a new creed of revolution, could all, at any moment, have laid their hands upon a weapon of some kind or another. Then, too, it must be remembered that their desire was not very difficult to gratify. They did not hope of themselves to win the freedom of Ireland. They only hoped to make a series of desperate efforts, to die if needs were, gallantly, and by their deaths to stimulate the national feeling of their country, and to convince the oppressor of their earnestness of purpose, and of their hatred of his rule. They set to work with all seriousness of purpose, and with a right good-will. It was the duty of every one of Joe Brenan's friends to swear in as many recruits as he could, and to get these recruits to bring in others to swell the total of insurrection. There were incessant nightly drillings in out-of-the-way places. There were incessant meetings of the revolutionary leaders and of their followers, organised under the pretence of temperance meetings, literary associations and the like. One spot in especial was a favourite place for secret drillings—the place known as Cork Park, in the region where the Cork and Bandon Railway now is, then slob land. Here there were continual drillings, where the great object was to get large bodies of men to obey readily the word of command, and to go through military evolutions swiftly and silently. Here, too, was a great advantage, that if at any time unwelcome persons—police or others—did make their appearance, any body of men could immediately and easily disperse, and be lost to sight in a few moments.

Many men were active in the movement whose names are still remembered in 'rebel Cork.' There was a smith named Bowes, a very Hercules in a leather apron, whose forge was a special centre of disaffection. There was a cobbler of the name of Mountain, a name grimly appropriate for the member of a party which desired to be regarded as the 'mountain' of Irish rebellion, who played a conspicuous part in the organisation, and who afterwards, if we remember rightly, underwent his trial for treason-felony. Another man who took a prominent place in the movement was Phil Gray, ostensibly a pedlar by profession, who was of rare service in conveying messages from one part of the country to another. At the smith's forge, in the cobbler's shop, in Mrs. Heron's supper-rooms, at the private dwellings of the youthful rebels, in all sorts of places in the city, the followers of Joe Brenan—who might almost have called themselves Youngest Ireland—met together and planned, and schemed, and hoped. They had their passwords, of course—their signs and counter-signs. If one recruit met another, and wished to be certain of his comradeship and brotherhood, he began by asking him, 'What's the news?' If the other were one of the League, he immediately made answer, 'The harvest is coming!' If this answer were not quite sufficient—if it seemed an answer that might possibly have been made by chance by some uninitiated one, for the harvest *was* near—he spoke again, interrogating thus: 'How are we to reap it?' If the man thus interrogated answered, 'We'll reap it with steel,' he was at once recognised as being of the company of the chosen.

What Joe Brenan was doing in Cork, others were engaged upon elsewhere. Youngest Ireland was busy in many parts of Ireland. Undoubtedly, however, the task that these young men had undertaken was attempted under conditions of more than usual difficulty. The failure of the forty-eight movement, the imprisonment and exile of its leaders—these in themselves were sufficient to dishearten a people reduced by famine to the verge of despair. The Young Ireland movement cannot be said to have taken hold of the popular mind. The people, upon whom in the end the success of a rising must depend, were not as a body prepared for, or even expecting, a rising at all. We are told, for example, that when Smith O'Brien, having at last resolved upon revolution, came in the course of his crusade to a certain village, the people there came out to meet him with chairs and tables, and set about the erection of a sort of platform, under the impression that he was merely going to hold a public meeting. We are told, too, that at the time when Mitchel was preaching the fiercest principles of insurrection, and was leaving behind him even the most vehement politicians of the *Nation*—even at this time the large bulk of the Irish peasantry, to whom the rising was most likely to appeal, knew as little of Mitchel as they did of Mahomet.

If there were such difficulties in the way of the Young Ireland movement, these difficulties stood ten, aye, a hundredfold greater in the way of the movement which succeeded to it. The young men who organised it, who took hand in it, who enrolled themselves proudly in its ranks, were patriotic, pure men. Gallant and devoted, they were prepared to do all that men could do for the cause that lay dearest to their hearts. But if the materials for a successful revolution might perhaps have been found in the Ireland of forty-eight, these materials were not to be found in the Ireland of the succeeding year. When one rising has failed, it is very difficult to rouse popular emotion or popular passions to the fever-heat of another insurrection.

Still, with all these difficulties in the way, the young men of the new movement were determined to go on. Anything, they thought, was better than a torpid acquiescence in defeat. So they met, and plotted, and planned, and drilled, and armed, and made ready for the signal which was to come to them, and which was to be the match which would fire the flames of rebellion in many parts of the country at the same moment. Unfortunately, the signal was not properly given. It reached some places and not others. The insurrection did not break out simultaneously. There were one or two abortive risings in different parts of the country. Joe Brenan did his part of the business. He rose at Cappoquin. He led his little body of insurgents to take the police barrack there. The police were prepared for their coming. There was a sharp, short exchange of shots, and then Joe Brenan saw that the thing was hopeless. His men dispersed. He himself flung away his revolver, and walked quietly from the scene of action and got into hiding, later on making good his escape to America.

That was the end of insurrection for a time. The little centres of conspiracy that had been waiting for the watchword that was to hurl them into action heard with despair of the disaster at Cappoquin and the failure of their hopes. There was nothing further to be done for the moment. For a time the national cause was defeated; for a time the foreign dominion was triumphant. Many of those who had been leaders and soldiers in this movement were destined to take part in first one and then another secret agitation, having an armed rising for its aim. One agitation for liberty in Ireland was no sooner extinguished than another began to burn in its place.

Joe Brenan's subsequent career was brief. He made his way to America—to New Orleans, that wonderful city on the Mississippi, which is still a marvellous combination of France before the Revolution, of tropical Creole life, and of modern American enterprise, and which was then still more striking and vivid in its contrast than it now is. There he founded a newspaper, and there he married—but not the love of his youth, not 'Mary of the *Nation*.' She died unmarried. Blindness came upon him, and he wrote some melancholy, beautiful verses upon the calamity which darkened his life. That life was not long. He died while he was still what may be called a young man. His life was not happy in the ordinary sense in which we value the word happiness. His dearest hopes were withered, the noon of his youth was darkened, and his life cut off in its bloom. But he did a good work worthily. He did his best to animate the national cause, at a time when the national cause seemed low indeed; and his name will always be held in honourable affection by his countrymen.

CHAPTER XIII.

THE IRISH BRIGADE.

THE failure of the Young Ireland movement flung Ireland back upon a long period of political apathy and domestic wretchedness. Starvation and misery forced the people into steady and incessant emigration. Eviction was in full swing, and between eviction and emigration it is estimated that almost a million of people left Ireland between 1847 and 1857. 'In a few years more,' said the *Times* exultingly, 'a Celtic Irishman will be as rare in Connemara as is the Red Indian on the shores of the Manhattan.' That the *Times* was not a true prophet was not the fault of the majority of the Irish landlords. Evictions took place by the hundred, by the thousand, by the ten thousand—evictions as much for grazier's purposes as for non-payment of rent, which in those evil days of famine and failure they could not pay. Winter or summer, day or night, fair or foul weather, the tenants were ejected. Sick or well, bedridden or dying, the tenants—men, women, or children—were turned out. They might go to America if they could ; they might die on the roadside if so it pleased them. They were out of the hut, and the hut was unroofed that they might not seek its shelter again, and that was all the landlord cared about. The expiring evicted tenant might, said Mitchel, raise his dying eyes to heaven and bless his God that he perished under the finest constitution in the world.

It is hardly a matter of surprise, however much of regret and reprobation, that the lives of the evicting landlords should often be in peril, and sometimes be taken. At that time the Ribbon organisation flourished. The Ribbon organisation, and kindred associations, were rendered inevitable by the conditions under which the Irish peasantry were compelled to live. Given a dominant landlord class, either of another race themselves, or supported by their adhesion to that other race ;

given the existence of a body of laws which allowed every right to the landlord and no right to the tenant; given long years of landlord tyranny and eviction, on the top of famine, and it was simply a matter of logical necessity that bodies like the Ribbon Society should come into existence and flourish. In them the peasant saw his only defence against the hateful landlord class, and the no less hateful law which sustained that landlord class in its worst actions.

There is a fine passage in Gerald Griffin's immortal novel, 'The Collegians,' which bears striking testimony to the way in which English law was then, and has been ever since, regarded by the Irish peasant. 'The peasantry of Ireland have, for centuries, been at war with the laws by which they are governed, and watch their operation in every instance with a jealous eye. Even guilt itself, however naturally atrocious, obtains a commiseration in their regard, from the mere spirit of opposition to a system of Government which they consider unfriendly. There is scarcely a cottage in the South of Ireland where the very circumstance of legal denunciation would not afford, even to a murderer, a certain passport and concealment and protection.'

There have been many secret societies in the modern history of Europe—the Tugendbund, the Carbonari, and the Camorra—but none have been more remarkable, more mysterious, or, for a time, more successful than the Ribbon Society. 'It is assuredly strange, indeed, almost incredible, that although the existence of this organisation was, in a general way, as well and as widely known as the fact that Queen Victoria reigned, or that Daniel O'Connell was once a living man; although the story of its crimes has thrilled judge and jury, and Parliamentary committees have filled ponderous bluebooks with evidence of its proceedings, there is to this hour the wildest conflict of assertion and conclusion as to what exactly were its real aims, its origin, structure, character, and purpose.'

For more than half a century the Ribbon Society has existed in Ireland, and even yet it is impossible to say how it began, how it is organised, and what are its exact purposes. Its aim seems chiefly to have been to defend the land-serf from the landlord; but it often had a strong political purpose as well. The late Mr. A. M. Sullivan statêd that he long ago satisfied himself that the Ribbonism of one period was not the Ribbonism of another, and that the version of its aims and character prevalent among its members in one part of Ireland often differed widely from that professed in some other part of the country. ' In Ulster it professed to be a defensive or retaliatory league against Orangeism; in Munster it was first a combination against the tithe-proctors; in Connaught it was an organisation against rack-renting and evictions; in Leinster it was often mere trade unionism, dictating by its mandates and enforcing by its vengeance the employment or dismissal of workmen, stewards, and even domestics.'

All sorts of evidence and information of the most confused kind has, from time to time, been given respecting Ribbonism, much of it the merest fiction. All that is certain is that it, and many other formidable organisations, existed among the peasantry of different parts of Ireland.

Many of the landlords themselves were in no enviable condition. Mortgages and settlements of all kinds, the results of their own or of their ancestors' profuseness, hung on their estates, and made many a stately showing rent-roll the merest simulacrum of territorial wealth. Even rack-rents could not enable many of the landlords to keep their heads above water. At length the Government made an effort to relieve their condition by passing the Encumbered Estates Act, by means of which a landlord or his creditors might petition to have an estate sold in the Court established for that purpose under the Act. Later, by a Supplementary Irish Landed Estates Act, the powers of the Court were increased to allow the sale of properties that were not encumbered. When Government has hitherto had to legislate for Ireland, it has usually displayed a pleasing alacrity in legislating for the advantage of the Irish landlord class, and a corresponding perfunctory unwillingness to legislate for the Irish peasant.

The vast body of the Irish people cared little or nothing for the legislation that was to the advantage of the landlord class. They regarded, and rightly regarded, that class as the curse of their country.

But the wants of the tenant closely concerned the Irish race; and in August, 1850, those who sympathised with the tenants' cause began to agitate for legislation. A conference was called by Dr., afterwards Sir, John Gray, the Protestant owner of the *Freeman's Journal*, by the Presbyterian barrister Mr. Greer, who later represented Derry in Parliament, and by Frederick Lucas, the Catholic owner of the *Tablet*. A conference of men of all classes and creeds was held in Dublin—'a conference,' Mr. Bright called it in the House of Commons, 'of earnest men from all parts of Ireland,' and a Tenant League was started. Everything was against the League The indifference of England and the prostration of the country after the famine and the rebellion, the apathy, even the hostility, of the Irish Liberal members were all combined against it. Then came the reorganisation of the Catholic Church in England, and Lord John Russell's 'Durham Letter,' which for the time made any political alliance between the Catholics and Protestants impossible.

But when, in 1852, the Whig Ministry went out, and Lord Derby, coming in with the Tories, dissolved Parliament, the chance of the Tenant Leaguers came. Some fifty tenant-right members were elected. It seemed for a moment as if a new era had dawned for Ireland. The country had for a time a large body of representatives pledged together for a common purpose of a truly national character. Many of the men who had been elected were men of the highest character, honour, and patriotism. Conspicuous among the champions of tenant-right was Charles Gavan Duffy, who has complained very inaccurately and unreasonably that the services of the tenant-right party have been under-rated and even ignored by the leaders of the modern political movement. There was a short and distinguished Parliamentary career waiting for Charles Gavan Duffy, before he went across the seas to find in a new world that fair fortune which was denied to him and to all national Irishmen in his own country.

Another conspicuous figure in the movement was Frederick Lucas, one of the most upright and pure-minded of politicians, a man whose name was destined to become very famous in Irish politics, and who was destined himself to become the leader of an Irish party expressing opinions which would have appeared strangely advanced to the tenant-righters, although they seem strangely behind the age to us of to-day. Isaac Butt was elected for Youghal; in Mr. John Francis Maguire, Ireland had a representative, eloquent, honest, and able—a man who might be called national in the sense that Irish members of Parliament in those days were national and who at all times did his best to be of service to his country.

Unfortunately for the country and the cause, the tenant-right party in the House of Commons contained members—and those unhappily among the most prominent—who were neither pure, nor honourable, nor patriotic. Among the most conspicuous of the tenant-right party in the House of Commons—the Irish Brigade, as it came to be called—was the once famous John Sadleir. His lieutenants were his brother, James Sadleir, Mr. William Keogh, and Mr. Edmund O'Flaherty: these men were all adventurers, and most of them swindlers. They were known as the Brass Band. John Sadleir was a man of remarkable ability, and still more remarkable audacity. He was absolutely unprincipled. He regarded the cause with which he was connected solely as a means of advancing the selfish personal interests of himself and of his accomplices. He was not merely a political adventurer, a Lismahago of the House of Commons; he was a swindler of no ordinary unscrupulousness, and no ordinary address. He got about him a gang of rascals like himself, no less unscrupulous, only a little less gifted in deceit and in fraud.

For a time this Sanhedrim of scoundrels deceived the Irish people by their pretensions and protestations. The

Sadleirs owned the Tipperary bank, one of the most popular banks in Ireland; they had plenty of money, and spent it lavishly; they started a paper, the *Telegraph*, to keep them before the public; they were good speakers, and they led good speakers; they were demonstratively Catholic, and for a time a good many people believed in them. Sadleir even succeeded in getting some honest men, who had been sent to represent Irish constituencies in Parliament, to believe in him and his lofty purposes, and so to further his secret aims by lending their respectability and their righteousness to him and his gang. Even however when the power of Sadleir was at its highest, he was distrusted by most intelligent Irishmen; and that distrust was soon justified.

Lord Derby went out of office, and Whig Lord Aberdeen came in, and the members of the noisy, blatant, Brass Band took office under him. John Sadleir became a Lord of the Treasury; Keogh was made Irish Solicitor-General; O'Flaherty Commissioner of Income Tax. There was fierce indignation, but they kept their places and their course for a time. Then they broke up. John Sadleir had embezzled, swindled, forged; he ruined half Ireland with his fraudulent bank; he made use of his position under Government to embezzle public money; he committed suicide—that is to say, he was supposed to have committed suicide, for there were many persons who believed then, and there are many persons who believe still, that the body which was found on Hampstead Heath, and which was consigned to the grave under circumstances of mysterious haste and secrecy, was not the body of John Sadleir.

In one of the greatest of German romances, the ' Flower, Fruit, and Thorn Pieces' of Jean Paul Richter, the hero passes himself off for dead, and seeks a new life far from his old home, leaving behind him an afflicted widow and sorrowing friends, under the conviction that he is no more. There were many persons who believed that John Sadleir, like another Siebenkäs, had died only in name, and was quietly enjoying the rewards of his deception in the security of self-chosen exile. The story is not very credible, but it will at least serve to show what public opinion at the time thought of John Sadleir, and of John Sadleir's ingenuity, and of John Sadleir's morality.

His brother James, his confederate, was formally expelled from the House of Commons, a punishment so rarely exercised in our time that it might almost be said to be non-existent. O'Flaherty hurried to Denmark, where there was no extradition treaty, and then to New York, where he lived —and, we believe, still lives—under another name, a familiar figure in certain circles of New York society, famous as a diner-out, as a good story-teller, and a humourist—a sort of combination of Brillat Savarin and the later Richelieu, with a dash of Gines de Pasamonte. Keogh, the fourth of this famous quadrilateral, their ally, their intimate, their faithful friend, contrived to keep himself clear of the crash. He was immediately made a judge, and was conspicuous for the rest of his life for his unfailing and unaltering hostility to any and every national party.

Only a Persius, or a Pascal, could do full justice to the history of this extraordinary quadrilateral. The story may, however, be summed up somewhat epigrammatically thus: There were once four men, close friends, companions, allies, partners in politics, partners in finance, bound in a brotherhood of common aims and common interests. One was a forger and swindler, who committed suicide; another was a swindler, who was expelled from the House of Commons, and who fled the country; the third embezzled public money, and also fled the country; the fourth was made a judge.

It is not to be wondered at that the lamentable end of the Brass Band, and the disasters of the tenant-right movement, should have produced another period of political apathy in Ireland as far as constitutional agitation was concerned. But there were other agitations on foot. Another experiment, which had been tried and failed in 1848, was to be tried again under new conditions.

CHAPTER XIV.

THE PHŒNIX CONSPIRACY.

AFTER the failure of the revolutionary movement of 1848, and of the slight attempt of the succeeding year, Ireland was left for a time unmoved by any active efforts at insurrection. But the revolutionary spirit was only quiescent, not extinct. It was destined to break out again in a fashion much more dangerous than that of the Young Ireland movement, under the leadership of men far more determined and desperate, and with results far more serious.

At the time when Smith O'Brien and his followers were skirmishing with the police at Ballingarry, there was among the insurgents a young man named James Stephens. Stephens was at that time about twenty-four years old. He was born in Kilkenny in 1824, of comparatively humble parents, who were able, however, to give their son a good education, of which he availed himself to the utmost. His mathematical tastes led him to devote himself to engineering ; and in his twentieth year he obtained an appointment on the Limerick and Waterford Railway, which was then being constructed. When the railway was completed he was thrown out of work for a while, and he came to Dublin to find occupation. The Young Ireland movement was in full swing at the time, and it soon drew the gifted young engineer into its charmed circle. Stephens was a clever young man, an ardent Nationalist, eager, like all the young Irelanders, to conquer or to die for his native country. He came very near to dying in that fight with the police at Ballingarry. From the cottage in which they had taken refuge, the police were firing as fast as they could upon their besiegers, and one of their bullets found its billet in James Stephens' body. He fell, rolled behind a hedge, and was left there, either unnoticed or regarded as dead, after Smith O'Brien and his party had dispersed, and the police had left the farm-house.

A few days later paragraphs in the newspapers announced to all that were interested that James Stephens was dead and buried 'Poor James Stephens,' so one paragraph ran, 'who followed Smith O'Brien to the field, has died of the wound which he received at Ballingarry while acting as aide-de-camp to the insurgent leader. Mr. Stephens was a very amiable and, apart from politics, most inoffensive young man, possessed of a great deal of talent, and we believe he was a most excellent son and brother. His untimely and melancholy fate will be much regretted by a numerous circle of friends.' Stephens' family and friends took good care to support by every means in their power the story of his death.

It would have been well for the English Government if the Ballingarry bullet had been surer in its aim, and if the newspaper paragraph had been true. But the news was not true. Stephens lay for some time where he had fallen. When he found himself alone, he bandaged his wound as best he could, exchanged clothes with a peasant, and after an interview with his sweetheart, which dangerously jeopardised his safety, sought hiding in the mountains. In the mountains he found a companion in misfortune, seeking, like himself, shelter from the harsh pursuit of the law. This was Michael John Doheny, the gifted child of a peasant race, the eloquent speaker and unselfish patriot.

The *Hue and Cry* of the day, which has left us so many grotesque, and some life-like portraits of the men who were wanted by the police, because they were Irishmen and enemies of the foreign dominion, thus describes Stephens' companion: 'Michael John Doheny, barrister, age about forty, height five feet eight inches, sandy hair, grey eyes, coarse, red face like that of a man given to drink, high cheek bones, wants several of his teeth, very vulgar appearance, peculiar, coarse, unpleasant voice, small red whiskers, dresses respectably.'

Doheny has left on record, in his fascinating 'Felon's Track,' the strange story of the six weeks of adventures and sufferings and privations which he and Stephens shared together while they were in hiding. In sunshine and storm, along sides of mountains, and across the cold courses of mountain torrents, through thick woods, and on bleak hill-sides, the refugees made their desperate way. Sometimes they were pursued by the police; sometimes, though rarely, they ran the risk of being delivered up to their enemies; sometimes they encountered cold looks from those who should have been their friends; but more often they found welcome and shelter and sustenance from the peasantry whom they had hoped to emancipate. The courage of the two men never for a moment deserted them through the whole time when, in Doheny's expressive phrase, they were under the shadow of the gibbet. Doheny was always ready whenever they sat and rested to write glowing verses. Stephens' mind was ever fertile in the formation of plans either for the furtherance of their own escape or for the purpose of kidnapping Lord John Russell.

Once, and once only, according to Doheny, did the courage of James Stephens seem likely to give way. This was when he learned that the woman to whom he was devoted was no longer true to him. But he rallied even against this stroke; his love for the cause and the country to which he had vowed himself was able to dwarf and conquer all other emotions, and he soon shook off the sick mood of despondency in which he had declared himself unwilling to make any further efforts to secure his safety.

When the little plan for carrying off Lord John Russell was baffled by the Prime Minister's unexpected departure, Stephens left Ireland in disguise, and made his way across England to France. In Paris he was joined some little time later by Doheny, who had left Ireland about a week after the departure of Stephens, and who made his way with more difficulty across England. The two were shortly reinforced by the arrival of a third Young Irelander, John O'Mahony. O'Mahony had lingered in Ireland for a considerable time after the failure of Smith O'Brien's rising. He commanded a rather large body of men and had control of some arms, and for a time he and his followers lurked among the mountains, hoping that something might yet happen to speed the insurrection to success. But nothing did happen. O'Mahony became convinced that for the time the revolution was over; he dismissed his guerilla army to drift to all the points of the compass, and made the best of his way to Paris. There he and Stephens remained for some years. Doheny had gone to the United States to make his way as a journalist and barrister, and to foster by all the means in his power the national cause.

It must not be supposed that all secret agitation died out in Ireland with the suppression of the Young Ireland movement, or of that later movement with which Fintan Lalor and Brenan were associated. Though many Young Irelanders and their accomplices who were not in the hands of the police sought safety in exile, the vast bulk of the conspirators remained at home. Of this large body the greater proportion dropped out of agitation and fell back into private life, and into the fulfilment of their ordinary daily tasks and daily duties. But a certain number still remained bound together by the bonds of secret association in certain of the larger cities. These small associations were centres of latent activity, ready to be employed at any time in widening their circle of agitation. Each of them was a focus from which the rays of revolution might be directed when the hour came, and brought the man with it. The hour and the man came with the decade of 1850, and the visit of James Stephens to Ireland.

The outbreak of the Crimean War, and the complications in which it involved England on the Continent and in the East, appeared to Stephens to offer happy opportunities for the renewal of active agitation. There is a story current that Russian agents sought out Stephens, and encouraged him to incite a new revolutionary movement in Ireland. This may or may not be true. It is doubtful whether at that time the Russian Government were sufficiently well aware of the seriousness of Irish discontent. But in any case, we may well believe that James Stephens needed no encouragement from Russian or other emissaries to induce him to seize the favourable hour, to seize the favourable moment, for again repeating Ireland's protest against her hard Government. So Stephens came over to Ireland, and made a tour of personal inspection of the country, accompanied by Thomas Clarke Luby. He saw for himself that the country was only outwardly quiescent; that the desire for national rights and national liberties was even stronger than it had been in 1848; that it only needed skill, and judgment, and patience to set on foot a movement which should do more effective service to the country than Young Ireland.

These small bodies of secret disaffection, which have been already mentioned, gave great support to Stephens in his visit, and received from him fresh inspiration for the spread of their propaganda. But if the rough outline of Stephens' plans was readily found, it took a long time to mature. The Crimean War passed away without awakening any active disturbance in Ireland; but the preparations for disturbance were surely and slowly progressing. In the town of Skibbereen there was a small club or reading-room, apparently of no great importance either as a literary or as a political centre. But it was destined to prove of very great importance, and gave its name to an unsuccessful conspiracy which was destined to be the parent of a far greater conspiracy.

This small body or association was called the 'Phœnix National and Literary Society.' Many of the young men of the town were its members: and it was apparently merely a kind of literary institute. It covered under its seemingly harmless appearance one of those small centres of secret agitation already mentioned. One of its most conspicuous members was Jeremiah O'Donovan, later known as O'Donovan Rossa. In the members of the Phœnix Literary Society, Stephens, then in Ireland, found ready and willing confederates; and from them and their institution came the name given to Stephens' organisation, then in process of formation. There was something in the title which appealed particularly and appropriately to the minds of Irish conspirators. Every Irish insurrectionary movement had risen, Phœnix-like, from the ashes of some preceding agitation. So the name Phœnix was adopted; and, had the Fates been propitious, it might have become the title of the greater movement which succeeded it, instead of living in history merely as the name of a prematurely-destroyed conspiracy.

A little before the time when James Stephens was finding welcome and sympathy, and a name for his organisation, at the hands of the Skibbereen Literary Society, another distinguished Irish rebel had returned to his native land. In 1856 Mr. William Smith O'Brien was allowed to return to Ireland under an unconditional amnesty. He had been for some time set free from absolute imprisonment; but it was only now that permission to return to his own country was accorded to him. The Government, which seldom did any gracious act except by halves, allowed Smith O'Brien to breathe his native air without fear of arrest as a felon; but it refused to allow him the rank and title which were his by right, as the brother of Lord Inchiquin. Smith O'Brien, we may feel sure, cared very little for any honours of which the Government were able to deprive him. The honour of a place of foremost affection in the hearts and minds of his countrymen the Government could not take away.

In the dead calm which seemed to come over Irish life, something like a ripple was produced in the return home of a Young Ireland leader. There were enthusiastic demonstrations in his honour, and he was earnestly entreated to once again represent an Irish constituency in the English Parliament. This, however, Smith O'Brien refused to do. The bright hopes of ten years earlier had faded away. He was not less national than he had been, but he was less sanguine of immediate success, and he was most unwilling to return to any active personal part in the cause. His interest in, and his affection for the country and the cause was as deep as ever; and a little later he made a tour of Ireland, in which he was received with enthusiasm wherever he went, and in the course of which he made an important speech on ground which was historic ground for him. At Clonmel, where he and so many of his companions had been tried and sentenced to death, he was presented with an address ; and he made a reply to the address which was full of a sad and lenient dignity and courage. He spoke sorrowfully of forty-eight and its failure; but he declared that he was as devoted now as he had been then to the principles which had led him to risk his life with the lives of his friends and followers in his country's cause.

The speech naturally created much interest; and it provoked an article in the London *Times* which was in its way a masterpiece of political folly, and of that curious misappreciation of facts, that lack of historical insight, which has always been the chief characteristic of English journalism in its speculations on Irish affairs. The *Times* was pleased to be somewhat scornfully amused over the utterances of the returned rebel. It pointed exultantly to the absolute peace, tranquillity, and contentment of Ireland; and it scoffingly assured Smith O'Brien, and such few persons as sympathised with him, that the days of rebels, and agitation, and conspiracy in Ireland were over, for good and all. At this time when these weighty words were being penned, at this time when the English Press was so confident that order reigned in Ireland, the Irish Executive was preparing to make a descent upon a formidable secret conspiracy which had been brought to its notice, and which was to be the parent of a conspiracy many times more formidable than any which had yet occurred in the history of the relations of the two countries.

It soon became bruited abroad that the Phœnix organisation was spreading rapidly; it soon came to be known, too, in that vague, indefinable way in which things do get to be known in political life before they actually occur, that the Government intended to make sharp and short work with the new conspiracy. Some Nationalists conceived it to be within their duty to make public protest against the new movement. Mr. Smith O'Brien, forgetting entirely, or apparently forgetting entirely, the history of his own struggle little more than ten years earlier with O'Connell, judged it advisable to write a letter to the *Nation*, appealing to the Irish people against the Phœnix conspiracy. Mr. John Dillon, wiser then, as he had been wiser ten years before, than his chief, refused to make any demonstration against the Phœnix Society, and considered that public interference was most inadvisable.

In all probability the Irish Government had made up their minds to crush out the conspiracy before Mr. Smith O'Brien's letter made its appearance. But such a letter would probably, in any case, have only encouraged instead of dissuading them from the course upon which they had resolved. On December 3, 1858, a viceregal proclamation warned the country that great danger was caused by the existence of a secret society. Within a few days this proclamation was followed up by a series of raids in different towns in Ireland, upon men known, or suspected to be, members of the Phœnix Society. There were a series of protracted trials, which revealed little or nothing, beyond the fact that in certain districts young men had banded themselves together into a secret organisation for the purpose of secret drilling, and that the organisation had an occult leader who was known as 'the Hawk,' and was pretty generally understood to be James Stephens.

One of the prisoners, Daniel O'Sullivan, a National School teacher, was brilliantly defended by the late Lord O'Hagan— then Mr. Thomas O'Hagan. The jury disagreed. O'Sullivan was tried again; and objecting to the unfairness with which the jury was packed, he refused to make any defence, was convicted, and sentenced to ten years' penal servitude. The other Phœnix prisoners were induced to plead guilty, and were released. Such was apparently the end of the Phœnix conspiracy. The Government fondly fancied they had done with it and all kinds of agitation for long enough. They did not dream that from the extinct association another conspiracy would arise, which would have its home in two hemispheres. 'The last of the Gracchi,' said Mirabeau, 'dying, flung dust to heaven, and from that dust sprang Marius.' From the dust of the exploded Phœnix conspiracy rose the far more formidable image of Fenianism.

CHAPTER XV.

JOHN DILLON AND JOHN BRIGHT.

The General Election of 1865 was in its results one of the most remarkable that have occurred during the whole of the Victorian epoch. It marked the passing away of an old order and the beginning of a new. Not long before it took place Mr. Gladstone had made himself conspicuous as the sympathiser with, and supporter of, advanced Radical ideas. The politician who had been looked upon in his youth as the rising hope of the stern and unbending Tories, had passed from Conservatism, through Conservative Liberalism, unto pure and undiluted Liberalism. He was even, in those days, regarded as a Radical. Mr. Gladstone's process of conversion showed that the tide of Liberalism was running high; the result of the General Election proved it still more conclusively.

Mr. Disraeli, with the keen political insight which at once perceives the chief historical characteristic of any great event, declared in a speech, shortly after the General Election, that the new Parliament had very greatly increased the power and the following of Mr. Bright. This was, indeed, the most conspicuous result of the election. Mr. Bright was at that time regarded as the champion of advanced thought, as the hero and the herald of Radical principles and Radical reforms. His position in the new Parliament was very strong. Death had taken from his side, shortly before the new Parliament came into existence, his friend and companion, Richard Cobden; but death had also, almost immediately after the birth of the new Parliament, taken away Lord Palmerston, who was the most serious barrier to the progress of the new ideas of which Mr. Bright was regarded as the apostle.

Men of rare gifts and rare genius came with that election for the first time into Parliamentary life, and rallied underneath Mr. Bright's banner. Most conspicuous among English members was John Stuart Mill, who had been successfully induced to come from his philosophic retirement in pleasant Avignon, and to dedicate for a season his fine intellect to the active service of the Radical party. Most conspicuous amongst Irish members was John Dillon.

John Dillon entered Parliament in 1865, as he had entered upon revolution in 1848, from a strong conviction of the duty he owed to his country. We have seen that he had not been anxious for revolution in the Young Ireland days; that he had opposed the premature explosion of insurrection as long as he could; but that when he saw a rising to be inevitable, he threw in his lot with it as composedly as if he had approved of it from the beginning, and shared heroically the consequences of a catastrophe which he had striven to avert. After the rising failed, he succeeded in making his escape, and he lived for many years in exile in the United States. In later years a general amnesty allowed him to return to his own country. It was urged upon him that he could be of service to his country by entering Parliament, and he accepted the duty.

Like many other Irishmen at that time, John Dillon was a great admirer and implicit believer in John Bright. Mr. John Dillon might very well believe that the Irish people and the representatives of the Irish people had a friend in Mr. John Bright. Mr. John Dillon was always a student of the political history of his time, and the utterances of Mr. John Bright might well have convinced a man of a more sceptical nature than Mr. John Dillon ever was, that Mr. Bright was a sustained and devoted friend to Ireland. There is no more instructive study for the Irish Nationalist of to-day than those volumes of Mr. Bright's collected speeches which contain his utterances delivered on Irish questions. They deserve to be read and re-read far oftener than they are. They have been called attention to from time to time by Irish politicians. A writer, some few years ago, at a period of acute political crisis, ventured to make public certain extracts from them which had a curious bearing upon Mr. Bright's conduct towards the Land League and its supporters. But it will not be out of place here, after some of the very recent utterances of Mr. Bright on the Irish question in and out of the House of Commons, to look over some of these Irish speeches of his, and see what it was that made Mr. John Dillon regard him with such admiration.

In the year 1845, in a speech on the Maynooth Grant question, Mr. Bright, who had then only been but a short time in the House, raised his voice to point out the wrongs of Ireland. ' I assert that the Protestant Church of Ireland is at the root of the evils of that country, The Irish Catholics would thank you infinitely more if you were to wipe out that foul blot, than they would even if Parliament were to establish the Roman Catholic Church alongside of it. They have had everything Protestant—a Protestant clique that has been dominant in the country; a Protestant Viceroy to distribute places and emoluments amongst that Protestant clique; Protestant judges who have polluted the seats of justice; Protestant magistrates, before whom the Catholic peasant could not hope for justice. They have not only Protestant, but exterminating landlords, and more than that, a Protestant soldiery, who, at the beck and command of a Protestant priest, have butchered and killed a Catholic peasant even in the presence of his widowed mother. All these things are notorious; I merely state them. I do not bring the proof of them; they are patent to all the world, and that man must have been inobservant indeed who is not perfectly convinced of their truth.'

Two years later, in 1847, Mr. Bright, in speaking on the Coercion Bill, for which he felt himself compelled to vote, but, although not without making a strong protest against the system of governing Ireland, addressed some reproaches to the Irish representatives in the House of Commons for their inaction. 'I am sure that 105, or even 30 English members, sitting in a Parliament in Dublin, and believing their country had suffered from the effects of bad legislation, would, by their knowledge of the case, their business habits, activity, union, and perseverance, have shown a powerful front, and by uniting together, and working manfully in favour of any proposition they might think necessary to remedy the evils of which they complained, they would have forced it on the attention of the House. But the Irish members have not done this. So far, then, they are and have been as much to blame as any other member of this House, for the absence of good government in Ireland.'

It is interesting to compare these utterances of what may be called Mr. Bright's youth with speeches made nearly forty years later. When the party whose presence he had so wished for, that party of united Irish members, showing a powerful front, united together, and working manfully in favour of any proposition they might think necessary to remedy the evils of which they complained, made their appearance in the English House of Commons, the reception they got from Mr. Bright was not of the kind which they might well have expected, from the speech of 1847. In the same speech he said: 'We maintain a large army in Ireland, and an armed police, which is an army in everything but name, and yet we have in that country a condition of things which is not to be matched in any other civilised country of Europe, and which is alike disgraceful to Ireland and to us.'

In the following year, 1848, almost immediately after the Young Ireland outbreak, Mr. Bright again made a speech about Ireland, and again enlarged upon the injustice of English rule. In this speech he touched upon a question destined to be of the utmost importance in the history of the relations between England and Ireland—the Irish in America. 'Driven forth by poverty, Irishmen emigrate in great numbers, and in whatever quarter of the world an Irishman sets his foot, there stands a bitter, an implacable enemy of England. That is one of the results of the wide-spread disaffection that exists in Ireland. There are hundreds of thousands—I suppose there are millions—of the population of the United States of America who are Irish by birth, or by immediate descent; and, be it remembered, Irishmen settled in the United States have a large influence in public affairs. They sometimes sway the election of members of the legislature, and may even affect the election of the President of the Republic. There may come a time when questions of a critical nature will be agitated between the Governments of Great Britain and the United States; and it is certain that at such a time the Irish in that country will throw their whole weight into the scale against this country and against peace with this country. These are points which it is necessary to consider, and which arise out of the lamentable condition in which Ireland is placed.'

In the same speech he said: 'At present there prevails throughout three-fourths of the Irish people a total unbelief in the honesty and integrity of the Government of this country. There may or may not be grounds for all this ill-feeling; but that it exists, no man acquainted with Ireland will deny. The first step to be taken is to remove this feeling; and, to do this, some great measure or measures should be offered to the people of Ireland, which will act as a complete demonstration to them that bygones are to be bygones with regard to the administration of Irish affairs, and that henceforth, new, generous, and equal principles of government are to be adopted.'

In the same speech, too, we find the following remarkable utterances: 'With regard to the parliamentary representation of Ireland, having recently spent seventy-three days in an examination of the subject, while serving as a member of the Dublin Election Committee, I assert most distinctly that the representation which exists at this moment is a fraud; and I believe it would be far better if there were not representation at all, because the people would not then be deluded by the idea that they had a representative Government to protect their interests.'

It is curious here to remember that when Ireland did get a body of delegates composing a less fraudulent representation, and possessing the confidence of the Irish people, they found no bitterer enemy than the man who had so ardently desired their existence in 1848. Mr. Bright concluded his speech with an eloquent peroration, which, coming at such a time, was perhaps of more value in keeping the spirit of agitation alive in Ireland than the fiercest utterances of the *Nation* or the *United Irishman*. ' Let the House, if it can, regard Ireland as an English country. Let us think of the eight millions of people, and of the millions of them doomed to this intolerable suffering. Let us think of the half million who, within two years past, have perished miserably in the workhouses, and on the highways, and in their hovels—more, far more, than ever fell by the sword in any war this country has ever waged ; let us think of the crop of nameless horrors which is even now growing up in Ireland, and whose disastrous fruit may be gathered in years and generations to come. Let us examine what are the laws and principles under which alone God and nature have permitted that nations should become industrious and provident.'

In the following year, 1849, the year of the abortive insurrection of Fintan Lawlor and Philip Grey, Mr. Bright made a speech which contains this famous passage : ' But the treatment of this Irish malady remains even the same. We have nothing for it still but force and arms. You have an armed force there of 50,000 men to keep the people quiet ; large votes are annually required to keep the people quiet, and large votes are annually required to keep the people alive. I presume the government by troops is easy, and that the—

> Civil power may snore at ease,
> While soldiers fire—to keep the peace!

'I shall be told,' said Mr. Bright, in the same speech, ' that I am injuring aristocratical and territorial influence. What is there in Ireland worth to you now ? What is Ireland worth to you at all ? Is she not the very symbol and token of your disgrace and humiliation to the whole world ? Is she not an incessant trouble to your Legislature, and a source of increased expense to your people, already overtaxed ? Is not your legislation all at fault in what it has hitherto done for that country ? The people of Ulster say that we shall weaken the

Union. It has been one of the misfortunes of the legislation of this House that there has been no honest attempt to make a Union with the whole people of Ireland up to this time. . . . Hon. gentlemen turn with triumph to neighbouring countries, and speak in glowing terms of our glorious constitution. It is true that abroad thrones and dynasties have been overturned, whilst in England peace has reigned undisturbed. But take all the lives that have been lost in the last twelve months in Europe amidst the convulsions that have occurred —take all the cessation of trade, destruction of industry, all the crushing of hopes and hearts, and they will not compare for an instant with the agonies which have been endured by the population of Ireland under your glorious constitution.'

There now seems a gap in Mr. Bright's speeches on Ireland, a gap of nearly twenty years. Once again insurrection is in the air; once again men are planning and arming secretly to attempt the regeneration of Ireland, and once again Mr. Bright comes forward, eloquent upon the injuries that Ireland has sustained, eloquent upon her wrongs, her sufferings, her humiliation.

'I believe that if the majority of the people of Ireland, counted fairly out, had their will, and if they had the power, they would unmoor the island from its fastenings in the deep, and move it at least two thousand miles to the west. And I believe, further, that if by conspiracy or insurrection, or by that open agitation to which alone I ever would give any favour or consent, they could shake off the authority, I will not say of the English Crown, but of the Imperial Parliament, they would gladly do so. . . . Sixty-five years ago this country and this Parliament undertook to govern Ireland. I will say nothing of the manner in which that duty was brought upon us except this—that it was by proceedings disgraceful and corrupt to the last degree. I will say nothing of the pretences under which it was brought about but this—that the English Parliament and people, and the Irish people too, were told that if they once got rid of the Irish Parliament they would dethrone for ever Irish factions, and that with a united Parliament we should become a united, and stronger, and happier people.' During these sixty-five years Mr. Bright went on to show that only three measures had been passed in the interests of Ireland. One of these was the Catholic Emancipation Act, which, as Mr. Bright proved, was only conceded out of fear of civil war; the other two were the measures for the relief of the poor and the sale of encumbered estates. 'Except on these two emergencies I appeal to every Irish member, and to every English member who has paid any attention to the matter, whether the statement is not true that this Parliament has done nothing for the people of Ireland. And, more than that, their complaints have been met—often by denial, often by insult, often by contempt.'

In the same speech Mr. Bright asked a question which had a peculiar pertinence at a time when the movement was chiefly organised by Irish-Americans. 'Why does every Irishman who leaves his country and goes to the United States, immediately settle himself down there, resolved to better his condition in life, but with a feeling of ineradicable hatred to the laws and institutions of the land of his birth?' Then comes a passage which really reads like a satire upon Mr. Bright's latest political pronouncements: 'Now, sir, a few days ago everybody in this House, with two or three exceptions, was taking an oath at that table. It is called the Oath of Allegiance. It is meant at once to express loyalty and to keep men loyal. I do not think it generally does bind men to loyalty if they have not loyalty without it. I hold loyalty to consist, in a country like this, as much in doing justice to the people as in guarding the Crown; for I believe there is no guardianship of the Crown in a country like this, where the Crown is not supposed to rest absolutely upon force, so safe as that of which we know more in our day, probably, than has been known in former periods of our history, when the occupant of the throne is respected, admired, and loved by the general people. Now, how comes it that these great statesmen whom I have named, with all their colleagues—some of them almost as eminent as their leaders—have never tried what they could do, have never shown their loyalty to the Crown by endeavouring to make the Queen as safe in the hearts of the people of Ireland as she is in the hearts of the people of England and Scotland?'

It is interesting to find that Mr. Bright considers loyalty to consist as much in doing justice to the people as in guarding the Crown, and it will be interesting to know, too, why he defines a party who are occupied in doing justice to their own people as a rebel party. Either Mr. Bright has forgotten his definition of loyalty, or he has changed his mind. Then came a passage that might have been, but was not, repeated by him during recent times of trial. 'You may pass this Bill,' said Mr. Bright—the House was discussing a Coercion measure—' you may put the Home Secretary's 500 men into jail; you may do more than this — you may suppress the conspiracy and put down the insurrection — but the moment it is suppressed there will still remain the germs of this malady, and from those germs will grow up, as heretofore, another crop of insurrection and another harvest of misfortune. And it may be that those who sit here eighteen years after this movement will find another Ministry and another Secretary of State, ready to propose to you another administration of the same ever-failing and ever-poisonous medicine.'

All these speeches that have been quoted were made during the lifetime of Mr. John Dillon. Listening to such speeches, or reading the reports of them, the true-hearted and simple-minded gentleman who represented Tipperary might very well have believed that Mr. Bright was one of Ireland's best friends. A great dinner was organised, chiefly by Mr. Dillon, to be given in honour of Mr. Bright, in Dublin. Mr. Dillon fully believed that the regeneration of Ireland was to be effected by union between the English Liberals and the leaders of opinion in Ireland. To effect this union he laboured for all the last years of his life; and this banquet to Mr. Bright was intended to be a sort of inauguration of the accomplished thing, and the herald of a happier state of things.

When all the preparations were completed for the banquet, at which, if we remember rightly, Mr. Dillon was to have taken the chair, Mr. Dillon suddenly died, and deprived Irish politics of one of the bravest and one of the sincerest of her soldiers and her statesmen. The banquet was not abandoned. It went on in spite of the loss which the two parties, who were thus to be politically bound together, sustained by Mr. Dillon's death. The chair was then taken by another Irish member, who was then regarded in England, and in Ireland, as a very advanced politician indeed, The O'Donoghue, who was, perhaps, a more appropriate chairman for any assembly at which Mr. Bright was going to speak than John Dillon could have been. Mr. Bright made a speech which he began by paying an eloquent tribute to the memory of the dead man. 'I speak with grief when I say that one of our friends who signed that invitation is no longer with us. I had not the pleasure of a long acquaintance with Mr. Dillon, but I shall take this opportunity of saying that during the last session of Parliament I formed a very high opinion of his character. There was that in his eye, and in the tone of his voice—in his manner altogether—which marked him for an honourable and a just man. I venture to say that this sad and sudden removal is a great loss to Ireland. I believe amongst all her worthy sons, Ireland has had no worthier and no nobler son than John Blake Dillon.'

Then Mr. Bright proceeded to examine the position of Ireland. 'There are some,' he said, 'who say that the great misfortune of Ireland is in the existence of the noxious class of political agitators. Well, as to that, I may state that the most distinguished political agitators that have ever appeared during the last hundred years in Ireland are Grattan and O'Connell, and I should say that he must either be a very stupid or a very base Irishman who would wish to erase the achievements of Grattan and O'Connell from the annals of his country.' Mr. Bright then proceeded to draw a graphic and powerful picture of the sufferings of Ireland and the Irish people, and he concluded his gloomy study thus: 'Bear in mind that I am not speaking of Poland suffering under the conquest of Russia. . . . I am not speaking about Hungary, or of Venice as she was under the rule of Austria, or of the Greeks under the dominion of the Turk, but I am speaking of Ireland—part of the United Kingdom—part of that which boasts itself to be the most civilised and the most Christian nation in the world.'

Under these conditions Mr. Bright was naturally not surprised at the statement which he quoted of an esteemed citizen of Dublin: 'He told me that he believed that a very large portion of what is called the poor, amongst Irishmen, sympathised with any scheme or any proposition that was adverse to the Imperial Government.' Then when the thoughts of every national Irishman were with his brethren in America, Mr. Bright gave this impetus to the Fenian movement. 'You will recollect that when the ancient Hebrew prophet prayed in his captivity he prayed with his window open towards Jerusalem. You know that the followers of Mahommed, when they pray, turn their faces towards Mecca. When the Irish peasant asks for food, and freedom, and blessing, his eye follows the setting sun; the aspirations of his heart reach beyond the wide Atlantic, and in spirit he grasps hands with the great Republic of the West.'

But Mr. Bright was not merely content with enlarging upon the sufferings of Ireland. He saw his way to a remedy and boldly enunciated it. 'If Irishmen were united—if your 105 members were for the most part agreed, you might do almost anything you like; you might do it even in the present Parliament; but if you are disunited, then I know not how you can gain anything from a Parliament created as the Imperial Parliament is now. The classes who rule in Britain will hear your cry as they have heard it before, and will pay no attention to it. They will see your people leaving your shores, and will think it no calamity to the country. They know that they have force to suppress insurrection, and, therefore, you can gain nothing from their fears. What, then, is your hope? It is in a better Parliament, representing fairly the United Kingdom—the movement which is now in force in England and Scotland, and which is your movement as much as ours. If there were 100 more members, the representatives of large and free constituencies, then your cry would be heard, and the people would give you that justice which a class has so long denied you.'

If John Dillon, over whose grave almost Mr. Bright was uttering these trumpet-notes of encouragement to the Irish people, could have known while he was yet alive that Mr. Bright would be the bitterest and most inveterate opponent of a body of Irish members who were united, and who were agreed, he would, we may feel convinced, have bitterly regretted that such a change could ever come over such a friend of Ireland.

There is little need to make citations from any further speeches of Mr. Bright's, but there is one more which may be regarded as belonging to the John Dillon period. It was spoken in Dublin only three nights after the banquet in that city. Mr. Bright said : ' I am very sorry that my voice is not what it was ; and when I think of the work that is to be done, sometimes I feel it is a pity we grow old so fast.' We, too, may be permitted to regret, nearly twenty years later, that Mr. John Bright grew old so fast—that he so soon shook off the belief and the courage of his nobler years. For the same speech concluded with these words : ' And if I have in past times felt an unquenchable sympathy with the sufferings of your people, you may rely upon it that if there be an Irish member to speak for Ireland, he will find me heartily by his side.' Yet there came a time when there were not one but many Irish members to speak for Ireland in the English House of Commons, and they found Mr. Bright not heartily by their side, but zealously, fanatically, opposed to them.

The Irish people can afford now to forgive, if not to forget, the enmity of John Bright. He is now the antagonist of the great Englishman who has borne the message of peace and love to Ireland. But because he was once a good friend to Ireland, because Ireland believed in him and admired him—then for the sake of that belief and that admiration we may be content to let him pass by in sorrowful silence.

CHAPTER XVI.

THE LAND QUESTION.

THROUGHOUT the history of Ireland no question has been so fruitful of wretchedness and of conspiracy among the Irish people, and of alternate remedial and repressive legislation on the part of the English Government, as the question of the land. By the incessant confiscations and settlements of Irish soil, the land became almost entirely vested in the hands of landlords, who, if not alien in blood, were at least alien so far as sympathy for their tenants was concerned. In fact, the vast proportion of the Irish people were merely tenants-at-will of these usurping landlords, the majority of whom had no other interest in their lands or their tenants than the amount of money which they could extort from them, and who were enabled to wring exorbitant rents from the wretched peasants to whom the land was an absolute necessity, whatever the price paid for its possession. Under such conditions it is easily conceivable that often the terms demanded were impossible to meet. In such cases the landlord had recourse to eviction. Eviction produced misery, and misery, disaffection—the disaffection gradually organising itself into secret societies and those famous Ribbon lodges, which have had such an important connection with the Irish Land question.

In no other civilised country in the world, perhaps, has such a system of land tenure existed as existed in Ireland. The landlord was absolutely master of his tenant, whom, as often as not, he ground down by deputy, living out of the country, and merely absorbing the rents. All enterprise and industry in the Irish peasant were simply at a discount; for any improvements which a tenant might effect upon his holding, and any increase in the producing power of the land which he might contrive, could only result, as he knew but too well, in the increase of the rent. Ever since the passing of the Union the position of the Irish peasant has constantly formed the subject of Parliamentary inquiry and the production of portentous Parliamentary reports. But only too often has the matter ended with the report of the Committee of Inquiry, without any practical legislation resulting. For a long time the only legislation on the subject was directed to the punishment and repression of the discontent which such a state of things naturally provoked. The greatest concession that was ever made was cruelly ironical in its provisions. It was an Act prohibiting evictions on Christmas Day and Good Friday, and the removal of the roof of a dwelling until the inhabitants had left its shelter.

In the year 1819 the Select Committee presided over by Sir John Newton sat to inquire into the matter. Its report called attention to the great distress of the needy agriculturalist, and earnestly advocated reform of the land law, and suggested the reclamation of land not under cultivation. But without avail. In 1823 another Committee reported upon the wretchedness of the labouring class, and urged reform as its predecessor had done, but again without avail. This report was followed in 1825 by a similar report of another Committee, which, like the other two, advocated agricultural reform, and like the other two, without success. In consequence of the Act of 1793 which extended the franchise to the forty-shilling freeholder, the landlord, greedy of power, divided his estate into a number of small tenancies in order to increase the number of votes under his command, and without regard to the injuries which his tenants sustained. Then by the Emancipation Act of 1829 the forty-shilling freeholder was deprived of the franchise, the landlord's interest in smaller holdings was gone, and the system of clearances which ensued was carried on again at the expense of the people.

In the same year as the Emancipation Act, 1829, a Mr. Brownlow introduced into the English Parliament a Bill for facilitating the reclamation of waste lands in Ireland, thereby bringing prominently before the Government the wretched condition of the tenant-farmer and the agricultural labourer. The Commons passed the Bill; and it was read a second time in the Lords; but the Select Committee to which it was referred shelved it for ever. An Arms Bill, however, proposed at the same time, though denounced by an English peer as vexatious and aggressive, was carried successfully.

In the year following Mr. Brownlow's futile attempt at remedial legislation, Mr. Henry Grattan, the son of the great Grattan, in concert with Mr. Spring Rice, who afterwards became Lord Monteagle, brought strongly before the attention of the Government the wrongs and hardships of the Irish peasant, and, like his predecessors, urged the reclamation of waste lands. The only outcome of Mr. Grattan's representations was the appointment of another Select Committee, which reported as the other Committees on the same subject had reported, and without any result.

In 1824 a Select Committee of the House of Commons recommended a valuation of the land in Ireland, and after an interval of six years this valuation was undertaken. In 1836 another Act was passed to insure uniform valuation, which enacted that the basis of all valuations was to be a fixed scale of agricultural produce contained in the Act. The instructions to the valuators showed a strong predisposition in favour of the landlord, the consequence being that the average valuation proved to be about twenty-five per cent. under the gross rental of the country.

In 1844 a Select Committee of the House of Commons was appointed to reconsider the question, with the result that in 1846 an Act was passed changing the principle of valuation from a relative valuation of townlands based on a fixed scale of agricultural produce, to a tenement valuation for poor-law rating to be made 'upon an estimate of the net annual value . . . of the rent for which, one year with another, the same might in its actual state be reasonably expected to let from year to year.' The same results, however, practically accrued from the two valuations. In 1852 another Valuation Act was passed, in which the former system of valuation by a fixed scale of agricultural produce was returned to; but Sir Richard Griffith's evidence in 1869 shows the valuation employed was a live-and-let-live valuation, according to the state of prices for five years previous to the time of valuation.

In 1830 famine was abroad and riot was rampant. It is curious to note that in the speech from the throne the King, while declaring that he was determined to crush out sedition and disaffection by all the means which the law and the constitution placed at his disposal, had no remedy for the poverty and distress which had bred the disaffection. The Ministry were attacked at this time by Mr. Hume, who denounced them for having violated by their coercive policy the promises which they made while in Opposition of a conciliatory policy towards Ireland. In 1831 Lord Althorpe proposed and carried a vote for 50,000*l.* to be advanced to the Commissioners for expenditure on public works in Ireland. The effect of this measure was, however, entirely negatived by the Arms Bill, which was introduced four months later by Mr. Stanley, and which Lord Althorpe stigmatised as one of the most tyrannical measures he had ever heard proposed.

An Act dealing with the question of sub-letting, prohibiting the letting by the lessee unless with the express permission of the proprietor, was now before the House. It was attacked by Dr. Boyle, who maintained that it was mere fatuity to expect the Irish peasants to submit tamely to eviction so long as their only means of livelihood depended upon the possession of their potato field. Though the Catholic Emancipation Act had removed the disabilities of representation from Catholics, yet it had also abolished the forty-shilling vote, and thus gave the landlords greater opportunities for clearance. The consequence was that the condition of Ireland was desperate to the last degree.

This terrible state of things was, as usual, met by the

Government with a fresh Coercion Bill. In 1834, indeed, an effort to do something for the Irish tenant was made by Mr. Poulett Scrope, but unsuccessfully; and in the following year Mr. Sharman Crawford, then member for Dundalk, moved for leave to bring in a Bill to amend the law relating to landlord and tenant. He reintroduced his measure in March 1836, obtained permission to bring in his Bill, and there the matter ended. He was followed, in 1837, by Mr. Lynch, who moved for permission to introduce a Bill on waste lands, but who met with the same amount of success as Mr. Sharman Crawford.

The first measure of real remedial value was the Artificial Drainage Act, passed in 1842, which did something towards reclaiming waste land, but which, until reinforced by the Summary Proceedings Act, was of small value. The year 1843 was a memorable one in the history of the Irish Land question, for it was then that, in response to the repeated importunings of Mr. Sharman Crawford, Sir Robert Peel appointed the famous Devon Commission. This Commission sat for two years, and at the end of its investigations reported, as all other Committees of Inquiry had reported, that the disastrous relations of landlord to tenant were the direct cause of all the poverty and suffering under which the Irish peasant laboured; and advised legislation which would secure to the tenant a just compensation for outlay of capital and labour.

Lord Devon, who was determined to secure some practical results to the inquiries of the Commission, if it were possible, on May 6, 1845, printed a number of petitions, in which he urged Parliament to assure to the industrious tenant the results and benefits of the improvements which he effected. In response to those appeals a Bill was brought in in the June of the same year by Lord Stanley, providing for compensation for disturbance. Owing to the violent opposition with which the Bill was encountered by Lords, Commons, and the Select Committee to whom it had been referred, Lord Stanley had to abandon it in the following month.

Mr. Sharman Crawford now introduced a Tenant-Right Bill which he had held back in 1843 in order to await the report of the Devon Commission. In 1846 a Bill brought forward by Lord Lincoln, prompted by Mr. Sharman Crawford, dealing with compensation for disturbance, passed the second reading, and then was lost sight of by the resignation of the Ministry. Mr. Sharman Crawford's Tenant-Right Bill was finally rejected on June 10, 1847, by a majority of eighty-seven; but it was brought forward again in the following year, and this time the adverse majority was reduced to twenty-three.

In 1848 a Bill, practically the same as that of Lord Lincoln's, which was lost in 1846, was introduced by the Irish Secretary, Sir William Somerville. It received the support of the Irish members; but the report upon the Bill was not prepared until too close to the end of the session for any further progress to be made; so, in order that the Irish people might not be disappointed by an absence of legislation, the Government suspended the Habeas Corpus Act.

In 1849 Mr. Horsman pleaded powerfully, but unsuccessfully, for the presentation of an address to Her Majesty, pointing out the condition of her Irish subjects. Sir William Somerville, early in the following year, reintroduced his Bill, which passed the second reading, was consigned to a Committee, and shelved, while Mr. Sharman Crawford again brought forward his Tenant-Right Bill, and again was defeated.

In 1851 a motion made by Sir H. W. Barron for a Committee of the whole House to inquire into the condition of Ireland, was lost by a majority of nine; and thus, though six years had elapsed, nothing had been done for Ireland since the report of the Devon Commission, except the Encumbered Estates Act, which was passed in the interest of the landlords.

On February 10, Mr. Sharman Crawford obtained leave to bring in a Bill to regulate the Ulster custom. But at this point the Liberal Government was ousted and supplanted by Lord Derby's administration, and Mr. Crawford's Bill was lost by a majority of 110. The new Government was not entirely supine on the Irish question, and the Irish Attorney-General,

Mr. Napier, drafted four Bills all bearing on the relations of landlord to tenant—a Land Improvement Bill, a Landlord and Tenant Law Consolidation Bill, a Leasing Powers Bill, and a Tenants' Improvements Compensation Bill.

In 1853 a Committee was appointed to consider these four Bills in conjunction with Mr. Sharman Crawford's Bill. It rejected the latter, and considerably modified, at the expense of the tenant, Mr. Napier's Compensation for Improvements Bill. Meanwhile the Government had again been vested in the hands of the Liberals, and although Mr. Napier, now in opposition, continued to give his strongest support to the Bills which he had introduced, the Tory party fought them tooth and nail.

In 1854 the Select Committee of the House of Lords, appointed to consider these Bills, condemned the Tenants' Compensation Bill, and only the other three were returned to the House of Commons. In the following year the Government adopted a Bill which Mr. Serjeant Shee endeavoured to bring in, and which was substantially identical with that Bill of Mr. Napier's which the Lords had rejected. The opposition of the land-owning class, however, was so violent that the Bill had to be abandoned.

In 1856 Mr. George Henry Moore, the leader of the Irish Parliamentary party, took up again Mr. Sharman Crawford's Tenant-Right Bill; but the opposition which it encountered from the Government was fatal to it. Mr. Moore reintroduced it in the following year, only to abandon it again.

In 1858 Mr. John Francis Maguire, who had succeeded to the leadership of the Irish party, again brought forward Mr. Serjeant Shee's Tenant Compensation Bill, but was defeated by a majority of forty-five. Though the Government displayed much apathy in remedying the grievances of their Irish fellow-subjects, they showed much more consideration for the Bengalee. They had just settled the Bengal Land question on the ancient principles of Indian law, thereby granting to the Indian subject much that was denied to the Irish subject.

At last, in 1860 was passed the famous Land Act, which

proved so unsatisfactory. This Act attempted to simplify the relations between landlord and tenant by sweeping away all the remains of the feudal connection, and by establishing an absolute principle of free trade and freedom of contract as opposed to tenure. But the principle of freedom of contract is wholly unsuited to the Irish Land question, and in so much as it was based upon this principle the Act was a failure. The tenants are compelled to take the land, often without any prospect of fulfilling their contract, because all other means of livelihood have been destroyed. The best terms they can make are practically those which the landlord chooses to impose. It is exactly the same principle as the State regulation of railway fares. Freedom of contract is not permitted in this case, because the passenger and the railway company are not free contracting parties. The latter holds a monopoly of what is practically a necessity to the former; and without State interference the passenger would have to submit to any charges the company thought fit to impose. The immediate effect of the Act was to produce an immense flood of emigration and to give rise to the Fenian conspiracy.

In 1866 a Bill brought in by Mr. Chichester Fortescue, to amend that of 1860, fell through, and in 1867 a like fate befell a Tory measure drawn up much on the lines of Lord Stanley's Bill of 1845.

Mr. Gladstone came into office in 1868, and early in 1870 introduced the only really beneficial measure since the report of the Devon Commission—the Bill to amend the Law of Landlord and Tenant in Ireland. But, though this Bill conceded to the tenant the privilege of litigation with his landlord, this really did not place him beyond the landlord's control, for the day went generally to the man who could hold out longest. The three objects of the Land Act of 1870 were to obtain for the Irish tenant security of tenure; to encourage the making of improvements; and the creation of a peasant proprietorship. With tenancies held under the Ulster tenant-right custom the Act did not interfere, but merely enforced the custom against the landlords of estates subject to it. The two chief features of this Ulster custom—so long and so greatly coveted by the Irish peasants of the other provinces—were permissive fixity of tenure, and the tenant's right to sell the good-will of his farm.

Those who drew up the Act of 1870 dare not affirm that its object was the creation of a peasant proprietorship--and, indeed, it was often denied that such was the object—or to give him any portion of absolute ownership. Its effect was stated as compelling bad landlords to act like good landlords; but what it really did was to make eviction too costly for any but the wealthier land-owners. Its provisions for compensation for disturbance were ineffectual, and the eight clauses attempting to create a peasant proprietorship were also futile. 'The cause of their failure is obvious,' says Mr. Richey, 'to anyone acquainted with the nature of the landed estates title which it was considered desirable for the tenant to obtain. A Landed Estates Court conveyance affects not only the parties to the proceedings, but binds persons, whether parties or not, and extinguishes all rights which are inconsistent with the terms of the grant of the Court. If by any mistake more lands than should properly be sold be included in the grant, or the most indisputable rights of third parties are not noticed in the body of the grant or the annexed schedule, irreparable injustice is done, and the injured parties have no redress.' The fact that the Court was not made the instrument for the perpetration of the grossest frauds is due solely to the stringency of its rules and the intelligence of its officers. Such was the condition of things that the Land Act of 1880 was schemed to ameliorate.

CHAPTER XVII.

FENIANISM.

THE suppression of the Phœnix movement stimulated, instead of retarding, the spirit of secret organisation in Ireland and in America. Stephens was not disheartened by a temporary defeat. The process of agitation, of enrolment, of organisation, went on with greater vigour than ever. And the new body was imbued with far greater vitality than the Phœnix conspiracy ever possessed, or had seemed likely to possess. Stephens in Ireland, and O'Mahony in America, were both working steadily for the same ends; and the result of their efforts was the Fenian organisation.

The title of the Fenian Brotherhood was not the title by which at first the body was known in Ireland. Stephens called the association of which he was the presiding genius the Irish Republican Brotherhood, and for a time the letters I.R.B. represented to Irish conspirators the name of their conspiracy. But O'Mahony, over in America, was something of a Gaelic scholar and student. He desired to give the organisation for which he was working a name which should recall some great historical association connected with the past glories of Ireland, and cast about in his mind for a suitable appellation. He bethought him of that wonderful semi-mythic chivalry of the Feni, companions of Fionn, the son of Coul, whose deeds were the pride and the marvel of pre-historic Irish history. From this legendary brotherhood of warriors and poets and heroes—warriors like Fionn himself, poets like Oisin and heroes like Diarmuid, the lover of Grainne —he borrowed their stately title to give it to the very real brotherhood of which he was, in a measure, the head. Thus, from the poetic fancy of the exiled Young Irelander, the most formidable of Irish conspiracies got its name of the Fenian Brotherhood.

The title was an attractive one. It was easy to remember,

It roused famous and fascinating associations, and it soon over-crowed the colder name devised by Stephens; till, in the end, the Fenians became the generally accepted designation of the world for the members of the I.R.B. The name passed at once into literature. It lives in passionate poems and stirring lyrics, in which the lengthy appellation of the Irish Republican Brotherhood could have found no place. The well-known poem, with its stirring refrain of 'Up and make way for the Fenian men,' would in itself be enough to fix and make permanent the title of any movement. The Tyrtæus of the latest of Irish conspiracies found his account in the term taken from the shadowy heroes of Irish antiquity. The Irish Republican Brotherhood might serve very well in eloquent speeches and elaborate addresses, but the Fenians was the term for poets.

The movement went on slowly but very surely. It received perhaps the most important of its earlier impulses with the funeral of Terence Bellew M'Manus. M'Manus had died away in America in exile. Fortune had not smiled upon him since the days when Meagher described him as the 'tall, dashing, soldierly fellow, with frank, bold, honest features, flushing with delight,' who, with a green cap on his head and a rifle in his right hand, joined the rebel muster at Ballingarry. He made his escape from his Australasian prison in 1851. 'Having been arrested,' says Gavan Duffy, 'by an excess of authority, for some supposed violation of convict regulations, he appealed to a bench of magistrates, and was set at liberty. Being thus free from any obligation to his jailers, he made his escape to San Francisco.' In California M'Manus's closing years were passed not too happily. He entered upon his old business. But the business habits of the New World, and especially of that very New World of California in those days, were not the business habits of the Old; and Terence Bellew M'Manus found it difficult for him to reconcile his own principles and theories with the rough-and-ready methods of that *terra nova*, the California of the Pioneers and of Bret Harte's 'argonauts.'

We are told that heavy shadows came to linger on the handsome face which once was all smiles and brightness. He lived poor, and he died poor in 1861. His family and his friends resolved that his body should be laid in the country he had loved so well, and for which he had sacrificed so much. The remains of the brave, brilliant, and gifted Young Irelander were conveyed in their coffin across the Atlantic, and were borne in solemn state through Dublin, to their final resting-place in Glasnevin, amidst the silent homage of assembled thousands.

'The incident,' says Mr. A. M. Sullivan, 'was so dramatic and touched such deep emotions, that the proceeding assumed a magnitude and solemnity which astonished and startled everyone. The Irish race in America seemed to make of the funeral a demonstration of devotion to the old land. The Irish at home were seized with like feelings, and on all sides prepared to give a suitable reception to the remains of him who, proscribed in life, might return only in death to the land he loved. It was a proceeding which appealed powerfully to the sympathies of the people; and Nationalists of all hues and sections mingled in the homage and patriotism which it was understood to convey.'

Another writer gives an interesting account of the passage of the funeral *cortège* through Dublin: 'Every spot that could call up a vengeful memory was included; no turning was neglected from which a silent bravado could be flung at the Government. It proceeded through Thomas Street, indissolubly associated with the memory of Lord Edward Fitzgerald, every head uncovering as it passed the house where that nobleman met his death, and the church where he was interred. A third, the most striking pause of all, was made at the scene of Emmet's execution. . . . A similar mark of respect was accorded to a house in High Street, where the remains of Wolfe Tone had been deposited previous to their removal to their last resting-place. In passing the Castle the procession slackened i's pace to the utmost, and lingered on its way in silent, but stern defiance. Then it took its course by the Exchange, through College Green, and in front of the Parliament Houses. Thence it wound through Westmoreland Street to Carlisle Bridge, and so to Glasnevin. The pall-bearers themselves were members of the Irish Republican Brotherhood.'

An immense number of recruits came into the Fenian ranks after the M'Manus funeral. During the six months which followed that memorable event the organisation is said to have no less than doubled its numbers in Ireland. One addition to the ranks could well have been spared. This was Pierce Nagle, who afterwards became so conspicuous and so infamous as the informer. A large number of American Fenians, too, came over with the body of M'Manus, and their presence in Dublin served to link very closely the kindred organisations of Ireland and America, and to encourage and stimulate the Irish agitation.

One very remarkable event which followed close upon the M'Manus funeral was a meeting that was held in the Rotunda in Dublin, to express sympathy with the American Federals. The meeting, which was ingeniously organised by members of the Fenian body, was addressed by one very peculiar patriot, and the chair was taken by another. The speaker was the late Mr. P. J. Smyth; the chairman was The O'Donoghue. At that time The O'Donoghue was an advocate of advanced nationalism, a point of view to which he again oscillated for a short time lately. It is interesting to read an account of the speech which Mr. P. J. Smyth, whose memory has been a good deal glorified by the Conservative Press, addressed to the meeting on that occasion :

'Having read the resolution which he was called upon to move, Mr. Smyth made a speech which abounded in sneers against England. The tone of his voice was pitched and his accent carefully suited to convey his meaning. He said that an insult had been offered to " our " flag – thereby capping the denial made shortly before by the chairman, that Irishmen accepted the flag of England as their own. He alluded to the mere Yankee captain, who was not of noble blood, but who, for all that, dared to fire a shot across the bows of a right-royal *British* steamer, although she was " under the flag that had braved a thousand years the battle and the breeze," thus forgetting that " *Britons* never failed," &c., and altogether regardless of the *British* captain, his storming, his swearing, and his exposition of *British* international law. After more of this kind of thing—the word *British* figuring in every sneering sentence—the speaker went on to observe that England had got up indignation meetings, but that Irishmen knew how to be indignant too. Here he looked round him with a peculiar expression. The look was understood, and elicited a storm of applause. Then came a panegyric on America, which introduced and strengthened the diatribe that followed against England, " the nation that had levelled their homes, banished them and scattered them as outcasts through the earth, and denied them the ordinary rights of mankind—even at that very hour forbidding Irishmen to bear arms. Thus," added Mr. Smyth, should Irishmen read the characters of the antagonists (England and America), " the one the best friend of Ireland, the other her inveterate enemy," and act accordingly. How the speaker expected his countrymen to act in case of war between the two countries, he showed a little later. When speaking of those already in the field on both sides in America, he declared that the moment England entered into a war with America, they (the Irishmen serving the North and the South) would forget all past differences and be arrayed against England. The speech closed with an enumeration of the difficulties and dangers threatening England, which drew forth reiterated cheers.' This was not the kind of speech which Mr. P. J. Smyth was accustomed to make in later years, when he had become first the panegyrist, and then the placeman of the Government he denounced.

The American civil war was a great nourisher of the Fenian movement. Thousands upon thousands of Irishmen fought upon either side in the great American Iliad. Whether under the Stars and Stripes or beneath the Stars and Bars, whether to the tune of 'The Bonny Blue Flag' or the still more menacing music of 'John Brown's Body,' vast numbers of Irishmen learnt the trade of war in one of its grimmest and sternest schools; learnt the familiar use of arms; learnt something of strategy; learnt, too, the art of commanding, and the more difficult art of obeying; and became familiar with all the duties and dangers of a soldier's life. When the war was over, it left many thousands of Irishmen dead on many desperate fields.

Of the Irish Brigade that followed Meagher so gallantly up the heights of Fredericksburg, few came back to tell the story of their wild charges under their beloved leader. In the ranks of the Confederate army Irishmen fought and died by the hundred and the tens of hundreds. But on either side, whether in the blue uniform of the Federal or the grey cloth of the Secessionist, the Irish soldier remained first of all an Irishman. There is a touching story told of one battle in which a Federal Irish regiment found itself opposed to an Irish regiment on the Confederate side, and of how the two regiments refused to join battle, and passed each other with mutual cries of 'God save Ireland!' Of such men as this the war left a goodly multitude, well-trained, well-seasoned, well-schooled in the use of arms. Such were the men whom the planners and promoters of the Fenian movement relied upon to make that movement triumphant.

The chiefs of the movement felt the time was approaching for the long-dreamed-of rising. A large amount of money was subscribed, and sent over to Stephens to be expended for the good of the cause. A little cloud of Irish-American officers, men who had served on both sides in the war, descended upon Ireland to organise the country, and act as heads of the rebellion. The preparations, however, in Ireland were not in a very advanced state, and the Irish-American officers found in most cases that very little was ready; that there were very few men for them to take command of; that there was little or nothing for them to do; and that their presence was rapidly arousing suspicions in the minds of the English Government. An attempt on Canada, which was, perhaps, one of the most hopeful of the Fenian schemes, fell through for want of proper management, and practically came to nothing.

Three men were conspicuous conspirators and followers of Stephens in the Fenian movement. These were Charles J. Kickham, John O'Leary, and Thomas Clarke Luby. Charles Kickham was a Tipperary man, intensely popular with the people of his own county. He had been intended for the medical profession, but an unhappy accident prevented him from ever hoping for success in such a career. He was a passionate sportsman; and one day, after returning from a long day's shooting in the hills, he was drying some wet powder before the fire, when a spark fell from the embers, and the powder exploded in Kickham's face. It was feared at first that he would lose his sight altogether; and when he had recovered, both sight and hearing were terribly injured. This misfortune, which only deepened the affection of the people, led him to devote his life to the study of literature. He wrote some charming stories, and some exquisite verses. He was an intense Nationalist, and when the Fenian movement first began to take shape in Ireland, he became an active member of the body.

In November 1860 some twenty-eight Tipperary men, who had formed part of the Irish brigade for the defence of the Pope, gave a public reception at Mullinahone, Kickham's native place, at which Kickham made a speech, and read an address to the friends of Ireland, signed by the twenty-eight members of the Papal brigade, and said to have been written by Kickham. In this address the signatories declared: 'We wish to let the world know that we are slaves, but not contented slaves. . . . We protest against this intolerable tyranny, and denounce to the world the hypocrisy of England in pretending to be the friend of freedom and oppressed nationalities.' Kickham made a speech after the address was read, which he concluded with some words which showed clearly enough his impassioned sympathy for the new agitation. 'I heard people say that the brigade men should be asked to scatter the seed during the spring, as in that case the harvest would surely be good. I hope they will scatter another kind of seed, broadcast too, and it will grow and ripen.'

The second of Stephens' supporters was John O'Leary. 'John O'Leary,' says Mr. A. M. Sullivan, 'was unquestionably one of the ablest and most remarkable men in the conspiracy. Intellectually and politically he was of the type of Wolfe Tone, Robert Emmet, and John Mitchel. . . . He was born in Tipperary town, and inherited on the death of his parents, for his share, a small property of some 300*l.* or 400*l.* a year. He was a graduate of the Queen's University, having taken out his medical degree in the Queen's College, Cork. He resided for some time in Paris, where his mind, his tastes, his manners, opinions, and principles, received impress and shape discernible in his subsequent career. He also visited America, and there formed the acquaintance of the men who were planning and devising the Fenian movement. He was a man of culture, and of considerable literary abilities. . . . He was reserved, sententious, almost cynical; keenly observant, sharply critical, full of restrained passion.' We believe that we are right in saying that Mr. O'Leary himself has stated that he never was a member of the Irish Republican Brotherhood.

The third of Stephens' ablest lieutenants was Thomas C. Luby. Luby, like Kickham, was a Tipperary man; like some of the most prominent of the leaders of 1798, he was a Protestant. Though he was a very young man when the movement of 1848 was going on, he had devoted himself to it, and had attached himself to the advanced section of the Young Irelanders who followed the lead of John Mitchel. He had come from Melbourne to France to join Stephens and O'Mahony, and he accompanied Stephens on the tour through Ireland that preceded the formation of the Phœnix conspiracy. Later on he became one of the editors of the *Irish Tribune*, a national newspaper which lived for a short time, and which preceded the *Irishman*. 'His politics,' says Mr. A. M. Sullivan, 'were a great affliction to his relatives, who were in a position to advance him, and who would have done so if he would but give up such dangerous doctrines. He preferred to struggle on for himself, holding by his principles, such as they were. This course he pursued unfalteringly to the last.'

Disaster after disaster came upon the Fenian movement. The best opportunity for a rising was in 1865, but the opportunity was lost. The history of other Irish insurrectionary projects repeated itself. In 1848 the followers of Mitchel appear to have imagined that the Government they were openly defying would forbear and hold its hand until all the plans and preparations of the insurgent party were perfected. Something of the same impression would seem to have influenced the councils and the actions of the Fenian leaders. Stephens established the *Irish People* newspaper, which numbered on its staff some of his best lieutenants, and the *Irish People* played much the same part in the history of the Fenian movement which the *United Irishman* played in the history of Young Ireland.

The Government allowed the *Irish People* to carry on its existence unimpeded up to a certain point. Then, suddenly, when Stephens and his friends were unprepared and unaware, it struck and struck sharply. As usual the hands of the Government were greatly strengthened by treachery in the ranks of their opponents. There was a man in the service of the *Irish People*, and in the confidence of Stephens, named Pierce Nagle. This man was a Government spy who made himself a profitable livelihood by retailing to the Castle authorities all the information he could get—and he had excellent opportunities of getting such information—about the plans of the Fenian leaders. In September, 1865, Nagle stole from one of Stephens' emissaries a letter from the head-centre to members of the movement in Tipperary. This letter he sent after some delay to the Castle, where a study of its contents showed the Executive that the plans of the Fenians were rapidly advancing, and that the Government must strike at once if it wished to strike in time. The letter in question ran thus :

'Dublin, September 8, 1865

'Brothers,—I regret to find the letter I addressed to you has never reached you. Had you received it I am confident all would have been right before this; because I told you explicitly what to do, and once you saw your way it is sure to me that you would have done it well. As far as I can understand your actual position and wishes now, the best course to take is to get all the working B.'s together, and after due deliberation and without favour to any one—acting purely and conscientiously for the good of the cause—to select one man to represent and direct you all. This selection made, the man of your choice should come up here at once, when he shall get instructions and authority to go on with the good work. There is no time to be lost. This year—and let there be no mistake about it—must be the year of action. I speak with a knowledge and authority to which no other man could pretend; and I repeat, the flag of Ireland—of the Irish Republic —must this year be raised. As I am much pressed for time, I shall merely add that it shall be raised in a glow of hope such as never gleamed round it before. Be, then, of firm faith and the best of cheer, for it all goes bravely on.—Yours fraternally,

'J. POWER.

'N.B.—This letter must be read for the working B.'s only and when read must be burnt.'

With such a document in their possession, the Executive felt confident of convicting its enemies, and it made its raid. On September 15 a police descent was made upon the offices of the *Irish People*; all the copies of the journal found therein were seized and conveyed to the Castle; and within a few hours all the more prominent Fenians were captured at their dwellings and secured in prison. All with one important exception. The head-centre himself, James Stephens, was not to be found. The Government had in their power all his principal lieutenants, but without Stephens their work was hardly half done. Fenianism, to the eye of authority, was crushable if Stephens were captured; with Stephens at liberty little or nothing had been accomplished.

There was the most intense excitement in Dublin when it became known that the Government had struck with all its force at the Fenian organisation; the excitement was increased an hundredfold by the news that Stephens was free and unfindable. For some hours it was feared that the arrests would be the signal for an armed rising. But the utmost precautions were taken by the Government. All over Ireland prominent Fenians were seized upon; all over Ireland forces of military and constabulary were held in readiness to meet any attempt at insurrection. Stephens was, indeed, a free man, but for the moment his movement was checkmated. It was perfectly easy for the Government to obtain convictions against the men in their power. When Luby was arrested a document was found among his papers, which was the most magnificent 'find' for the Government, and was in itself enough for their purpose. It was a paper written by the head-centre entrusting his authority to a triumvirate of his most trusted friends:

'I hereby empower Thomas Clarke Luby, John O'Leary, and Charles J. Kickham a Committee of Organisation or Executive, with the same supreme control over the home organisation, England, Ireland, and Scotland, that I have exercised myself. I further empower them to appoint a Committee of Military Inspection and a Committee of Appeal and Judgment, the functions of which Committee will be made known to every member of them. Trusting to the patriotism and abilities of the Executive I fully endorse their actions beforehand. I call on every man in our ranks to support and be guided by them in all that concerns the military brotherhood.

'J. STEPHENS.'

Even without such a document, however, the Government had on their side all the evidence they desired. Their trusty spy, Nagle, had been arrested, for form's sake, along with his deluded comrades, and for some days he kept up his character as a Fenian prisoner. As soon as he was wanted, however, he exchanged the cell for the witness-box, and made his appearance as the inevitable informer to give Queen's evidence against the men who had believed in him.

In the meantime the Dublin police were racking their brains to discover the whereabouts of Stephens. It was not until November that they learned that the man whose capture they so eagerly desired was, and had been, within their grasp all the time since their raid upon the office of the *Irish People*. In a peaceful unsuspected gentleman, with a taste for gardening in a mild way, living in the suburbs of Dublin—Mr. Herbert, of Fairfield House, Sandymount—the police at last discovered the long-lost head-centre.

On Saturday, November 11, 1865, Fairfield House was surrounded by a strong force of police, and Stephens was arrested at last. With him were captured Charles J. Kickham, Hugh Brophy, and Edward Duffy, who has been called the life and soul of the Fenian movement west of the Shannon. A vast mass of important documents were seized at the same time. An exultant Executive was now convinced that all further danger from the dreaded organisation was over for good and all. In Ireland, in England, in America, and, indeed, all over the civilised world, the tidings of the capture of the famous head-centre were received with intense excitement. But the excitement occasioned by the capture of Stephens was as nothing when contrasted with the excitement caused by a piece of news which followed close upon it—the news of Stephens' escape.

Stephens' escape! The escape of the head-centre of the Fenian conspiracy from the hands that had caught him at last, after seeking for him so long and so eagerly in vain! The escape of the Government's most valuable prisoner from one of the strongest of Government prisons! The escape of James Stephens within exactly a fortnight of his capture! It seemed incredible, but it was true, nevertheless. On

Saturday, November 11, the police laid hands on Stephens; on Saturday, the 25th, he had slipped through their fingers and was free again, out of their power and wholly vanished. 'The earth has bubbles as the water has, and he is of them,' the perplexed Lord Lieutenant might well have said, with Macbeth, when he learned of the astonishing disappearance of his prize.

Nothing in the whole history of wonderful escapes from durance, from Benvenuto Cellini or Casanova to Latude, is more remarkable than the escape of Stephens. The prison-breaking feats recorded of English Sheppard or French Cartouche sink into insignificance beside it. The dearest captive that Castle authority could have closely shut in its surest stronghold had passed out of its power as easily as if bolts and bars were things of air, and massive walls mere film or gossamer. Stephens might well have boasted, more literally than the poet Lovelace, that 'stone walls do not a prison make nor iron bars a cage.' He was gone, no one in authority knew how, and left not a trace behind. Then came such a mounting and riding for such a hunt as had not been run in Ireland since the days of ninety-eight. But not all the king's horses nor all the king's men could get James Stephens within the grip of the law again. He hid safely for a while in the vicinity of Dublin, and then made good his escape to France.

The escape of Stephens seemed little short of miraculous at the time. We know now that Fenianism had made its way within the walls of Richmond Prison. If the Government had their servants in the ranks of the Fenians, the Fenian oath bound many who were apparently in the service of the Government. Two of these, it is said, were warders in Richmond Prison, and it was by their aid that Stephens' escape was effected. It may be that the knowledge of this fact was in the mind of Stephens when, at his examination on November 15, he boldly declared that he 'defied and despised any punishment that British law could inflict upon him.' The words seemed idle breath when they were uttered; their meaning was understood on the wild, wet morning when Dublin woke up to find that Stephens was once again at liberty.

But if Stephens was gone, the Executive had other prisoners, and could deal with them. Luby and O'Leary were sentenced to penal servitude for twenty years; O'Donovan Rossa to penal servitude for life. There were more and more arrests, more and more convictions; blow after blow was dealt at the Fenian organisation; internal quarrels, too, weakened it. But it still existed, still held together; the dread of a rising was almost daily present to the mind of authority in 1866. Well it might be present. Over across the Atlantic wild work had begun. The Fenians in America invaded Canada on the 31st of May, 1866, and enjoyed for some brief hours the honour of victory. They occupied Fort Erie; they defeated the Canadian Volunteers who came against them; they captured some English flags, and saw their own green banner floating over a captured position in British territory. But the United States, which under other conditions might have been willing enough to hold aloof if not to facilitate the invasion, interfered to enforce the neutrality of the frontier, arrested most of the Fenian leaders, and extinguished the invasion.

Another daring attempt was actually made some time later on English soil. Some of the Fenians in England planned the capture of Chester Castle. The scheme was to seize the arms in the Castle, to hasten on at once to Holyhead, to take possession of such steamers as might be there, to cut the telegraphic communication between the islands, and invade Ireland before the authorities could be prepared for the blow. Once in Ireland, the pressure of such a force would facilitate the general rising, and anything might be hoped for. The plan was daring and ingenious, but it was betrayed by the informer Corydon, and came to nothing.

At last the general rising in Ireland, which had been so long expected, came in the early months of 1867. It was premature, abortive; but, while it lasted, desperate. Through Corydon and their other informers the Government were acquainted with most of the Fenian plans, and were able to meet them at almost every point. Everything seemed against the insurrection: the very elements fought against it. Snow, that rare accompaniment of winter in the mild climate of Ireland, fell incessantly during those stormy March days of 1867, and practically buried the rising in its white shroud.

The last struggle of the Fenian insurrection of 1867 was made in England, and that last struggle forms the saddest chapter in the whole story. Soon after the rising in Ireland the Manchester police arrested on suspicion two men. The prisoners proved to be Colonel Thomas J. Kelly, who had taken a conspicuous part in the leadership of the Fenian movement after Stephens' arrest and escape, and Captain Deasy, another prominent Fenian. Their seizure was a great gain to the Government and a great blow to the Fenians. The members of the organisation in Manchester met together and resolved upon a bold attempt to rescue their captive leaders. A body of men were told off for the purpose. As usual, some inkling of the Fenian purpose reached the Government, and some precautions were taken by the Manchester authorities.

On Wednesday, the 18th of September, Kelly and Deasy were removed in the prison van from the court to be taken to the county jail at Salford. The prisoners were handcuffed in separate compartments of the van; a guard of twelve policemen accompanied it. On the road the van was stopped by a body of armed Fenians, who drove off most of the police and attempted to break it open. The policeman inside the van, Sergeant Brett, refused to surrender the keys, and the Fenians, driven by time, and dreading reinforcements for the police, resorted to the familiar expedient of blowing open the lock with a pistol shot. The shot thus fired accidentally and mortally wounded Brett. One of the women prisoners inside the van took the keys from the dying man's pocket and handed them out to the rescuing party. The van was then opened, entered, Kelly and Deasy were brought out, and heavily manacled as they were, were hurried away by some of their rescuers.

While all this was going on the majority of the rescuing party were engaged in keeping off with levelled revolvers the police who had returned, and the large crowd that had rapidly formed. When Kelly and Deasy were safely out of danger, this little ring of men about the van broke up and each sought safety for himself. The fugitives were hotly pursued, and several of them were captured and savagely handled by the crowd. It is worth while noticing that none of the armed Fenians used their weapons in their own defence. The only shot fired was fired with no deadly purpose; the death of the policeman was absolutely an accident. Whether the rescuers would or would not have taken life if they could not effect their object otherwise is matter of opinion; their justification for so doing is matter for argument; the fact remains that the solitary shot fired was fired for the purpose of breaking open the van door, and that Sergeant Brett was killed by mistake. Yet for this shot three men were hanged.

The captured rescuers were William Philip Allen, Michael Larkin, Michael O'Brien, Thomas Maguire, and Edward Condon. All five were tried for the wilful murder of Brett; all five were found guilty; all five were sentenced to death. The state of the English mind at the time was one of unreasoning anger. These men had defied the law; they had rescued two Fenian prisoners; they were rebels and the friends of rebels; let them die the death. What is called public opinion was expressed by a clamour for an example. The public mind, curiously inconsistent, flames into easy sympathy with revolution abroad, but blazes into deadly fury at any hint of revolution at home. Had the men of Manchester been Hungarian volunteers rescuing some Magyar leaders from Austrian hands; had they been Venetians plucking some follower of Manin from Teuton jailers; had they been Poles contending with Russians, or Southern Secessionists fighting with the Federal Government, the Press would have been loud in its praise of the heroism of their deed, and would have heeded little if some Austrian or Russian or Federal soldier had fallen in the scuffle. But the Fenians who tried to rescue their fellows, and who killed a man by mistake, were, in the judgment of the general public at that time, nothing but common murderers, for whom no plea could be maintained, to whom no pity could be extended.

It must not be forgotten, however, that in that season of frantic panic some minds were found calm and just; that through all the wild clamour for death some voices were raised loud and clear for mercy. Mr. John Bright made many efforts. Mr. John Stuart Mill exerted himself strenuously and courageously to save the Manchester men from their doom. The English poet, Mr. Algernon Charles Swinburne, wrote and published a passionate appeal to his countrymen for mercy, an appeal which deserves the gratitude of all the generations of Irishmen.

> Freeman he is not, but slave,
> Whoso in fear of the State,
> Asks for council of blood,
> Help of gibbet or grave;
> Neither is any land great
> Whom in her fear-stricken mood
> These things only can save.
>
> Lo! how fair from afar,
> Taintless of tyranny, stands
> Thy mighty daughter, for years
> Who trod the wine-press of war;
> Shines with immaculate hands,
> Slays not foe, neither fears,
> Stains not peace with a scar.

Thus Mr. Swinburne sought to sprinkle cool patience upon the heat and flame of the distempered public mind, conjuring it to mercy by the image of the great, victorious Republic. In vain poet and philosopher and politician—the three great men, and all those who thought with them, strove bravely and strove unsuccessfully to stay the hands of the executioner. Two of the five condemned men were pardoned—Maguire, who after his sentence was proved to have had nothing to do with the rescue, and Condon. Allen, Larkin, and O'Brien were hanged on November 23, 1867. The manner of their death is recorded in Mr. T. D. Sullivan's touching poem, 'God save Ireland!'

CHAPTER XVIII.

DISESTABLISHMENT AND EDUCATION.

THE Government had put down the Fenian insurrection, but that insurrection had memorable consequences, and a memorable influence upon the statesmen of England. There were English statesmen sufficiently endowed with political foresight to appreciate that although a Fenian rising had been put down, the political difficulty which Fenianism represented was as great and as complicated as ever. It did not, indeed, need a statesman to be a very political Lynceus to perceive that the mere suppression of revolution after revolution was not, in the long run, the most satisfactory method of governing a country. The very fact of a country being in a condition of latent revolution and intermittent rebellion was in itself enough to teach such statesmen as were willing to learn, that something or other was wrong in this portion at least of that complex piece of State machinery, which its admirers were accustomed to regard as the most perfect piece of political mechanism on the face of the earth, the Government of Ireland.

Mr. Gladstone was then, as he is now, the most advanced thinker and the most keen-sighted statesman in the English House of Commons. Then, as now, he was far ahead of his fellows in appreciating the inevitable in politics. The younger men who have grown up around him are not quicker to see what must be done at a great crisis, nor more ready to do it. At the time when the Fenian insurrection was lying dead beneath its white shroud of snow, Mr. Gladstone was the one man in English statecraft who was keen enough to perceive what the Fenian rising meant, and to grasp the vast importance of the lesson it had taught him. Mr. Gladstone had the genius to appreciate the fact that a nation which could make such repeated efforts to shake off a bondage which had been gradually lightening, must be suffering from some very serious, some very intolerable, grievances. So Mr. Gladstone looked a little more closely into the question, and saw that the most intolerable grievances from which the Irish people were suffering were the Irish Church question and the Irish Land question.

The condition of Ireland with regard to what was called the Irish Church question was one of the greatest scandals in modern history. One of the most Catholic among Catholic countries, Ireland had languished for generations under the most savage system of Penal Laws levelled against her faith; and even now, at a time when the nineteenth century had lived more than half its life, Catholic Ireland was compelled against its will to maintain a foreign Church, and to hear it spoken of, in bitter mockery of themselves and of their creed, as the Irish Church.

One of the most remarkable of all the many remarkable facts in connection with the long struggle of Ireland against the English rule, is the way in which the Irish people have maintained through all the darkest pages of their history their devotion to their national Church. That Church, whose missionaries and whose martyrs alike maintained the principles of religion and of education for Western Christianity in evil times—that Church had implanted in the hearts of her Irish children the deepest and the most passionate attachment to her.

A well-known writer has made use of the beautiful allegory with which Moore conveys the attachment of Ireland to her own Church. '" The Irish Peasant to his Mistress" is the name of one of Moore's finest songs. The Irish peasant tells his mistress of his undying fidelity to her. "Through grief and through danger" her smile has cheered his way. "The darker our fortunes, the purer thy bright love burned;" it turned shame into glory; fear into zeal. Slave as he was, with her to guide him he felt free. She had a rival, and the rival was honoured, " while thou wert mocked and scorned." The rival wore a crown of gold ; the other's brows were girt with thorns. The rival wooed him to temples, while the loved one lay hid in caves. " Her friends were all masters, while thine, alas ! are slaves ! " " Yet," he declares, " cold in the earth at thy feet I would rather be, than wed one I love not, or turn one thought from thee ! " '

The poet has described with all a poet's beauty the strength, the profundity, and the purity of the Irish peasant's devotion to the Catholic Church, and his loyal refusal, through long generations of temptation and of persecution, to abandon her for the rival creed which was sought to be imposed upon him by foreign arms. The writer already quoted has shown the poetic and religious character of the Irish nature. ' For him, as for Schiller's immortal heroine, the kingdom of the spirits is easily opened. Half his thoughts, half his life, belong to a world other than the material world around him. The supernatural becomes almost the natural for him. The streams, the valleys, the hills of his native country are peopled by mystic forms and melancholy legends, which are all but living things for him. Even the railway has not banished from the land his familiar fancies and dreams. The " good people " still linger around the raths and glens. The banshee even yet laments, in dirge-like wailings, the death of the representative of each ancient house. The very superstitions of the Irish peasant take a devotional form. They are never degrading. This piety is not merely sincere; it is even practical. It sustains him against many hard trials, and enables him to bear in cheerful patience a life-long trouble. He praises God for everything, not as an act of mere devotional formality, but as by instinct ; the praise naturally rising to his lips. Old men and women in Ireland, who seem to the observer to have lived lives of nothing but privation and suffering, are heard to murmur, with their latest breath, the fervent declaration " that the Lord was good to them always." '

This intense spirit of devotion to his creed was accompanied in the Irish peasant by a strong and unconquerable loyalty to it. The infernal ingenuity of the Penal Laws might well have seemed calculated in the minds of hostile statesmen to root out the Irish faith from the hearts of Ireland, to annihilate for ever the Catholic Church in Ireland. But the Penal Laws at their worst only seemed to strengthen the hold of the Catholic Church over her children, and to deepen and widen the affection of her children for the Catholic Church. Even when the Penal Laws had ceased to exist, when they had become only a hideous record of blundering tyranny and misgovernment, the trials of the Catholic Church in Ireland were not at an end. The strength of the attachment of the Irish people for their Church was not to be left untested. A man was no longer liable to have his property confiscated, or his children stolen from him, or to run the risk of imprisonment or exile, because he professed the Catholic creed; the priest had to go no longer in fear of his life; it was no longer a legal sin for Catholic masters to teach Catholic children; but all the indignities that a powerful and dominant party could offer, through the Church it sought to impose upon the Irish people, were freely offered; and all the disadvantages that could be flung in the way of the Catholic Church were so flung persistently.

The Protestant Church in Ireland was kept alive as a State Church out of the substance of the people, to whom it could offer nothing, to whom it was only the representative of oppression and injury and insult, and to whom its ministers were only part and parcel of Ascendency. Ascendency could and did maintain for long enough the State Church in Ireland against the wishes of the Irish people, and in a large measure upon money extorted from the unwilling Irish people. But there was one thing it could not do—it could not make the Irish people abandon their own faith and worship at foreign altars. When the leprous servant of the Assyrian king came to the Hebrew prophet, and was made pure of body, he sought the permission of the holy man to bend his knee in the house of Rimmon. What the companion of the king was willing to do for the sake of preserving the royal favour, the Irish people refused to do to win the pleasure of Ascendency. The Irish Church existed, a huge anomaly of State-imposed religion, which the vast majority of the people who were compelled to support it refused to have anything to do with, and which remained one of the bitterest of the many bitter grievances which kept alive the detestation of English dominion in Ireland.

Many attempts, more or less half-hearted and pottering, had been made in the House of Commons from time to time to approach this Irish Church question with some idea of settling it, and a Commission had even been appointed to make some kind of investigation of the matter. But the first serious blow struck against the Established Church was struck by Mr. John Francis Maguire, in a debate in March 1868, on a series of resolutions dealing with the condition of Ireland, which he submitted to the House. Mr. Maguire was an Irish member of great ability and of great integrity. He was not an advanced politician in the sense in which we speak of advanced politicians to-day. He was not an advanced politician twenty years ago; but he was genuinely devoted to the interests of his country, and loyally determined to serve those interests in every way compatible with his own opinions as to what her best interests were. He was the proprietor of the most important paper in the South of Ireland—the *Cork Examiner*—and he had made himself a strong position in the House of Commons by his independence and his courage and his Parliamentary ability.

In the course of the speech in which he introduced his resolutions, Mr. Maguire made a special and powerful attack upon the principle which sanctioned the Established Church in Ireland. In the debate which followed, the then Irish Secretary, Lord Mayo, made a somewhat mysteriously-worded speech, in which he threw out hopes that a way might be found of introducing religious equality in Ireland without making a sacrifice of the Established Church, and he considerably surprised his hearers by an occult phrase about 'levelling up, and not levelling down.'

What Lord Mayo actually meant by the half-hints he

threw out, whether he was giving a kind of tentative expression to some idea on the part of the Government, or was merely uttering a speculation of his own, must remain an unsolved political problem. But the speech and the words made it plain to Parliament, and to politicians outside Parliament, that the existence of the Established Church in Ireland was from that moment down an open question.

The debate suddenly assumed a new aspect when Mr. Gladstone, as leader of the Opposition, rose and announced himself an opponent of the Established Church in Ireland. Mr. Maguire immediately withdrew his resolutions, and Mr. Gladstone brought in a series of resolutions of his own, the effect of which would be to sweep away the Established Church in Ireland. The debate which followed upon the introduction of these resolutions was one of the most remarkable that has ever taken place in the House of Commons. On both sides the feelings of politicians were keenly, even bitterly aroused. On both sides the battle was fought stubbornly, even desperately.

Mr. Lowe made a fierce attack, which has now become famous, upon the Irish Church. He compared the Irish Church to ' an exotic brought from a far country, tended with infinite pain and useless trouble. It is kept alive with the greatest difficulty and at great expense in an ungenial climate and an ungrateful soil. The curse of barrenness is upon it. It has no leaves, puts forth no blossom, and yields no fruit. Cut it down; why cumbereth it the ground?' The opinion which was expressed by Mr. Lowe in these fiercely eloquent words proved to be the opinion of the majority in the House of Commons. The resolutions were carried by large majorities. The Government was defeated upon a question of vital importance, and Mr. Disraeli appealed to the country.

The General Election of 1868 was remarkable for the expectations it formed, and the way in which these expectations were not answered. It had been expected that the Parliament chosen upon the General Election would have a strongly Radical and even Democratic element introduced into it. Expectation was not realised. The most advanced Radical in the previous Parliament, Mr. John Stuart Mill, was not re-elected for Westminster. Of the many advanced Radical candidates who came forward with Mr. Mill's support and approval, none were returned. It had been confidently expected by advanced politicians that a certain number of working-men candidates would find seats in the new Parliament. And many working-men candidates offered themselves to constituencies, but in no case was any one of them returned.

The new Parliament of 1868 presented few bright features of difference from the preceding Parliaments. It had no more of a Democratic complexion than any of those which had gone before; but it was sufficiently advanced in its views to place the Liberal party in power, and to enable Mr. Gladstone to carry into effect his purpose of eradicating the Establishment in Ireland. The proposals of the Government were that the Irish Church should almost at once cease to exist as a State establishment, and should pass into the condition of a free Episcopal Church. As a matter of course, the Irish bishops were to lose their seats in the House of Lords. The clergy and laity of the Church were to elect a governing body from themselves, which the Government was to recognise and incorporate. The English and Irish Churches were no longer to be connected, and the Irish Ecclesiastical Courts were to be done away with. With regard to the protection of the life interests of those holding office in the Irish Church, and with regard to the disposal of the fund which would return to Government when all such holders of office had been indemnified, there were various intricate provisions. In considering such claims as these the Government did not err on the side of parsimony.' But the opposition by which they were confronted was so powerful, that they were almost compelled to paralyse some part of it by compensating with a free hand all those who were about to lose the dignity attaching to the position of a clergyman in a State Church.

When all these claims had been met and settled, there yet remained in the hands of the Government a considerable sum of money, which they determined to devote to the alleviation of inevitable suffering in Ireland. The Conservative Opposition fought the Ministerial proposals step by step and point by point with defiant pertinacity. They knew well enough that the Government would have its way, and that the Established Church in Ireland was doomed; but they argued and wrangled and debated unwearyingly none the less. One of the great points raised by the opponents of the Ministerial measure was based on the Act of Union. The 5th article of that Act was incessantly quoted, dwelt upon, alluded to in the early debates. That article provided 'that the Churches of England and Ireland as now by law established be united into one Protestant Episcopal Church, to be called "the United Church of England and Ireland," and the doctrine, worship, discipline, and government of the said United Church shall be and shall remain in full force for ever as the same are now by law established for the Church of England, and the continuance and preservation of the said United Church as the Established Church of England and Ireland shall be deemed and taken to be an essential and fundamental part of the Union.'

The argument, of course, had no validity in it. The Act of Union is fortunately as liable to be set aside as any other measure. Of late days Ireland's enemies have made use of this alteration in the Act of Union to strengthen their argument for a reduction of the Irish representation. They argue that the mere fact that the Act of Union provides for a certain representation in Ireland can no longer be appealed to as a definite argument against the reduction of Irish representation, because, as the Act of Union has been altered in one particular, it may be altered in another. This point is easily answered. It is perfectly in accordance with all the principles of justice for one nation to alter the terms of conditions that she has imposed upon another nation when the alteration is for that other nation's benefit. It would be directly in defiance of all principles of justice for a dominant nation to make such alterations to the injury of the other country.

All the ingenuity and all the obstinacy of the Conservative

party could not defeat, could not long delay, the determination of the Government. On July 26, 1869, the measure which disestablished the Irish Church received the royal assent and became law.

The Liberal Government which came into office in 1868 deemed itself destined to settle for ever any grievances which Ireland might have to complain of. Mr. Gladstone admitted frankly and freely enough that Ireland had grievances to complain of; but if he was convinced of the existence of injustices in the existing condition of things, he seemed scarcely less convinced of the possibility of removing them in the space, if not of a single session of Parliament, at least in a single Parliament. The Government came into power with the practical recognition of the fact that Ireland and the Irish question were to be the important themes of legislation. English statesmen had recognised this fact before the Parliament of 1868; but it is only since the Parliament of 1868 that the statesman who then made himself the champion of Irish wrongs has fully worked out the problem and found the solution of the Irish difficulty.

Mr. Gladstone was in a mood for great legislation in the beginning of 1869. He approached Parliament with a list of measures long enough to startle the most enthusiastic of his followers, and to arouse from Mr. Bright the criticism that the Government were attempting to drive six omnibuses abreast through Temple Bar; a criticism which was criticised in its turn by another politician, Mr. W. E. Forster, who observed that six omnibuses might be unable to pass through Temple Bar abreast, but they might pass very successfully one after another. Of the six omnibuses, three may be said, to pursue Mr. Bright's ingenious allegory a little further, to have been painted green and lettered Ireland.

The three most important measures which Mr. Gladstone had undertaken to pilot in safety through the two Houses of Parliament were devoted to Irish questions, and these Irish questions were of pressing and urging importance. The most immediate question, which like a great wave had swept the previous Government out of office and carried Mr. Gladstone to power on its crest, was the question of the Disestablishment of the Irish Church. We have already seen how that great reform was effected. The second great question was the Land question, and we have already touched upon the principal points of the Land Act of 1870. The Land Act of 1870 was a very important measure, although it rendered very little immediate service to the Irish people, although it was at the best but a weak and imperfect piece of legislation, although it was not the first chapter, but merely one of the first lines in the record of reforms demanded by the system of land tenure in Ireland. It was one step in the steady march of progress.

Happily for the world, the statesmen who extolled the Land Act of 1870, and went into ecstasies over it, and dwelt upon its many merits, and expatiated upon its effect, while those for whose relief it was intended failed to discern its blessings, were of a different mould from the Prime Minister who created it. Having, however, accomplished the Disestablishment of the Irish Church, which was a great measure, and passed his Land Act, which was a small measure, Mr. Gladstone turned with fresh purpose to his third enterprise, the solution of the great question of Irish Education. Those three questions dealt with, Mr. Gladstone appeared to hope that Irish disaffection and Irish discontent would vanish for ever from the fair face of the island. It had always been the delusion of English statesmen to fancy that every small concession of Ireland's just demands is to silence for ever any allusion to demands which are left unsatisfied. Like Pan, in the hymn of the English poet, ' Gods and men, they were all deluded thus,' and they regarded with stern disapproval the contumacious and persistent nation which, when it is offered some small plateful of legislative porridge, has the audacity to come up with a hungry face and ask for more. This line of policy is now the exclusive property of the Tory party.

The third side of Mr. Gladstone's triangular policy with regard to Ireland faced the question of University Education in Ireland. Parliament met on February 6, 1873. The Royal Speech announced that 'A measure will be submitted to you on an early day for settling the question of University Education in Ireland. It will have for its object the advancement of learning in that portion of my dominions, and will be framed with a careful regard to the rights of conscience.'

On February 13 Mr. Gladstone introduced his Irish University Education Bill, and explained it to an eager and attentive House of Commons. The position of Irish University education was very serious. Ireland possessed—she could not be said to boast of—two Universities. One was the University of Dublin, which was then a distinctly and even defiantly Protestant organisation; the other was the Queen's University, which had been established under the odd delusion that a University body entirely given over to secular instruction would satisfy the educational desires of the Irish people. This strictly secular system was condemned by the authority of the Catholic Church, and it was practically a failure. Ireland from an educational point of view presented this extraordinary appearance to a curious investigator. In a country in which the vast, the overwhelming majority were Catholics, there were two chartered Universities, one which was opposed to the Catholics, and the other to which Catholics were opposed. Under the conditions it ought not to have been very difficult for any body of statesmen to see their way out of the difficulty. The Catholics asked for a University of their own. Nothing, one would think, could be simpler than to accede to the wishes of the majority of the Irish people and charter a Catholic University.

But Parliamentary ideas were strongly opposed to so simple and sensible a solution of the difficulty. Government had always recognised grudgingly and sorely against its will the Catholic demand, not merely for education, but even for existence. If it could it would have liked to shut its eyes to the fact that a majority of the Irish people are Catholics. It had always acted in the long course of its connection with Ireland on a policy based on this belief, or at least upon this assumption. So the majority of the Parliament were unwilling to grant a charter for a merely Catholic University; and those amongst its members who did not admit, or did not choose to admit, that their objection was levelled against Catholics as Catholics, adduced a variety of more or less flimsy reasons for refusing to satisfy the natural demands of a Catholic country.

One argument was, that if a charter were granted to a Catholic University there would be a distinct risk of lowering the national standard of education in the two islands. Another equally invalid argument was, that the grant of any funds for the purpose of supporting a Catholic University would be spending the public money on a purely sectarian body. With arguments as vague and as valueless as these, English statesmen had for long enough persistently rebutted all claims of Irish Catholics to be educated according to their own ideas in their own country.

Mr. Gladstone now appeared upon the Parliamentary scene with the resolute determination to settle if he could a hitherto complex question—a new Alexander solving the knot; a new Œdipus answering the riddling interrogations of the Sphinx. He recognised the difficulty; he saw the necessity for some remedy; and he did his best to devise the right remedy. Hopeful was the tone of Mr. Gladstone's speech on February 13, 1873, when he explained to the attentive Commons the principles of his Irish University Education Bill.

Unfortunately, however, the Bill itself did not quite answer to the hope of its introducer, and did not appear to Irish Catholics, and their representatives in the House of Commons, to be so satisfactory a settlement of the vexed question as it appeared to the Prime Minister. Mr. Gladstone proposed to make the Dublin University the central University of Ireland, and to make it not merely an examining, but a teaching body. Trinity College was to be separated from the Dublin University, and the theological faculty separated from Trinity College. Trinity, the Colleges of Cork and Belfast, and the existing Catholic University—an institution which was supported entirely by a voluntary fund, and which had no charter—were all to become affiliated colleges of a newly-created University. The Galway College was to be wiped out of existence altogether. The theological faculty, which had hitherto existed in connection with Trinity College, was to be given to a representative body of the Disestablished Irish Church, together with a fund for carrying out the purposes for which the theological faculty had hitherto existed. The new University was to have no chairs for theology, moral philosophy, or modern history. The governing body of the University was to be composed in the first instance of twenty-eight ordinary members, to be nominated in the Act. Vacancies were to be filled by the Crown and by co-option alternately for ten years; after that time four members were to retire annually—one successor to be named by the Crown, one by the council, one by the professors, and one by the senate. In addition to the ordinary members, the affiliated colleges would be allowed to elect one or two members of council, according to the number of pupils in each college. The money to sustain the University was to come in proportionate allotments from the revenues of Trinity College, a very wealthy institution; from the Consolidated Fund, the fees of students, and the surplus of Irish ecclesiastical property. Trinity College and each of the other affiliated colleges would be allowed to frame schemes for their own government.

Such was the plan by which Mr. Gladstone trusted that he had succeeded in threading the labyrinth of the Irish University question; such was the scheme by which the Prime Minister hoped for a moment that he had succeeded in reconciling opposing principles and satisfying contending claims—only for a moment, however. When the excitement of the particular sitting in which the Bill was introduced had passed away, the Prime Minister discovered that his method was not the right one.

The first reception accorded to the Bill in the House of Commons was of a nature to deceive its introducer. A great many speakers said a great many civil things about the proposed scheme, and a few dissentient voices were raised. But if few dissentient voices were heard that night there was no lack of dissentient opinion, which soon enough found tongue. The measure which was meant to please everybody pleased nobody. Englishmen of most creeds objected to the Bill. The vast Nonconformist body protested against any endowment for the purposes of Catholic denominational education. They received no endowment, they argued, and therefore no other sectarian body ought to receive it. The Irish Protestants, already sore over the disestablishment of their Church in Ireland, protested loudly against the proposed interference with their old-established University system. The Irish Catholics declined definitely and distinctly to accept the proposed measure, which did not meet their demands. It did not satisfy their wishes. It made no answer to their claims. They wanted a Catholic University, and that Catholic University Mr. Gladstone's measure did not propose to give them.

The outcry against the measure steadily increased in volume. In all parts of Ireland all parties protested against it. The Roman Catholic prelates held meetings to oppose the scheme, and joined in a declaration which contained the following passages expressing their views: 'That, viewing with alarm the widespread ruin caused by godless systems of education, and adhering to the declarations of the Holy See, we reiterate the condemnation of mixed education as fraught with danger to that divine faith which is to be prized above all earthly things. . . . That the distinguished proposer of this measure, proclaiming as he does in his opening speech that the condition of Roman Catholics in Ireland with regard to University education is "miserably bad," "scandalously bad," and, professing to redress this admitted grievance, brings forward a measure singularly inconsistent with his professions, because, instead of redressing, it perpetuates that grievance, upholding two out of three of the Queen's Colleges, and planting in the metropolis two other great teaching institutions the same in principle with the Queen's Colleges. . . . That, as the legal owners of the Catholic University, and, at the same time, acting on behalf of the Catholic people of Ireland, for whose advantage and by whose generosity it has been established, in the exercise of that right of ownership, we will not consent to the affiliation of the Catholic University to the new University, unless the proposed scheme be largely modified; and we have the same objection to the affiliation of other Catholic colleges in Ireland.'

A second reading was speedily and persistently opposed. Mr.—now Sir—Lyon Playfair made himself conspicuous in his opposition—on the ground that it was unreasonable and absurd to exclude modern history from any national University, and in which he talked wildly about sacrificing free inquiry to ecclesiastical dictation. Dr. Playfair did not recollect that Mr. John Stuart Mill, a thinker who was, to put it mildly, at least as gifted and as far-seeing as Dr. Playfair himself, considered history as one of those branches of knowledge which are best left to private study. He did not reflect, too, that the teaching of modern history might present some difficulties in an Irish University of the kind proposed by Mr. Gladstone, the members of which would hardly be likely to look with the same eye upon any of the events of Irish history. Dr. Playfair's opposition was in itself a matter of small importance, but it served to show the variety of men and minds arrayed against the scheme.

On the same day when Dr. Playfair delivered his somewhat unfortunate protest, a deputation of Irish members waited upon Mr. Gladstone to inform him that they were bound to support denominational and religious education against secularisation. A little later a Pastoral from Cardinal Cullen was read in all the Irish Catholic churches, which described Mr. Gladstone's Bill as endowing 'non-Catholic and godless colleges to those who for centuries have enjoyed the great public endowments for higher education in Ireland, and then, without giving one farthing to Catholics, it invites them to compete in their poverty, produced by penal laws and confiscations, with others who, as the Prime Minister states, are left in possession of enormous wealth. The new

University scheme only increases the number of Queen's colleges, so often and so solemnly condemned by the Catholic Church and by all Ireland, and gives a new impulse to that teaching which separates education from religion and its holy influences, and banishes God, the Author of all good, from our schools.'

The opposition came to a head on March 11, on the fourth night of the debate on Mr. Bourke's amendment. The House was crowded to its fullest; both sides were animated by the keenest emotions of anxiety and expectation. The general impression that the Government was about to sustain a defeat was visible on the faces of most men. Mr. Disraeli, fired and animated by a triumphant consciousness of impending victory, made one of his most brilliant and most paradoxical speeches. 'We live in an age,' said Mr. Disraeli, 'when young men prattle about protoplasm, and when young ladies in gilded saloons unconsciously talk atheism. And this is the moment when a Minister, called upon to fulfil one of the noblest duties that can fall upon the most ambitious statesman—namely, the formation of a great University—formally comes forward and proposes the omission from public study of moral and mental philosophy.' He described the new council of twenty-eight persons, which was to form the governing body, as coming to be 'very much what you have in the House—two parties organised and arrayed against each other, with two or three trimmers thrown in on each side.'

From assaults upon the particulars of the Bill, Mr. Disraeli proceeded to a direct attack upon the author of it. 'You have now,' said Mr. Disraeli, 'had four years of it. You have despoiled churches. You have threatened every endowment and corporation in the country. You have examined into everybody's affairs. You have criticised every profession and vexed every trade. No one is certain of his property, and no one knows what duties he may have to perform to-morrow. I believe that the people of this country have had enough of the policy of confiscation.'

P

The speech was extravagant. It was levelled against the measure, not because it was not Irish enough, but because it was too Irish, Mr. Disraeli thought. But it delighted Mr. Disraeli's followers, whose views it expressed perfectly. The description which Mr. Disraeli gave of the measure in his concluding sentences was one which exaggerated the views of every opponent of the Bill. 'I must vote,' said Mr. Disraeli, 'against a measure which I believe to be monstrous in its general principles, pernicious in many of its details, and utterly futile as a measure of practical legislation.'

Mr. Gladstone concluded the debate, and accepted defeat with a dignified and statesmanlike composure. In concluding, Mr. Gladstone was eloquent in his appeal to the sacred name of justice. 'To mete out justice to Ireland according to the best view that with human infirmity we could form, has been the work—I will almost say the sacred work—of this Parliament.' Such measure of human infirmity as Mr. Gladstone admitted to himself then, has not prevented him, fortunately, from meting out in a later day justice to Ireland in the way that the Irish people themselves most desired.

In the face of almost inevitable defeat, Mr. Gladstone still persisted in regarding his measure as one which might be law. 'As we have begun,' he said, 'so let us go through, and with a firm and resolute hand let us efface from the law and the practice of the country the last—I believe it is the last—of the religious and social grievances of Ireland.' There was something exceedingly pathetic, there was something almost tragic, in the picture of a great English statesman seriously striving with all his heart and soul to remove from the Irish people all the political and all the social grievances of which they had to complain, and striving unsuccessfully then. Experience has taught Mr. Gladstone, in the twelve years that have gone by since that eventful March morning, that Ireland's political and Ireland's social grievances are only to be effaced from the minds and memories of her children by Home Rule. Mr. Gladstone addressed a few words of dignified reference to the Irish members who had supported him in his two previous measures, and who had gone against him in this, and were helping to overthrow him, as more than twelve years later another body of Irish members were again destined to turn him from office.

About two o'clock on the morning of the 12th the division took place, and the Government were defeated by a majority of three. Mr. Gladstone immediately resigned office, but Mr. Disraeli declined to accept it; and Mr. Gladstone had to return to power with a shaken majority and a damaged party.

CHAPTER XIX.

THE HOME RULE MOVEMENT.

THE Fenian insurrection had been put down; most of its leaders were in prison or in exile; many were dead. The Government and the Government party in Ireland believed that another ten or twenty years of apathetic acquiescence in their rule was secured to them. Indeed, for the few years that immediately succeeded the collapse of the rising of 1867 there seemed to be every prospect of such hopes finding fulfilment. The years immediately following upon the Fenian outbreak were years without a history for Ireland. Somebody has said, foolishly enough, that the country is happy which has no history. Ireland had no history in the national sense in these years of evil, and yet she could hardly be called happy. Landlordism, that had been frightened out of its wits by the apparition of what it and its kind called the revolutionary spectre in its midst, was taking its revenge for its alarm by fresh and persistent oppression of the peasantry, whom evil chance had delivered into its hands. Rack-renting and evictions flourished; and for a time it seemed as if the landlord party were to have it all their own way, and as if national aspirations had been flung back for a generation.

Just, however, when things were looking their blackest,

there came a new gleam of hope. A movement was inaugurated which was destined to develop into something very much more powerful than its early founders ever dreamed of or desired; which was destined after fifteen years of varying and stormy fortunes to cause the overthrow of an English Ministry, and to bring the Irish demand for national independence very definitely into what English statesmen are fond of terming the field of practical politics. In the May of 1870 a meeting was held in an hotel in Dublin, which was attended by representative Irishmen of almost all classes of society and almost all phases of political and religious opinion. The majority, however, was composed of Protestant Conservatives. The meeting was summoned to consider the political position of Ireland, and to debate the question as to what ought to be done to advance her interests.

The presence at that meeting of so large a body of Protestant Conservatives is not difficult of explanation. The Irish Protestants were inspired at that time with mingled feelings of alarm at and hatred of Mr. Gladstone and Mr. Gladstone's recent Irish policy. The disestablishment of what was called the Irish Church had caused that fierce irritation which men always feel when they have been suddenly deprived of rights and privileges over a foreign population. Some of the Irish Protestants, therefore, who attended that meeting in Dublin in the May of 1870 were animated chiefly by a dislike and dread of Mr. Gladstone, and by the gradually-dawning conviction that, on the whole, they might hope to fare better at the hands of the Irish people themselves than at the hands of their patrons across St. George's Channel. Others there were, however, men not in one sense of the term Nationalists, who saw more clearly than English statesmen could or would see, that the desire for national independence was one of the deepest-rooted feelings in the Irish heart. These men had sufficient political foresight to perceive that no measures of disestablishment, no small concessions here and small ameliorations there, would in any degree satisfy the aspirations of the Irish people. It was not small concessions that the Irish people were asking for, but the just demand to be allowed to have their voice heard in the administration of their own affairs.

Some, therefore, of those who attended the meeting were prepared to meet the Irish demand half-way. They saw there were only two alternatives before the English Government—either to concede to Ireland some measure of self-administration, or to keep on for ever struggling at greater or less intervals with active or intermittent rebellion. Of the two alternatives they preferred for their own peace, and for the peace of the country, that the principle of self-government should be conceded. There were others at the meeting of more advanced views—Fenians and friends of Fenians—who recognised the fact that for the time any acquirement of their rights by a strong hand was out of the question, and who were, therefore, prepared to go in with a constitutional movement, and strive to attain some measure of national independence. There was one man present at that meeting—a man of distinction and of a rare ability that at times seemed closely akin to genius—who was fated to be for a season the leader of the new movement.

Mr. Isaac Butt was at that time a man of fifty-five years of age, whose life had been devoted to law and politics, and occasionally to literature. He had begun his political career as a strong opponent of nationalism, and had been chosen by the Irish Protestant Conservatives to fight their fight and plead their cause for them against O'Connell himself, in the days when Repeal was the watchword of the national party. O'Connell, at the end of a debate, had prophesied that the time would come when his eloquent young opponent would be found 'in the ranks of the Irish people,' and the prophecy of O'Connell had come to pass. Mr. Butt in course of time found himself the legal and the political champion of Irish nationalism. He was a lawyer of the greatest skill and subtlety—a skill and subtlety worthy of Daniel O'Connell himself; and at the time of the meeting in Dublin, and for many years previously, he was practically without a rival at the Irish

Bar. In 1848 he had played a prominent part in the defence of Smith O'Brien and Thomas Francis Meagher at Clonmel; and at the time of the Fenian risings he defended many of the most conspicuous of the political prisoners.

He became as years went on more and more of a Nationalist, and less and less of an adherent of the Conservative party. The Conservatives, with that unwisdom which at times characterises them in their dealings with their adherents, had somewhat neglected Isaac Butt. The Conservative party have always an innate distrust of brilliant men—even when the brilliant men belong to their own country, and rise from their own ranks. All the successes that the Conservative party have achieved in modern times have been due to the enterprise and genius of one or two brilliant men whom the Conservative party as a whole has at first sourly mistrusted and disliked, and only accepted in the end with reluctant resignation to the inevitable. The steady-going Conservative chiefs as a rule like steady-going followers. They have a vague dread of abilities of the kind which they characterise as showy; and when they avail themselves of such abilities they are seldom grateful for the services that have been rendered them. So the Conservative leaders somewhat unwisely neglected Mr. Butt.

One Conservative leader, keener than his fellows, in at least appreciating the services of Mr. Butt, recommended the party, in a letter to a colleague, 'to buy Butt.' This cynical piece of advice showed that the writer understood the value of Mr. Butt's allegiance; but it showed also that the writer did not quite understand Mr. Butt's character. Mr. Butt was by no means the Englishman's ideal of a prudent politician. He was not a keen, cool, hard-headed man of business. He was not always very wise in the way in which he ordered his own personal affairs. He was often enough in difficulties, which are very embarrassing to a politician, and, perhaps, still more embarrassing to a politician's friends. But he was emphatically not a man to be bought, though the cynical Conservative counsellor seemed to think he was. His political record is wholly free from such a suspicion. In any case, the Conservative party made no attempt to buy Butt, in which they were wise, and made no attempt to conciliate him, in which they were foolish. He gradually dropped away from his alliance with them; he disappeared from political life altogether for a time, and when he came to the front again he came as the inaugurator of a new departure in Irish politics, as a leader of the Home Rule movement.

He was a genuinely eloquent and brilliant speaker, and he made a brilliant speech at the meeting in Dublin, at which he urged on his hearers the common union of all policies and all parties for the one goal of Irish self-government. It was he who proposed the resolution declaring ' that the establishment of an Irish Parliament with full control over our domestic affairs was the only remedy for the evils of Ireland;' and the resolution was carried unanimously. A committee was immediately formed to draw up a series of resolutions to constitute the platform of the Home Rule party. It is curious and interesting to study now what these resolutions were which then seemed so terrible in their audacity in the eyes of English statesmen.

' I.—This association is formed for the purpose of obtaining for Ireland the right of self-government by means of a National Parliament.

' II.—It is hereby declared, as the essential principle of this association, that the objects, and THE ONLY OBJECTS, contemplated by its organisation are:

' To obtain for our country the right and privilege of managing her own affairs, by a Parliament assembled in Ireland, composed of Her Majesty the Sovereign, and her successors, and the Lords and Commons of Ireland;

' To secure for that Parliament, under a federal arrangement, the right of legislating for and regulating all matters relating to the internal affairs of Ireland, and control over Irish resources and revenues, subject to the obligation of contributing our just proportion of the Imperial expenditure;

'To leave to an Imperial Parliament the power of dealing with all questions affecting the Imperial Crown and Government, legislation regarding the colonies and other dependencies of the Crown, the relations of the United Empire with foreign States, and all matters appertaining to the defence and the stability of the empire at large.

'To attain such an adjustment of the relations between the two countries, without any interference with the prerogatives of the Crown, or any disturbance of the principles of the constitution.

'III.—The association invites the co-operation of all Irishmen who are willing to join in seeking for Ireland a federal arrangement based upon these general principles.

'IV.— The association will endeavour to forward the object it has in view by using all legitimate means of influencing public sentiment, both in Ireland and Great Britain, by taking all opportunities of instructing and informing public opinion, and by seeking to unite Irishmen of all creeds and classes in one national movement, in support of the great national object hereby contemplated.

'V.—It is declared to be an essential principle of the association that, while every member is understood by joining it to concur in its general object and plan of action, no person so joining is committed to any political opinion, except the advisability of seeking for Ireland the amount of self-government contemplated in the objects of the association.'

But the movement which was then inaugurated spread rapidly by one of the surest tests which can be applied to any political movement—the test of the elections. It was soon found that Home Rule had a great hold upon the mass of the Irish people. A curious proof of the condition to which Ireland had been reduced is afforded by a study of the names of the men who were then returned to Parliament as leaders in the front rank of the Irish movement. Mr. Mitchell-Henry and the late Mr. P. J. Smyth are not exactly politicians of the kind that Irish nationalism of to-day looks upon with any great favour. The late Mr. P. J. Smyth, as we have seen, had never outgrown the traditions of the 1848 movement, in which he played no conspicuous part. Of late years, shortly before his death, he came to be distinguished chiefly as a bitter and unscrupulous enemy of those who were recognised as the leaders of the Irish people.

But at the time when the Home Rule movement was still in its dawn, the election of Mr. P. J. Smyth and the election of Mr. Mitchell-Henry were hailed with jubilation as proof of the amount of vitality in the country. The election of Mr. John Martin for Meath, and of Mr. Butt himself for Limerick, gave fresh impetus to the advancing movement, which now began to be regarded with equal enthusiasm in Ireland and indignation in England. The demand of the Home Rule party was not a very appalling one. It was clear and simple enough. It did not, indeed, plead for the restoration of Grattan's Parliament, for the restoration of a Parliament which practically ignored the rights of Catholics in a Catholic country was hardly likely to appeal even to the moderate politicians who first began the Home Rule agitation. What they asked was a separate Government for Ireland, still allied with the Imperial Government, on principles such as those which regulated the alliance between the United States of America. The proposed Irish Parliament in College Green would have borne much the same relation to the Parliament at Westminster that the Legislature of every American State bears to the head authority of the Congress in the Capitol at Washington. All that related to local business it was proposed to delegate to the Irish Assembly; all questions of Imperial policy were still to be left to the Imperial Government.

There was nothing very startling, very daringly innovating, in this scheme. In most of the dependencies of Great Britain, Home Rule systems of some kind were already established. In Canada, in the Australian colonies, the principle might be seen at work upon a large scale; upon a small scale it was to be studied nearer home in the neighbouring

Isle of Man. One of the chief objections raised to the new proposal by those who thought it worth while to raise any objections at all, was that it would be practically impossible to decide the border-line between local affairs and Imperial affairs. The answer to this is, of course, that what has not been found impossible, or indeed exceedingly difficult, in the case of the American Republic and its component States, or in the case of England and her American and Australasian colonies, need not be found to present unsurpassable difficulties in the case of Great Britain and Ireland. But this demand, modest as it was, aroused the wildest indignation and the most vigorous opposition in England. English journalists and politicians alike mistook the importance of the movement. They cried out almost unanimously that England would never listen to such a demand, that it was no use making it, as it would never be entertained or even investigated.

This attitude of uncompromising refusal only served to give further strength to the Home Rulers. 'If the Home Rule theory,' says Mr. Lecky, ' brings with it much embarrassment to English statesmen, it is at least a theory which is within the limits of the Constitution, which is supported by means that are perfectly loyal, legitimate, and which, like every other theory, must be discussed and judged upon its merits.' This was exactly what English statesmen and politicians sternly refused to do in the early years of the decade of 1870. They would have none of the Home Rule theory. They would not admit that it could possibly come within the limits of a constitutional question. ' Home Rule never could and never shall be granted, so what is the use of asking it?' they said.

This was the temper in which Home Rule was at first received in and out of Parliament. Even much later, politicians who piqued themselves on being practical, and who had been gradually forced to consider the possibility, if not the necessity, of some scheme of local government for Ireland, still strove to fight off the consideration of the question by saying, 'What is the use of discussing the question of Home Rule until you who support it present us with a clear and definite plan for our consideration?'

This form of argument was hardly less unreasonable than the other form of uncompromising antagonism. The supporters of Home Rule very fairly answered, 'We maintain the necessity for establishing a system of local government in Ireland. That cannot be done without the Government; till, therefore, the Government is willing to admit that Home Rule is a question to be entertained at all, it is no use bringing forward any particular plans. When it is once admitted that some system of Home Rule must be established in Ireland, then will be the time for bringing forward legislative schemes and plans, and out of the multiplicity of ideas and suggestions creating a complete and cohesive whole.'

The principle of Home Rule obtains in every State in the American Union, though the plan of Home Rule in each particular State is widely different. The principle of Home Rule obtains in every great colony of the Crown, but the plan pursued by each colony is of a very different kind. Now that the people of the two countries have practically agreed together to allow Ireland to manage for herself her own local affairs, it will be found very easy to shape a scheme exactly deciding the form which the conceded Home Rule is to take. But to bring forward the completed scheme before a common basis of negotiation was established would have been more the duty of a new Abbe Sieyès, with a new theory of irregular verbs, than of a practical and serious politician.

But, whether English statesmen liked it or not, were compromising or uncompromising in their attitude towards it, the Home Rule movement was an accomplished fact. Every day increased the popular interest and the popular support accorded to the new organisation. After the General Election of 1874, some sixty members were returned for Irish constituencies who had stood before their constituents as Home Rulers. Most of them were what would be called to-day very moderate Home Rulers. Indeed, many of the names in that sixty would not suggest to the politician of to-day the idea of any very active or very daring political reputation. But for a time the Home Rule party in Parliament appeared a very formidable body, indeed, in the eyes of English Ministers and English members of Opposition. But with all his sixty men, and all his own ability and eloquence, and with all the enthusiasm of the country behind him, and with all the strength that lies in a new movement, Mr. Butt did not make much use of his opportunities. The Home Rule party was in existence, but its existence was not an active one. Mr. Butt and his followers had proved the force of the desire for some sort of National Government in Ireland, but the strength of the movement they had created now called for stronger leaders. A new man was coming into Irish political life who was destined to be the most remarkable Irish leader since O'Connell.

Shortly after the General Election of 1874, a vacancy caused by a Government appointment left Dublin County open to a contest. A young Irish Protestant landlord came forward to fight for the seat as a Home Rule candidate. At that time little or nothing was known in Ireland of the new man who was to become the leader of the Irish people. Mr. Parnell was a member of the same family as the English poet, Parnell, and the two Parnells, father and son, John and Henry, who had stood by Grattan to the last in the struggle against the Union. He was the grand-nephew of Sir Henry Parnell, the first Lord Congleton, the advanced Reformer and the friend of Lord Grey and Lord Melbourne. He had been educated entirely in England. He had been for some time at Cambridge University, and had travelled much in America. In 1871 he had settled down on his estates in Avondale, within whose boundaries is to be found Moore's Vale of Avoca with its meeting waters, and was apparently about to content himself with the career of an Irish country gentleman. But it would have been as possible for a Napoleon to remain a simple sub-lieutenant as for Mr. Parnell to pass his days as a quiet country gentleman. So his unsuccessful Dublin contest of 1874 brought him for the first time into public notice in Ireland.

It is curious to have to record that when Mr. Parnell addressed his first meeting in the Dublin Rotunda he was exceedingly nervous, and practically broke down, so that, we are told, the persons who were present on the occasion prophesied of him that if he ever got into Parliament he would only play the part of a silent member. In 1875 Mr. Parnell stood again, on the death of John Martin, as candidate for Meath, and was successfully returned after a stiff contest. That Meath election marks the date of a new and important epoch in the histories of Ireland and England.

At first Mr. Parnell attracted absolutely no notice in the House of Commons; one member of the numbers who were simply regarded as the rank and file, and whose position in the representative assembly was of little importance to themselves, and of no importance to anyone else. Presently, however, Mr. Parnell began to force himself a little upon public attention. He began to ask questions, to make speeches, to show he had a very keen and ready appreciation of the duties of Parliamentary life, and a very remarkable power of assimilating and interpreting the rules of the House itself. His name began to be talked about. English members talked with some curiosity of the pale slight young man who sat for an Irish constituency, and who was beginning to cause some ferment among the Irish representatives in the House of Commons.

The presence of the member for Meath seemed to be quickening the Irish Parliamentary party into a new existence, and animating it with a fresh and unexpected activity. Mr. Butt's placid leadership, his well-ordered and regulated field nights for the discussion of Irish questions, which were immediately allowed to drop into complete oblivion until the next set scene was ready, had reconciled English members very much to the presence of the Home Rule party in the House of Commons. It did no harm; it took up a night now and then, it is true; but it had one or two good speakers

—its leader in especial was a very eloquent man—its members were many of them pleasant enough, and so the English parties on both sides of the House had come to tolerate the Home Rulers, and to listen to their periodical display of patriotism with a kind of good-humoured compassion. All this easy-going, jog-trot, old order of things was now undergoing a change beneath their very eyes, and the change was due to the agitating presence of the young man who represented Meath.

In 1877 the House first came definitely into conflict with the new factor in Irish politics, when the Home Rule members made a determined stand against the principle of bringing on important business late at night, or rather early in the morning. On this point they fought vigorously, employing all the rules of the House that assisted them; moving the adjournment of the debate and the adjournment of the House alternately, and very seriously interfering with the old Ministerial privilege of rushing work unnoticed through the House of Commons at an unseemly hour in the morning. The House of Commons, as a body, bitterly resented the action of Mr. Parnell and those who acted with him, and sought to express its resentment in its time-honoured, old-fashioned way, and the time-honoured, old-fashioned way failed utterly, as such ways will sometimes when applied unwisely to new conditions which are too strong for them.

In old days a member of the House who pursued any line of policy unpopular to the majority was rapidly howled and shouted into silence. The majority, to do it justice, did its very best to howl and shout Mr. Parnell down, but failed hopelessly. It had howled and shouted down Sir Charles Dilke and Mr. Auberon Herbert a few years before when these two members proclaimed themselves Republicans to an astonished and insulted Senate; but Mr. Parnell and his half-dozen colleagues were not to be howled or shouted down. If the House shouted and howled while they were talking so much the worse for the House, and so much the greater waste of time. They went on talking till the House was tired, or they quietly or composedly moved motions of adjournment, which had to be tested by a process of long divisions, and which could not be howled or shouted out of existence.

The term 'obstruction' has been applied very frequently and very angrily to the policy which Mr. Parnell and his followers pursued then, and to the policy which Mr. Parnell and his increasing number of followers have had occasion to pursue from time to time in the years that came after. Indeed, there appears to be a kind of popular, loose impression abroad that obstruction was invented by the Parnellites; that until the unlucky hour which introduced the member for Meath into the House of Commons such things as talking against time, dilatory motions, and the whole machinery of obstruction had never been employed—had never been so much as heard of. As a matter of fact it had often been employed before, with good effect, long before Mr. Parnell ever came into the House of Commons. Mr. Gladstone himself had once announced his determination of opposing an obnoxious measure by every means which the forms of the House permitted to him. The Tory party had often enough shown themselves to be past masters in the art of obstruction. A very gifted and brilliant Irish politician, Sir John Pope Hennessy, recently Governor of the Mauritius, was, during the period of his successful Parliamentary life, more than once conspicuous for the skill and ability of his obstructive tactics. In point of fact, obstruction, like everything else beneath the sun, was not a new method of Parliamentary warfare. The Irish members did not invent obstruction. It had been practised often before, for special purposes, by Liberals and Tories alike. But they applied the method with considerable ingenuity and consistence.

Equally ignorant, equally unfair, is the popular, loose impression that Mr. Parnell obstructed for the pure joy in obstruction, merely for the pleasure of delaying business—any business—and without any definite purpose whatever. This is, of course, so amazing, so astounding a misconception, that it seems extraordinary that it ever should be necessary to contradict it. The obstruction of 1877 was levelled against a most unjust and unbusinesslike method of going through Parliamentary work, and one which pressed with particular unfairness upon Irish members. The opposition which Mr. Parnell and those who sided with him raised to the Prison Code, and to the Army and Navy Mutiny Bills, rendered a most signal service to all those Bills. 'Whoever,' says Mr. A. M. Sullivan, 'will take into his hand the Prison Code of this country, and the Army and Navy Mutiny Bills as they stood before Mr. Parnell and his audacious band began operations on them in March 1877, and compare those three codes with what they were as they emerged from that purifying ordeal, will be struck with amazement and admiration.'

But the worst of it is, that the hostile critics of Mr. Parnell and his friends and his followers never will take the trouble to inquire into the accuracy of any of their allegations. The soldier who wears the English uniform, the sailor who serves in the English navy, whether he be English, Irish, Scotch, or Welsh, have the best of reasons to be grateful to Mr. Parnell and his allies for the beneficial changes which they introduced into the Government measures. A record of the debate on the Prison Bills tells the same tale.

One of the most well-known cases of early obstruction belongs to the famous South African debate; and there are few Englishmen now who will not be inclined to regret that the efforts of Mr. Parnell and his followers on that occasion did not prove successful. That was one of the few occasions on which the members of the Irish party did not fight their fight alone. They had with them the leading lights of the English Radical party below the gangway. Sir Charles Dilke, Mr. Leonard Courtney, and Mr. Edward Jenkins—who was then a Radical and a Home Ruler, though he has now become a Conservative and an enemy to Home Rule—fought in the South African debate as vigorously as any of the Irish members, and were as fertile in the employment of the resources of obstruction.

The Bill over which the battle was fought was Lord

Carnarvon's South African Confederation Bill, which provided facilities for the voluntary union of the Colonies, and for the appointment of a Governor-General, a Ministry, a Legislative Council, and a House of Assembly, each Council to be presided over by a Chief Executive officer. The Bill was introduced in the Lords, through which it passed rapidly enough, and came down to the Commons. Before it had reached its second reading, news came of the annexation of the Transvaal by Sir Theophilus Shepstone, the British Commissioner in South Africa. The Bill and the annexation were alike strenuously opposed by Mr. Leonard Courtney, Sir Charles Dilke, and Mr. Edward Jenkins, as involving a complete reversal of the policy of twenty years previously, when the Orange River territory had been given up.

The opponents of the Bill urged—and urged with a wisdom which proved prophetic—that the annexation would involve the country in increased expenditure, and inevitable war. Some of the Irish members acting with Mr. Parnell, in their position as members of an Imperial body, agreed with the English Radicals, and supported them with all their strength and fought the fight as stubbornly as they could. They were bitterly opposed to the Bill and to the annexation, and they were determined to combat both by all the means in their power. The old House of Commons tradition that Irish members should only interfere on Irish questions, and should leave great Imperial matters to be settled by the English members alone, was in itself an ingenious argument for Home Rule; but it was not one which Irish members, compelled to attend an English Parliament, were bound to act upon. So Mr. Parnell and his followers steadily opposed the Bill in Committee step by step, stage by stage, and point by point.

At the end of July there was a sitting of then unparalleled length, which endured for exactly twenty-six hours. Other and longer records have since completely defeated this; but at the time it was one of the longest sittings the House of Commons had ever held, and it was looked upon as little less than a prodigy and a portent; and a portent it certainly was. Motion after motion of adjournment was made, divided on, and defeated, the temper of the House with every division proving hotter and angrier, and the Parnellites more and more determined. In the course of the struggle Mr. Butt seized an opportunity for severing himself from the unpopular action of his fellow-members, and of practically ending his own career as a possible leader of an Irish party. He repudiated the claim of the Irish members who were acting with Mr. Parnell to represent the Irish party; and he declared that if he thought they did he would retire from political life altogether. 'I would retire,' he said, 'from Irish politics, and from a public broil in which no man can take part with dignity to himself or advantage to his country.'

It mattered very little then what opinion Mr. Butt might hold or express to Mr. Parnell and to those who thought and acted with him. Mr. Butt's career was coming to an end with such services as he had rendered. His leadership had done little to advance the cause of the country, and if his words of renunciation gained for him the applause of the English benches, they had no effect in guiding the conduct or affecting the policy of Mr. Parnell and the party that was growing up around him. In the end, of course, numbers triumphed, and the unlucky South Africa Bill became law.

The obstruction, if it had been successful, would have prevented an unfortunate war and much bloodshed, and some humiliating defeats, and some ignominious treaties. It was silenced by the sheer force of numbers, and from that time forth any comment that any member of the advanced Irish party offered upon any measure was described as a systematic policy of obstruction. The obstruction of 1877 had, however, one good effect. It brought to the front rank of Irish politics the most remarkable Irish politician of the century, and gave the Irish people what they had been long looking for, and what they had been long looking for in vain—a leader who was worthy of the cause.

Any history of that wild and stormy period of obstruction

would be incomplete which failed to do justice to the ability, the courage, and the loyalty of Mr. Biggar. When Mr. Parnell was still a young, almost unknown and untried, member of the House of Commons, unsifted in the perilous enterprise of facing hostile and howling majorities, Mr. Biggar sat by his side, faithfully and undauntedly, through all the brunt of the battle. In one of the best modern historical novels in the English language—' The Cloister and the Hearth '—the hero is comforted, through a long period of sorrow, strife, and danger, by a gallant companion, who shares his sufferings, helps him to face his dangers, fights his enemies, and at all times and seasons is clapping him encouragingly on the back, and repeating to him the watchword, ' *Courage, camarade, le diable est mort !* '

In the same spirit of gallant brotherhood Mr. Biggar occupied his place by the young man who was fighting his first fights in a hostile assembly. With imperturbable composure, with unalterable good humour, with an apparently marvellous and unwearying staying-power, Mr. Biggar proved himself the very ideal lieutenant of the leader of a small minority against overwhelming odds. Those who remember that wild night ten years ago think even now, with unfeigned amazement, of the composed way in which, at four o'clock on that stormy morning, Mr. Biggar quietly adjourned to the library to seek a little needful slumber, and presently came back, after a due interval of time, as fresh as ever, to carry on the fight. That South African night might not inappropriately be regarded as the birth night of a new Irish Parliamentary party.

Meanwhile all dispute or discussion with regard to the leadership of Mr. Butt was settled by the death of Mr. Butt himself in 1879, and Mr. Shaw was chosen leader in his stead. Mr. Shaw became leader in difficult times. The Land question was coming up again. Mr. Butt, shortly before his death, had predicted its reappearance, and been laughed at for his prophecy, but he was soon proved to be right. The condition of the peasantry was still very bad, their tenure of land precarious. A new land agitation was inaugurated by a new man. Mr. Michael Davitt was the son of an evicted tenant. He had lost his arm while a boy in a machine accident in Lancashire. When a young man he joined the Fenian movement, was arrested, and sentenced to fifteen years' penal servitude. Seven years later he was let out on ticket-of-leave. During his imprisonment he had thought much of the means of bettering the condition of Ireland, and had come to the conclusion that by constitutional agitation, not by force of arms, the improvement could be best accomplished. Mr. Davitt went to America, planned out there a scheme of land organisation, and returned to Ireland to put it into practice. He found the condition of the Irish peasant very wretched. For three years the harvest had been going from bad to worse, and there was danger of a serious famine. Mr. Davitt and his friends organised land meetings in various parts of Ireland; the new scheme was eagerly responded to by the tenant farmers in all directions.

In October, 1879, the Irish National Land League was formed. Mr. Davitt and some other Land Leaguers were prosecuted for speeches made at some of the land meetings, but the prosecutions were abandoned. Mr. Parnell went to America to raise funds to meet the distress; the Lord Mayor of Dublin, Mr. E. D. Gray, M.P., raised a furd at home; so did the Duchess of Marlborough. The Government passed certain relief measures. The severity of the famine was stayed, but neither the Government nor the public and private relief was able to prevent a great amount of suffering. Such was the condition of affairs in Ireland when Lord Beaconsfield wrote his letter to the Duke of Marlborough, in which he attacked the Liberal party for their compromises with Irish faction and disaffection.

Quite unexpectedly, in the early March of 1880, Lord Beaconsfield issued a political manifesto. The political manifesto took the form of a letter to the Duke of Marlborough, in which Lord Beaconsfield announced his intention of promptly dissolving Parliament, and of appealing to the constituencies for their verdict upon his policy and the policy of his opponents. The letter covered a vast variety of topics, but it was practically a hostile pronouncement against the Irish Parliamentary party, then under the nominal leadership of Mr. Shaw and the virtual leadership of Mr. Parnell. It was no question of foreign policy which drove Lord Beaconsfield into an appeal to the country, which cannot be described as premature, but which was certainly unexpected at the time when it was made. Ireland was the theme of Lord Beaconsfield's letter. The difficulty about Ireland was the first topic touched upon by him in the last letter of political importance he was ever destined to write. Lord Beaconsfield frankly recognised the growth of the Home Rule movement, and characterised it as dangerous, 'scarcely less disastrous than pestilence or famine.' According to Lord Beaconsfield it had been insidiously supported by the Liberal party, who sought to destroy the 'Imperial character' of England by a 'policy of decomposition,' which Lord Beaconsfield called upon all 'men of light and leading' to struggle against.

As we read this letter now, at a distance of seven years from the time when it was first given to the world, it is difficult to avoid smiling at the way in which history repeated itself, only with a slight eccentric transformation of the *rôles* of the two great parties in England. Then, in 1880, it was Lord Beaconsfield who thundered and anathematised against the wily and treacherous Liberals who were dallying with the seditious phantom of Home Rule, and who were going to give up the empire to chaos and old night, in order to please the Irish people and the handful of their representatives.

Seven years have passed by; new Ministries have come into power and have fallen from power; and there is a fresh appeal to the country impending, and we hear over again the same accusation of dalliance with Irish disaffection and alliance with Irish leaders. But this cry comes this time from Liberal as well as from Tory lips. Certain of the men whom Lord Beaconsfield so vehemently accused of a desire to disintegrate the empire, and to destroy England's Imperial character by a policy of decomposition, in which they were assisted by Ireland and the Irish members, are now applying the same thing as vigorously and as violently to Mr. Gladstone's followers and Mr. Gladstone's lieutenants in the leadership of the Radical party. It is the Radicals, we are told now, who are pledged to the hilt to the Irish party, who have packed cards with treason, and who are destroying the empire by a policy of decomposition. The words are the words of Lord Beaconsfield, but the voice is the voice of Mr. Chamberlain. But whatever language is addressed by one English party to another the position of the Irish people and their leaders remains the same. Their power has changed, however, marvellously.

When Lord Beaconsfield issued his fiery letter to the Duke of Marlborough the Irish party in the House of Commons was few in numbers, was, as a body, feeble of purpose, was, indeed, a house divided against itself. Mr. Shaw, who was its nominal leader—' Sensible Shaw,' as he was called by his friends and admirers—was regarded by everyone as a solid, practical man of business; but he was not the kind of man who was calculated to shine as a leader of an active and energetic political minority in an assembly like the House of Commons. Mr. Parnell was the real leader; and round Mr. Parnell all that was strong in purpose and in principle of the Irish Parliamentary party was forming itself into a group that became the core of a later and more successful party.

Lord Beaconsfield, with the keen political foresight that was usually characteristic of him, saw the real strength of the little band of men that were clustered round Mr. Parnell; but his insight was not keen enough to allow him to estimate that strength at its full value. He saw that they were dangerous, but he made the mistake of thinking that they could be crushed out of existence; and he accordingly struck at them with all his strength in his pronouncement to the Duke of Marlborough. The Irish party promptly took up the challenge. A manifesto was immediately drawn up by the Irish leaders, and circulated broadcast wherever an Irish voter was to be found, calling upon every man who believed in the national cause and the national leaders to lend a hand in flinging the Tory party from office. That call was responded to with a promptness which must have appeared menacing to any English statesmen of either party who were watching the contest with sufficient calmness to appreciate the gravity of the appeal to the Irish Parliamentary party, and the answer which the Irish voters gave to it.

At the time undoubtedly the sympathies of a large portion of the Irish people in England went with the Liberal party; but they recorded their votes for the Liberal candidates on this occasion for the first time, not because they were Liberal candidates but because they were opposed to the Tories. The Irish vote throughout the United Kingdom was acting in accordance with the advice and entreaty of men to whom a scornful and irritated majority denied the right of speaking for the Irish people at all. In giving that advice the Irish leaders acted wisely; in following it the Irish people acted admirably. It was essential at that time for the safety of the national movement, for the integrity of the national party, that the challenge of Lord Beaconsfield should be taken up, and that the Tory Government should be driven from office. The personal leanings of Irishmen in England to one or other of the great parties were wisely put aside in recognition of the fact that it was far more important to further Irish interests than to pay heed to the quarrels of Whig and Tory. There were plenty of Irishmen in England who, if they had been left untrammelled by any other consideration, would gladly have recorded their vote in favour of the Tory candidate, but who, in obedience to the appeal of leaders whose judgment they relied upon, whose action they admired, and whose opinions they supported, went with a light heart to the polling-booth and voted for the Liberal representative.

Undoubtedly the Irish vote, given as it thus was, practically solid for the Liberal party, counted for much in the result of the General Election. Undoubtedly, in the face of the advantage of gaining that vote, English Liberal statesmen and Liberal politicians of all classes said a good deal more or a good deal less than they precisely meant on the Irish question. Either they expressed their sympathy with a warmth which cooled down with amazing rapidity when they found themselves in office, or they discreetly kept their disapproval of the Irish demands well in the background until the contest was safely over.

The result of the election greatly altered the appearance of the Irish party in Parliament. The action of Ireland showed decisively and conclusively that the heart of the Irish people was with Mr. Parnell and the advanced men who supported him, rather than with the moderate Home Rulers who were represented by Mr. Shaw. Mr. Parnell himself was elected for no less than three constituencies, and decided to take his place in the House of Commons as the representative of the city of Cork. The story of the Cork election is one of the most remarkable in the whole history of the General Election of 1880. We know now how largely Mr. Parnell's candidature for Cork, and in consequence his success there, was due to the interest and the action of one of his most brilliant and gifted lieutenants. The result had an effect almost beyond the hopes of the advanced party. The seat was a difficult one to win; and it was won under conditions which made victory exceptionally difficult and exceptionally advantageous. It impressed the sense of Mr. Parnell's popularity through Ireland upon Englishmen almost more than all the other elections put together. In nearly all the other elections Mr. Parnell's candidates were as a matter of course returned, and when the Irish party assembled at St. Stephen's it was seen that Mr. Parnell could count upon the alliance and the adhesion of a large majority of those who had come to Westminster as members of the Home Rule Party.

The division of the party between those who sided with Mr. Parnell and those who held by Mr. Shaw made itself at once apparent. Mr. Parnell and his followers were of opinion that it was the duty of any Irish national party in the English House of Commons to seat itself in opposition to any Government, Whig or Tory, that might be in office. The Irish vote had helped to return the Liberals to office, not so much from devotion to the Liberals as in order to answer Lord Beaconsfield's challenge. The good intentions of the Liberal party had, indeed, been freely expressed towards Ireland; but the Irish members who were with Mr. Parnell were not quite sure of the value of these good intentions, which come so readily into the political mind at the time of an election, and which fade away so often without any fulfilment or performance. Those, therefore, who followed Mr. Parnell, who had already been formally chosen as leader of the Irish Parliamentary party at a meeting in Dublin, seated themselves below the gangway on the Opposition side of the House. Mr. Shaw and the minority of moderate Home Rulers took up their places, as loyal adherents of the Government, below the gangway on the Ministerial side of the House.

The new Irish party, which followed the lead of Mr. Parnell, has been often represented by the humourist as a sort of Falstaffian 'ragged regiment,' and its members described as rivals of Lazarus in the painted cloth, to whom the mere necessities of life were luxuries, to obtain which they would follow any leader or advocate any cause. From dint of repetition this has come to be almost an article of faith in some quarters. Yet it is grotesquely without foundation. A large proportion of Mr. Parnell's followers were journalists. Journalists, unfortunately, seldom amass large fortunes, but the occupation is not usually considered dishonourable by Englishmen, and the journalists who belonged to the Irish party were, to put it mildly, sufficiently intelligent to be able to obtain their livelihood by their pens.

Mr. T. P. O'Connor, for example, was a young Irishman who had come to London, and was making his way in English journalism. He was a strong Radical, and had gained a reputation by an exceedingly able 'Life of Lord Beaconsfield.' Mr. Sexton, who was destined to prove himself one of the foremost debaters in the House of Commons, began life in the employment of the Waterford and Limerick Railway Company. When he was some twenty years of age he became a writer for the *Nation*, a newspaper which had upheld through long years and under disheartening conditions the traditions of Nationalism which had made it famous in 1848. He had been a writer for the *Nation* for some years when the General Election came. Mr. Sexton, like most young Irish journalists who ever wrote for the *Nation*, had taken the keenest interest in Irish politics. He was sent to Sligo to oppose Colonel King Harman, an influential landlord and a nominal Home Ruler. So great was the popular feeling for the growing Nationalist party, that an almost unknown young writer with the eloquent tongue was returned by a triumphant majority over the wealthy landlord, his opponent, who had come to regard a seat for Sligo as an item of his personal property. Mr. T. D. Sullivan was another Irish journalist, the owner of the *Nation*, eminent in Ireland, and not in Ireland alone, as a true poet of the people.

Mr. Healy was not returned to Parliament at the General Election. He did not enter the House of Commons until November, 1880, but he may fairly be described with the party he was so soon to join, and of which he was already a valuable adherent. Mr. Healy came to England at sixteen years of age, a poor young man, with his way to make in the world. Almost self-educated, he had taught himself, beside French and German, Pitman's shorthand, and through his knowledge of phonography he obtained a situation as shorthand clerk in the office of the Superintendent of the North-Eastern Railway at Newcastle. Later on, he came to London as the confidential clerk of a manufactory, and as weekly correspondent of the *Nation*. In this capacity he made the acquaintance of Mr. Parnell, whom he accompanied on his American tour in 1879. From that time Mr. Healy became one of the most prominent of the young men who were working for the Nationalist cause. He was soon to prove the possession of true political genius, and to become one of the most brilliant and one of the most important of the Irish Parliamentary party.

Mr. James O'Kelly was a journalist who had been a

soldier and a special correspondent in all parts of the world. He served in the Foreign Legion of the French army against the Arabs at Oran, under Maximilian in Mexico, and had narrowly escaped being shot by the Spaniards at Cuba. He was yet to peril his life in the red deserts of the Soudan. After accompanying the Emperor of Brazil on his tour through America, and following the fortunes of the war with the Sioux chief, Sitting Bull, Mr. O'Kelly came to England, and at once took an active part in the Home Rule movement then inaugurated by Mr. Butt.

Another journalist, one of the most able among the Irish members, was Mr. E. D. Gray, the proprietor of the *Freeman's Journal*, probably the most valuable newspaper property in Ireland. Mr. William O'Brien, one of the most trenchant writers and sincerest patriots who ever served Ireland, entered Parliament later. He and Mr. Justin M'Carthy were both journalists.

Those who were not journalists in the Irish party were generally what is called well-to-do. Mr. Dillon had inherited property from his father. Mr. Biggar had retired from a very successful connection with the North of Ireland bacon trade. Mr. Richard Power was a country gentleman of position; so was Mr. Mulhallen Marum; so was Mr. John Redmond; so was Mr. William Redmond, who was elected later; so was Mr. Sheil; so was Mr. Metge. Mr. Arthur O'Connor had been in the War Office for many laborious years, and had retired upon a pension. Dr. Commins was a successful Liverpool lawyer, Mr. John Barry was a prosperous business man; so was Mr. Dawson. Mr. Leamy was a solicitor of independent means. Colonel Nolan was an artillery officer of distinction. One of the most remarkable figures in the ranks of the Irish party was Colonel The O'Gorman Mahon, with whose career we are already familiar.

It is obvious, therefore, that the Irish Parliamentary party was a very solid political body, containing within its ranks a large number of men of very remarkable ability, and a very goodly proportion of men of ample means and of position in the conventional social sense. It contained, for its numbers, a proportion of really admirable speakers, all ready, many genuinely eloquent, which either of the two great parties might have envied.

The Liberal party, whose triumphant return to office was due in so large a measure to the Irish vote, was not a little surprised at the attitude taken up by the Irish Parliamentary party who followed Mr. Parnell. They could not understand why the party who helped to vote them into office should sit in opposition. They did not appreciate the full force of the new departure. They did not realise that henceforth there was to be an Irish party in the House of Commons which would not pledge itself in any way to either of the two great English parties, but would fight entirely for its own cause, and which was always in opposition to any Government which did not grant full and complete justice to Ireland.

But though the Irish party sat in opposition to the Liberal party which they had helped to return to power, there did not at first appear to be any likelihood of any serious disunion. In the previous Parliament the Irish members and the Radical members had been thrown into frequent alliance; during the General Election the bonds of sympathy between the English Radicals and the Irish people seemed to have been strengthened. The Irish vote in England had been given to the Liberal cause. The Liberal speakers and statesmen, without committing themselves to any definite line of policy, had maintained friendly sentiments towards Ireland; and though, indeed, nothing was said which could be construed into a recognition of the Home Rule claim, still the new Ministry was known to contain men favourable to that claim.

The Irish members hoped for much from the new Government; and, on the other hand, the new Government expected to find cordial allies in all sections of the Irish party. The appointment of Mr. Forster to the Irish Secretaryship was regarded by many Irishmen, especially those allied to Mr. Shaw and his following, as a marked sign of the good intentions of the Government towards Ireland.

From the very first, however, it became obvious that there was little chance of any practical friendship between the Liberal party in power and the Irish party in opposition. The opening record of the new Ministry was marked by a series of blunders in their dealings with the various phases of the Irish question. The Queen's Speech contained some important announcements; but it was remarkable for yet more important omissions.

The Queen's Speech announced that the Peace Preservation Act would not be renewed. This was a declaration of considerable moment. From her Union with England Ireland had hardly ever been governed by the ordinary law. Since the opening of the century stringent coercive measures of every description had succeeded, accompanied, and overlapped each other with incessant persistence. Now the Government were to boldly attempt to govern Ireland without having recourse to exceptional and repressive legislation.

The Queen's Speech, however, referred to Ireland only in one other particular—namely, that a Bill should be brought in for the extension of the Irish borough franchise. The borough franchise in England was very much lower than in Ireland, the latter system being based upon the old principle still extant in English and Irish counties. Every householder in England exercised the privilege of the franchise, without regard to the value of the house in which he lived. The right to vote was conferred by any place in which he and his family lived, whether lodging, or room separately held. In Ireland, on the contrary, the house in which a man lived had to be of a certain value, had to have a certain rental, before its occupier might exercise the franchise. No house in an Irish borough the yearly rental of which was not 4*l.* or more could qualify for a vote.

In England and Ireland alike there was a standard of value which had to be reached before an occupier had the privilege of voting. This condition of things the advocates of the new Reform Bill proposed to change. But extension of the borough franchise did not seem to the Irish members in 1880 the most important form that legislation for Ireland could take just then. The country was greatly depressed by its recent suffering; the number of evictions was beginning to rise enormously. The Irish members thought that the Government should have made some promise to consider the Land question, and above all should have done something to stay the alarming increase of evictions. Evictions had increased from 463 families in 1877, to 980 in 1878, to 1,238 in 1879; and they were still on the increase, as was shown at the end of 1880, when it was found that 2,110 families were evicted.

An amendment to the Address was at once brought forward by the Irish party, and debated at some length. The Irish party called for some immediate legislation on behalf of the Land question. Mr. Forster replied, admitting the necessity for some legislation, but declaring that there would not be time for the introduction of any such measure that session. Then the Irish members asked for some temporary measure to prevent the evictions which were undoubtedly rapidly on the increase, and appeals were made to the Government not to lend landlords military aid in carrying out evictions; but the Chief Secretary answered that while the law existed it was necessary to carry it out, and he could only appeal to both sides to be moderate.

For a short time matters went on slowly in this manner, the Secret Service vote and the Irish Relief Bill giving opportunities for animated debates, in the course of which the Irish Secretary several times declared his belief that the improved condition of Ireland would render it unnecessary to resort to many of the old-fashioned methods of governing Ireland. Evictions speedily increased, however, and Mr. O'Connor Power introduced a measure for the purpose of staying evictions. The Government, however, refused this measure, but brought in a Compensation for Disturbance Bill of its own, which embodied some of the points in the Irish Bill. The Bill authorised County Court Judges in Ireland till the end of 1881 to allow compensation to tenants evicted for non-payment of rent, in cases where failure of crops had produced the insolvency.

Mr. Forster described this as nothing more than an extension of the Act of 1870, by making eviction for non-payment of rent, in cases where tenants were really unable to pay, a disturbance within the meaning of that Act. Mr. Forster moved the second reading on June 25, denied that it was a concession to the anti-rent agitation, and denounced in forcible terms the outrages then taking place in Ireland. At the same time he admitted that the annual rate of evictions had already more than doubled the average rate in 1877. This was the point at which the difference between the Irish people and the Government became strongly marked. It was destined to become more marked yet. From that moment for five years the natural links between the English Liberals and the Irish Nationalists were severed.

CHAPTER XX.

THE LAND LEAGUE.

IN order to properly understand the exact position of affairs in Ireland at the moment when Mr. Gladstone took office in 1880, it is no harm to recapitulate some of the events that took place under the preceding Ministry, or even earlier. When Mr. Gladstone went out of office in 1874, he had passed two great Irish measures, and had tripped himself and his administration up over a third. The measure which overthrew him was the Irish University Education Bill; the measures which he carried disestablished the Irish Church, and created the Land Act of 1870.

The Land Act of 1870 endeavoured, first, to give the tenant some security of tenure; second, to encourage the making of improvements throughout the country; and third, to promote the establishment of a peasant proprietorship. It sought to further the first and second of these aims by legalising the

Ulster tenant right on farms where it already existed, and by allowing compensation for disturbance and for improvements to evicted tenants on farms where the Ulster tenant-right system did not prevail.

Up to this time the Ulster tenant-right custom was not recognised by law, and as it differed widely in different estates, it was not very easy to define strictly. Roughly speaking, however, it maintained, for those who were bound to it by time and tradition, first, that the tenant was not to be evicted so long as he paid his rent and acted properly, his landlord having indeed the right of raising the rent from time to time, though not so high as to destroy the tenant's interest; second, that the tenant who wished to leave his holding had a right to sell his interest in the farm, subject to the landlord's consent to receive a new purchaser as a tenant; third, that if the landlord wanted to take the land himself, he must pay a fair sum for the tenant right.

It may be fairly said that, wherever the Ulster tenant-right custom existed, the relationship between landlord and tenant was reasonably good. On estates where the custom or anything like it did not prevail, the tenant had practically no rights as against the landlord. The majority of Irish tenancies were tenancies from year to year. These might at any time be ended by the landlord after due notice. A comparatively small proportion of tenancies were let on leases which gave the tenant security of possession for a considerable period, so long as he could pay the yearly rent, or the landlord did not press too heavily for arrears. In neither case had the tenant any right to claim on eviction compensation for disturbance, or for any improvements he might have made in the land; and in Ireland, except on a few 'English-managed' estates, the improvements were always made by the tenants. In the yearly tenancies the landlord had always the power of raising the rent when he pleased; in estates held on lease he could raise it at the expiration of the lease, and, as a rule, the landlord or his agent always did so raise the rent whenever the exertions of the tenant had made the land of more value than when he had entered it.

Undoubtedly one of the reasons for the wretched condition of so many Irish farms and cabins was that the tenant feared, and often justly feared, that the smallest sign of well-being, the least evidence of improvement of any kind, would be taken by the landlord or his agent as a sure sign that he might safely raise the rent. Raising the rent was the one great dread of the tenant. So great was the poverty of the average tenant that, in many cases, it was almost impossible to pay any rent at all, and the prospect of having the existing rent raised was terror. The Irish peasant is, as a rule, profoundly unwilling to emigrate. He loves his land with a passion which defies starvation, and he will make any sacrifices and run any risks to remain at home. Of those who do emigrate, the majority always dream of returning, and many do return, to their native land. The land is the love, but it is also the life, of the Irish peasant. If he remains in Ireland, he has nothing else to live upon, and he is ready to take the land on any terms the landlord chooses to make, trusting to Providence to see him safely through with his rent at the due time, or hoping that the landlord may be found easy-going and unexacting. Furthermore, the Irish peasant is in his heart convinced that the land is really his; that the landlord to whom he pays his rent and the agent to whom he touches his hat are alike, whatever their nationality, the representatives of a hostile rule, of a coercion which is no conquest.

Evictions were the great misery of the peasantry. Evictions were often for non-payment of rent, often because the landlord wished to clear the ground, and was anxious to get rid of his tenants whether they paid their rent or not. In the years from 1849 to 1882 inclusive, the evictions have been on an average of more than three thousand families a year. The highest rates of eviction were in 1849 and 1850, the two years immediately following the rising of 1848, when the rates were 16,686 and 19,949 families in each year. The rate was at its lowest in 1869, when the number of evicted families was only 374. From 1865 to 1878 inclusive, the number of evictions never got into the thousands; in 1879 they were over 1,000;

in 1880, over 2,000 ; in 1881 and 1882 over 3,000. The Land Act of 1870 did not lessen evictions, as great numbers of the tenantry in all parts of the country were in heavy arrears of rent. In many estates it was practically compulsory for the rent to be in arrears by a process known as the hanging gale, by which the tenant had always a year's or half a year's rent due and hanging over him, thus giving him completely into the landlord's power as regarded eviction.

One of the objects of the Land Act of 1870 was to create a peasant proprietary, through the clauses known by the name of Mr. Bright. Something of the kind had already existed on a very small scale. When the Irish Church was disestablished, the Church Temporalities Commissioners were given the power to aid occupying tenants of Church lands in purchasing their holdings when it was wished. These tenants were allowed, on payment of one-fourth of the purchase-money, to leave three-fourths of the purchase-money on mortgage at four per cent., the principal and interest to be repaid in half-yearly payments, extending over a period of thirty-two years. Nearly three-fourths of the tenants occupying Church lands did in fact thus purchase their holdings. It was with the intention of increasing such facilities for the purchase of holdings that the Bright clauses were introduced. A landlord and a tenant might come to an agreement under the Act by which the tenant could purchase his holding, and receive a Landed Estates Court conveyance.

The very fact, however, that a Landed Estates Court conveyance is absolutely binding in its character, and gives its possessor an absolute title to the land acquired, to the disregard of any subsequent claims that might be made after the sale was effected, made the process a costly one. To prevent any mistake in the transfer of the land, or injury to any third parties, careful investigations had to be made, and elaborate requirements gone through, all of which made the process of transfer costly and troublesome. The expenses were often from ten to thirty per cent. of the price of the farm ; in some extreme cases the cost of the transference was very considerably greater than the actual price of the purchased land. Moreover, the tithe rent-charges, quit-rents, and drainage charges, to which most Irish estates are subject, remained with the land instead of being transferred to the money in court, and were a fruitful source of trouble to the new purchasers.

All these various conditions combined to make the working of the Bright clauses far more limited and unsatisfactory than had been intended by their framers. Thus the Act failed practically to establish a system of peasant proprietorship on anything like an extended scale, or indeed on any scale large enough to judge of its working by. It did not give the ordinary tenant any great degree of security of tenure. It allowed him, indeed, the privilege of going to law with his landlord, but as in most cases the tenant had little or no money, while the landlord could fight out the case from court to court, appeal to the law was a privilege of no great value to the tenant. The chief thing actually accomplished by the Act was the legalising of the excellent Ulster custom.

The passing of the Land Act, instead of settling the Land question in Ireland, was destined to give it a fresh impetus. The year that saw it passed saw also the formation of an Irish organisation which was to be the cause of bringing every phase of the Irish question more prominently before the notice of England than at any time since O'Connell, if not, indeed, since the Union. On May 19, 1870, two months and a few days before the Land Act became law, a meeting was held in Dublin of representative Irishmen of all opinions, and of all political and religious creeds. The object of the meeting was to form an organisation to advocate the claims of Ireland to some form of Home Government. The words 'Home Rule' were used by some one, and they became at once the shibboleth of the new party.

The increase of evictions in Ireland, following as it did upon the wide-spread misery caused by the failure of the harvests and the partial famine, had generated—as famine and hunger have always generated—a certain amount of lawlessness. Evictions were occasionally resisted with violence; here and there outrages were committed upon bailiffs, process-servers, and agents. In different places, too, injuries had been inflicted upon the cattle and horses of land-owners and land-agents, cattle had been killed, horses houghed, and sheep mutilated. These offences were always committed at night, and their perpetrators were seldom discovered. There is no need, there should be no attempt, to justify these crimes. But while condemning all acts of violence, whether upon man or beast, it must be remembered that these acts were committed by ignorant peasants of the lowest class, maddened by hunger, want, and eviction, driven to despair by the sufferings of their wives and children, convinced of the utter hopelessness of redress, and longing for revenge.

It was difficult to get these poor peasants to believe in the good intentions of the Government at any time, and unfortunately just then the good intentions of the Government were not very actively displayed. The Compensation for Disturbance Bill was carried in the Commons after long debates in which the Irish party strove to make its principles stronger, while the Opposition denounced it as a flagrant infringement of the rights of property. It was sent up to the Lords, where it was rejected on Tuesday, August 3, by a majority of 231. The Government answered the appeals of Irish members by refusing to take any steps to make the Lords retract their decision, or to introduce any similar measure that session. From that point the agitation and struggles of the past four years may be said to date.

It is impossible to estimate how much suffering might have been avoided if the Government had taken a firmer line with the House of Lords in August 1880. The House of Lords is never a serious opponent to the will of a powerful and popular Ministry; and if it had once been shown that the Government were determined to carry some measure for the relief of evicted tenants, it would have soon ceased to make any stand against it. But though the Government, through the mouth of Mr. Forster, had admitted the alarming increase of evictions and the agitated condition of the country, they refused to take any further steps just then. They promised, indeed, to bring in some comprehensive measure next session, and they appointed a Committee to inquire into the condition of the agricultural population of Ireland. On this commission they absolutely refused, in spite of the earnest entreaties of the Irish members, to give any place to any representative of the tenant-farmer's cause.

This was a curious illustration of the Irish policy of the Government during the early part of its rule. Though the Irish members who followed Mr. Parnell might surely have been regarded as expressing at least the feelings of a very large section of the Irish people, their wishes were as little regarded as if they had represented nothing. It seems difficult to believe that during the whole of Mr. Forster's occupation of the Irish Secretaryship, he never once consulted any member of the Parnellite party on any part of his Irish policy; never asked their advice, or even their opinion, on any Irish affairs whatever. It is still stranger that he pursued almost the same principle with regard to the Irish members who sat on his own side of the House—moderate men like Mr. Shaw and Major Nolan.

The speeches of the Land League leaders became more and more hostile to the Government. At a meeting in Kildare, in August, Mr. John Dillon made a speech in which he called upon the young farmers of Ireland to defend evicted Leaguers threatened with eviction. He looked forward to the time when there would be 300,000 men enrolled in the ranks of the Land League; and when that time came, if the landlords still refused justice, the word would be given for a general strike all over the country against rent, and then 'all the armies in England would not levy rent in that country.'

On Tuesday, August 17, Sir Walter Barttelot called the attention of the Chief Secretary to this speech. Mr. Forster described it as wicked and cowardly; but, while he declined to prosecute Mr. Dillon for it, he announced that the Government were watching the Land League speeches very carefully. Mr. Dillon immediately came across from Ireland to reply to the Chief Secretary's attack.

Mr. Dillon was one of the most remarkable men in the national movement. He was the son of John Dillon, the Young Irelander and rebel of 1848, with whose history we have already made ourselves familiar. When the 'Young Ireland' rising failed, John Dillon the elder escaped to France, and afterwards to America, and in later years he came back to Ireland, and was elected to Parliament for the county of Tipperary. He earned an honourable distinction in the House of Commons, where his great aim was to strengthen the alliance between the Irish members and the English Radicals, and he won the cordial admiration of Mr. John Bright. Mr. Bright, as we have seen, paid eloquent tribute to the memory of John Dillon in a speech which he delivered in Dublin at a banquet which Mr. Dillon had organised to Mr. Bright. Mr. Dillon was to have presided at the banquet, but he died suddenly a few days before it took place. 'I venture to say,' said Mr. Bright, in words which may well be repeated, 'that his sad and sudden removal is a great loss to Ireland. I believe among all her worthy sons Ireland has had no worthier and no nobler son than John Blake Dillon.' Mr. Dillon, the son, was a much more extreme man than his father. He did not display the sympathy with English Radicalism which his father felt, and he appeared to have little or no belief in Parliamentary action. He was quite a young man, and had been elected for the county of Tipperary at the General Election while absent himself in America.

Mr. Dillon rose in the House of Commons on Monday, August 23, and moved the adjournment of the House in order to reply to Mr. Forster's attack upon him. The manner of his speech was no less remarkable than its matter—quiet, perfectly self-possessed. With a low, passionless voice and unmoved face, Mr. Dillon met the charges against him. He professed his absolute indifference as to what the Irish Secretary might choose to call him; but he denied that his speech was wicked in advising the farmers of Ireland to resist an unjust law. He laid at Mr. Forster's door the difficulties and the possible bloodshed that might be caused by the increasing evictions and the unjust course the Government was pursuing.

Mr. Forster replied by analysing the Kildare speech, and repeating his former charges. He accused Mr. Dillon of advising his hearers not to pay their rents, whether they could afford to or not; he charged him with something like sympathy with the mutilation of animals, because, instead of denouncing the houghing of horses and cattle that had taken place, he had said that if Mayo landlords put cattle on the lands from which they could get no rent, the cattle would not prosper very much. He quoted sentences from Mr. Dillon's speech, that 'those in Parliament faithful to the cause of the people could paralyse the hands of the Government, and prevent them from passing such laws as would throw men into prison for organising themselves. In Parliament they could obstruct, and outside of it they could set the people free to drill and organise themselves;' and that 'they would show that every man in Ireland had a right to a rifle if he liked to have a rifle.'

A long and bitter debate followed, in which Irish, Liberal, and Conservative members took part. The Irish members, in almost every case, appealed to the Government even now to do something for the tenants; the Liberals replied, justifying the action of the Government. The next day, Tuesday, the 24th, another Irish debate arose on a motion of Mr. Parnell's on the Parliamentary relations of England and Ireland. On the following Thursday, in Committee of Supply, another Irish debate arose on the vote for the Irish constabulary estimates. This was in many ways a memorable debate. It was from the defence Mr. Forster made in this debate of the use of buckshot as ammunition for the Irish constabulary that the nickname of 'Buckshot' arose, which will, in all probability, be associated with his name as long as his name may be remembered. Furthermore, this debate was the first of several famous all-night sittings, which mark at intervals the career of the administration. The debate had begun on Thursday afternoon; it was protracted all through Thursday night and over Friday morning, and only came to an end shortly before 1 p.m. on the Friday, when the Government consented to an adjournment of the debate until the following Monday.

On the Monday, after further debate from the Irish members, the vote was finally carried. The Irish case against the constabulary was in some measure recognised by Mr. Forster, who stated that, although it was quite impossible then for the Executive to consent to the general disarmament of the constabulary force, yet Her Majesty's Government felt bound not to rest until they had placed Ireland in such a position as no longer to need the presence of this armed force. In some of Mr. Forster's speeches there were menacing allusions to the possibility of the revival of the abandoned coercive measures; but, on the other hand, Mr. Forster declined to promise to urge the calling of a winter session in case the evictions increased, in order to deal with the question. On September 7, the House was prorogued.

The rejection of the Compensation for Disturbance Bill and the inaction of the Government gave fresh impulse to the agitation in Ireland. Evicting landlords, encouraged by the failure of the Government measure, swelled the list of evictions; and, on the other hand, all landlords, good and bad alike, became the objects of popular antipathy. The Land League leaders, members of Parliament and others, advised the tenants' passive resistance of eviction and non-payment of rent, in the hope that, by a sort of general strike on the part of the tenantry, evictions might be delayed until the following session saw the introduction of the promised Ministerial measure. In fact, the Land League advised the tenants to form a sort of tenant trades union, for resisting not merely evictions, but the exactions of what they considered an unjust amount of rent above Griffith's valuation.

Griffith's valuation played such an important part in the

politics of this time, and was so frequently alluded to, that it may be well to give some idea of what it was. The valuation of Ireland was undertaken in 1830 on the recommendation of a Select Committee of the House of Commons in 1824. To insure uniform valuation an Act was passed in 1836 requiring all valuations of land to be based on a fixed scale of agricultural produce contained in the Act. The valuators were instructed to act in the same manner as if employed by a principal landlord dealing with a solvent tenant. The average valuation proved to be about twenty-five per cent. under the gross rental of the country. In 1844 a Select Committee of the House of Commons was appointed to reconsider the question, and an Act passed in 1846 changed the principle of valuation from a relative valuation of town lands, based on a fixed scale of agricultural produce, to a tenement valuation for poor-law rating to be made ' upon an estimate of the net annual value . . . of the rent for which, one year with another, the same might in its actual state be reasonably expected to let from year to year.' The two valuations gave substantially the same results. In 1852 another Valuation Act was passed, returning to the former principle of valuation by a fixed scale of agricultural produce; but Sir Richard Griffith's evidence in 1869 shows the valuation employed was a 'live-and-let-live valuation, according to the state of prices for five years previous to' the time of valuation.

Griffith's valuation was indeed but a rough-and-ready way of estimating the value of land. In many cases it was really above the worth of the land; in other cases it was below it. Still it was a reasonable basis enough, certainly far more reasonable than the rates of the rack-rents. The Land League speakers condemned all rents above Griffith's valuation—only, it must be remembered, in the period of probation while the Government was preparing its Land measure—and under their direction a practical strike was organised against the landlords extorting high rents. It ought to be borne in mind that the failure of the Government to pass its Compensation for Disturbance Bill, coupled with its announcement that it practically intended to reopen the Land question and introduce a new Land Bill, had driven the bad landlords in Ireland to desperation. They thought that the interval between the measure that had failed and the measure that was to come was the only time left to them, and they went to work vigorously to get all the money they could out of the land before the crash came, and the Government, in the formulas of the Opposition, 'interfered with the rights of property.'

It certainly did seem hard that the tenants should have been left by the Government at the mercy of landlords who were incited to make the most out of their tenancies before the new Land Act fell upon them. But as the Government had done nothing, the Land League advised the people to stand out for themselves; to pay no rent, and passively resist eviction. The supporters of the Land League had another enemy besides the landlord, in the person of the land-grabber, the man who took a farm from which his neighbour had been dispossessed. The strike was supported by a form of action, or rather inaction, which soon became historical.

Captain Boycott was an Englishman, an agent of Lord Earne, and a farmer at Lough Mask, in the wild and beautiful district of Connemara. In his capacity as agent he had served notices upon Lord Earne's tenants, and the tenantry suddenly retaliated in a most unexpected way by, in the language of schools and society, sending Captain Boycott to Coventry in a very thorough manner. The population of the region for miles round resolved not to have anything to do with him, and as far as they could prevent it not to allow any one else to have anything to do with him. His life appeared to be in danger; he had to claim police protection. His servants fled from him as servants fled from their masters in some plague-stricken Italian city; the awful sentence of excommunication could hardly have rendered him more helplessly alone for a time. No one would work for him; no one would supply him with food. He and his wife had to work in their own fields themselves in most unpleasant imitation of Theocritan shepherds and shepherdesses, and play out their grim eclogue in their deserted fields with the shadows of the armed constabulary ever at their heels.

The Orangemen of the North heard of Captain Boycott and his sufferings, and the way in which he was holding his ground, and they organised assistance and sent him down armed labourers from Ulster. To prevent civil war the authorities had to send a force of soldiers and police to Lough Mask, and Captain Boycott's harvests were brought in, and his potatoes dug by the armed Ulster labourers, guarded always by the little army. When the occupations of Ulstermen and army were over, Captain Boycott came to England for a time, but in the end he returned to Lough Mask, where, curiously enough, he is once again at peace with his neighbours, and is even popular, perhaps because he showed that he was a brave man.

The events at Lough Mask, however, gave rise to two things—to boycotting on the part of the Land League, and to the formation of a body known as emergency men, chiefly recruited from the Orange lodges. The business of the emergency men was to counteract, wherever it was possible, the operations of the League, by helping boycotted landlords and land-agents to gather in their harvests. Boycotting was freely employed by the League. It meant the practical excommunication of rack-renting landlords, evicting agents, and land-grabbers. No sympathiser with the League was supposed to have any dealings with the boycotted individuals; they were not to be worked for, bought from, sold to. The principle of boycotting was not aggressive; nothing was to be done to the obnoxious person, but, also, nothing was to be done for him. This was strictly legal. The law cannot compel a man to buy or sell with one of his fellows against his will. The responsible leaders of the Land League never countenanced other than legal agitation. Mr. Michael Davitt again and again put on record in public speeches his uncompromising opposition to all intimidation. 'Our League does not desire to intimidate any one who disagrees with us,' he said; 'while we abuse Coercion we must not be guilty of

Coercion;' and he made frequent appeals to his hearers in different parts of Ireland to 'abstain from all acts of violence and to repel every incentive to outrage.' 'Glorious indeed,' he said, 'will be our victory, and high in the estimation of mankind will our grand old fatherland stand, if we can so curb our passions and control our actions in this struggle for free land, as to march to success through privation and danger without resorting to the wild justice of revenge, or being guilty of anything which could sully the character of a brave and Christian people.'

Unfortunately, these good counsels were not always obeyed. Famine and eviction had sowed evil seed; men who had been evicted, men who were starving, who had seen their families and friends evicted, to die often enough of starvation on the cold roadside—these men were not in the temper which takes kindly to wise counsel. Outrages have invariably followed in the track of every Irish famine, and they followed now this latest famine. There were murders in different parts of the country; there were mutilations of cattle. These outrages were made the very most of by the enemies of the Land League. Scattered agrarian murders were spoken of as if each of them were a link in the chain of a widely-planned organisation of massacre. People found their deepest sympathies stirred by the sufferings of cattle and horses in Ireland, who never were known to feel one throb of compunction over the fashionable sin of torturing pigeons at Hurlingham.

But while most of the persons who acted thus knew little and cared less for the real condition of Ireland, there was one man who was studying the country with all the sympathy of one of the noblest natures now living on the earth. General Gordon—then known best to the world as 'Chinese' Gordon, destined now, perhaps, to be remembered chiefly as 'Soudan' Gordon—was in Ireland examining the Irish question for himself with kind, experienced eyes. He wrote a letter to a friend, which was published in the *Times* on December 3, 1880. 'I have been lately over the south-west of Ireland,' General

Gordon wrote, 'in the hope of discovering how some settlement could be made of the Irish question, which, like a fretting cancer, eats away our vitals as a nation.' After speaking of the 'complete lack of sympathy' between the landlord and tenant class, General Gordon went on: 'No half-measured Acts which left the landlords with any say to the tenantry of these portions of Ireland will be of any use. They would be rendered—as past Land Acts in Ireland have been—quite abortive, for the landlords will insert clauses to do away with their force. Any half-measures will only place the Government face to face with the people of Ireland as the champions of the landlord interest.'

General Gordon then proposed that the Government should, at a cost of eighty millions, convert the greater part of the south-west of Ireland into Crown lands, in which landlords should have no power of control. 'For the rest of Ireland I would pass an Act allowing free sale of leases, fair rents, and a Government valuation. In conclusion, I must say from all accounts, and my own observations, that the state of our fellow-countrymen in the parts I have named is worse than that of any people in the world, let alone Europe. I believe that these people are made as we are, that they are patient beyond belief, loyal, but at the same time broken-spirited and desperate, living on the verge of starvation in places where we would not keep our cattle. . . . Our comic prints do an infinity of harm by their caricatures. Firstly, the caricatures are not true, for the crime in Ireland is not greater than that in England; and, secondly, they exasperate the people on both sides of the Channel, and they do no good. It is ill to laugh and scoff at a question which affects our existence.' It is impossible to avoid reflecting with melancholy bitterness on the different aspect that the Irish question would now wear if a man like Chinese Gordon could have been sent to administrate the country in the place of the egotistical and ill-conditioned politician who succeeded to, and was more noxious than, famine.

Still there were outrages, and Ireland was disturbed.

The Land League claimed that it did much to prevent outrage; that the unavoidable violence consequent upon the famine and the evictions would have been far greater but for them; that secret conspiracy and midnight outrage were notably diminished by their open agitation. The Government, on the other hand, declared that the Land League was guilty of inciting to outrage. A State prosecution was commenced against the officials of the League—Mr. Parnell, M.P., Mr. Dillon, M.P., Mr. T. D. Sullivan, M.P., Mr. Sexton, M.P., Mr. Biggar, M.P., Mr. Patrick Egan, Treasurer of the Land League, Mr. Thomas Brennan, Secretary of the Land League, and some eight others—on a charge of seditious conspiracy. The jury were unable to agree, and the trial came to nothing.

In the meantime the country was becoming daily more agitated, and Mr. Forster daily more unpopular. His appointment had at first been hailed with satisfaction by many of what may be called the popular party, and with anger and alarm by the landlords, who regarded him as the herald of startling land changes. But Mr. Forster soon became as unpopular with the national party in Ireland as ever Castlereagh had been. They alleged that he was completely under Castle influence; that he only saw through the eyes and heard through the ears of Castle officials; that he came out prepared to be popular and settle everything at once, and that his vanity was keenly hurt by the disappointment; that, finding the forces he had to deal with were difficult and complex, he could only propose to deal with them by crushing them down. He was soon known to be in favour of a revival of the policy of Coercion. Lord Cowper, the Lord Lieutenant, was an amiable, but by no means a strong, man; in the Cabinet he feebly echoed Mr. Forster's opinions, and in the Cabinet Mr. Forster was able to carry the day on Irish matters when he proposed the revival of Coercion. It was soon blown abroad that the Government intended to bring in a Land Bill for Ireland, and to balance it with a Coercion Bill; furthermore that they intended to bring in the Coercion Bill first, and the Land Bill afterwards.

Parliament met on Thursday, January 6, 1881. It found the Radicalism of the Ministry strengthened by the appointment of Mr. Leonard Courtney as Under Secretary for the Home Department. The Queen's Speech was able to announce the conclusion of the Afghan war, and the intention not to occupy Candahar, an intimation that sounded most unpleasantly in the ears of the Imperial party. The Boer war was spoken of; the Greek frontier was declared to be under the consideration of the great Powers; mention was made of certain measures of domestic interest, chief among them being the Bills for the abolition of flogging in the army and the navy. But undoubtedly the most important part of the royal speech referred to Ireland. The multiplication of agrarian crimes, and the insecurity of life and property, demanded the introduction of coercive measures; while, on the other hand, the speech admitted that the condition of Ireland called for an extension of the Land Act principles of 1870. A measure for the establishment of county government in Ireland was also mentioned.

The debate on the address in the House of Lords was chiefly remarkable for a brilliant and bitter speech from Lord Beaconsfield. In the eight months that had elapsed since the new Ministry had come into power, much had happened to embarrass them and dim their triumph. Lord Beaconsfield was naturally not willing to spare his antagonists the recapitulation of their difficulties. In the lifelong duel between Mr. Gladstone and Lord Beaconsfield there came in the end to be an amount of accusation and recrimination of so personal a nature as almost to recall the traditions of the days of Bolingbroke and Walpole. Mr. Gladstone's Midlothian speeches had struck hard at Lord Beaconsfield, and Lord Beaconsfield was not now likely to let slip the chance of retaliation upon his antagonist. He dwelt with scornful emphasis upon the complete repudiation of Tory policy which had been so loudly trumpeted when Mr. Gladstone came into office. What had their principles of repudiation brought the Government? he asked. Retreat from Afghanistan, abandonment of Candahar, a Berlin Conference which had reopened the closed Eastern question and nearly plunged Europe into war.

But Lord Beaconsfield was naturally most exulting when he came to the relations of the Government with Ireland. He had been mocked at for his prognostication of danger; the new Ministry were satisfied with the condition of Ireland, and were prepared to govern it without the worn-out Tory methods of Peace Preservation Acts: and now, after little more than half a year of trial, the Government were coming before the House, confessing their failure, and seeking to be strengthened once again by those coercive measures which they had so lightly rejected with every other portion of the policy of their predecessors. Lord Beaconsfield had a clever case, and he made the most of it. With a brilliant maliciousness which recalled the days when Mr. Disraeli was still a young man with the world before him, Lord Beaconsfield appealed to the Lords not to do anything in this juncture which might weaken the Administration in their late effort to deal with their Irish difficulty.

Almost at the same time that Lord Beaconsfield was attacking the policy of the Government in the Lords, Mr. Gladstone was defending it in the Commons. He dwelt upon the happy conclusion of the Montenegrin difficulty; he was hopeful of a fortunate settlement of the Greek difficulty; he passed lightly over the Afghan war, touched upon the Boer war, and justified the Government in not making the Basuto war—with which they had nothing to do, and for which they were in no measure responsible—their own. But the chief point of Mr. Gladstone's speech, as indeed of every speech delivered then and for a long time to come, was of course the Irish question. The Prime Minister denied that the Ministry had any reason to feel humiliation at what had taken place. He justified them in not calling Parliament together earlier, on the ground that they were determined to do their best with the existing law before appealing for stronger measures. In a few remarkable sentences he censured the late Government for the manner in which they had chosen to act upon the existing law : they put the law into effect against four men, three of whom were utterly insignificant. 'One of them, indeed,' Mr. Gladstone added, thinking of Mr. Davitt, 'has since proved himself to be a man of great ability, but was not then of much note.' 'The late Government did not aim their weapons at the chief offenders, but contented themselves with charging comparatively insignificant men, and, having charged them, did not bring them to trial.' 'The method of threatening without striking is, in our opinion,' said Mr. Gladstone, amid the loud cheers of his party, 'the worst course of action that could have been adopted;' and he pointed to the State trials then going on as a proof of the more decided action and stronger purposes of the new Ministry. He considered that they had done their duty in watching the country for a while under the operation of the ordinary law. He thought they had now waited long enough, but could not admit that they had waited too long, though he declined to allow that the coercion which he thought necessary was any remedy for the grievances of Ireland. Hence the announcement with regard to the new Land Act. He claimed that the Land Act of 1870 had not been a failure; but he confessed that the provisions of the Act 'have not prevented undue and frequent augmentations of rent which have not been justified by the real value of the holding, but have been brought in in consequence of the superior strength of the landlord.'

Mr. Forster had given notice before Mr. Gladstone spoke of the introduction of Bills for the better protection of persons and property in Ireland, and to amend the law relating to a carrying and possession of arms; and Mr. Gladstone had announced his intention of moving that these Bills should have priority over all other business. But these Bills were not destined to be introduced for some days to come. The address was still to be disposed of, and there were many amendments to it to be considered and discussed, several of these being moved by Irish members and relating to Irish affairs. But as, according to Thackeray, even the Eastern Counties' trains come in at last, so, too, the debate on the address came to an end at last. On Thursday, January 20, after eleven days of debate, the report of the address was agreed to amid general cheering.

But already the Irish members had roused the anger of the Government. Most of the speeches on the address had been Irish speeches, the speeches of Irish members on the various Irish questions. Before the debate had concluded, Lord Hartington had attacked the obstructive policy of the Irish members, and warned them that their action might compel the House to come to some understanding by which the process of business should be facilitated. If every day added to the debate on the address staved off the introduction of Coercion, so too, Lord Hartington urged, it delayed the introduction of the promised Land Act. Lord Edmond Fitzmaurice and Mr. Thorold Rogers formed themselves into a sort of amateur committee on obstruction. They plunged into records of old rulings, they became learned in antique principles of procedure and venerable points of order, and they addressed to the *Times*, three days before the debate on the address concluded, a long letter in which they pointed out the existence of certain seventeenth-century orders of the House. One of these ruled that 'if any man speak impertinently, or beside the question in hand, it standeth with the order of the House for Mr. Speaker to interrupt him, and to know the pleasure of the House whether they will further hear him;' an order which was sanctioned and strengthened by later rulings.

On Monday, January 24, 1881, Mr. Forster introduced his first Coercion measure. Mr. Forster made out a long and elaborate case in justification of the measure. He presented a return of outrages to the House of Commons which looked alarming at first, but which Mr. Labouchere showed to be somewhat curiously manufactured. In many cases outrages were of the simplest description; in many more the number was swelled by an ingenious process of subdivision, so that one outrage was made to stand for several, by the simple process of multiplying any given offence by the number of men committing it. The total number of agrarian outrages in Ireland in the year 1880 was 2,590. Returns of agrarian crimes in Ireland had been made since 1844, but not before, and the highest return since that date was for the year 1845, the first year of the great famine, in which year the list of outrages numbered 1,920, or thirty-five per cent. less than in 1880. Excluding threatening letters, the number of outrages in 1880 was 1,253, as contrasted with 950 in 1845, or thirty-two per cent. higher. Moreover, as the population of Ireland was only 5,000,000 in 1880, to 8,000,000 in 1845, the proportion of outrages in 1880 was really more than double the proportion of outrages in 1845. There were, indeed, few cases of murder, or attempts at murder; the outrages were chiefly intimidation by personal violence, by injury to property and cattle, and by threatening letters. The number of outrages of this kind had greatly increased during the last three months of 1880, and the area of intimidation was extending. One hundred and fifty-three persons were under the personal protection of two policemen on the first day of the new year, and 1,149 persons were watched over by the police.

Mr. Forster urged that the existing law was not strong enough to grapple with this system of intimidation. The instruments of this intimidation were, however, well known to the police; they were generally old Fenians and Ribbonmen, the *mauvais sujets* of their neighbourhood, dissolute ruffians and village tyrants. The new Bill would give the Lord Lieutenant power by warrant to arrest any person reasonably suspected of treason, treasonable felony, or treasonable practices, and the commission, whether before or after the Act, of crimes of intimidation or incitement thereto. By this means the Government would be able to lay their hands upon the *mauvais sujets*, the village tyrants, and, by depriving the Land League of its police, render it powerless.

Naturally an animated debate followed. The Irish Nationalists, of course, opposed the measure. Moderate Irishmen, like Dr. Lyons, Mr. Givan, Mr. Richardson, and Mr. Litton, either opposed the precedence of coercive to remedial measures, or urged the introduction of a Bill to stay unfair eviction pending the introduction of the remedial legislation. Mr. Bradlaugh did not consider that a case had been made out for a Coercion Bill. The Conservative party, of course, supported the Government. The debate was adjourned on the Monday night, and its resumption was interrupted for a couple of days by the first all-night sitting of the year. On the day after Mr. Forster's introduction of the Coercion Bill, Mr. Gladstone moved to declare urgency for the Coercive Bills, and so give them precedence over all other public business. The Irish Nationalists at once set themselves to opposing this by every means in their power. The new standing order prevented the taking of many divisions, as it allowed individual members only two motions for adjournment; so the Irish members confined themselves to making speeches, which were incessantly interrupted by calls to order from the chair.

Mr. Biggar, at a comparatively early period of the debate, got into a conflict with authority which led to his being suspended from the sitting; whereupon he immediately withdrew, and, ascending the heights of the strangers' gallery, watched the conflict with unwearying interest from that elevation, as Ivanhoe followed from his turret the fortunes of the Black Knight and his fellows. The struggle, indeed, was sufficiently interesting to be worth sitting out. It was fought—this being but a first essay for the year—with sufficient good-humour on both sides. The hours waned, but there came no waning in the animation of the speakers on both sides. Members came and went; ingenious little plans of relays for relieving guard were arranged. Morning came, and brought with it a fog scarcely less obscure than night. It was not bright enough till eleven o'clock to extinguish the gas. Very dismal the chamber showed when daylight did come, as unwashed, unbrushed, with weary, sleepy faces and tumbled clothes, the members faced each other. For three hours more the fight went on, and then, at two o'clock, Mr.

Gladstone's motion was agreed to, and the House, not unnaturally, immediately adjourned to wash, eat, and sleep.

This was but the prelude to a series of stormy scenes in the House, each one surpassing its predecessors in bitterness and unpleasantness. The debate on the Coercion Bill was resumed on the Thursday, and was remarkable for a speech from Mr. Bright. Mr. Bright had kept silence—with the exception of a protest against obstruction—since the beginning of the session, and it had been whispered that he was so silent because he was not in accord with his colleagues on the Irish question. He was roused from his silence by a speech of The O'Donoghue's. The O'Donoghue was at this period of his varied political career an ardent supporter of Mr. Parnell. He sat in opposition to Government, and made himself conspicuous as an aggressive patriot and unfailing opponent of the Government. He declared that the Land League differed in no respect from the Anti-Corn Law League, and taunted Mr. Bright by asking what trials followed the agitation and the denunciation of landlords which belonged to the movement of which Mr. Bright and Mr. Cobden were the heads.

A little later in the debate Mr. Bright rose and spoke. In a speech of great bitterness Mr. Bright attacked the conduct of the Irish Parliamentary party. He denied angrily that any parallel existed between the action of the Land League and the Anti-Corn Law League. With all the indignation of which Mr. Bright is a master, and with more than his usual vehemence, he flung himself in a very fury of passionate oratory upon the Irish opponents of the Government. It almost seemed as if Mr. Bright were determined to make it plain, by the very rage and whirlwind of his passion, how completely unfounded were those rumours which hinted that he was at odds with his colleagues in the Cabinet on the Irish question. He assailed his opponents with all the eloquence at his command; and though the speaker was now old, the strength and power of that eloquence were still sufficiently impressive, even to those at whom all its fierce invective was levelled.

The severance of the extreme Irish party and the Government was now complete. Mr. Bright, who had often supported Ireland before and was looked upon as a true friend by the Irish people, was now one of the bitterest opponents of the whole national movement and of its Parliamentary leaders. The Irish national press was fiercely exasperated to find Mr. Bright supporting Coercion for Ireland. He had indeed voted for Coercion before in his younger days, but he had always been eloquent against it, and his utterances were brought up against him by the Irish papers. They reminded him that in 1866 he had described Coercion for Ireland as an 'ever-failing and ever-poisonous remedy;' and they asked him why he recommended the unsuccessful and venomous legislation now. They pointed to his speech of 1849, in which he said: 'The treatment of this Irish malady remains ever the same. We have nothing for it still but force and alms.' They quoted from his speech of 1847: 'I am thoroughly convinced that everything the Government or Parliament can do for Ireland will be unavailing unless the foundation of the work be laid deep and well, by clearing away the fetters under which land is now held, so that it may become the possession of real owners, and be made instrumental to the employment and sustentation of the people. Honourable gentlemen opposite may fancy themselves interested in maintaining the present system; but there is surely no interest they can have in it which will weigh against the safety and prosperity of Ireland.'

Such a passage as this might have served, it was urged, as a motto for the Land League itself. What other doctrine did the Land League uphold but that the land should become the possession of real owners, and be made instrumental to the employment and sustentation of the people? Might not the Land League have fairly asked the Government what interest it could have in the present system of land which would weigh against the safety and prosperity of Ireland? Had not Mr. Bright told them too, in 1866, that 'the great evil of Ireland is this: that the Irish people—the Irish nation

—are dispossessed of the soil, and what we ought to do is to provide for and aid in their restoration to it by all measures of justice'? He disliked the action of the Irish members now because they were acting against the Liberal party; but had he not said, in 1866, also: 'If Irishmen were united, if you hundred and five members were for the most part agreed, you might do almost anything that you liked;' and further said: 'If there were a hundred more members, the representatives of large and free constituencies, then your cry would be heard, and the people would give you that justice which a class has so long denied you'? 'Exactly,' replied his Irish critics. 'We have now a united body of Irishmen, the largest and most united the House has ever seen, and you do not seem to look kindly upon it. You do not seem to be acting up to your promise made in Dublin in 1866.' 'If I have in past times felt an unquenchable sympathy with the sufferings of your people, you may rely upon it that if there be an Irish member to speak for Ireland, he will find me heartily by his side.' At the same speech in Dublin, Mr. Bright said: 'If I could be in all other things the same, but in birth an Irishman, there is not a town in this island I would not visit for the purpose of discussing the great Irish question, and of rousing my countrymen to some great and united action.' 'This is exactly what we are doing,' said his Land League critics; 'why do you denounce us now? Why do you vote for Coercion Acts to prevent the discussion of the great Irish question?'

The next day, Friday, January 28, while the impression of Mr. Bright's speech was still fresh in the minds of the House, Mr. Gladstone made a speech which, viewed as a piece of Parliamentary attack, certainly far surpassed it. With all his eloquence Mr. Gladstone flung himself against his enemies, justified the introduction of Coercion in the disorganised condition of Ireland, and bitterly denounced many of the speeches of Mr. Parnell and Mr. Biggar. From a dramatic point of view the scene in the chamber was singularly impressive. If the sheer force of eloquence and anger and the support of a powerful and enthusiastic majority could have done it, the opposition would have come to an end then and there, and the Coercion Bill been carried at once. Never since the night when Sir Charles Dilke made his famous speech, and Mr. Auberon Herbert announced himself too as a Republican, had the House witnessed such a scene, though since then stormy scenes have been less infrequent. Mr. Gladstone was playing the part of Jupiter suppressing the revolted gods. Wine, says Macaulay, was the spell which unlocked the fine intellect of Addison. Passion is the spell which most surely unlocks Mr. Gladstone's skill as an orator of attack. The fury of his indignation swept over the House and stirred it to its depths, arousing tumultuous enthusiasm in the majority of his hearers, and angry protest from the minority he was assailing. The pale, unmoved face of Mr. Parnell occasionally showed through the storm as he rose to correct the Prime Minister in his quotations from his speeches, and was howled and shouted, if not into silence, at least into being inaudible.

Vague rumours floated about the House of Commons on the Monday evening that there would be troublesome work ere night, but at first there seemed no promise of the excited and strenuous fighting which kept the weary Commons awake through successive days. The Irish members were determined to resist the Coercion Bill in every stage to the utmost. They challenged Fate, in the shape of the Ministry, to come into the lists and fight it out, and the result was the longest sitting then on record. The hours came and went, the gray dawn stole on the heels of night, and ugly night again came breathing at the heels of day, and found the Commons still wrangling, still dividing, still calling to order, still stupidly sleeping or vainly trying to follow the arguments of the various speakers. The scene was full of interest to those—and there were some —who had the courage to see it out from the watch-towers of the Speaker's gallery.

As the time went on the appearance of the House was not without elements of humour. One member of the Third

Party, as the Irish party were called, found the atmosphere cold, and insisted upon addressing the House in a long ulster, resembling the gaberdine of Noah in the toy-shop arks. On the Treasury bench Lord Hartington, grimly erect, doggedly surveyed the obstructives. He was curiously in contrast with Mr. Forster, who sat doubled, or, rather, crumpled up, in an attitude of extreme depression. The occupants of the front Opposition bench wore an air of bland unconcern. 'This is not our fault,' they seemed to say, ' but it is not uninteresting, and we do not mind seeing you through with it.'

At ten minutes to five o'clock on the Tuesday morning the Speaker left the chair ; the clerk at the table gravely informed the House of the unavoidable absence of Mr. Speaker, and his place was taken by Mr. Lyon Playfair. Still the debate went on. Irish member succeeded Irish member in lengthy speeches, interrupted by incessant calls to order from all parts of the House and from the chair. Somewhere about six o'clock the motion for the adjournment of the debate was defeated by 141 to 27 : majority, 114. The debate was then resumed on the original motion, and Mr. Healy immediately moved the adjournment of the House. At twenty-five minutes past one on Tuesday afternoon the deputy-chairman left the chair, which was reoccupied by the Speaker.

A small side discussion sprang up at this point, Mr. Parnell contending that, by the standing orders of the House, the Speaker had not the right to return to his place after that place had been taken by the deputy-chairman, until the next sitting of the House, a point which the Speaker ruled was based on a misconception of the order. At ten minutes to three the motion for the adjournment of the House was divided upon, and was lost by a majority of 204 ; the numbers being, ayes, 21, nays, 225. Still the debate went on, without any sign of flagging determination on either side. The adjournment of the debate was then moved by Mr. Daly, and this question was fought out for some time and divided upon —23 to 163 : majority against, 140. The debate was then resumed on Dr. Lyon's amendment to the main question, and the adjournment of the House moved. At half-past eleven on the Tuesday night the Speaker again left the chair, and his place was again taken by Mr. Lyon Playfair. At midnight Sir Stafford Northcote appealed alike to the chair and the Government to do something to put an end to the obstruction. A little later on the debate was enlivened by a wordy wrangle between Mr. (now Sir Frederick) Milbank and Mr. Biggar. Mr. Milbank complained that Mr. Biggar had used offensive language to him in the chamber, and, in consequence Mr. Milbank, later on, in the lobby, addressed opprobrious terms to Mr. Biggar. Mr. Biggar denied having used the words attributed to him, whereupon Mr. Milbank apologised to the House.

By this time a fresh division had been taken, and the motion for adjournment negatived by 22 to 197: majority, 175. At ten minutes to five on Wednesday morning the second unsuccessful attempt to count the House was made. At nine o'clock the Speaker resumed the chair, and, immediately rising, made perhaps one of the most remarkable speeches ever delivered from the chair. The Speaker observed that the motion to bring in the Bill had been under discussion for five days, and that during that time most of the opposition was purely obstructive. By the existing rule nothing could be done to stop this obstruction; but the Speaker was prepared to take upon himself the responsibility of ending it by declining to call upon any more members, and by putting the questions at once from the chair. This announcement was received with tumultuous cheering, and the Speaker then put the motion for Dr. Lyon's amendment, which was defeated on a division by 164 to 19: majority, 145. The Speaker then proceeded to put the main question. An Irish member rose, but the Speaker refused to hear him. Then the whole Irish party stood up, shouted for some seconds the cry of 'Privilege!' —which had not been heard in the House since the day when Charles I. came looking for his five members—and, bowing to the chair, left the chamber in a body. The Bill was immediately brought in by Mr. Forster. Mr. Forster then explained to the House that on the previous Friday he had given into the hands of Mr. Gladstone a speech which he believed to be by Mr. Parnell, and which Mr. Gladstone quoted from as being by Mr. Parnell, but which was, as a matter of fact, delivered by another person. The House then adjourned until twelve o'clock of the same day, when it met again to discuss the second reading of the Coercion Bill.

The Irish members who had left the House in a body that morning did not, however, intend to follow the example set them by Pulteney and his followers, in the early part of the last century, and secede from the House for any length of time. When the House met again at mid-day, they returned to their places in order to criticise the action of the Speaker in bringing the debate to a close on his own motion. The Speaker, however, ruled that the matter was not a question of privilege, and could not be discussed then, but must be brought forward on a specific motion. The adjournment of the House was then moved by Mr. A. M. Sullivan, and supported by Mr. Joseph Cowen, Mr. Labouchere, Lord Randolph Churchill, and Mr. Shaw, and argued upon until nearly six o'clock, when it was defeated on division by 278 to 44 : majority, 234 ; after which, it being six o'clock, and the day being Wednesday, the House of necessity adjourned.

The next day, however, witnessed a still more exciting scene, compared with which any mere prolongation of debate seemed tame and colourless. At question time Mr. Parnell suddenly rose and asked if it was true that Mr. Michael Davitt had been arrested that day at one o'clock. There was a murmur of surprise, followed immediately by a deep silence as Sir William Harcourt rose to reply. 'Yes, sir,' was the answer of the Home Secretary, amid the wildest cheering from both sides of the House. Had some new conquest or some great victory been announced, it could not have been greeted with greater rapture. Human nature and human voices have their limits, and certainly the limits of human voices were severely taxed that day when it was definitely announced that Michael Davitt was once again in prison.

When the cheering abated, Sir William Harcourt went on to state that the Irish Secretary and he, after consultation with their colleagues and the law officers of the Crown, had come to the conclusion that Mr. Davitt's conduct was incompatible with the conditions of his ticket-of-leave. Mr. Parnell tried to find out what condition of ticket-of-leave Mr. Davitt had broken, but the Speaker called upon Mr. Gladstone, who was waiting to submit to the House his urgency motion. Mr. Gladstone had risen and begun to speak when Mr. Dillon rose also to a point of order. What the point of order was the House was not fated to hear; for amid much noise and shouting from all parts of the House, the Speaker rose and declared Mr. Gladstone in possession of the House. Mr. Dillon, instead of sitting down when the Speaker rose, and then rising again to make his point of order clear, remained standing with folded arms facing the speaking Speaker, and demanding his privilege of speech. A few seconds of excited confusion followed, few members of the House remaining silent. The majority shouted against Mr. Dillon. The Irish minority shouted scarcely less loudly for him. 'Name him,' vociferated English members; to which the Irish members responded by shouting, 'Point of order.' Then the Speaker gravely named Mr. Dillon for disregarding the authority of the chair, not, as he afterwards explained, for rising to a point of order while Mr. Gladstone was speaking, but for remaining on his feet after the Speaker had risen. Mr. Dillon now sat down, and Mr. Gladstone, rising, immediately moved the usual formula, familiar enough even then, but destined within the next half-hour to become much more familiar, that the offending member should be suspended from the service of the House for the remainder of the sitting. A division was taken and Mr. Gladstone's motion carried by 395 to 33: majority, 362. The Speaker then called upon Mr. Dillon to withdraw. Mr. Dillon rose again and strove to speak, but the shouts with which he was greeted rendered him practically inaudible. He was understood to announce that he refused to withdraw. The Speaker immediately called upon the serjeant-at-arms to remove Mr. Dillon. At first Mr. Dillon refused to move, but at a signal from the serjeant several attendants advanced into the House, whereupon, as if accepting this as symbolic of sufficient force to remove him by physical strength, Mr. Dillon got up and left the House. All that happened immediately after was an incoherent medley. Mr. A. M. Sullivan spoke amid vehement clamour against the Speaker, who explained that he had named Mr. Dillon, not for interrupting Mr. Gladstone on a call to order, but for remaining on his feet when the Speaker rose.

Mr. Gladstone now made a further effort to go on with his speech, and was at once interrupted by The O'Donoghue, who loudly moved the adjournment of the House. The Speaker taking no notice of this, Mr. Parnell jumped up and called out that he moved that Mr. Gladstone should be no longer heard. Amid stentorian cheers from his own party and indignant shouts from the rest of the House, Mr. Parnell reiterated his motion in defiance of the warning of the Speaker, and was immediately named. Mr. Gladstone again made the motion for expulsion, which was carried by a majority of 405 to 7, the Irish members refusing to leave their seats and vote. On the reassembling of the House, Mr. Parnell refused to withdraw until the serjeant-at-arms had gone through the same ceremony with him as with Mr. Dillon, when he retired amid the plaudits of his party.

It must here be remarked that, whatever may be the opinion as to the wisdom, policy, or propriety of Mr. Parnell's conduct on this occasion, there was absolutely nothing 'disorderly' in the Parliamentary sense about it. But a little time before Mr. Gladstone had moved, and moved successfully, that a member should be no longer heard, and it had been urged in defence of that motion that it was perfectly permissible, although it had not been made in Parliament for something like a couple of centuries. Now, if it was permissible for Mr. Gladstone to put this venerable rule into action against an Irish member, it was equally permissible for an Irish member to put it into practice against Mr. Gladstone. We are not speaking now of the good or bad taste of such a line of action, nor do we need to be reminded of the impossibility of carrying on the business of any legislative assembly if any member might interrupt it by motions that other members be not heard. But the Prime Minister had himself revived this antiquated form; he had drawn it out from the dust of centuries in order to silence an unwelcome speaker; it had received the full sanction of Parliament, and until Parliament repealed or altered it, it was in full force. As the rules binding the House of Commons affect all members equally—as no member, whether he be at the head of the Government or not, has any privilege whatever of making any motion which is denied to any other member—it is clear that Mr. Parnell was as much in his Parliamentary right as Mr. Gladstone in moving that a member should not be heard. So much for the mere question of the motion, the revival of which Mr. Gladstone was himself probably the first to regret.

After the division had been taken, and the leader of the Irish party removed, Lord Richard Grosvenor, the Liberal Whip, announced that the Irish members had refused to leave their seats and enter the division lobby, a line of action which Mr. Gladstone immediately expressed a hope that the Speaker would find some means of dealing with. He was, however, once more interrupted, this time by Mr. Finigan, member for Ennis, who, following the example of Mr. Parnell, again proposed that Mr. Gladstone should be no longer heard. The Speaker named Mr. Finigan; Mr. Gladstone, for the third time, made the suspension motion, and a division was again taken, and the motion carried by 405 to 2, the Irish members again expressing their protest against the whole proceeding by remaining in their seats and refusing to vote. The Speaker cautioned them that he would regard this abstention as defiance of the authority of the chair, and the Clerk of the House took down their names.

When Mr. Finigan had been removed from the House, after the same fashion as Mr. Dillon and Mr. Parnell, the Speaker called the attention of the House to the conduct of the Irish members, and 'named' them at once. There were twenty-eight of them in all. Mr. Gladstone immediately rose and moved for their suspension in a body, and the motion was carried by 410 to 6, the abstaining members, as before, refusing to vote. Then came a strange scene, such as had never been witnessed in the House of Commons before. The name of each member was read out in turn by the Speaker, as he called upon him to withdraw. Each member called upon answered to his name with a short speech condemning the action of the Government, and refusing to go unless removed by superior force. To each member making such announcement, the serjeant-at-arms advanced and touched him solemnly on the shoulder. In most cases the member so touched at once rose and walked out; one or two exceptionally stalwart members, however, refused to go until the serjeant-at-arms approached them with such a muster of attendants as made it evident that he commanded sufficient force to compel withdrawal. For half an hour this process of naming, speech-making, and removal went on. At length the bulk of the Irish members were expelled, and had rallied in the conference room, where they drew up an address to the people of Ireland, urging them to remain quiet in spite of the indignity offered to their representatives. Then, for the fourth time, Mr. Gladstone rose and essayed to go on with his motion.

But, in the meantime, some few Irish members who had not been present hitherto in the House had arrived, and through their opposition shared their comrades' fate. First Mr. O'Kelly, then Mr. O'Donnell, moved that Mr. Gladstone be no longer heard, and were named, suspended, and removed, while three others—Mr. Molloy, Mr. Richard Power, and Mr. O'Shaughnessy—went through the same process for refusing to take part in the division, and remaining in their seats while the division went on. Then, none of the Irish members who followed the lead of Mr. Parnell being left in the House, Mr. Gladstone began his urgency motion for the sixth time, and proceeded with it without further interruption.

After the *coup d'état* by which the Speaker brought the

debate on the introduction of the Coercion Bill to an end, the Government felt the necessity of altering the rules of the House so far as to meet with such emergencies in the future in a more legal manner. A set of rules was accordingly drawn up, nominally by the Speaker, for the regulation of the business of the House when the state of public business should be declared urgent. These rules limited the occasions and the scope of motions for adjournment of either the House or the debate, gave the Speaker power of calling the attention of the House to continued tediousness and irrelevancy on the part of a member, and of taking the general sense of the House on any debate, and, if supported by a three-fourths majority, of putting the question without further debate. The rules further prevented the possibility of debate on the motion for the House to go into committee on any matter declared urgent, and limited members to a single speech. These rules were laid on the table of the House by the Speaker on Wednesday, February 9, 1881. The long-argued-about principle of *clôture*—or closure, to give what has become an English institution its English name—was of course conceded in the rule which allowed the Speaker, when presiding over a debate governed by the urgency rules, to appeal to the general sense of the House, and, if supported by a three-fourths majority, to put the question at once from the chair without any further debate.

The debate on the Coercion Bill was not concluded very rapidly. On Wednesday, February 23, 1881, the Bill was still in committee, and Mr. Gladstone, in order to accelerate its progress, moved that on the next day at seven the debate should come to an end, and the third reading be moved without discussion on any amendments that might be left unconsidered at that time. There was no debate permissible upon this motion, which was moved by Lord Hartington in the absence of Mr. Gladstone, who was confined to his room for a few days by an accident—he had slipped on the ice near his house, and hurt his head—and was carried by 371 to 53: majority, 318. At seven o'clock, accordingly, the debate was cut short by the Speaker; the remaining amendments were divided upon without debate, and the third reading moved for by Mr. Forster. The third reading was carried in the Commons the next day, Friday, February 25, by 231 to 36 : majority, 245. The Bill was then sent up to the House of Lords, where it passed rapidly through all its stages ; was read a third time on Wednesday, March 2, and received the royal assent by commission on the same day.

The Arms Bill was introduced in the Commons on Tuesday, March 1, by Sir William Harcourt, in the absence of Mr. Forster ; and its third reading was carried on Friday, March 11, by 236 to 26 — majority, 210 — and was passed in the Lords on the following Friday. During its passage through the Commons there were some heated debates on the relationship of the American Fenians with the Irish Land Leaguers, in one of which, on Thursday, March 3, Mr. Healy suffered suspension for charging the Home Secretary with breaches of truth and usual disingenuousness. Mr. O'Donnell was suspended on Tuesday, March 8, after a dispute with Mr. Playfair on a point of order.

In the meantime the excitement in Ireland was increasing. While the Coercion debates were going on, Mr. Parnell had gone across to Paris, accompanied by Mr. O'Kelly, and obtained an interview with Victor Hugo, who was expected to issue some manifesto in favour of Ireland. Victor Hugo compared Ireland to Poland struggling against Russia, but he wrote nothing on the subject, either in prose or verse. The interview, however, provoked a remonstrance from the great Catholic organ, the *Univers*, which warned Mr. Parnell that it was not well for the leaders of a Catholic cause and country to seek for the alliance of men like Victor Hugo and his friends. Mr. Parnell had an interview with M. Rochefort on the one hand, and with the Archbishop of Paris on the other. Just at that moment, when people were saying that there would be a split between the Nationalists and the Catholic clergy on account of the friendship of M. Rochefort, an event occurred which served to show how much the Irish priests and the Irish people were in agreement as to the Land League and the national cause

T

generally. In Ireland a Ladies' Land League had been formed, with Miss Anna Parnell—a sister of Mr. Parnell—for its president. Its object was to assist the existing Land League in every possible way—by raising funds, by inquiring into the cases of eviction, and by affording relief to evicted tenants. As soon as this new organisation came into existence it was assailed by Archbishop M'Cabe of Dublin. In an angry pastoral he denounced the participation of women in the strife of politics as at once immodest and wicked. Mr. A. M. Sullivan, one of the most Catholic of Irish Catholic members of Parliament, immediately wrote a reply defending the Ladies' Land League, and justifying and approving of the manner in which the women of Ireland proposed to come to the assistance of their husbands, fathers, and brothers. Mr. A. M. Sullivan's letter had not long been written when the Ladies' Land League found a still stronger ally, and Archbishop M'Cabe a still more formidable opponent, in Archbishop Croke, of Cashel. From the rock which has reminded so many travellers of the Athenian Acropolis, Archbishop Croke launched an epistle which Jerome might have envied for its vigorous distinctness. The Archbishop of Cashel had nothing but praise for the Ladies' Land League, and for their eloquent champion. In a moment Archbishop Croke was the hero of the national party in Ireland. They greeted him with joy as a proof that the Church was on their side; and when he went, shortly after, on a sort of tour of inspection through a great part of Ireland, he was received everywhere with a display of the most enthusiastic homage and devotion.

Long before Archbishop Croke had come so prominently to the front, many of the priests had shown their sympathy with, and approval of, the Land League doctrines; but after the action of the Archbishop of Cashel, their sympathy and approval became more openly and markedly displayed. Day by day the ranks of the League were swelled by Irish ecclesiastics of all orders. It might be fairly said that, roughly speaking, all the younger priests throughout the country were in cordial sympathy with the Land League, and a very large number of the elder priests as well. It was this sympathy between the priests and the people which gave the Land League a great part of its strength; it was the eagerness of the people to be in accord with their priests which made them receive Archbishop Croke's pronouncement with so much delight, and listen to his counsels with as much readiness as if they had come from the lips of Parnell or Davitt.

When the Coercion Acts were carried, Mr. John Dillon went over to Ireland and began a series of speeches in different parts of the country, supporting the League and assailing the Government. On the one side, the League was being upheld from pulpit and platform; on the other, the Executive was choking its prisons with its arrests of 'suspected' Land Leaguers. Evictions had not decreased, and there were frequent collisions between the police and the people, and blood was spilled on both sides. At first the Government arrests were confined to members of the League, who, although prominent enough in their own localities, were little known outside of Ireland. But Mr. John Dillon's action soon attracted the notice of the Government; and, after a speech which he delivered at Grangemaller, near Clonmel, in May, which counselled an extreme form of boycotting, he was arrested and put into prison. A short while before, the Government had roused great indignation among the Irish ecclesiastics by arresting and imprisoning Father Eugène Sheehy, of Kilmallock. These were the most important arrests made, at first, under the new Coercion Acts. The Land League was still flourishing. Mr. Sexton, M.P., hurried to Dublin from London to take Mr. Dillon's place at the head of the League in Ireland.

When the Coercive Acts had passed into law, every one's thoughts turned at once to the promised Land Act. But there were some other matters to be disposed of before the new Land Bill could be introduced. There was a debate on Candahar. The Army Discipline Bill, definitely abolishing flogging for soldiers, had to pass through its various stages. Then there was the Budget, which had of necessity to be disposed of before any other possible topic could be discussed.

On Monday, April 4, Mr. Gladstone made his financial statement in a speech of over two hours. The Budget being finally disposed of, the ground was now clear for the Land Bill, which was introduced, accordingly, by the Prime Minister on Thursday, April 7, 1881.

The history of the new Land Bill was curious. The measure which Mr. Gladstone laid before the House on April 7 was not the measure, or indeed anything like the measure, which the Government had originally intended to offer to Parliament. Another Bill had been prepared, of a less comprehensive nature. The draft of this Bill had been submitted by a member of the Ministry to a prominent Liberal member, who was very properly regarded as an authority on the Land question in Ireland, and who has since been one of the most eminent legal members of a Liberal Ministry, with the request that he would make any suggestions he thought fit as to its possible improvement. The member consulted returned the draft Bill promptly, saying that the only improvement he could suggest would be to put the proposed measure behind the fire. The Government apparently acted upon this summary advice; at least, if they did not put their valueless land scheme actually behind the fire, they speedily prepared a new and more advanced measure. Even the new Bill was mild enough, and bore very little resemblance to the form it came to assume later on.

Mr. Gladstone introduced the Bill on April 7, 1881, in a long, elaborate, and exceedingly eloquent speech on what he then not inappropriately called 'the most difficult and the most complex question' which he ever had to deal with in the course of his public life. Roughly speaking, the Bill proposed to deal with the Irish Land question on the basis of what was known as the three F's—fair rent, fixity of tenure, and free sale. Mr. Gladstone denied that either the iniquity of the existing land laws, or any sympathy with the extreme views of some of the Irish land reformers, or the bad conduct of Irish landlordism in general, called for the new attempt at legislation. It was the 'land hunger,' or rather the land scarcity; it was certain defects in the Land Act of 1870, and it was the rack-renting and evictions of a limited number of landlords which had inspired the action of the Government.

The Government was not in want of guidance in the step it was taking. A commission—the Richmond Commission—had been appointed by the previous Government to inquire into the Land question. Another commission—the Bessborough Commission—had been appointed by the existing Government for the same purpose. These two Commissions had begot, not two reports, but a perfect 'litter' of reports. There was naturally an agreeable diversity of opinion among these various reports. One member of the Richmond Commission, Mr. Bonamy Price, was for applying, 'in all their unmitigated authority,' the principles of abstract political economy to the very exceptional Land question of Ireland, 'exactly as if he had been proposing to legislate for the inhabitants of Saturn or Jupiter.' Of the four commissioners who made up the Bessborough Commission, only two agreed to sign what may be called the main report: Mr. Shaw signed one collateral report, The O'Conor Don signed another, and Mr. Kavanagh signed a third. Out of this multiplicity of counsel, however, Mr. Gladstone found that, with the exception of Mr. Bonamy Price, the whole body of both commissions were agreed in supporting the constitution of a court for the purpose of dealing with the differences between landlords and tenants in Ireland with regard to rent.

The establishment of such a court was to be then one of the principal features of the new measure. Appeal to this court was to be optional, and not compulsory. Every tenant from year to year coming under the description of 'present tenant' could go before the court and have a judicial rent fixed for his holding. This judicial rent was to last, in the first instance, for fifteen years, during which no eviction would be possible, except for non-payment of rent or distinct breach of specific covenants. When the fifteen years expired, landlord or tenant might apply to the court for a revision of the rent. If the tenancy were renewed, the same conditions as to eviction were to hold good. In the case, however, of the tenant wishing to sell his tenant right, the privilege of preemption, at the price fixed by the court as the value of the tenant right was reserved to the landlord. The Bill acted retrospectively with regard to tenants against whom process of ejectment had been begun but not concluded. The Ulster tenant, while remaining under the privilege of his custom, was to be allowed the protection of the general provisions of the Bill for controlling augmentation of rents. The new court, which was also to perform the functions of a land commission, was to consist of three members, one of whom was always to be a judge or ex-judge of the supreme court. It was empowered to appoint sub-commissions as courts of first instance, to hear applications and fix fair rents.

The second part of the Bill passed entirely from the region of the three F's into the difficult question of peasant proprietary. The court, as a land commission, was empowered to assist tenants to purchase their holdings, and furthermore to purchase itself estates from willing landlords, for the purpose of reselling them when three-fourths of the tenants were ready to buy. The court might advance three-fourths of the purchase-money to tenants, and was not to be prohibited from advancing the whole sum when it saw fit. Tenants availing themselves of these purchase clauses would obtain a guaranteed title, and would only have to pay a very small sum for legal costs. Emigration was to be included among the purposes for which advances might be made. Such were the more striking features of the new measure.

The Bill was read a first time without opposition, and immediately after, on the following day, the House adjourned for the Easter recess. When it reassembled on April 25 the second reading of the Land Bill was moved at once. The debates were long and bitter. The Conservative party as a body opposed the Bill with unwearying vigilance and vehemence. They characterised it again and again as a measure of communism, of socialism, of brigandage; and they exhausted their ingenuity in efforts, if not to defeat the Bill altogether, at least to delay it as long as possible, and to minimise as much as might be its 'revolutionary' nature. The Irish members, on the other hand, were no less energetic in their efforts to widen the scope of the Bill, and make it of a character more markedly beneficial to the tenant class. Their efforts were more successful than those of the Conservative party. The general principles of the Bill remained the same, but its scope was widened, and its powers of application strengthened to a surprising degree. The Bill in the final form in which it was presented to the House of Lords in the end of July, after months of protracted debate, might be not unfairly characterised as in large part the creation of Mr. Healy and the Irish party, of Mr. Charles Russell and certain of the Ulster members.

The sleeper in the Arabian story scarcely underwent a more remarkable metamorphosis when he assumed the care and dignity of the Kalifeh than was experienced by the new Bill in its passage from the Treasury bench to the Upper House. It is only necessary to compare the original draft of the Bill with its final form to see how important these alterations were. The famous Healy clause was constructed to exclude altogether the valuation of improvements made by the tenant in estimating the amount to be fixed as a judicial rent. On the other hand, an amendment by Mr. Heneage was agreed to, excluding what are called 'English-managed' estates from the operation of the Healy clause. The court was empowered by another provision to quash leases contracted since 1870, which might be shown on examination to have been drawn up with a view to dodging or defeating the objects of that measure. The emigration proposals, which were extremely obnoxious to the Irish party, were very largely modified. The total expenditure for this purpose was limited to 200,000*l*., not more than a third of which was to be spent in any single year. A clause was introduced allowing the commissioners to make advances to tenants for the purpose of clearing off arrears of rent which had accrued for three years.

On July 29 the Bill was read a third time in the House of Commons, and was carried up to the House of Lords, where it was read a first time for form's sake, without opposition, the same evening. After two nights' debate it was read a second time without division, in obedience to Lord Salisbury's counsels. In committee, however, the majority in the Lords fell upon the measure. They reduced the Bill to a nullity by comprehensive interpolations and additions. They altered, they amended, they substituted, till the Bill resembled Wallenstein's horse as shown to Brown, Jones, and Robinson. The head, legs, and part of the body are new, all the rest is the real horse. The Bill in this 'real-horse' condition was returned to the Commons. The Ministry accepted a few of the least important amendments, modified some others, and firmly rejected those which struck at the vitality of the measure. It was sent back to the Lords again, and once again the Lords, with that marvellous infatuation which is the peculiar privilege of the Upper House in its struggles with the Commons, proceeded to make the measure useless by reinstating the objectionable amendments and interpolations. The Bill was then sent down to the Commons. The Ministry made a further pretence of considering the question. The more dangerous amendments which the Lords had restored were struck out, but the Ministry made certain concessions. In the first form of the Healy clause, for instance, the Government had insisted upon a proviso that the tenant should not be allowed the value of improvements for which he had been paid by the landlord. The Government now conceded the addition 'or otherwise compensated.' Under these words, Irish courts can, as in the case of Adams and Dunseath, rule that length of enjoyment is to be taken into account as an element in considering the value of a tenant's improvement. The Bill was then handed back to the Lords.

By this time public feeling was thoroughly aroused at the prospect of a serious constitutional struggle between the two Houses. Liberal meetings were held in all parts of the country, at which the Government were vigorously encouraged to make no concessions, to fight the fight out to the end. The Lords blustered, but their courage was shaken. Two of the most comprehensively destructive of the Lords' amendments had been moved by the Duke of Argyll and Lord Lansdowne. On August 16, when the Bill came before the Lords for the third time, Lord Salisbury still assumed a semi-defiant attitude. Perhaps on the whole, he said, their lordships had better accept the Bill, unless, indeed, the Duke of Argyll and Lord Lansdowne pressed their amendments. In that case, Lord Salisbury would certainly vote for them, and for resistance to the imperious Commons. But the Duke of Argyll was conveniently absent. Lord Lansdowne sat in his seat and made no sign. Lord Salisbury had sounded his trumpet, and no knight challenger galloped into the arena. So, with something of an ill grace, Lord Salisbury bade those of his inclining hold their hands, and the Land Bill of 1881 became law. The House of Lords had gained nothing by their opposition, but, for the moment at least, they were saved from the consequences of direct collision with the Commons.

Mr. Cowen had been a persistent opponent of the coercive policy of the Government. He had spoken against it again and again; he had supported the Irish members time after time with his voice and with his vote in opposing the Bills. At the meeting in Newcastle-on-Tyne, on Monday, August 29, 1881, he attacked the Government with all his energy and all his eloquence. It had been found useless, he said, to argue with the master of many legions, even when that master argued on the extraordinary paradox that the only way in which the law could be maintained in Ireland was by its being superseded. The Land Act had failed as a means of pacification. It was too abstruse and complicated for plain men to understand, and its fair proportions were hidden by the repulsive screen of the Coercion Act. While he strongly condemned the wild writings and wild threats of the American Fenians, he attributed the fault of such writings and threats mainly to the action of the English Government itself.' 'No more barbarous or inhuman treatment had been attempted against political prisoners in modern days in Western Europe than was meted out by the English Government to the Fenians. . . . By their treatment we converted men who might have been our friends into foes.' The outrages in Ireland, on account of which the Government had demanded Coercion, were, Mr. Cowen contended, shamefully exaggerated. The reason for the exaggeration was this: the Irish Executive feared that a Liberal Parliament would not pass a Coercion Bill, and that they could only get it by showing that the country was greatly disturbed, and law superseded. They therefore made no attempt to use the ordinary law with a view to restrain incipient excess, and their strategy succeeded. There was no constitutional country in Europe. Mr. Cowen concluded, in which such a state of things obtained as it did in Ireland. It was a scandal to our civilisation, and a disgrace to our statesmanship.

The convention at Newcastle was followed up by another convention in Ireland, in the Dublin Rotunda, a convention of delegates from the various branches of the Land League all over Ireland. The convention represented the public feeling of Ireland, as far as public opinion ever can be represented by a delegated body. The descendants of the Cromwellian settlers of the north sat side by side with men of the rebel blood of Tipperary, with the impetuous people of the south, with the strong men of the midland hunting counties. The most remarkable feature of the meeting was the vast number of priests who were present. A great number of priests, young and old, spoke at the convention; all were warm in sympathy with the League and its leaders; all were ready to deal with the Bill as these leaders wished. Mr. Parnell explained his views to the convention. He announced that the League was willing to use the Bill as far as it went, but that the existence of the Bill did not put an end to the work of the Land League; it had still to be vigilant; it had to experiment upon the newly-founded land courts with test cases, and in every way to watch over the interests of the tenant farmers.

Not of the tenant farmers alone; the Irish labourers were to be thought of as well. The condition of the labourers in Ireland was very bad, and their complaints had gradually been taking organised shape. They were now formally recognised by the League, which became henceforward a Land and Labour League.

The convention was singularly quiet; the speeches were all moderate in tone; the attitude of the League as represented by its delegates was pacific and constitutional. But the country undoubtedly was in a disorganised state. The fierce anger that the Coercion Acts and their operation had aroused was creating a wide-spread disorder, with which it seemed at first as if Coercion itself could not successfully cope. The Land League leaders maintained always that they had the country entirely under their control, and that as long as they were to the front they could keep the disorder and violence in check. How far they could have carried this out—how far they could have overmastered the forces that were now at work in Ireland—it is impossible to say, for they were not given the opportunity of carrying out their promises.

The action of the Government during the couple of months following upon the rising of Parliament is wholly inexplicable. They cannot have thought that the condition of the country was dangerous, for they saw fit to set free Father Sheehy, a step which it is difficult to believe they would have taken if they considered the country to be seriously disturbed. Yet, before the release of Father Sheehy, Mr. Parnell had received in Dublin the greatest tribute of popular enthusiasm that had been accorded to any Irish leader since the days of the Liberator. He had been attending meetings in the country. He returned to Dublin one night towards the end of September. He was met at the station by an enthusiastic crowd bearing torches, and was drawn through the Dublin streets to the Land League offices in Sackville Street. From the windows of these rooms Mr. Parnell and Mr. Sexton delivered speeches to the vast, excited audience, who choked the whole of Sackville Street; and on the speeches made that night part of the Government case was afterwards made to rest.

Yet it was after this demonstration and after those speeches that the Government thought proper to set Father Sheehy at liberty, although they must have known that he was scarcely likely to remain quieter after his experiences of a prison than he was before he entered it. Is it to be credited that the Government considered the country to be seriously disorganised and disturbed, and yet deliberately let loose among such elements of revolution an agitator who was doubly popular, and therefore doubly dangerous, because he was a priest, and was regarded by the people as a martyr? Father Sheehy at once commenced a vigorous crusade against the Government, and his entry into Cork, in company with Mr. Parnell, resembled a Roman triumph.

For a while after the session came to an end there appeared to be a lull in political excitement. The session had been so stormy that it was, not unnaturally, hoped that it might be succeeded by a lengthened period of repose.

Up to this time nothing new had taken place in Ireland. The convention had been held, and had passed off quietly. Mr. Parnell had spoken in Cork and Dublin; the Land League was advising the tenant farmers to wait for the submitting of their cases to the land courts until the test cases of the League had been decided; the Land League itself was in full activity, and seemed more popular than ever. Suddenly a series of events took place with great rapidity, which were more startling than anything that had preceded them. Early in October Mr. Gladstone entered upon what was called his Leeds campaign. It was, in point of fact, a campaign against the Irish Parliamentary party, and against Mr. Parnell in particular. On Friday, October 7, 1881, Mr. Gladstone was at Leeds receiving an address from the mayor and town council, and he made a speech.

This speech was remarkable for the manner in which it singled out a political opponent for all the energy of Mr. Gladstone's powers of attack. Mr. Gladstone began by replying to the Conservative taunts over their victory at Durham. In Durham the victory had been won, it was said, by the Irish vote, and Mr. Gladstone at once turned to the Irish question. After declaring that the condition of Ireland for generations, perhaps for centuries, its prosperity and happiness, or its loss of all rational hope of progress, depended upon its reception of the Land Act, Mr. Gladstone proceeded to draw a contrast between the conduct of politicians of the school of 1848, like Sir Charles Gavan Duffy, and even of some advanced men of to-day like Mr. John Dillon, with the conduct of Mr. Parnell and his followers. Sir Charles Gavan Duffy was delighted with the new legislation; Mr. John Dillon, rather than attempt to plunge his country into disorder by intercepting the operations of the Land Act, had withdrawn from politics; while Mr. Parnell, in carrying out his policy of plunder, was doing his best to arrest its action. 'Mr. Parnell,' said Mr. Gladstone, slightly confusing his Scripture history in the vehemence of the moment, desired 'to stand, as Moses stood, between the living and the dead, but to stand there not as Moses stood, to arrest, but to spread the plague.'

Such a speech, made at such a time, naturally created the greatest excitement. Lord Salisbury attended a meeting at Newcastle-on-Tyne on the following Tuesday, in which he pointed out humorously that Mr. Gladstone was unjust to Mr. Parnell. 'When Mr. Gladstone complains that Mr. Parnell has deserted him, I think he forgets it is mainly due to the organisation over which Mr. Parnell presides that he is now Prime Minister of England. . . . Mr. Gladstone's complaint of Mr. Parnell for preaching the doctrine of public plunder seems to me a strange application of the old adage that Catiline should not censure Cethegus for treason.' In such terms the head of the Opposition bantered the head of the Government; but in Ireland the speech aroused replies that had little spirit of banter in them.

At a meeting in Wexford on the Sunday following Mr. Gladstone's speech at Leeds, Mr. Parnell delivered a speech of vehement attack upon the Prime Minister. It was a curious duel of words, unlike anything that English political life had been accustomed to: a Prime Minister levelling a bitter personal attack upon a political opponent, and the opponent retorting in terms of equal fierceness. Mr. John Dillon was not behindhand in replying to the Prime Minister. Mr. Gladstone had held him up as an honourable contrast to the conduct of Mr. Parnell, and Mr. Dillon angrily and scornfully repudiated the compliments of the Prime Minister. He had not, he assured the Prime Minister, retired from politics to allow free play to the Land Act. On the contrary, he deeply regretted that he had not been able to stand between his country and the Land Act altogether.

Mr. Gladstone's speech had aroused the greatest excitement in Ireland, and, indeed, in England too. People felt that such a pronouncement could not have been uttered merely *pour rire*—that something more was to come of it; and something more came. A few days after Mr. Parnell and Mr. Dillon had replied to the attack, the Government replied by a veritable *coup d'état*. A descent was made upon all the prominent Land League leaders in Dublin on Thursday, October 13. Mr. Parnell was arrested in Morrison's Hotel, and conveyed to Kilmainham early in the morning. Mr. Sexton, M.P., Mr. O'Kelly, M.P., Mr. Dillon, M.P., Mr. O'Brien, and Mr. J. P. Quinn, Secretary of the Land League, were arrested in rapid succession, and conveyed to Kilmainham Prison. Warrants were out for Mr. Biggar, Mr. Healy, and Mr. Arthur O'Connor. Mr. Biggar and Mr. Arthur O'Connor got over to England, where Mr. Healy was, and orders were conveyed to them from their leader not to return to Ireland to certain arrest, but to remain in England, where they might be useful in keeping the agitation alive.

These wholesale arrests startled the whole civilised world. Continental countries, used to struggles with revolutionary parties, congratulated themselves on the discovery that England, the proud mother of free nations, had her difficulties as well as they, and could only meet them with the old methods.

In England itself the *coup d'état* was received with satisfaction, almost with rejoicing, by the generality of the supporters of the Government, though it is hardly necessary to say that advanced Radicals like Mr. Jesse Collings, Mr. Thompson of Durham, Mr. Labouchere, Mr. Storey, and Mr. Joseph Cowen did not share in this satisfaction, and that the rejoicing was not unanimous even in the Cabinet. Mr. Gladstone was present at an entertainment given by the Corporation of the City of London at the Guildhall on October 13. Mr. Gladstone made a speech which might be regarded as the epilogue to his Leeds address. In the middle of an eloquent appeal to the principles of law and order the Prime Minister produced a telegram which he had just received, and in tones of triumphant exultation announced to his hearers the arrest of Mr. Parnell.

The effect was curious. Had Mr. Gladstone informed his audience of the conquest of some foreign foe, of the successful conclusion of some long and hazardous war, or the consummation of some honourable and long-looked-for peace, his words could not have aroused a greater frenzy of enthusiasm. Every man in the crowded hall sprang to his feet and cheered till he could cheer no longer. 'Our enemies have fallen, have fallen,' said Mr. Gladstone; and the tumultuous applause with which he was greeted from political opponents, as well as political allies, must have assured him that he had wrestled well, and overthrown more than his enemies.

Across the Irish Sea everything was confusion. Arrests followed arrests; excited meetings were held all over the country; a Ladies' Land League, even a Children's Land League, and a Political Prisoners' Aid Society strove to keep the agitation alive; there were slight riots here and there; the Government took the most elaborate precautions against a possible popular rising. Suddenly the walls of Dublin were placarded by a proclamation calling upon the Irish people to pay no rent while their leaders were in prison. This document was signed by Charles S. Parnell, President, Kilmainham Jail; A. J. Kettle, Honorary Secretary, Kilmainham Jail;

Michael Davitt, Honorary Secretary, Portland Prison; Thomas Brennan, Honorary Secretary, Kilmainham Jail; John Dillon, Head Organizer, Kilmainham Jail; Thomas Sexton, Head Organizer, Kilmainham Jail; Patrick Egan, Treasurer, Paris.

The No-Rent manifesto was dramatically effective, but it was not generally acted upon; its framers can hardly have expected that it would be. The clergy were entirely against it. Even the most national of Irish ecclesiastics, Archbishop Croke of Cashel, condemned it unhesitatingly. A general strike of rent all over Ireland might have been a great political move if it had been possible, but it was not possible. The No-Rent manifesto was a direct challenge to the Government, and the Government retaliated by declaring the Land League an illegal body, by proclaiming its meetings, and by arresting its remaining official, Mr. Dorris, and sending him to Dundalk Prison. Many women, members of the Ladies' Land League, were put into prison in different parts of the country. The most advanced of the national newspapers, *United Ireland*, was shortly afterwards proscribed, and for the time being practically suppressed. It carried on a fitful existence, printed now in Paris, now in Liverpool, and smuggled over as well as might be to Ireland, where it was sold surreptitiously, and seized by the police whenever they could lay hands upon it. The Government had done their best to stifle the Land League, to crush it out of existence altogether, and they appeared to have succeeded. They really seemed to think that by abolishing an association and suppressing a newspaper they could silence a national agitation, and summarily dispose of a complicated and vexatious problem.

As soon as Mr. Parnell was imprisoned the Lord Chancellor removed his name from the Commission of the Peace for the county of Wicklow. An effort was immediately made by the national section of the Dublin Corporation to confer the freedom of the city upon Mr. Parnell and Mr. Dillon. After a stormy discussion, in which Mr. Gray, M.P., and Mr. Dawson, M.P., led the national party, against Mr. Brooks, M.P., who opposed the proposal, the motion was lost by the casting vote of the Lord Mayor, Dr. Moyers. The proposal was only delayed. With the new year a new Lord Mayor was elected, Mr. Charles Dawson, M.P., a strong Nationalist. This time the national party in the Corporation were in a large majority, and by a large majority the customary vote of thanks to a retiring Lord Mayor was refused to Dr. Moyers, for the part he had taken in defeating the freedom of the city proposal. This proposal was now revived and carried successfully. Such an act on the part of the Corporation of a city that had always been remarkable for what was called its 'loyalty,' which meant its subservience to Castle influence, was in itself deeply significant of the hold the national leaders had got upon the heart of the country. But a message from Heaven would not have appeared significant to Mr. Forster if it had not accorded with his pre-established opinions of the way Ireland ought to be governed.

The suppression of the Land League did not make Ireland quiet. The imprisonment of the responsible leaders of the national party had removed all check upon the fierce and dangerous forces which are always at work under the surface of Irish politics. The secret societies, which had almost ceased to operate during the rule of the Land League, came into play again the moment the restraining influence of a popular, constitutional, and open movement was removed. Outrages increased daily, and were exaggerated out of all proportion to their increase, until, to those at a distance, Ireland appeared to be sinking into a condition of hopeless anarchy. The Chief Secretary had had his way; he had put into prison men, women, priests, according to his pleasure, and yet an obstinate island and an ungrateful people refused to justify him by being pacified. Order did not reign in Warsaw.

CHAPTER XXI.

COERCION.

THE year 1882 opened with a grim sense of disquiet in Ireland, of which we find a gloomy record in the 'Annual Register.' 'Though the Land League was suppressed, though its chief leaders were in prison, the condition of the country was worse than ever, and seemed to have become more and more hopelessly disorganised day by day. Undoubtedly the imprisonment of Members of Parliament like Mr. Parnell, Mr. Dillon, and Mr. O'Kelly had succeeded in breaking the power of the Land League, but it had done little or nothing towards restoring the country to quiet. The members of the many secret societies that abound in Ireland had found their favourite forms of action terribly restrained by the more open agitation established and carried on by the Land League. Now that there was no longer a Land League, the secret societies had it all their own way, and outrages of various kinds multiplied alarmingly in all parts of the island where the influence of these occult bodies extended. A new and dangerous organisation, headed by a mysterious individual known as "Captain Moonlight," distinguished itself for midnight maraudings, farm-burnings, mutilations of cattle, and similar crimes.

'At last the police arrested a man named Connell, who seems to have been drifting about the Cork hills and the Killarney mountains, dressed in a sort of military costume, and levying a kind of black-mail upon the peasantry. Papers were found on the man, orders for shooting, and clipping, and the like, all signed "Captain Moonlight," which seemed to show that he was no other than Captain Moonlight himself. Captain Moonlight, to save himself, promptly turned informer, gave evidence which led to a great many arrests, and then disappeared and was heard of no more.

'But the arrest of Captain Moonlight did not necessarily mean the stoppage of moonlighting, nor the cessation of outrages, nor, unfortunately, of incessant rumours and stories of outrages of the most exaggerated kind. Archbishop Croke, the leader of what may be called the national majority among the priesthood, declared that a large number of outrages were invented or grossly exaggerated for the mere purpose of inflaming public feeling and injuring the Land League. Archbishop Croke, though a Nationalist, was by no means an extreme man. He had never failed to denounce wild action of any kind; he had always used his influence for the preservation of peace and order. His opinion, therefore, was well worthy of serious consideration, and it must be admitted that while the condition of Ireland was bad enough, rumours and exaggerations of all sorts were in circulation, with and without intent, which made it appear a good deal worse than it really was.

'Arms were frequently seized by the police, and the authorities were convinced that the importation of weapons into Ireland was being successfully carried on on a very large scale. The two most serious crimes which marked the beginning of the year were the murder of two bailiffs in Connemara, and the shooting of an informer in Dublin. The first of these murders occurred in January, when two of Lord Ardilaun's bailiffs, an old man and his grandson named Huddy, were sent to collect rents in a part of Connemara known as Joyce's country, from the fact that through constant intermarriages all, or almost all, the peasants of the district bear the name of Joyce. Into the Joyce country they went, and in the Joyce country they disappeared; search was instituted, the waters of Lough Mask were dragged, and the bodies of the Huddys found. They had evidently been shot, and then tied up in sacks with stones and flung into the Lough. For many months no clue to the murderers was obtained, and it was not until the end of the year, at the time of another terrible crime in the Joyce country, that the murderers of the Huddys were discovered.

'Late in February an informer named Bernard Bailey was shot dead in Skipper's Alley, Dublin, at a time when the place was crowded with people, when the lamps were lighting, and policemen on duty in the immediate neighbourhood. But the assassins were not discovered, and the offer of a reward of 500*l.* failed to elicit any information. Bernard Bailey was a labourer who was supposed to have given information which led to an extensive seizure of arms by the police in Brabazon and Cross Kevin Street, in the preceding December. He had received several threatening letters, and had, it is said, lived for some time entirely in the police-barracks, which he left to go into the workhouse. On Saturday, February 25, he went out into the street, and was immediately killed.

'Towards the end of 1881 a proposal had been brought before the Corporation of the city of Dublin, by Mr. Charles Dawson, M.P., that the freedom of the city should be conferred on Mr. Parnell and Mr. Dillon, then in Kilmainham Prison. The question was fiercely contested, and Mr. Dawson's proposal was finally defeated by the casting vote of the Lord Mayor, Dr. Moyers. The new year, however, gave Dublin a new Lord Mayor in the person of Mr. Dawson himself, and the question at once came up again. Dr. Moyers was punished for his casting vote by being refused by a large majority the usual vote of thanks accorded to a retiring Lord Mayor. Then the proposal to give the freedom of the city to Mr. Parnell and Mr. Dillon was brought forward by Mr. T. D. Sullivan, M.P., and, in spite of an opposing amendment by Mr. Brookes, M.P., on the ground that to do so would be to support the No-Rent manifesto, was carried by a majority of 29 to 23. The defeated members of the Corporation talked of further resistance —even hinted that as Messrs. Dillon and Parnell were not burgesses, they could not legally receive the freedom of the city; but on having it pointed out to them that this argument would, if successful, necessitate the removal of the names of Mr. Gladstone, of President Grant, and other distinguished persons who were not burgesses, from the roll, they forbore to press the point, which, indeed, it seems had in reality little to support it. The Corporation, or rather the Parnellite majority in the Corporation, asked the Lord Lieutenant to allow Mr. Parnell and Mr. Dillon to attend at the City Hall to receive the freedom of the city, but the request was of course refused.

'Though the Land League was suppressed, the Ladies' Land League declined to admit defeat. Women had played a great part in history before, had marched to Versailles at the heels of Shifty Usher Maillard, had disarmed military opposition, had conquered a king. Would the Irish constabulary be more ungallant than those Gardes Françaises? Would a Lord Lieutenant be more difficult than a Louis Capet? Such, or similar thoughts, may be supposed to have animated the minds of the Lady Land Leaguers when they announced that, in despite of all proclamations and prohibitions, they would hold their meetings all over the country on New Year's Day; would meet Mr. Forster at Philippi. Miss Parnell came over from England to preside at the meeting in the League rooms in Sackville Street, Dublin, at which there were many speeches made, and allusions to the uncrowned king of Ireland. Similar meetings took place on the same day in every part of Ireland where a Ladies' Land League had a branch organisation to raise its head. One or two Lady Land Leaguers were arrested in consequence here and there, but practically the Government thought it wisest to ignore the existence of the Ladies' Land League rather than extinguish it by any violent suppression. So the Ladies' Land League lingered on throughout the year, until it was finally abolished by the national leaders, Messrs. Parnell and Dillon, whom, if report were at all well-founded, the Lady Land Leaguers regarded with very little favour in the end, as temporising and half-hearted politicians.

'Mr. Forster, of course, was more unpopular than ever. Threatening letters snowed on him; one at least was more than threatening, and might have exploded had not aroused suspicion taken proper precautions. Yet for all his unpopularity he was able to make a journey of inspection into County Clare, then much disturbed, to go about among the people unescorted, and make earnest, well-meaning appeals to them, which were well enough received, to support the Executive in carrying out the law. It is to be regretted that Mr. Forster had not acted more in this manner from the beginning. Like most of his acts since he took the office of Chief Secretary, it was done too late. The Executive, as advised by Mr. Forster, always used the means at its disposal, whether of coercion or of conciliation, just too late for either to be of effective service. It was no use for Mr. Forster now to go among the disturbed districts and make sensible speeches; the mischief had been done, and was not now to be mended by any efforts of his.

'Meanwhile, the popularity of the men in prison only increased. Dublin had given them the freedom of her city, and other Irish cities were not slow to follow her example. Cork conferred its freedom on Mr. Dillon; freedoms came in to the Kilmainham prisoners from all directions. Mr. Parnell and Mr. Dillon could exercise all the privileges of freemen in an embarrassing variety of places when once they came out of Kilmainham. But when this coming out of Kilmainham was to take place, no man could say.

'A curious bye-election served to show that the Land League and its leaders were not losing popularity in the country. Mr. A. M. Sullivan, Member of Parliament for Meath, felt himself compelled for his health's sake to resign his seat in the early part of the year. The name of Mr. Michael Davitt was at once brought forward, and the founder of the Land League was elected without opposition. He was not of course allowed to take his seat. The Solicitor-General showed that as Mr. Davitt was a convicted felon working out his sentence in Portland Prison at the time of the election, he was by that fact disqualified, as O'Donovan Rossa in 1870 and John Mitchel in 1875 were disqualified. A new Land League candidate was immediately proposed-- Mr. Sheil, formerly member for Athlone—and was returned without opposition.

'On April 2 a terrible murder took place. Mr. Smythe, a large landowner in Westmeath, had become very unpopular with his tenants, and his life had been for some time threatened. On April 2 he was returning from church in a carriage with his sister-in-law, Mrs. Henry Smythe, and Lady Harriet Monck, when he was fired at by three men with blackened faces, who made no attempt to conceal themselves, and who successfully escaped. The shots missed Mr. Smythe, but struck his sister-in-law in the head, killing her instantly. The circumstances of this murder were exceptionally ghastly, for it had always hitherto been maintained that, no matter how unpopular a landlord might be, he was always safe so long as he was in the company of a woman, and threatened landlords often lived long by availing themselves of so simple a precaution. Mr. Smythe wrote a very bitter letter to Mr. Gladstone, laying the guilt of the blood upon him and his Ministry. Mr. Gladstone replied in a singularly temperate letter, expressing his profound regret and sympathy, and kindly ignoring the wild personal charge made against himself. Mr. Smythe then addressed an indignant circular to his tenants, accusing them all of complicity in the murder, directly or indirectly, and telling them that in future the rents were to be paid to a non-resident agent, "who can make no future allowances, nor do anything on the property not strictly required by law."

'The fear of assassination led many persons to take careful measures to protect themselves. Of all these, perhaps, the most characteristic and complete was that of Major Traill, R.M., who, in a letter to the *Daily Express*, gave a curious picture of his daily life. He always went about with a guard of two policemen, one armed with a Winchester rifle, carrying twelve rounds ready and fifteen extra rounds in pouch, and the other armed with a double-barrelled gun loaded with buckshot and eight extra rounds; he himself carried a revolver and six spare rounds, and his groom carried a revolver and five spare rounds. At no moment of the twenty-four hours was a revolver out of reach of his hand, and his wife had a revolver too, and knew how to use it. Being thus guarded against any attempts at assassination, Major Traill dryly concluded, " The man who attempts my life and lives to be tried by a jury is entitled to their merciful consideration as a brave man."

'But if Major Traill was perfectly justified in taking all possible precautions to defend his life or to sell it as dearly as might be, there was no such justification for an extraordinary circular which Major Clifford Lloyd thought fit to issue later in the year. In this document the police were told that if they should "accidentally commit an error in shooting any person on suspicion of that person being about to commit murder," the production of the circular would exonerate them. Of course such a document, which practically authorised any policeman to shoot on sight anyone whom he fancied might possibly be going to commit murder, could not be tolerated by the Executive. Even allowing to the constabulary the best intentions, it is easy to see that in troublous and excited times harmless persons—beggars by the roadside, labourers in the field, belated wayfarers, anybody at all—might have been shot down by an excitable constable with a revolver in his hand and such a circular in his pocket. Between this and any amount of such precautions as Major Traill and others like him were taking there was all the difference in the world, and the circular had to be withdrawn.

'Early in the year a very remarkable publication was made under the official authority of the Irish Land Commission. This was the reprint of articles which appeared in the *Freeman's Journal*, under the title of " How to become owner of your own farm : why Irish landlords should sell and Irish tenants should purchase, and how they can do it under the Land Act of 1881."

'Those who thought this heading rather remarkable for a work issued with the authority of the Government-appointed Commission, found much more cause for wonder on reading the pamphlet itself. There they found a vigorous and able exposition of the principles of peasant proprietorship, interspersed with enthusiastic commendation of the Land League as " the most widespread, the most powerful, and in its effects, we believe, the most enduring organisation of our time," and allusions to the cause for which "Parnell and Dillon and Davitt laboured and suffered." Naturally such a pamphlet, issued with official authorisation, and at a time when the Land League was suppressed as illegal, and Parnell, Dillon, and Davitt were in prison, created no small excitement in Ireland. An inquiry was immediately instituted ; the pamphlet was found to be written by Mr. George Fottrell, an able and rising Dublin solicitor, who had been appointed Secretary to the Irish Land Commission. Mr. Fottrell, while defending the pamphlet as well calculated to advance the cause of peasant proprietorship, which the Commission had at heart, immediately resigned his secretaryship, and the pamphlet was withdrawn from official circulation at once.

' The Government had great difficulty in dealing with the chief of the Land League journals, *United Ireland*, and with the large introduction into Ireland of the New York *Irish World*, a journal of the fiercest and most pronounced opinions. *United Ireland* was suppressed, and was being seized incessantly, but it continually made its appearance in some form or other. Sometimes it was printed in Dublin under conditions of great difficulty, and sold or rather smuggled about; then it was printed in Paris and exported to Dublin, where it was generally seized on arrival ; then again it was taken over to Liverpool to be set up, and introduced from there surreptitiously into Ireland. All the activity of the police could not prevent the circulation of the paper in some form or another. Week after week it kept on appearing, encouraging the agitation to continue, and assailing the Government in unmeasured prose and vigorous cartoons.

' The *Irish World* was a much wilder journal than *United Ireland*, and the copies sent to Ireland by post were generally seized by the English postal authorities, to the great indignation of the staff of the *Irish World*, who inquired indignantly : " Is a thick-headed, shock-haired, leaden-hearted old reprobate like Forster going to succeed in keeping out the light, or are we to see America triumphant and defeating this hirsute Forster ? " In one sense America, as represented by the *Irish World*, was triumphant, for with all the zeal and watchfulness of the Government, it could not prevent the frequent introduction of the journal into Ireland.

' Early in April the rumour suddenly ran through Ireland that Mr. Parnell had been released from Kilmainham. The greatest joy was expressed at the news, and bonfires blazed in every village in the three provinces; but the excitement was allayed by the later information that Mr. Parnell had indeed been released, but only on parole for a few days, in order that he might go to Paris to attend the funeral of a relative. The terms of Mr. Parnell's parole engaged him not to take any part in political matters or demonstrations of any kind, and it is needless to add that the conditions were absolutely observed. Mr. Parnell did not return to his prison quite as soon as was expected, and the absurd scare got possession of some minds in Dublin that the Land League leader did not mean to come back at all. Such baseless apprehensions were, however, promptly dissipated by Mr. Parnell's return to Kilmainham on April 24.

' This temporary liberation was but the herald of freedom for the imprisoned Land Leaguers. For some time, indeed, the Government had been greatly embarrassed by the necessity for keeping Mr. Parnell, Mr. Dillon, and Mr. O'Kelly in prison. The hoped-for reformation in the country which that imprisonment was to effect had not taken place; on the contrary, the country was evidently getting more and more hopelessly disorganised; and, at the same time, the responsibility of keeping so many men imprisoned merely as "suspects" increased daily. Many offers were made to the three leaders in Kilmainham of liberation on condition of their leaving the country, or even of going across to France for a short time and returning to Ireland when they pleased. The imprisoned Members declined all conditions of the kind. In the meantime, ever since the temporary release of Mr. Parnell, many-tongued rumours had been circulating in Dublin. It was whispered that Mr. Dillon was to be released. The statement was denied, was whispered abroad again, and again denied. It was clear that some curious political event was going to happen, but few outside the Government circle were prepared for the startling character that the event was to wear. On May 2, Ireland was electrified by the news that Mr. Forster and Lord Cowper had resigned; that Mr. Parnell, Mr. Dillon, and Mr. O'Kelly were to be immediately released unconditionally; nay, more, that Michael Davitt was once more to become a free man, and that the Government had undertaken to bring in an Arrears Bill on the lines of a measure drafted by Mr. Parnell himself.

'What was the cause of this strange Ministerial change of front? This was the question everyone set himself to ask and answer to the best of his ability during the days immediately following the amazing news. The Government explanation itself was, one might well think, sufficiently clear and reasonable to satisfy curiosity, without any further gropings for hidden motives and secret reasons. Mr. Gladstone and his Ministry had imprisoned certain men at a certain time because they believed it was for the good of both countries that they should do so.

'The condition of the country since had led Mr. Gladstone to the conclusion that the ends he had in view for the pacification of Ireland and the settlement of the Irish question would be further advanced by releasing the imprisoned Members. Mr. Gladstone had been conspicuous all through his political career for his willingness to recognise when he had made an error, and his willingness to sacrifice those personal feelings of pride which have so often led Ministers to pursue an unlucky course, simply because they had begun and were too proud to draw back. But so simple an explanation would not satisfy the wiseacres who always know more of Ministerial purposes than the Ministers themselves, and an imaginary " Kilmainham Treaty " was at once invented, in which it was supposed that Mr. Gladstone and Mr. Parnell had made many mutual pledges to assist and countenance each other, and that the liberation of the prisoners was the fulfilment of the first article of the convention. Nothing in the subsequent history of the year showed anything to justify the assumption of the existence of any such negotiations, even were the repeated denials of Mr. Gladstone and Mr. Parnell not to be considered sufficiently conclusive.

'Mr. Forster, however, was entirely opposed to Mr. Gladstone's new policy. Having entered on one particular line of action, he was for following it up to the end, regardless of consequences; and he refused to be any party to the new arrangement. He resigned, and Lord Cowper resigned with him. Lord Spencer was appointed Lord Lieutenant, and Lord Frederick Cavendish, second son of the Duke of Devonshire and brother of Lord Hartington, was appointed Chief Secretary in Mr. Forster's stead.

'For the first time since Mr. Gladstone's Ministry took office there seemed to be a cordial understanding between the Government and the Irish party. Each side seemed to have awakened to the fact that its opponents were honest and honourable men, really trying to do their best, and that the welfare of Ireland was the real desire of each. If such an understanding could have been arrived at earlier the history of the past two years might have been very different; but the impartial observer is compelled to admit that on both sides —on the part of the Ministry as well as on the part of Mr. Parnell and his followers—there was a certain impatience, a not unnatural incredulity as to the good intentions of the other, which widened day by day the breach between the great Liberal majority and the small Irish minority. Now, however, all this seemed to be at an end; the unhappy quarrel seemed concluded. The Government appeared to accept the fact that it was impossible to govern Ireland without taking into account some of Ireland's ideas as expressed by her representatives. Ireland appeared well pleased to admit that the Liberal party were as sincerely anxious to benefit the country now as they had often done before. All over Ireland there was a feeling of joy that the time of trouble had passed away; that misunderstandings had ceased; that the new era had begun at last. Indeed, it seemed like a new era. The imprisoned leaders were released, were actually consulted by the Government; **the Chief Secretary** who, with the best intentions, had succeeded in making himself as unpopular as Castlereagh, **was out of office**; the reign of Coercion was to cease, and new and much-desired legislation was to be undertaken immediately. It would be difficult to over-estimate the good effect that the change produced in Ireland. But unfortunately there were men in the country to whom reconciliation was hateful, who hated the constitutional agitation with all their hearts, and who dreaded nothing so much as its triumph. During the suppression of the Land League the secret societies which fostered such feelings had grown and thriven. While the Land League was in existence their influence had dwindled away; the moment the power of the Land League was destroyed, the secret societies again asserted themselves and their dangerous methods. So much to explain the catastrophe which suddenly destroyed so many bright hopes of peace and reconcilement between the two countries.

'On Saturday, May 6, Lord Frederick Cavendish arrived in Dublin, to be present at the entry of the new Viceroy, Lord Spencer. When the ceremony was over he took a car to drive to the Viceregal Lodge in the Phœnix Park. On his way he passed Mr. Burke, a well-known Castle official of many years' standing. Lord Frederick Cavendish got off the car, dismissed it, and walked with Mr. Burke through the Phœnix Park. It was a bright summer evening, between seven and eight, scarcely less light than at noonday. There were many people in the Park. Lord Frederick Cavendish and Mr. Burke were walking along the principal road—a wide highway for walking and driving, with flat grassy stretches at each side, and trees here and there. It seems almost incredible that in such a place, a park full of people, and at such a time—the clear bright evening of a summer day—two men could have been suddenly set upon by armed assassins, and literally been cut to pieces without anyone noticing what was going on, and without any opposition being offered to the escape of the murderers; yet that is precisely what did happen. Lord

Frederick Cavendish and Mr. Burke had got to within a few yards of the Phœnix Monument, they were within sight of the windows of the Viceregal Lodge, which lay at their right a few hundred yards away. Some boys on bicycles who passed them were the last to see them alive. The bicyclists drove round the Phœnix Monument, passed a cart with some four men on it driving rapidly away, and came back to find Lord Frederick Cavendish and Mr. Burke lying on the ground dead, and covered with wounds. When the alarm was given the bodies were soon recognised, but all trace of the assassins had disappeared, and such efforts as were made in the excitement of the hour to track them down were futile. It soon transpired that several persons were witnesses of the ghastly murder, who had no idea what they were witnessing. One man who was walking with his dogs at some little distance off saw what he believed to be a group of roughs struggling together in the road; he saw a couple of men fall and some others drive away without any feeling of surprise; nor had he, until he arrived at the spot where the dead bodies were lying, the slightest idea that he had been looking at one of the most horrible tragedies on record. It is even more painful to know that from the windows of the Viceregal Lodge Lord Spencer himself was looking out of one of the windows, and saw with unconcerned eyes the scuffle on the road some hundred yards away, little thinking that what seemed to be the horseplay of half a dozen roughs was in reality the murder of two of his colleagues.

'The effect that the news produced in Ireland and in England was one of universal horror. The leaders of the National party, Mr. Parnell, Mr. Dillon, and Mr. Davitt, at once issued an address to the Irish people and to the world, expressing their horror and despair at the shameful crime which had brought disgrace upon their country. The manifesto concluded: " We feel that no act has ever been perpetrated in our country, during the exciting struggles for social and political rights of the past fifty years, that has so stained the name of hospitable Ireland as this cowardly and unprovoked assassination of a friendly stranger, and that until the murderers of Lord Frederick Cavendish and Mr. Burke are brought to justice, that stain will sully our country's name."

'The feelings expressed in this manifesto were generally shared in Ireland. In Cork, a meeting chiefly composed of Nationalists and Land Leaguers, passed unanimously the following resolution:

'"That this meeting of the citizens of Cork, spontaneously assembled, hastens to express the feelings of indignation and sorrow with which it has learned of the murders of Lord Frederick Cavendish and Mr. T. H. Burke last night, and to denounce it as a crime that calls to Heaven for vengeance; to repudiate its authors, whoever they may be, with disgust and abhorrence, as men with whom the Irish nation has no community of feeling; and to convey our condolence with the families of the murdered."

'Similar resolutions were passed in all parts of Ireland, and the sincerest regret and horror appeared to prevail all over the country. But the murderers could not be found. . . . During the weeks immediately following the murder the police made many arrests, but in no cases were they able to establish any evidence of guilt in the prisoners. Later in the year a man named Westgate gave himself up in a South American port as one of the murderers, and was brought to Ireland to be examined; but it was soon found that his confession was false, it being clearly proved that he had sailed from Ireland some days before the murder had been committed.

'Mr. G. O. Trevelyan was appointed as the new Chief Secretary for Ireland. The Government immediately passed an exceptionally stringent and severe Crimes Act.

'Whatever the value of some of the powers conferred by the Bill might be, proof of the uselessness of "curfew-clause" legislation was given in June by two terrible murders which were committed long before sunset. On June 8, Mr. Walter Bourke and his military escort were shot at from behind a loopholed wall near Gort, and both killed. On the 29th of the month Mr. John Henry Blake, Lord Clanricarde's agent, and Mr. Keene, his steward, were shot also from behind a loopholed wall near Lough Rea, and both killed. In neither case was any clue to the assassins discoverable.

'The 15th of August was the occasion of a great national celebration in Dublin. On that day the great statue of O'Connell, cast from designs by Foley, which had been set up in the end of Sackville Street opposite the O'Connell—formerly Carlisle—Bridge was to be unveiled. On the same day the Exhibition of Irish Arts and Manufactures was to be opened. The history of this Exhibition was somewhat curious. Towards the end of 1881 the scheme of an Exhibition of Irish Manufactures in Dublin was proposed by some of the leading Dublin citizens, amongst whom Mr. Dawson, M.P., the Lord Mayor Elect, and other Irish members were conspicuous.

'These gentlemen had determined that the Exhibition should be entirely of a national character, and though they would undoubtedly have received Government assistance for their scheme, they chose to trust to their own exertions to carry the thing through, and they gave considerable offence in many quarters by their refusal to solicit or accept either Castle or Royal patronage for their undertaking. It was confidently predicted that an Exhibition got up under these conditions must of necessity be a disastrous failure. Nothing of the kind had practically been done without Castle countenance ever since there was a Castle, and the experiment was condemned in many quarters before it was attempted. But the founders of the scheme were not to be daunted. Headed by Mr. Dawson, they certainly worked hard for the success of their project, and by August 15 the Exhibition, which was entirely the work of the national party, was actually ready.

'The Exhibition, which was erected at the back of the Rotunda, was really a very pretty building of glass and iron, and it contained a display of Irish art and manufactures which was highly creditable to the artistic and industrial efforts and resources of the country. There was some fear that the day of the celebration would be disturbed by some fierce outbreak in Dublin, in consequence of the number of persons who would come into the city from the surrounding country. Commendation is due to Mr. Trevelyan and the authorities, who, while taking every precaution to be in readiness in case of any outbreak, made no display whatever of military or constabulary force. In Sackville Street, where the chief events of the day were to take place, there were no policemen visible; the town was apparently left in the trust and charge of the people themselves, and the result fully justified the wise action of the authorities. All the day the most perfect order was maintained everywhere. No rioting or unseemly displays of any kind occurred. The great procession, some miles in length, of Dublin guilds and trades, headed by the popular members of Parliament, went its appointed course from Stephen's Green through the city, and down Sackville Street to the foot of the veiled statue of O'Connell, through streets so densely filled by enthusiastic crowds no whit disheartened by an occasional rainfall, which indeed served only to heighten the national character of the proceedings. The statue was unveiled; the Exhibition was opened and was immediately crowded with curious visitors; and the whole day passed off without leaving any unpleasant memory of any kind behind it.

'The next day the long-deferred freedom of the city of Dublin was conferred upon Mr. Parnell and Mr. Dillon in the City Hall. Some considerable excitement was caused during the ceremony by the arrival of the news that Mr. E. D. Gray, M.P., the owner of the *Freeman's Journal*, and High Sheriff of Dublin, had just been committed to prison by Justice Lawson for contempt of Court. A man named Francis Hynes had been tried for a murder and condemned to death. A letter was published in the *Freeman's Journal* by Mr. O'Brien, the editor of *United Ireland*, declaring that on the night before the finding of the verdict the jury, who were in the Imperial Hotel where Mr. O'Brien was stopping, had behaved in a very noisy manner under the influence of drink. The *Freeman* published an article on this letter written by Mr. Gray, and commenting very severely upon the conduct of the jury. Mr. Gray was accordingly summoned before Mr. Justice Lawson for contempt of Court, and was condemned to three months' imprisonment, to pay a fine of 500*l*., and at the expiration of his imprisonment to find bail for 5,000*l*., and two sureties in 2,500*l*., under penalty of a further imprisonment of three months. Mr. Gray went to prison. Many of the Irish members in Dublin immediately went back to London, where the Parliament was just drawing to a close, to make the case known there; a proclamation, signed by the Lord Mayor and Mr. Parnell, was posted in all parts of the town calling upon the people to make no disturbance in consequence of the arrest. A public subscription was immediately started to meet the fine, which was promptly paid off. To dispose of this matter at once, we may say that Mr. Gray was kept in prison for a couple of months, and then released by Mr. Justice Lawson. The whole matter was afterwards made the subject of an inquiry by a Committee of the whole House of Commons, which, however, decided to take no action in the matter, on the ground that Judge Lawson was within his rights and privilege in what he had done.

'On August 17 a terrible outrage took place in Maamtrasna, in the Joyce country, which was connected with the murder of the Huddys in the early part of the year. A party of disguised men entered the house of a family named Joyce, consisting of a man, his wife, mother, two sons, and a daughter, and massacred them all with the exception of one son, who was severely wounded. The murderers had some reason to fear that the Joyce family knew of the murder of the two bailiffs whose bodies had been found in Lough Mask, and might betray it, and they tried to prevent this by a wholesale massacre. Three alleged murderers were convicted and condemned to death, and executed on December 15. Five others pleaded guilty and were condemned to death, but the death-penalty was commuted by the Lord Lieutenant. The alleged murderers of the Huddys, two men named Higgins and a man named Michael Flynn, were then discovered on the evidence of an informer, tried, and Flynn and one of the Higgins were sentenced to death.

'During the greater part of August the Irish Executive was much embarrassed by what threatened to be, and what in certain districts became, an actual strike on the part of the Irish Constabulary. The Constabulary had been agitating for increased pay and some other reforms in the service. The Inspector-General of Constabulary unfortunately characterised the conduct of the men, who had rendered the Government great service during two very trying years, as "disloyal"—a word which roused the greatest indignation throughout the whole force, and which had to be apologised for later. The Viceroy made several promises of redress of grievances which quieted the agitation for a short time, but it soon broke out again, chiefly in Limerick and in Dublin. On September 1 there was an almost general strike of policemen in Dublin. Special constables had to be hastily enrolled. For the time Dublin might almost have been called the City of Proclamations, for every wall bore placards—some from the Lord Lieutenant calling upon loyal citizens to come and enrol themselves as special constables; some from the Lord Mayor, Mr. Dawson, M.P., entreating all citizens to keep order. In fact, during this period of the strike the Lord Lieutenant and the Lord Mayor figured for a time as rival and hostile potentates. The Lord Mayor did not at all approve of the special constables enrolled by the Viceroy, and was anxious to organise a body of his own, and the Lord Lieutenant objected strongly to any such step on the part of the Mayor. The timely surrender of the Constabulary and the return of the policemen to their duty put an end to a very unpleasant crisis. There was actual rioting on more than one day, and the military had to be called out to clear Sackville Street at the point of the bayonet.

'The extreme Nationalists lost an old leader in August by the death of Mr. Charles Kickham. Mr. Charles Kickham was an author and journalist who had taken part in the Fenian organisation of 1867, was arrested, tried, and sentenced to fourteen years' penal servitude. After remaining three and a half years in Portland Prison he was released, but his health, which had always been delicate, was much weakened by his imprisonment, and for the remaining years of his life he took no part in Irish politics, but lived quietly outside Dublin, occasionally writing a little for some of the national papers. A large funeral procession was organised to do honour to his remains.

'Some slight excitement was caused in the early part of September by the arrest of Mr. Henry George, the correspondent of an American paper, and Mr. Joynes, an assistant-master at Eton who were travelling together in Ireland. The arrest was a mere mistake, and the two gentlemen were at once released; but Mr. Joynes wrote an amusing account of the adventure to the *Times*, and afterwards published a little book upon the Irish question, which led to disagreements between himself and the head-master of Eton, and to Mr. Joynes's retirement from his position as assistant-master.

'On October 17 an Irish National Conference was held in the Ancient Concert Rooms, Dublin. The object of the conference was to form an organisation which should unite into one body all sections of the Irish party, whether Nationalists, Land Leaguers, or Home Rulers. The new body was styled the Irish National League, and its programme was undoubtedly of the most comprehensive nature, for, in the words of Mr. Parnell, its objects were " national self-government, land-law reform, local self-government, extension of the Parliamentary and municipal franchises, and the development and encouragement of the labour and industrial interests of Ireland." This formation of the National League on the ruins of the old Land League recalled curiously enough the historical parallel of O'Connell's societies for the promotion of Catholic Emancipation, which the Government was always suppressing and the Liberator always re-creating under a new name.

'At first the new organisation seemed likely to cause some dissension among the national party. Mr. Michael Davitt was well known to hold very different views from those of Mr. Parnell himself on the Land question. While Mr. Parnell for the time contented himself with making peasant-proprietorship the basis of his demands, Mr. Davitt was an enthusiastic advocate of the nationalisation of the land, and he had a considerable following in the country. Mr. John Dillon, too, was supposed to be in favour of more advanced views than the leader of the Parliamentary party, and this impression was confirmed by the sudden announcement that Mr. Dillon intended to resign his seat in Parliament. The cause alleged was ill-health, and it was indeed well-known that Mr. Dillon's physical condition was far from good, but it was immediately bruited abroad that there was a split in the national camp. A little later, however, Mr. Dillon was induced to withdraw his resignation at the request of Archbishop Croke, but he shortly after left the country to recruit his health in warmer climates. Mr. Davitt, though he still adhered to the principle of nationalisation of the land, and advocated it warmly on every platform where he spoke, offered no opposition to the new organisation, and all appearance of disunion among the party was averted. But the threatened split proved a temporary split among the national Irish across the Atlantic. The *Irish World* and its followers not only espoused Mr. Davitt's theories, but fiercely attacked Mr. Parnell and the Parliamentary party, while most of the Land League branches throughout the States adhered to Mr. Parnell's policy.

'The Corporation of Dublin were again conspicuous in November. One of the body proposed that the freedom of the city should be conferred on Sir Garnet Wolseley, in recognition of his distinguished services in the Egyptian campaign. This was strenuously opposed by the more extreme members of the Corporation, and a story was circulated to the effect that Sir Garnet Wolseley had expressed a wish for a rising of " the Paddies," that he might get a chance of putting them down. As the story, though improbable, found many believers, some friends of Sir Garnet Wolseley thought it worth while to write to him, asking if there was any truth in the tale. Sir Garnet Wolseley at once replied that there was no truth in it, and added, "I trust I may not live to see civil war in any part of Her Majesty's dominions; but should such a calamity ever befall us as a nation, I hope I may not have anything to do with it. Although I am not any politician, no Irishman could wish to see Ireland loyal, peaceful, contented, and prosperous more than I do." In view, however, of the strong feeling manifested, the proposal to confer the freedom of the city on Sir Garnet Wolseley was withdrawn.

'On November 11 a period of considerable absence of outrages was broken, and Dublin society was much alarmed by a mysterious attempt to assassinate Mr. Justice Lawson. The Judge was walking on the north side of Merrion Square, about five o'clock in the evening, when one of his escort of four men, two detectives and two army pensioners, who always accompanied him of late, observed that a suspicious-looking man was apparently dodging the Judge. This man was then observed to put his hand to his breast, when he was seized by the one of the escort who had first observed him, and was found to be holding a loaded seven-chamber revolver in his hand. He was at once disarmed and given into custody. He was afterwards tried and sentenced to ten years' penal servitude.

'Towards the end of November, Dublin was the scene of several more outrages. On the night of November 25, an attack was made on several detectives by armed men in Abbey Street, and one of the detectives was killed. The next evening a man named Field, who had been juror in the trial of a man named Walsh, who was executed for the murder of a policeman at Letterfrack, was attacked by assassins outside his own house in North Frederick Street in the dusk of evening, and stabbed several times and left for dead. The assassins escaped, and no trace of them could be found, but their victim, though his case was considered hopeless at first, did finally recover from his injuries.'

CHAPTER XXII.

ORANGE AND GREEN.

IN December of 1882, according to the same authority, the Irish Executive had turned its attention to certain speeches delivered by Mr. Michael Davitt, Mr. Healy, M.P., and Mr. Biggar, M.P., which appeared to the Castle authorities to call for prosecution. 'On January 2, Mr. Biggar's case came before the Waterford Sessions, Waterford having been the scene of his offending utterances. The prosecution, however, came to nothing. Mr. Biggar had made a very violent attack upon Lord Spencer, and had passed the severest strictures upon the conduct of the jury in the Hynes case; but, however much his remarks might have offended against the canons of political good taste, there was nothing in them to justify the interference of the law. Mr. Biggar was committed for trial at the Spring Assizes, after being allowed to find bail and give securities in small amounts; and nothing further was heard of the matter.

'The Executive would, perhaps, have displayed greater discretion if they had treated the speeches of Mr. Biggar, Mr. Davitt, and Mr. Healy with politic indifference from the beginning. Failing this, the wisest course might have been to let the matter drop in all three cases. An unsuccessful prosecution is, indeed, always bad for an Executive, but it is not the worst that can befall it. A successful prosecution may sometimes have more disastrous consequences. It proved so in this instance. The Executive, fearing that its action with regard to Mr. Biggar might make it appear too easy-going, determined to push things farther in the cases of Mr. Davitt, Mr. Healy, and Mr. Quinn, a secretary of the National League. They were called upon to find securities for their good behaviour, or to go to prison for six months.

'To men in their position there was of course no alternative. To have consented to find securities would have been to admit that they were wrong, and to discredit them for ever in the eyes of the people to whom they were appealing. In sending them to prison, on the other hand, the Castle authorities were only increasing their opponents' popularity and power in the country a thousandfold. Mr. Davitt had, indeed, passed a large part of his life in prison, but every fresh incarceration made him more and more of a martyr in Irish eyes, and he invariably came out of confinement a far more potent political force than he had entered it. Mr. Healy, on the other hand, although one of the most popular of the Parnellite party in Ireland, was one of the few leading Nationalist members who had not suffered imprisonment for his opinions. It was, dramatically, the one thing wanting to his career, and the temporary inconvenience of six months' seclusion was but a trifle in contrast with the increase of influence and authority which was certain to accompany it.

'But the prosecutions did something more than merely increase the personal and political popularity of Mr. Davitt and Mr. Healy. The opponents of the national movement were always most anxious to see a split in the Parnellite ranks. Such a split they thought had occurred after the formation of the new national League, when Mr. Davitt made proclamation of marked difference of opinion with Mr. Parnell, and was severely censured by Mr. T. P. O'Connor for doing so. There did, indeed, seem at moments the possibility of the National movement being divided into the two camps of the Parnell party and the Davitt party. But any such division, if it existed at all, was completely put an end to by the imprisonment of Mr. Davitt and Mr. Healy. The necessary intercourse caused by common imprisonment between Mr. Davitt and one of the ablest of Mr. Parnell's lieutenants was in itself enough to solder close the two powers in the national party. In the excitement and enthusiasm caused by the imprisonment all small differences were forgotten, and, as a matter of fact, when Mr. Davitt finally came out of prison, he gave in his adherence cordially to the National League, with which, at its first inception, he appeared to be at odds. It is, indeed, one of the most remarkable things in Mr. Davitt's connection with the agitation in Ireland that the originator of the Land League has always been content to act loyally with Mr. Parnell, and has steadily rejected the many opportunities of setting himself in opposition.

'Of course the Executive could not allow its action to be influenced by such considerations as these, if the speeches of either Mr. Davitt or Mr. Healy seriously called for strong measures. But the offending orations were hardly of sufficient magnitude to justify the temporary martyrdom of their speakers. They had said nothing very new or very surprising, and in making an example of them, the Executive only succeeded in making Mr. Davitt more popular than before, in raising Mr. Healy to the front rank among the politicians of the Parnellite party, and in effectually preventing for the time any suggestion of a split between the followers of Mr. Parnell on the one side, and the adherents of Mr. Davitt on the other.

'The Government was engaged on yet a third prosecution, the results of which were equally favourable to the Nationalists. *United Ireland* was the paper of all others in Dublin which expressed most frankly the opinions of the advanced party in Ireland. At the time of the Government descent upon the Land League this journal was promptly proscribed, and for a long time made its appearance with the greatest difficulty, being printed now in Paris, now in Liverpool, and smuggled into Ireland as chance permitted or opportunity offered. It now made its appearance again, and was as active as ever in its support of the extreme national party. Its editor was Mr. William O'Brien, a young man of education and ability, conspicuous among the prominent non-Parliamentary followers of Mr. Parnell for his " irreconcilable " opinions.

'He had, it will be remembered, come forward at the time of the Hynes trial to give his testimony to the riotous conduct of the jury at the Imperial Hotel on the night previous to the verdict. After the execution an article appeared in *United Ireland* entitled " Accusing Spirits," in which a bitter attack was made upon the Government of Lord Spencer. On

January 15 Mr. William O'Brien was committed for trial for having, in the phraseology of the indictment, published a false, malicious, and seditious libel for the purpose and with the intent of bringing the government of the country and the administration of the law into hatred and contempt, and in order to incite hostility against the same, and for the purpose of disturbing the peace of the country, and of raising discontent and disaffection among the Queen's subjects.

'At this time Mr. William O'Brien was a candidate for the small constituency of Mallow, one of the most peculiar constituencies in the South of Ireland. It was very small; it was popularly held to be very rotten. During the old Parliament it had been represented by a very moderate Home Ruler, Mr. John George MacCarthy. That a Home Ruler of any shade should be able to sit for Mallow seemed remarkable enough, but it was pretty generally admitted that a Home Ruler would have no chance again. At the General Election Mr. William M. Johnson, an Irish Liberal lawyer, had been elected by a considerable majority over his Conservative opponent. When, on the formation of the Ministry, Mr. Johnson, as the new Solicitor-General for Ireland, went down again to Mallow, a Home Rule candidate was run in opposition to him. The result was discouraging enough to the Home Rulers. Mr. Johnson was returned by a larger majority than before, while the Home Rule candidate got very considerably less votes than had been won by Mr. Johnson's Conservative rival. Now, in the beginning of 1883, Mr. Johnson, having accepted other duties, was leaving Parliamentary life; Mallow was again vacant, and the national party, apparently forgetful of their former rebuff, were bringing forward, not a nominal Home Ruler, but one of the most aggressive and uncompromising champions of the principles of Mr. Parnell.

'The struggle was watched by both sides with the keenest interest. The defeat of Mr. O'Brien would undoubtedly be a very severe check to the aspirations of the Nationalist party; his success would be a decided triumph for them. The issue seemed doubtful until the beginning of the *United Ireland* trial. With his committal for trial Mr. O'Brien's chance of election became a certainty. Two days after the formal committal he was returned at the head of the poll by a majority of seventy-two votes over Mr. Naish, the new Solicitor-General for Ireland, and the Nationalists had scored their greatest success since the election of Mr. Parnell for Cork City. The trial itself came to nothing, owing to the disagreement of the jury.

'During the week of the Mallow election several executions took place, which were the subject of much comment in the Nationalist Press and on Nationalist platforms. Patrick Higgins, Thomas Higgins, and Michael Flynn were hanged for the murder of the Huddys in the Joyce country in the early part of the previous year; Sylvester Poff and James Barrett were hanged for the murder of Thomas Brown near Castle Island. Considerable belief in the innocence of Poff was expressed in Ireland, and a wide-spread sympathy for the dead man was finding vent in bitter criticisms of the administration of justice, when a series of events, the most startling and the most impressive that had yet occurred in the history of Ireland under the new Government, diverted public attention from everything except certain proceedings in the Dublin Police-court and in Kilmainham Court-house.

'On January 13 Dublin was surprised by a mysterious police raid on various houses, resulting in the arrest of no less than seventeen persons, most of them in an humble way of life, but one of them, a well-to-do tradesman, and recently elected Town Councillor, by name James Carey, of whom the year was to hear more. The arrests were made in consequence of a series of inquiries which had been going on at the Castle, under the peculiar statutory powers allowed by the Crimes Act, of examining witnesses without bringing any specific charges against individuals, and so obtaining information not otherwise to be got at. The seventeen prisoners were at once charged with conspiracy to murder certain Government officials and other persons. Attempts were made on behalf of many of the prisoners to obtain bail, but bail was in every instance steadily refused. Two days later three more men were arrested.

'The news of these arrests created great excitement on both sides of St. George's Channel. In Ireland all who belonged to the disaffected portion of the community were inclined to believe that the authorities had made one more needless blunder in arresting a number of inoffensive men, and putting them to unnecessary annoyance and indignity by repeated examinations. The refusal of bail was regarded as a special grievance, and the complaints against the harshness of the Executive were many and bitter. Others, however, were more disturbed by doubt as to whether the Castle had really been fortunate enough to place its hand upon any of those unknown criminals who were held responsible for the mysterious murders of the preceding year. While they hoped, with the London *Times*, " that there is at length a probability of securing the clue to a series of atrocious crimes, perpetrated with a cold-blooded deliberation and remorseless purpose not easily paralleled, save among the fanatics of Nihilism," they felt that it did not follow that even now the Government was in the possession of legal proof. Any such doubt was soon to be removed. On January 20, the prisoners were brought before the court, and it was made known that one of their number, Robert Farrell, a labourer and an old-time Fenian, had turned informer. Farrell's evidence was startling. Something had always been known by the outer world of the Fenian organisation, but Farrell's revelations disclosed the existence of an organisation inside that, a mysterious inner circle, composed of men carefully selected from the larger body, and organised for the assassination of Government officials and others. The scheme of this inner circle was managed with an ingenuity that would have done credit to a Nihilist committee. Its members were unacquainted with the bulk of their associates; each man only knew the colleague who swore him in, and who was known as his "right," and another introduced by himself, and who was styled his "left." The chief business of this inner circle, as far as

Farrell's knowledge of it went, was to try and assassinate the then Chief Secretary, Mr. Forster. Farrell described with great coolness and elaborate minuteness of detail a series of plans to take Mr. Forster's life, each of which only failed through some mere chance, some bungle in the working of a preconcerted signal, or some error in the calculation of the hour at which the Chief Secretary's carriage would pass by an appointed spot. Farrell himself was never a member of the inner circle, nor was he ever present at any meeting called for the purpose of planning the murder of any one; but he admitted being implicated in certain attempts on the life of the Chief Secretary. He furthermore stated that one of the prisoners, Hanlon, had given him a circumstantial account of the attempt to murder Mr. Field.

'Farrell's evidence aroused the most intense excitement everywhere. It was whispered abroad that the Government expected to elicit from this inquiry information not merely with regard to the attack on Mr. Field, but the murders in the Phœnix Park, and public curiosity was strained to its highest. On the 27th evidence was given implicating Joseph Brady, Timothy Kelly, John Dwyer, Joseph Hanlon, and a car-driver, Kavanagh, in the Field attack. One of the witnesses, Lamie, was, like Farrell, an informer who had been a Fenian. He gave some curious evidence of the formation of vigilance committees to see that the orders of the Directory were carried out. One of these vigilance committees had been broken up by the fight in Abbey Street, when apparently a Fenian, named Poole, was being marked for assassination. The work was interrupted by the detectives, and in the scuffle that followed Sergeant Cox was killed.

'On February 3 the inquiry first was directed towards the Phœnix Park murders. Knives were produced which had been found in James Carey's house, deadly-looking weapons, such as are used by surgeons for amputation. The medical men who had examined the bodies of Lord Frederick Cavendish and Mr. Burke considered that the knives corresponded to the nature of the wounds inflicted. A chairmaker and his wife, who lived at the strawberry beds, identified Edward O'Brien and Joseph Brady as being in the Phœnix Park on the day of the murder. The keeper of a deerkeeper's lodge testified to seeing a car with Joseph Brady on it pass out of the Chapelizod Gate on the evening of the murder. Another witness had seen Brady and M'Caffrey in the Park on the evening of the murder. On February 10 Michael Kavanagh, the car-driver, turned informer. His evidence was startling. On May 6, 1882, he drove Joe Brady, Tim Kelly, and two other men, whose names he did not know, but one of whom he identified as Patrick Delaney, to the Phœnix Park. There they found James Carey; there Carey gave the signal for the murder of Mr. Burke and Lord Frederick Cavendish by raising a white handkerchief. Kavanagh saw the murder committed; then his four passengers got on again to the car and he drove off as fast as he could, returning to the city in a roundabout way. On the night of the Field outrage he drove Brady and Daniel Delaney to Hardwicke Street, where Tim Kelly and Hanlon were, and after the assault he drove Brady and Kelly away.

'But the crowning surprise came on February 17, when James Carey entered the court as an informer. This Carey had conducted himself all through the course of the investigations thus far with cool effrontery. His position among the other prisoners was peculiar. He belonged to a somewhat better class in life than the rest. His place on the Town Council he owed to the fact that he was an ex-suspect. He had been arrested under the old Coercion Act on suspicion of being concerned in an outrage in Amiens Street. After his release he stood at the municipal elections for Town Councillor, and was elected by a very large majority over a Liberal and Catholic opponent.

'His demeanour during the early part of the investigation was noisily defiant. He protested loudest when he was first arrested; we hear of him swaggering out of the prison van to the first examinations smoking a cigar, ostentatiously dressed to mark the distinction between his position and that of his fellow-prisoners ; again we hear of him losing his temper and assaulting the Governor of Kilmainham Jail. But after the evidence of Farrell and Lamie his audacity appears to have broken down. He determined to save his own neck at any hazard, and he turned informer.

'Carey, on his own showing, was the worst of the assassins. He had lured other men into the organisation, had plotted murders, had arranged the Phœnix Park assassination, and given the signal when the deed was to be done. It was at his suggestion that knives were chosen as the weapons to be employed in committing the crime.

'In 1861 Carey had joined the Fenians, and was a prominent member until 1878. In 1881 the Invincibles were formed, outside the Fenian body, though composed of men drawn from its ranks. The oath which Carey took as leader of this body pledged him to obey all the orders of the Irish Invincibles, under penalty of death. At the head of the organisation appeared to be a mysterious person, whose name Carey never knew, but who was always called "No. 1." He gave most of the orders, he seems to have supplied the money. After the attempts on Mr. Forster failed, and when Mr. Forster and Earl Cowper resigned, it was No. 1 who settled that Mr. Burke was to be the victim.

'Carey's evidence practically closed the inquiry. The prisoners were at once committed for trial. The trials began in April, and did not last very long. Brady, Curley, Fagan, and Kelly were found guilty, the latter after the jury had twice disagreed, and were sentenced to death. Caffrey and Delaney pleaded guilty, and were sentenced to death. Delaney's sentence was commuted to penal servitude for life. The five others were hanged. Mullett and Fitzharris were sentenced to penal servitude for life, and the remaining prisoners to various periods of penal servitude.

'Carey's evidence failed to connect the Land League as a body with the "Invincibles." When it first became known that James Carey had turned informer, and that he had apparently inculpated the Land League in his evidence, public curiosity on both sides of the Irish Sea held its breath. What might not come next! The wildest improbabilities were gravely suggested; the enemies of the Land League exultingly announced that the time had at last come when the secrets of the nefarious body were to be revealed, and its flimsy pretence of constitutional agitation finally torn away from it, while others went even so far as to hint with unmistakable clearness that the true heads of the Invincibles would now be found among the ranks of the Irish Parliamentary party.

'These predictions, however, were not verified. Some humble members of the Land League were accused by Carey of being concerned in the Phœnix Park assassination, but his evidence absolutely failed to show any connection between the Land League, as an organised body, and the Invincibles. Carey accused the wife of a secretary of the English branch of the Land League—a man named Frank Byrne—of having brought over weapons from London to Dublin for assassination purposes, but on being confronted with the woman, who was immediately arrested, Carey at once declared that she was not the woman he meant. A man named Sheridan, who had figured in the debates on the Kilmainham Treaty, and another named Walsh, who were implicated by Carey's evidence, got away to the United States. Frank Byrne and Walsh were in France at the time when the disclosures were made in Kilmainham Court-house. They were arrested in reply to the appeal of our Government, and examined, but were speedily set at liberty, on the ground that there was no case to justify their extradition, and made their way to America.

'A curious piece of evidence came out in the trial in support of the claim made by the leaders of what may be called the Parliamentary part of the national movement, that their action, far from having anything in common with the actions of the secret societies, was actually inimical to these, and was in consequence bitterly obnoxious to them. One of the assassins kept a diary, in which he recorded from time to time his opinions of the political events going on around him, and one of these records gave, in clear and direct language, full expression to the writer's scorn and contempt for Mr. Parnell, and those who, like him, were practising the methods of constitutional agitation.

'The trial made it evident that the death of Lord Frederick Cavendish was a mischance, wholly unplanned and wholly unintentional. While the horror of the murder was first fresh in men's minds, it seemed obvious that Lord Frederick Cavendish had been sacrificed by the irreconcilable party as an immediate answer to the message of peace which Mr. Gladstone was sending to the distracted country.

'The Government had recalled a thoroughly unpopular and unsuccessful Chief Secretary, and were sending in his place a young man of ability, of unprejudiced sympathy with the work entrusted to him, who was known to be in the most complete agreement with Mr. Gladstone. It seemed almost certain that his murder was the deliberate answer of the secret societies to any attempt on the part of England to hold out the hand of fellowship to Ireland.

'It is gratifying, as far as anything in the hideous tragedy can be gratifying, to find that this theory was erroneous. The evidence of the chief criminal made it clear that the Phœnix Park murder, horrible though it was, was not so absolutely horrible as it had first appeared. The assassination was entirely aimed at Mr. Burke, a man who was well known to be one of the most dangerous enemies the secret societies had in all the range of Castle authority. He was believed to have all the threads of their workings in his hands; it was at him the blow was levelled, not at the friendly stranger. Lord Frederick Cavendish was murdered not because he had come with a message of conciliation to those who would not be conciliated, but because he was walking in the company of a man marked for death.

'The murderers of Mr. Burke did not even know who his companion was—did not learn till later that the brave man who had fallen in the effort to save his companion was the new Chief Secretary. The levity of destiny shows only too painfully in the chance which killed Lord Frederick Cavendish, and deepened the darkness of the gloom in which the struggle between the two countries was going on. But the horror of the murder is somewhat lessened by the knowledge that the Phœnix Park assassins had not compassed the death of one who, judged even by their own dark canons, was innocent of all offence against the country which, in their error, they believed themselves to be serving.

'One result of the trials was to fully justify the Government in any action which had resulted in the substitution of a new Chief Secretary for Mr. Forster. However excellent Mr. Forster's intentions, however praiseworthy his motives, the result of his administration was not success. With all the instruments of coercion in his hands, he did not know how to employ them properly. It reads like the grimmest of satires upon his term of office to know that at a time when the jails were choking with the number of Mr. Forster's " suspects ; " when, according to his own belief, he had every dangerous man in the island under lock and key, his own life was in incessant danger at the hands of men of whose existence and purposes he was guilelessly unaware. Only a succession of chances, that read almost like providential miracles, saved him, time after time, from men whom a word of his, or a stroke of his pen, could at any moment have clapped in safe keeping, had he the slightest suspicion of their existence. The law gave him power to arrest on suspicion, but he had no suspicion of the only body of men whose plans were really dangerous, whose actions were really deadly.

'The informer's own fate was dramatically tragic. For some time he remained in Kilmainham Prison. His life would not have been worth an hour's purchase had he been turned out free into the streets of Dublin, and yet, with reckless effrontery, he wrote letter after letter to the Town Council, of which he was a member, announcing that he would soon take his seat amongst them again. Meanwhile preparations were being made to get him out of the country. He really seems to have been unwilling to go, to be deeply angered against the Castle authorities for refusing to pay him any reward. At last he seemed to be got rid of, to have disappeared; no one, it was thought, knew whither. Most people conjectured that he would be successfully buried from knowledge or pursuit in some Crown colony, or possibly in the wardership of some Government prison, where, under an assumed name, he might probably escape detection for the term of his natural life.

'Suddenly, one day towards the end of July, came a startling telegram from the Cape, from the representatives of the firm of Donald Currie, announcing that James Carey, the informer, had been shot dead on his arrival at the Cape by a man named O'Donnell, who had travelled out with him on the same ship from England for the purpose of killing him. At first the news was doubted. There was something grimly dramatic about the way in which the informer was struck down, that at first people refused to believe it. But the news was soon corroborated. O'Donnell was brought to England, tried, found guilty, and executed early in December. It is as well to conclude the list of the year's executions at once by mentioning that on Tuesday, December 18, Joseph Poole, convicted of the murder of a suspected informer named Kenny, was hanged in Dublin.

'After the ghastly revelations in Kilmainham Court-house there came a season of comparative quiet in Ireland. So terribly had the public ear been crammed with horrors in Dublin, that a series of trials going on in Belfast raised little excitement, and passed off comparatively unnoticed. Yet at any other time these trials would have roused the keenest attention. A murder conspiracy was being unravelled—a conspiracy scarcely less deadly than that of Dublin, though its aim was the assassination of local landlords rather than of prominent Government officials. As usual, the evidence of an informer was necessary to complete the Government case, and a James Carey was found to bring guilt home to the North of Ireland conspirators in the person of one Patrick Duffy. Ten of the twelve men brought to trial were sentenced to ten years' penal servitude; of the remaining two, one received seven, the other five years of imprisonment.'

In conformity with the habit of Parliament under the new administration, a long debate sprang up upon the address. People who objected to the policy of the Government in Egypt and in Zululand, or who objected to other actions of the Government, or who wished to point out what the Government ought to do, expressed their opinions with sufficient copiousness. Mr. Gorst was the first to bring Ireland prominently forward by an ingenious amendment, expressing a hope that no further concessions would be made to lawless agitators in that country. This at once aroused all the old Kilmainham treaty excitement. In these debates Mr. Gibson, as he then was, and Mr. Plunket were always in their element. Like the great twin brethren who were always supposed to have a special eye to the safety of Rome, and to interfere in person where the fortunes of the 'Nameless City' were going badly, Mr. Gibson and Mr. Plunket were ever in the van of the Conservative battle when an Irish question gave them the chance of showing that the Conservative party really had some of the old fighting spirit left in them.

The Kilmainham treaty was the greatest of blessings to these two gentlemen. The curious resemblances that existed between them increased their likeness to the Dioscuri, and lent a piquant attraction to any of their united attacks upon the Ministry accused of unholy compact with the Third Party. Both represented the same constituency, both were clever lawyers, both were exceptionally able speakers, both had peculiarly eighteenth-century faces, both prided themselves on their gifts of satiric speech, both were endowed with a certain quality of theatrical display which enabled them to make the very most of even the slightest rhetorical opportunity, both were law officers of the Crown under the late Administration.

But just as Castor was not wholly like Pollux, or Pollux like Castor, so Mr. Gibson and Mr. Plunket had certain points of difference, which serve perhaps only to heighten the general similitude. Mr. Gibson was, perhaps, the harder hitter; Mr. Plunket the more poetically minded. Mr. Plunket was more showy than solid ; Mr. Gibson more solid than showy. On this occasion both speakers were in full force. Mr. Gibson attacked everybody fiercely—the Government, the Irish members, and especially Mr. Herbert Gladstone, who had made a speech at Leeds which stirred Mr. Gibson to a passion of indignation. The Dioscuri raised the Kilmainham ghost again, showed that it had been neither laid nor exorcised by all the debates that had been devoted to it, and succeeded in bringing up Mr. Forster. Mr. Forster had a peculiar affection for the Kilmainham treaty topic. It enabled him to gratify his sense of injury against the colleagues who did not properly appreciate his worth and his ability. Mr. Forster's speech was a long attack upon Mr. Parnell, interrupted at one point not undramatically. Mr. Forster had used words which, whatever they were meant to convey, gave to their hearers the impression that he charged Mr. Parnell with conniving at murder. Mr. O'Kelly immediately and impetuously interrupted him by crying out thrice, ' You lie! ' and was at once suspended. This debate took place on Thursday, the 22nd, and the next day Mr. Parnell replied in a brief, quiet, composed speech, in which he coldly repudiated Mr. Forster's insinuations.

In the course of the debate some ingenious use was made by Mr. Forster's opponents of former utterances of his own, and journalistic comments upon them. Mr. Forster had made a speech in March, 1864, defending Mazzini as a man of high character, whose friend he should not be ashamed to be, as he was not ashamed to be his acquaintance. This declaration was made after long quotations had been read in the House from Mazzini's letter on ' The Theory of the Dagger,' in which he had written, ' Blessed be the knife of Palafox ; blessed be in your hands every weapon that can destroy the enemy and set you free. The weapon that slew Mincovitch in the arsenal initiated the insurrection in Venice. It was a weapon of irregular warfare, like that which three months before the Republic destroyed the minister Rossi in Rome.'

These were the utterances of the man whom Mr. Forster considered of high character, whose friendship he would not repudiate. The quotation of these passages was appropriate. They were not brought forward to convey the idea that Mr. Forster approved of political assassination; that, of course would have been absurd. The intention was to show how easily such accusations are trumped up, and also how liable English statesmen are to commend, or at least to condone, principles of revolution in foreign states, which they view in a very different light when they are applied at home. The Kilmainham treaty was not heard the last of in this debate. It came up again and again. Whenever adventurous members of the Opposition had nothing better to do or to talk about they turned to the Kilmainham treaty, and made it the sempiternal text for attacks upon the Government. But no amount of indignant inquiries or pertinacious onslaughts succeeded in eliciting any further facts as to the alleged 'treaty.' The Government had given its explanation, and declined to amplify it to suit the sensational and mysterious suggestions of an incredulous Opposition.

Early in March the Parliamentary party lost one of its most remarkable, and certainly one of its most picturesque figures, by the resignation of Mr. John Dillon. Mr. Dillon's appearance singled him out at once, whether on the back benches of the House of Commons, or on the crowded platform of an Irish meeting, as a man remarkable among his fellows. His grave, melancholy face, his intensely dark hair and eyes, gave him as we have said a curiously Spanish air, more appropriate to those stately faces that smile from the canvases of Velasquez in the great gallery of Madrid than to a nineteenth-century member for Tipperary. He was one of the few followers of Mr. Parnell whose appearance in any sense corresponded to the ideal picture of a member of a revolutionary party. Those who watched him in the House of Commons felt instinctively that he would have found more fitting surroundings in some Jacobin convention, some Committee of Public Safety of the year 1793. Mr. Dillon's character did not wholly belie his appearance. He was among the extremest of the extreme section of Mr. Parnell's following. His speeches had raised fiercer controversy than those of any of his colleagues. The son of a rebel of 1848, he inherited all, and more than all, the uncompromising spirit of Young Ireland, and he did not, in his early days in the House of Commons profess any profound blessing in Parliamentary agitation. Thirty years earlier he would have flung himself enthusiastically into the movements of the national party; have matched passions with Mitchel; perhaps have striven to emulate the glowing oratory of Meagher, and have followed Smith O'Brien from London to Ballingarry, and from Ballingarry to Van Diemen's Land. He should have played the father's part, the father the son's. John Dillon the elder had a belief in the sympathies of English statesmen and politicians, of which his son inherited no jot. Had the elder Dillon lived to carry out his cherished purpose of effecting a lasting union between the representatives of Irish nationalism and the leaders of the English Liberal party, the story of Irish politics for the last twenty years might have been very different.

John Dillon the younger was rumoured to be at odds with Mr. Parnell on many points. People talked of him as being anxious to set himself up as a rival to Mr. Parnell, as scheming to wrest the leadership away from him. Mr. Dillon never showed the least sign of any such purpose. Whenever he found that his ideas were not in complete unison with those of his chief, instead of thrusting himself forward and declaring his own views, he simply held aloof and was silent. In the end his health gave way, and retirement from political life became inevitable. He had desired to resign more than once before, but had been restrained by his friends; now, however, the condition of his health rendered rest imperative. He resigned his seat, and went away to recover his strength in Italy and Colorado; and his vacant place was filled by Mr. Mayne, who was of course an ardent Parnellite.

In April, 1883, a measure was introduced and passed into law with almost unrivalled rapidity. This was the Bill for amending the law relating to explosives, which was introduced by Sir William Harcourt on Monday, April 9, passed through all its stages in the Commons in less than two hours, was sent to the Lords, and received the royal assent the next day.

There was reason for this unusual haste. Much had been said and written for some time by a section of Irish-Americans in New York about the introduction of dynamite into the political difficulties between England and Ireland. Threats to blow up London buildings were uttered at meetings of the advocates of dynamite, and printed in their journals, but at first little heed was paid to these utterances. On the night of Thursday, March 15, 1883, however, an attempt was made to blow up the offices of the Local Government Board at the corner of Whitehall and Charles Street. No great damage was done, and no lives were lost, but a great many windows were broken. The wall and one room of the Local Government Offices were considerably shattered, and for a time considerable alarm was created. A simultaneous attempt to blow up the *Times* office failed through the fortunate accidental overturning of the infernal machine used, which prevented it from operating. The same attempted explosions by dynamite in Glasgow appeared to be in fulfilment of these threats, but they did not arouse much public excitement. The Government immediately offered the reward of 1,000*l*. for the apprehension of the criminals, but no clue was obtained, and no information given.

It was confidently expected that the attempts would be repeated, and every precaution was taken. At all the public offices, important public buildings, and the residences of statesmen, a military guard was placed, or where it existed before was doubled. For some little time after the event London presented an unwontedly military air. The presence of so many soldiers in places where formerly no other guardianship than that of the policeman was required lent London something of the appearance of a Continental city. These precautions, however, were not long maintained, and in a short while London resumed its wonted aspect. The dynamite difficulty was not at an end, unfortunately. In the first week in April, 1883, the police succeeded in discovering a conspiracy, in arresting eight men concerned, and in seizing a large quantity of nitro-glycerine, which was manufactured in Birmingham, and was being secretly conveyed to London.

It was impossible to identify the men arrested with the perpetrators of the attempt upon the Local Government Board and the *Times* office. But their connection with the Irish-American advocates of dynamite was clearly established. To meet what seemed like a wide-spread conspiracy the Explosives Bill was hurried through Parliament. Four of the prisoners were sentenced to penal servitude for life: two were acquitted. These sentences and the comprehensive powers of the new measure did not, however, prevent further dynamite crimes. The police made seizures of nitro-glycerine in Leicester, and in Cupar, in Fife. Men were arrested in Glasgow on the charge of being concerned in the outrages of January. Four men were sentenced to penal servitude for life for introducing explosive substances into England at Liverpool. On October 30, 1883, two explosions took place on the Metropolitan Railway: one between Westminster and Charing Cross, the other between Praed Street and Edgware Road. Both occurred almost at the same time, about eight o'clock in the evening; both did considerable damage to property, and many human beings were injured, though no one fatally. No trace of the perpetrators of this outrage was discovered.

Towards the end of February in 1884 a yet bolder outrage was attempted, which happily only partially succeeded. At a little after one on the morning of Tuesday, February 26, an explosion took place in the luggage-room of Victoria Station, which wrecked a large part of the station, and destroyed a considerable amount of property. Though it was at once assumed that this was part of a dynamite plot, the destruction of everything in the luggage-room was so great that absolute proof might have been difficult to obtain. The discovery of infernal machines at Charing Cross, Ludgate Hill, and Paddington stations supplied the necessary proofs. In the luggage-room of each of these stations a portmanteau was discovered containing a large quantity of dynamite connected with a pistol and a clock timed to go off at a certain hour. In each of these cases the defective nature of the machinery employed had happily prevented catastrophes which would in all probability have been far more dangerous than that at Victoria Station. An attempt was made later on Blackfriars Bridge. Early in 1885 two explosions took place in Westminster, one in the great hall and one in the chamber of the House, which did great damage and seriously injured two policemen.

No language can be too strong in condemnation of these criminal attempts. The freedom and the future of Ireland are not to be worked out by means abhorrent to all Christian men. Every Nationalist, every one who believes that the hour of Ireland's regeneration is daily, even hourly, drawing nearer, who believes that in the immediate future the Parliament of Ireland will be restored to her, can only feel horror at such deeds. The cause of Ireland is not to be served by the knife of the assassin and the infernal machine of the dynamitard.

'In the month of May a fresh stimulus to popular excitement was given by the case of the *Kerry Sentinel*. The proprietor of this paper was Mr. Timothy Harrington, who had suffered imprisonment in the preceding year for a speech he delivered, and who was rewarded for his imprisonment by being elected to represent Westmeath in Parliament, while still confined in Mullingar Jail. The offence with which the paper was charged was the issue of certain seditious proclamations alleging to emanate from the " Invincibles," calling upon the people to assemble in a particular place for the purpose of being sworn in, and threatening those who refused with the fate of Lord Frederick Cavendish and Mr. Burke. The sub-inspector of constabulary who examined this document noticed that there were some lines at the top, impressed by type but not marked in ink, which had evidently nothing to do with the purport of the proclamation. On carefully investigating these lines, he read the words, " Yours very truly, Michael Davitt." As a letter from Mr. Michael Davitt had appeared in the *Kerry Sentinel* and in no other local paper, the sub-inspector at once concluded that the "Invincible" manifesto had been printed in the offices of the *Kerry Sentinel*. He accordingly directed the seizure of the newspaper under the powers allowed him by the Crimes Act. Mr. Edward Harrington, editor of the paper and brother of the proprietor, with a number of his compositors, was prosecuted. The case of the defence was that the document, though undoubtedly printed in the offices of the *Kerry Sentinel*, was so printed without the knowledge of any of the responsible authorities of the paper; that it was done in all probability as a joke, as otherwise the offenders would scarcely have been careless enough to let it be so easily known where the proclamation was printed, or where the alleged meetings of " Invincibles " were to take place.

'Mr. Edward Harrington, however, and his foreman were sentenced to six months' imprisonment, and two compositors to two months' imprisonment each. Energetic efforts were made in Parliament by Mr. Harrington and his friends to have the sentence mitigated, but the efforts were unsuccessful, and Mr. Harrington suffered the full term of his imprisonment, not being set at liberty until early in the following January.

'Curious proof of Mr. Parnell's increased popularity was given in July. On June 4 Mr. Healy, together with Mr. Davitt and Mr. Quinn, was allowed to leave Richmond Prison, after serving four out of the six months of imprisonment ordered in the sentence. A month later Mr. Healy was elected member for Monaghan county, one of the strongholds of Ulster. Six months earlier, any one who should have said that it would be possible for a Parnellite politician to represent an Ulster county would have been laughed at heartily for his folly; but the seemingly impossible had come to pass.

'The choice of the Nationalist candidate was in itself

peculiar. Instead of attempting the attack upon Ulster with some mild-mannered politician, the Nationalists put forward one of the most extreme and uncompromising of Mr. Parnell's lieutenants. Mr. Healy had, however, special qualifications for the position. He was well known to be a master of the Land Act, to have worked long and hard at it in the House of Commons, and to be the author of the Healy clause. He had been personally complimented at Westminster by the Prime Minister himself upon his knowledge of that measure, a knowledge not only far beyond that of his own leader, or of any of his colleagues, but said at the time to be beyond that of any member of the House, with the exception of Mr. Gladstone himself, and of Mr. Law. When Monaghan was left vacant by the resignation of Mr. Litton, appointed to a place of profit under the Crown, the Nationalists resolved to contest the seat, and to put Mr. Healy forward as their champion.

'The campaign was skilfully managed. Mr. Healy went through the county Monaghan, accompanied by Mr. Parnell, making speeches everywhere on the Land question. Little was spoken of beyond the services rendered by Mr. Healy to the Land Bill, and the strong necessity that existed for still further amending and improving that measure. Vexed questions were kept in the background; the Land question alone was insisted upon, and on the Land question Monaghan county was won for the Parnell party. A very little later, seat after seat in Ulster was to be won upon Home Rule and Home Rule alone. The feelings with which this victory were regarded in England were sufficiently represented by a cartoon in *Punch*, in which Mr. Parnell was represented as cutting a square piece marked Monaghan out of Mr. John Bull's overcoat, and observing, "Bedad, I've been and spoilt his Ulster anyhow."

'Mr. Healy's vacant place in Wexford was immediately filled by Mr. Redmond, brother of the member for New Ross, who was elected in his absence, by a large majority over the Liberal candidate, The O'Connor Don, an Irish gentleman of old family and great position in Wexford. Mr. Redmond, the newly-elected member, was an exceedingly young man, not long of age.' At the time of his election he was in Australia with his brother, carrying on an active campaign in favour of the national cause.' The Parnellite party was strengthened later on in the year by the return of Mr. Small for Wexford county, of Mr. Lynch for Sligo county, and of Mr. McMahon for Limerick.

'On July 4 a banquet was given by the Mayor and Corporation of Cork to celebrate the opening of the Industrial Exhibition. The city of Cork had been very anxious to obtain the privilege of being the scene of the Royal Agricultural Society's Show for 1883. When, however, it was decided that the Agricultural Show was to be held in Limerick, the Cork Corporation resolved to hold an Industrial Exhibition, as some compensation to themselves and their fellow-townsmen for the loss of the other attraction. The arrangements for the Exhibition were successfully carried out; it was opened by Lord Bandon with great success on July 2, and the banquet was the justifiable celebration of a well-organised and happily-completed enterprise.

'It was not a little curious to find the name of Mr. Parnell prominent among the distinguished guests, who included Lord Bandon and the Earl of Dunraven, as well as moderate Home Rulers like Mr. Shaw and Colonel Colthurst, who had but little reason to love the party which Mr. Parnell represented. That Mr. Parnell should be present at the banquet was only natural; he was member for the city, and the Mayor and Corporation were strongly national. But it was surprising to find men of such markedly different opinions, prominent members of the landlord class, which it was Mr. Parnell's aim to destroy, consenting to take part in any ceremony in which he had a share. The fact, slight though it was, served to show how very much the position of Mr. Parnell had been strengthened of late.

'Early in August the Government, after pleasing one party in Ireland by the Tramways Act, succeeded in giving more

general satisfaction by accepting the tender of the City of
Dublin Steam Packet Company for the carriage of the mails
as heretofore between Holyhead and Kingston. This fine line
of boats was exceedingly popular with those whose business
in life frequently called upon them to cross St. George's
Channel, and there was general discontent expressed in Ireland
when it was announced that the Government, in renewing the
contract for the carriage of the mails, was about to accept the
tender of another company, whose boats might be less suitable
for passenger traffic. The dissatisfaction was so general that
the Government consented to reconsider its decision, and the
result was that the contract was renewed with the original
Company. It was a curious experience for the Government
to have to deal with a question on which practically the whole
of Ireland was in agreement, and they undoubtedly acted
wisely in taking a step which gave satisfaction to Irishmen of
every variety of political party or opinion.

'By the death of Mr. Hugh Law in September, the Government lost a zealous and valuable public servant, and the Irish Lord Chancellorship one of the ablest holders of that office. Mr. Law's name will be especially remembered for the signal service he rendered to two Liberal Governments, first by his drafting of the Bill disestablishing the Church in Ireland, and secondly by his drafting and management of the Land Bill of 1880.'

Towards the end of the year the old Orange and Green
feud was revived in Ireland with peculiar animosity. It had
never, indeed, died out, but of late years its old ferocity seemed
to have faded. Ever since 1795, when the first Orange lodge
was founded in Armagh, after the 'Battle of the Diamond,'
Orangeism had become an important factor in the political
situation of Ireland. The Orangemen were the legitimate
successors of the old English 'garrison,' of the chivalry of
the Pale, of the Cromwellians of the plantations, of the
Scotch 'settlers.' The guiding principle of Orangeism was
antagonism to Catholicism. It supported the Penal Laws
while they still existed; it struggled hard against their repeal;

it represents to-day the spirit which animated and inspired the Penal Laws.

The entertaining inspector of police who has introduced himself to contemporary literature as 'Terence M'Grath,' gives, in his 'Pictures from Ireland,' a sketch of a typical Orangeman, which, coming from such a source, cannot be considered to be biassed by any undue prejudice against the Orange institutions. 'From the time when he was old enough to throw a stone at a Catholic procession on Patrick's Day, the most stirring incidents of McGettigan's life have been connected with the annual commemoration of the two victorious engagements fought by the much-lauded and sorely execrated monarch. . . . The village of Juliansborough is a well-known Protestant stronghold; and, though a Roman Catholic chapel stands about half a mile away, no one of that benighted faith would have the audacity to pass through the village to his devotions during the month of July. . . . The principles of the Orange Society are "civil and religious liberty," and McGettigan flatters himself that he adopts them to the fullest extent. . . . But with "Papishers" it is a different thing. That every one of these followers of the Scarlet Woman is destined to eternal perdition is as firm an article of belief with William McGettigan as that the evening and the morning were the first day; and he feels that, in doing all that in him lies to obstruct the religious practices of Popery, and otherwise make the lives of the Papishers a burden to them, he is simply doing his duty as a good citizen. . . . Patrick's Day passed, McGettigan bears no violent malice against his Catholic neighbours. He has even walked to market on more than one occasion with members of that faith. But with the heat of June his sentiments become less dormant, and with the first of July sets in a period of intolerance that, for thirty days at least, subverts his reason.

'During this time a Sister of Mercy with a cup of water in the desert would be an unwelcome sight; and a general inclination to wade knee-deep in Catholic blood is accompanied by a worship of the Orange lily as real as the "idolatry" that he so bitterly condemns. . . . The clergyman of his church has a certain influence with him, but it is in exact opposition to that pastor's attitude towards the Orange Society. The basis of his faith is the warrant and rules of his lodge, and while cursing his Roman Catholic opponents he never imagines that his religion is as much a religion of hatred as the gloomy frenzy of the Puritans or the tribal ferocity of the ancient Jews. . . . In his political principles he is torn by conflicting emotions. . . . He approves of tenant right, fixity of tenure, freedom of sale, and vote by ballot. So far he is Liberal, but he votes with the Conservatives; for is not the extension of the franchise a Liberal proposal that would, in proportion to the lowness of level at which the line is drawn, increase the number of Catholic votes? And did not the Liberals disestablish the Church that seemed to McGettigan an evidence of Protestant ascendency that gratified his vanity, and assented to the principles of the Orange Society, in which all sections of Protestants could meet on common grounds? McGettigan calls himself a thorough Loyalist, but his feelings towards England are exactly identical with his feelings and attitude towards the Church. He is loyal to Protestant England because she represents to him Protestantism *versus* Popery. If she became Roman Catholic he would hate her with all his heart; and if she grants Home Rule he will vote for the removal of the Union Jack from Orange processions.' Such is the picture, drawn in no unfriendly spirit, by a writer as bitterly opposed to the national party as McGettigan himself, of the Orange agitation of the North of Ireland, the member of a secret society as fatal in its way to the well-being of the country as the Ribbon lodges themselves. How little the loyalty of the Orange Society could be depended upon was shown in 1835, when the Orange plot to place the Duke of Cumberland upon the throne instead of Queen Victoria was discovered and defeated.

'Mr. Parnell's victory at Monaghan aroused the greatest excitement in the North of Ireland. The Orange lodges were resolved to challenge Mr. Parnell's alleged power in Ulster, and whenever a Nationalist meeting was organised for any Ulster town an opposition Orange meeting was got up for the same time and place. Such demonstration and counter-demonstration on the part of the Green and Orange parties was in the highest degree prejudicial to the public peace. For generations the hostility between Orange and Green had run too fiercely to be smoothed down by the soft-spoken lyric of Thomas Davis, and the feeling had now been exceptionally stimulated by what the Orange lodges regarded as the Parnellite invasion of Ulster. In the month of September Orange and Green meetings were held at Dungannon and Omagh, and only the effective presence of military and constabulary prevented some serious breach of the peace.

'At this critical juncture Sir Stafford Northcote, as leader of the Opposition, undertook a crusade into Ulster against the Irish policy of the Government. The English Conservative press commended Sir Stafford Northcote highly for repeating Mr. Gladstone's Midlothian tactics in Ulster; while Liberal journalism contented itself chiefly with good-humouredly bantering the leader of the Opposition on his Irish crusade. Sir Stafford Northcote was never meant to be an agitator, nor were his crusade speeches in themselves of a very dangerous character. But they succeeded in arousing all the old party passions. The Monaghan election had been a severe blow to the Orange garrison in Ulster, and they were eager to efface its recollection by any means in their power. Orange riots followed Sir Stafford Northcote's progress through the North of Ireland. In one of these a convent in Belfast was attacked, and the lady superior, who was ill, died of the alarm and the excitement. Sir Stafford Northcote and the speakers who accompanied him inflamed the Orange mobs they addressed, not merely against the Nationalist party, but against the Government which supported, abetted, and basely yielded to the demands of the national party. The very fact of such a crusade being undertaken roused the Orange lodges to enthusiasm. Other speakers, less temperate and judicious than Sir Stafford Northcote, did much by impetuous and unreasoned harangues to rouse the spirit of faction, and for a time the situation in Ulster almost suggested the beginning of a civil war.

'Whenever a Nationalist meeting was called a counter Orange demonstration was summoned, and in spite of all the efforts of the authorities violent physical contests often took place between the followers of the two factions.' The Orange party were inspired by the double purpose of fighting the Nationalists and harassing the Government. Whenever a national meeting was announced to be held in Ulster the Orange party immediately organised a counter-meeting, to oppose what they chose to call the invasion of their county.

To appreciate properly the situation, it must be remembered that even in Orange Ulster something like half of the population were Catholics, and that when the new franchise came into effect the majority of votes would no longer be the privileged possession of the supporters of the Orange lodges. The Nationalist leaders always found in Ulster large audiences of Nationalists; Mr. Healy's election for Monaghan showed that Orangeism could not always turn the scale against the men who had made the Land agitation. It was perfectly clear that if National and Orange meetings were held on the same day and in the same locality without precautions, it would be impossible to preserve peace. The Orange leaders wrote and spoke in a way which showed that they were determined to rival the wildest utterances ever made on the national side. A national meeting was announced to be held in Rosslea, in Fermanagh, on October 16, 1883. Lord Rossmore, the Grand Master of the Orangemen of the county Monaghan, and a justice of the peace, signed a proclamation calling upon the Orangemen to oppose the meeting. It was evident that a crisis was at hand, and the Irish Executive poured a large force of military and police into the district, who succeeded in keeping the two crowds apart in spite of the attempts of Lord Rossmore to bring about a collision.

The account of the proceedings of the Orange meeting on that day is extraordinary. 'Some pistol-shots were fired into the air in the outskirts of the crowd, and immediately the fire was taken up by several hundred persons throughout that vast assemblage. Pistols and revolvers were produced on all sides, and a continuous fusillade was maintained for nearly fifteen minutes. The leaders endeavoured to stay the deafening discharge, but for some time without effect.' Lord Crichton and other Orange leaders on the platform were obliged to stoop down for fear of being shot by their own adherents. 'When the excitement subsided several Protestant clergymen came to Lord Crichton and asked him could he prevail on the Orangemen to stop firing. Lord Crichton, spreading out his hands, called out in as loud a voice as he was able to command, "For God's sake, men, will you listen to what I say, and stop the firing?"' Lord Rossmore's speech, which was interrupted at one point for some ten minutes by the firing of hundreds of revolvers, was specially violent. 'He thought it was a great pity that the so-called Government of England stopped loyal men from assembling to uphold their institutions here, and had sent down a handful of soldiers, whom they could eat up in a second or two if they thought fit.' For Lord Rossmore's conduct he was removed from the commission of the peace by the Government, to the great indignation of the Orange lodges and their leaders. The tenor of Orange talk became more violent. A circular, signed by Captain Charles Alexander, advised the Orangemen in every district to enrol themselves into an armed volunteer force, to provide stores of arms, and to create, in fact, a complete military organisation. Lord Enniskillen, the Orange Grand Master, repudiated the circular on the ground that it contained 'proposals of an illegal character;' but the fact that such a circular could have been issued, and such proposals seriously entertained, is in itself sufficiently curious.

'The Executive did their best to deal with the serious difficulty in an impartial manner. Whenever it was considered that meetings thus organised and counter-organised would lead to disturbance, they adopted the plan of proclaiming both meetings. One prominent Orangeman, Lord Rossmore, who had distinguished himself by his efforts to disturb the peace, and by his defiance of the law's authority, was promptly removed from his position as justice of the peace—a step which, while it roused the greatest anger in the Orange lodges, served to show even the most extreme of its opponents that the Executive was holding its scales with justice, and was prepared to tolerate no infringement of the law from any political party in the island.

'The English press on the whole was pretty unanimous in its condemnation of the action of the Orange leaders. The journals devoted to the Ministry were, naturally, especially warm against a series of assaults directed quite as much against the existing Government as against the Irish Nationalists; and even the most strenuous journalistic adherents of the Opposition were compelled to censure the manner in which the politicians of the school of Lord Rossmore had chosen to defend their principles. A paper like *Punch*, which may be regarded as expressing pretty fairly what the bulk of the country feels at any given moment on any given question, was especially severe in its condemnation of the Orange policy, and of the professing loyalty which was even more dangerous to law and order than avowed disloyalty.

'When the year ended the situation in Ulster was still unsettled. Lord Rossmore, smarting under his dismissal from the justiceship of the peace, was becoming more violent than ever in his attacks upon the Government. Orange manifestoes of exceptionally warlike character were freely circulated, and a pair of meetings, Nationalist and Orange, which were announced to be held at Dromore on the first day of the new year, were looked forward to by impartial politicians with well-justified alarm.' The counter-meetings were held at Dromore, in Tyrone, on January 1, 1884. Police and military held the ground to prevent hostilities; but several attacks were made upon the Nationalists by the Orangemen, who had to be driven back by the bayonets of the police and the sabres of the cavalry. In one of these encounters a young Orangeman named Giffen, who had been brought in—like many others—from another district to swell the Orange levées for the occasion, was mortally wounded and died shortly after. The Government then adopted the plan, whenever Orange and Green counter-meetings were announced, of proclaiming both meetings; breaches of the peace were thus prevented, though the Nationalist party strongly protested against a policy which allowed the Orangemen to silence any national meeting by merely announcing opposition, and thus calling down a Government proclamation on both alike.

'One of the latest events of the year was also one of the most remarkable—the solemn presentation to Mr. Parnell of the long-collected, much-discussed testimonial. A banquet to Mr. Parnell was given in the Rotunda, Dublin, on Tuesday, December 11. The testimonial, originally intended to be limited to some fourteen thousand pounds, had swelled to some thirty-eight thousand pounds. Mr. Parnell's speech on this occasion came, like so many other of his utterances, upon the world somewhat in the nature of a surprise. It had been confidently expected in many quarters that the tone of Mr. Parnell's speech would be, if not exactly conciliatory towards the Government, at least uttered in no unfriendly or unsympathetic spirit. The speech, however, was given in most uncompromising terms.

'Mr. Parnell began by contrasting the position of the Irish question at that moment with its position three years before, when the Land League was founded. But though much had been done since to further the well-being of Ireland, there was yet much to do. There must be no more coercion, and there must be no more emigration. On this latter point Mr. Parnell had the strong support of the majority of the Roman Catholic bishops in Ireland, who, in a circular issued in July, had declared themselves very strongly opposed to the Government emigration policy. Mr. Parnell sharply censured the conduct of Mr. Trevelyan. Between Mr. Trevelyan and Mr. Forster there was this great difference, that while Mr. Forster always tried to overwhelm his opponents by saying that his great ambition was to enable every one in Ireland to do what they had a legal right to do, Mr. Trevelyan's great ambition appeared to be to prevent anybody in Ireland from doing what he had a legal right to do. In support of this charge, he adduced the case of the imprisonment of Mr. Timothy Harrington, of the seizure of the *Kerry Sentinel* and the imprisonment of its editor—" as well might you flog a schoolmaster because an idle schoolboy drew an idle picture on his slate "— for the proclamation of the Nationalist meetings in the North of Ireland.

'But, in spite of the Government, the national position was a strong one, and its cause a winning one. Even coercion could not last for ever, but if it were to be renewed it should be by a Tory and not a Liberal Government. "Beyond a shadow of doubt it will be for the Irish people in England— separated, isolated as they are—and for your independent Irish members, to determine at the next General Election whether a Tory or a Liberal English Ministry shal rule England. This is a great force and a great power. This force has already gained for Ireland inclusion in the coming Franchise Bill. We have reason to be proud, hopeful, and energetic, determined that this generation shall not pass away until it has bequeathed to those who come after us the great birthright of national independence and prosperity." Such was the tenor of Mr. Parnell's utterances.

'The emphatic vigour of this speech naturally roused the greatest excitement in both countries. The *Freeman's Journal*, after declaring that the banquet would "live in the memory of all who were present, and in the records of the time, as the most magnificent of Irish national demonstrations," added that Mr. Parnell's speech "demolishes the fictions about pacts and treaties with the Government like so many houses of cards." The English papers for the most part were surprised by Mr. Parnell's tone. The *Times* declared that "no more uncompromising defiance was ever flung in the face of a nation or a Government," but consoled itself by believing that Mr. Parnell had "overrated his strength," while his attack upon the Irish Executive might " be taken as a proof that Lord

Spencer's administration in Ireland is an obstacle the Land League party cannot get over."

'Perhaps the most remarkable utterance of the London press, however, was an article in the *Pall Mall Gazette*, entitled " The Master of the Situation." It said, " The young Irish squire of English education and American descent " was " in some respects the most interesting figure in the empire . . . One of the youngest members of the House of Commons . . . he is, beyond question, one of the most powerful. . . . He is not only the chief of a devoted party, as much the ' uncrowned king of Ireland ' as in the days before Kilmainham, but he aspires, not without solid ground for his ambition, to play the part of a Parliamentary Warwick, and to pose as the master of the situation in the Imperial Parliament." " Onehalf of our recent mistakes," the *Pall Mall* went on to say, " have arisen from our not taking sufficient account of Mr. Parnell and the people who think with Mr. Parnell. . . . It would be equally irrational to wax wroth at what is described as his ' malevolent language,' or the ' brutality ' of his vituperation. We gave them the plank bed, the solitary cell, and prison fare. They give us in return ' vulgar obloquy and truculent abuse.' So far as the exchange goes we have so much the best of it that we need not be too squeamish about the quality of their compliments." The article concluded by saying that though " Mr. Parnell's claim to be master of the situation cannot be fully recognised until he gives proof that he can hold together a party which has never before been held together for any length of time," yet, " should Mr. Parnell really unite Irishmen, and teach them submission and loyalty to their own leader, he will do more for Ireland than anything he has as yet even attempted." '

CHAPTER XXIII.

HOME RULE.

It is not necessary for my present purpose to give more than a cursory glance at the events since the Conservative accession in 1885. The difficulties of the Government were growing greater. Mr. William O'Brien succeeded in exposing a terrible record of offence on the part of certain officials of Dublin Castle—a record which showed the existence of a horrible condition of corruption in certain phases of viceregal society. Mr. William O'Brien, in the face of great difficulty, proved his case with a result which caused a considerable scattering of certain Crown officials. It became daily and hourly more obvious that the Irish difficulty was only growing greater. Mr. Trevelyan, weary of a post for which he was quite unsuited, gave up the Irish Secretaryship for the Chancellorship of the Duchy of Lancaster, and was succeeded in Dublin Castle by Mr. Campbell Bannerman. Mr. Campbell Bannerman had not a very long term of office.

The Government had exhausted its mandate, and was near its doom. It fell, curiously enough, not upon any of the great questions with which it had dealt, not upon its Irish policy nor its policy in Egypt, but upon Mr. Childers' Budget. On June 8, 1885, the Government was defeated by a majority of twelve, and a few days later Lord Salisbury accepted office, and Lord Randolph Churchill became to all intents and purposes the leader of the Conservative party. At first the attitude of the new Government was friendly towards Ireland. Its leaders expressed themselves severely upon Lord Spencer's administration.

The new Viceroy, Lord Carnarvon, was known to have strong Home Rule leanings. The attitude of conciliation did not last very long. After a vexed existence of a few months it became obvious that the Conservative Government were more anxious to be out of office than in. It was soon apparent that, overburdened by its difficulties, the Conservative Government was riding for a fall. It was doomed to die like its predecessor, actually if not nominally upon the Irish question. It had dallied with that question helplessly, aimlessly, inconsistently. In the person of Lord Carnarvon the Government coquetted with Home Rule, interviewed Irish leaders, and promised, in that delightfully indefinite way which is the joy of Conservative statesmen, all sorts of speedy blessings for Ireland. The negotiations which Lord Carnarvon opened up with the Home Rule leaders are matters of history.

It was not, indeed, in Lord Carnarvon's power to pledge the Government of which he was a member to any particular course of action ; it would hardly have been in Lord Salisbury's power to do so much ; but it would be idle to consider as serious the feeble defence raised in certain Conservative quarters, when the secret was no longer a secret, that Lord Carnarvon was simply making a stroke off his own bat out of a purely personal curiosity to learn what Mr. Parnell's opinions upon the Irish question were. Mr. Parnell's opinions upon the Irish question were fairly well known, and it would be absurd indeed to suppose that the Lord Lieutenant of Ireland, in seeking out a formal interview with the leader of the Irish people, had attached no greater significance to the act than would belong to a meeting between two wholly obscure and uninteresting private individuals.

However, the Conservative Government, after well-nigh committing itself to a policy of Home Rule through the speeches of its leaders and the action of its Viceroy, took fright. Those who were chiefly responsible for directing its action saw or thought they saw that Ireland was too unpopular to be safely patronised yet, and the Government swung round the political circle with amazing alacrity.

Lord Randolph Churchill, imitating the example of Lord Iddesleigh, organised a crusade in the North of Ireland. Lord Iddesleigh was a mild man and an urbane politician, but he succeeded in sowing the seeds of riot and disturbance in the North of Ireland. If he could accomplish so much, what might not Lord Randolph Churchill accomplish? He did accomplish much. He stirred up all the worst passions; he incited to riot and civil war; he prophesied for the Orange party laurel victory if they were firm in denying the law and authority of Parliament; he cheered their hearts with stirring citations from the poet Campbell, and leaving behind him any number of texts on which appeals to riot and outrage might be based, returned home in triumph.

Sir Michael Hicks-Beach announced the intention of the Government to ask for power to suppress the National League. This was a dramatic touch intended for the gallery, which Sir Michael knew well enough could come to nothing. On January 27 the Government were defeated by a majority of seventy-nine on Mr. Jesse Collings' amendment to the Queen's Speech, and Mr. Gladstone returned to power.

It was known by this time that Mr. Gladstone's views upon the Irish question had been greatly extended. Mr. Gladstone had never been a hard-and-fast opponent of Home Rule, and it was obvious to those who had studied his career with any care for the last few years, that his mind was more and more inclining in favour of the extension of local government in Ireland, in the direction desired by the Irish people, as the only possible solution of the Irish difficulty. Rumours of all kinds had spread abroad during the duration of Lord Salisbury's Government as to the nature of Mr. Gladstone's views upon the Irish question, and as to the precise form in which Mr. Gladstone would, when he had the power, shape his plans for the better government of Ireland.

All doubts were soon to be set at rest. The new Gladstone Government at once adopted an attitude of the strongest sympathy with Ireland. Lord Aberdeen, who was appointed Lord Lieutenant, was destined to be one of the very few Viceroys whose names are dear to the Irish people. It was soon known that the Government had a Home Rule Bill in preparation; soon known too that the projected measure was the cause of many dissensions in the Cabinet, which eventuated in the retirement of Mr. Chamberlain and Mr. Trevelyan from the Ministerial ranks. All manner of rumours as to the precise nature of the measure which was to mark a new era in Irish history were abroad ; all speculations were satisfied on Thursday, April 8, 1886.

The history of modern times affords no parallel to the exciting scene which the House of Commons presented on that afternoon. There were many members whose memories of the struggles on that battle-ground went back to the days when Lord Palmerston was summarily dismissed from office in 1851, and to the wild excitement which followed Mr. Lowe's hour of more than Roman triumph, when his purple face and silver hairs flamed comet-like across the political horizon, and carried destruction to Mr. Gladstone's Government in its wake. There are even some who recalled the feverish passions, the bitter animosities, and fiery enthusiasms of the days of the first Reform Bill. But no man's memory could conjure from the past any scene of excitement comparable to that which St. Stephen's witnessed on that memorable Thursday.

When the time came for the Speaker's little procession to enter the Chamber, it seemed to be threading its way to the table with difficulty through a human sea. The House has been crowded before often enough during its history. Recent years have more than once witnessed occasions on which it has been described as full to overflowing. But such fulness was almost emptiness as contrasted with the choking closeness with which it was packed on April 8, 1886. The officials of the House have assured curious inquirers that never before has there been any instance of the floor of the House being filled with chairs for the accommodation of its members. There were twenty-eight chairs on the floor on Thursday. Could their number have been multiplied by ten they would not have been equal to the demand there was for them. One of the most peculiar features of the event was the voluntary suffering which legislators inflicted upon themselves in order to obtain good places for the great occasion. One member actually got to Westminster at half-past five in the morning : the majority of the Irish members were there by six. Members who arrived at eight found that they were too late to obtain a good seat, and by a little after nine o'clock there was not a place of any kind to be had. Such unwonted attendance was a decisive tribute to the absorbing interest of the day.

The aspect of the Chamber when Mr. Gladstone entered was exceptionally curious. Almost all those on his own side, even rebellious Whigs and disaffected Radicals, rose to their feet and hailed him with applause—an example that was instantly followed by all the Irish members. By an odd chance the composition of the House was such that it appeared as if the whole House rose to greet Mr. Gladstone. The explanation of this curious phenomenon was in this wise. The Irish members present in full force had not only occupied all the seats below the gangway on the Opposition side of the House, but had flowed across the Rubicon of the gangway and occupied a surprisingly large proportion of the seats above it. Thus a large bulk of the Conservative members were driven into the upper galleries, into the twenty-eight seats on the floor of the House, and into the standing places below the Bar and behind the Speaker's chair.

It was this combination of fortuitous circumstances which gave such an apparently comprehensive character to Mr. Gladstone's welcome, and which must have been not a little puzzling to the unsophisticated eyes of strangers in the galleries.

The oratorial capacity of Mr. Gladstone was never more strikingly manifest than during the course of the three hours and twenty-five minutes which his speech occupied. He was excessively pale and his voice was very hoarse at first, but he soon assumed complete command over its tones, and then the House listened to one of the greatest speeches of our century. The inflections of the voice were marvellously controlled: the tones rose and fell, now in what seemed like almost sibyllic exultation, anon dying down to some pathetic whisper, low but perfectly audible; every gesture furthering the dramatic intensity of the words the speaker was using. On Mr. Gladstone's own following the Prime Minister played as upon some favourite instrument. Even the large proportion of the disaffected forgot their differences for the moment—actually lost their heads under the glamour of the performance—and cheered as lustily as the rest. Only the Conservatives sat stiffly and unmoved.

Neither the history of the reign nor the history of the century afford any parallel to the scene of this day. The records of contemporary events afford many examples of great and stirring moments in the chronicle of the Commons Chamber at Westminster. The introduction of great measures of social political reform, the debates which have been big with the fates of Ministers, and which have resulted in the overthrow of administrations that seemed yesterday to be deeply rooted in popular favour, the explanations consequent upon momentous resignations, all these varied means of arousing intense political excitement have each in their turn thronged the panelled room with members and lined the walls with the breathless spectators of epoch-making episodes. But the rise of no measure and the fall of no Minister have ever stirred St. Stephen's to such fever-fire of excitement as that which animated it all through the long hours of that Thursday's life. Neither the introduction of the first Reform Bill, with all the fervid emotions of the consequent debates, nor the excitements of such Parliamentary catastrophes as the dismissal of Lord Palmerston in 1851 and the defeats of Mr. Gladstone in 1866 and 1885, can be fairly said to offer even a distant parallel to the passions, the enthusiasm, the fear and hope and fury and exultation which swept the surface and stirred the depths of the greatest legislative assemblage of modern times.

Most of those present had taken part in all the thrilling incidents that have marked the stormy course of Parliamentary history for the past six years. The House of Commons has outwatched the stars while the battle for Irish rights has raged below; night has faded into dawn and dawn become noon, and the day's strength waned into evening, and through night to dawn again, while some fierce Parliamentary struggle has been fought out. The representatives of the Irish nation have been again and again expelled from the Chamber amidst wild scenes of passion and tumult. Few who shared in those tumultuous emotions will forget the two fateful hours in which successive Ministries fell on the cause of coercion before the votes of an united Irish party. All these scenes and incidents are graven upon men's memory, but no one of them, not the fiercest and stormiest, could for a moment compare with the keen, almost agonising, excitement and the vast historical dignity of the scene which the House of Commons presented at four o'clock on the afternoon of Thursday, the ever-memorable 8th of April.

One great fact rises distinctly, star-like, out of all the confusion and passion and heart-burning and heart-uplifting of that memorable day—the fact that a great English Minister, the foremost and most famous statesman of his age, has recognised, speaking to an attentive Senate, to an attentive nation, to an attentive world, the right of the Irish people to self-government. That great historic fact is at once the triumph and the justification of an oppressed but an unconquered nationality.

Whatever may be thought of the particular measure which Mr. Gladstone has introduced, whatever may be its ultimate fate in the House of Commons or in the House of Peers, whatever modifications, improvements, extensions, it may be found capable of sustaining are all but details, vastly important in themselves, but for the moment unimportant in contrast with the stupendous, the monumental importance of the recognition by the foremost of English statesmen of that right of Ireland to make her own laws for her own people, which for so many centuries has been so persistently, so bloodily, denied to her. There are certain hours in the lives of great men which are in themselves epochs, hours when a single speech is more momentous, more far reaching, than half a dozen revolutions. Such was the hour which but a year ago reversed the verdict of seven centuries; such was the speech in which Mr. Gladstone apologised for the folly of eighty-six years of false and fatal union, and frankly recognised, late in the day, indeed, but not too late, that Ireland contained a people 'rightly struggling to be free.'

The great Prime Minister had the advantage of addressing the greatest speech of his life to the largest audience that was ever gathered together within the precincts of the popular assembly. An observer in one of the choking spaces set apart for strangers, looking down upon those packed benches, upon that floor where, for the first time within memory of man, seats had been placed for members upon the blocked gangways, upon the thickly-clustering groups behind the Speaker's chair and below the bar, upon the overflowing passages and groaning galleries, might well have imagined that so full a House could scarcely be made fuller even by the addition of a solitary individual. In sober fact, it would have been hard indeed to find room for another human being in the dense assemblage, or for the over-taxed and enervating atmosphere to afford him a life-sustaining supply of oxygen, if room had been found for the sole of his foot.

But crowded though the Chamber was, and crowded, too, with perhaps the most remarkable throng of men that has ever been gathered together within the walls of Westminster, it was for some of those present more closely crowded and with a yet more eminent congregation. The mind's eye of many an Irish member, gifted for the moment by fancy with the powers of second sight, peopled it with further presences. As the gaze wandered over that vast sea of human faces they seemed to change to faces scarcely less familiar, though they have long been strange to sunlight and starlight, and in a moment a new and more Imperial Parliament, a Parliament not of the quick but of the dead, was summoned, and this new 'call of the House' evoked from the long avenues of the past a world of stately shadows. The Irish benches, crowded with enthusiastic colleagues rallying in exultation around the chosen leader of their country and their cause, seemed to give place to a legion of mighty and mournful phantoms.

The white-haired, blind old man, whose stalwart frame

was bowed by sorrow and whose sightless gaze had in it such a wistful pathos, was not he the exiled Earl whose grave in Roman earth is now the shrine of so many pilgrimages? Near him, his soldier's face writhed with pain or poison, came the great kinsman of his House, Owen Roe. Sarsfield, with the blood of Landen on his breast and hand ; Talbot of Tirconnell's weary, haughty face ; Roger Moore, handsome, chivalrous, devoted ; William Molyneux, with the ' Case of Ireland ' in his grasp ; the small fervid figure of the Dean of St. Patrick's, with ' fierce indignation ' blazing in his wild dark eyes ; Lucas, with his volume clasped in his embrace ; the gallant bearing of Charlemont ; Grattan, in the uniform of the Volunteers ; Flood, restless and repentant ; Curran, swaying with stormy eloquence—these and many others floated by in proud succession.

With them were yet livelier and loftier presences. Edward Fitzgerald, his comely body gashed with more scars than Cæsar's, and by baser hands ; Tone, with that grim wound in his throat ; Bagenal Harvey and Father John ; the Brothers Sheares, in death as in life undivided ; and Emmet, with the livid circle round his young neck. On they came, the long line of martyrs who had died to defeat the fatal principle which the Act of Union formulated, and who seemed now to rise from their graves at the sound of the knell of that principle.

Nor were the phantoms of such fancy confined alone to one side of the House, nor to the Irish benches. Across the floor, even on the seat where the Ministers of the hour were grouped together, the eye of fancy seemed to discern the benign shadows of the illustrious dead. Chesterfield and Fitzwilliam stood there side by side. The genius of Charles James Fox seemed to hover like an inspiring influence about the bowed form of the Prime Minister, and the likeness of Burke leaned over to prompt his brilliant biographer and follower with his silver voice, and to encourage him with his golden counsel. A few more ominous and forbidding shapes were huddled together in angry companionship upon the

Opposition side of the House, lurking furtively in the dark spaces behind the Speaker's chair. Cornwallis and Castlereagh and Pitt, Stafford and Essex, and Perrot, and Bagnal, Cromwell and William of Nassau, with such baser spectres as Sirr, and Swan, and Higgins, emerged momentarily from the darkness and vanished again with the fitful confusion of a dream.

All this ghostly army, multiplying in bewildering rapidity, swayed and floated silently forward, their pale faces shining with wild emotions of hope and exultation and hate. Then a great cry rose up, a fierce, tumultuous yell of triumph and salutation ; the grey ghosts seemed to shudder at the sound, and swiftly vanished as the clamour rose to their place of shades. St. Stephen's was itself again, and the assembled, living, breathing multitude were—the majority of them—cheering themselves hoarse in welcome of Mr. Gladstone, who had just risen to his feet. Irishmen who listened to the orator, and heard the impassioned words in which an English Minister, for the first time in the face of all the world, recognised the rights of the Irish people, felt that indeed the mighty dead might well be content with that day's business, and might, indeed, if it were permitted to them, quit their resting-places to share in the triumph of a day which marks an epoch in Irish history—an epoch which seems as if it were destined to end the old evil order of repression and revolution, and open the new order of freedom and of hope.

At this point my record pauses. Everyone knows the fortunes of the particular measure which Mr. Gladstone introduced ; everyone might, I should imagine, be able to predict the inevitable results of the introduction of that measure. The Irish question has passed since the 8th of last April into a wholly new phase. The struggles not merely of five years but of eighty-five years, not merely since the Union but for many centuries, are practically at an end. Those were the struggles of the Irish people, alone, unaided, to plead their cause and to obtain justice. With the recognition by a great English Prime Minister of the justice of Ireland's

A A

appeal and the righteousness of her cause, the whole aspect of the longest political struggle in history changes. A vast proportion of the English people are henceforward in sympathy with the Irish people; all those who are most closely identified with the cause of progress, the love of liberty, and the interests of civilisation are eager to allow to Ireland the right to manage Irish affairs according to Irish ideas. This is a great triumph for Ireland and England alike. England no less than Ireland should be eternally grateful to the great statesman who has undone so much evil, who has healed so great a hurt, who has atoned for so much injustice, who has united two hostile nationalities, and has, while freeing Ireland from her unhappy servitude, strengthened the empire which it is his duty to serve.

INDEX.

ABERCROMBIE, Sir Ralph, sent over to take command of the troops in Ireland, 49

Aberdeen, Lord, his viceroyalty of Ireland, 20, 21; one of the few Viceroys dear to the Irish people, 346

Addison, Joseph, 264

'All the Talents,' ministry of, 83; their resignation, 84

Althorpe, Lord, carries a vote for public works in Ireland, 171; on the Arms Bill, *ib.*

American Civil War, 181–182

Amurath succeeding Amurath, 83

Anne, Queen, statesmen of, 9, 15

Aristophanes, 111

Arminius, 6

Armstrong, Captain, 50

Athlone, capture of, 1

Aughrim, rout of, 1

Austerlitz, battle of, 82, 83

BACK Lane Parliament, concessions to, made with one hand and taken away with the other, 42, 43

'*Baratariana*,' 25, 26, 29

Baretti, Joseph, 31

Barrington, Sir Jonah, his eloquent description of the last scene in the Irish House of Commons, 64

Barron, Sir H. W., motion of, 173

Bastille, fall of the, 40

Beaconsfield, Lord, on Sheil, 99; his letter to the Duke of Marlborough, 228–230; appeal to the country on the Irish question, 228–231; his keen political foresight, 230; his brilliant and bitter speech against Mr. Gladstone's Government, 255, 256

Beauclerk, Topham, 31

Bedford, Duke of, succeeds Lord Harwicke in the Lieutenantship, 83; earns a dishonourable immortality, *ib.*

Beresford, Lady Frances Maria, married to Henry Flood, 23

Berwick, Duke of, 4

Bessborough Commission, the, 277

Biggar, Mr., his loyalty and devotion to Mr. Parnell, 227; the ideal lieutenant of the leader of a small minority, *ib.*; a successful trader, 235; suspended, 260, 264; wordy wrangle between him and Mr. Milbank, 266; prosecution of, for a violent attack upon Lord Spencer, 311

Bodenstown churchyard, 55

Bolingbroke, 32

Bond, Oliver, 43, 46; seizure of, 49, 50; death in Newgate, 51, 58

Boswell's Life of Johnson, 31

Boulter, Primate, 24

Bowes, Lord Chancellor, 10

Bowes (smith), a Hercules in a leather apron, 137

Boycott, Captain, treatment of, by Lord Earne's tenantry, 250; assisted by the Orangemen of the North, 251

'Boycotting,' its principle not aggressive, 251, 275

Boyle, Dr., on the eviction of Irish peasants, 171

Boyne Water, fight by, 1

Boynton, 'the languishing,' married to the Duke of Tirconnel, 2

Bradlaugh, Charles, 260

Brenan, Joseph (Joe Brenan), 134; a man of many and varied gifts, 135; loved by 'Mary of the *Nation*,' *ib.*; at Mrs. Heron's

BRE

supper-rooms, 135, 136, 138; his insurrection, 139; escapes to America, 140; marries, but not 'Mary of the *Nation*,' *ib.*; his blindness and death, *ib.*

Bret Harte, his 'argonauts,' 178

Brett, Sergeant, accidentally killed by the rescuers of Kelly and Deasy, 191-192

Brian Boroimhe, 125-126

Bright, John, 144; his power and following greatly increased, 156; regarded as the champion of advanced thought and the apostle of the new ideas, *ib.*; his speeches on Irish questions, 157-164; surprising change of front in his later utterances, 157, 158, 163, 164, 167, 168; his conduct towards the Land League and Home Rulers, 158, 159, 161, 163, 164, 167, 168; his tribute to Mr. John Dillon, 165, 246; his efforts on behalf of the men of Manchester, 193; criticism of Mr. Gladstone's list of measures, 202; his speech in support of Mr. Forster's Coercion Bill, 261-263

Brillat Savarin, 147

Brophy, Hugh, 188

Browning, Robert, quoted, 186

Brownlow, Mr., his Bill for reclamation of waste lands in Ireland, 170; a futile attempt at remedial legislation, *ib.*

Buckingham, Duke of, 2

Bunting, Mr., his collection of the national music of Ireland, 67

Burgh, Hussey, 28, 33; fine simile of, 30, 62

Buried cities, 17

Burke, Edmund, genius of, 10; on the Penal Code, 14; the greatest of Irishmen, 18; his famous letter, 25; on Sir Hercules Langrishe, 28, 31; his reply to the Duke of Bedford, 83; richly-coloured periods of, 127; his silver voice and golden counsel, 352

Burke, Mr. T. H., assassination of, in Phœnix Park, 301-303, 317-319, 321

Butler, Simon, 43

Butt, Mr. Isaac, 145; character and career of, 213; unwisely neglected by the Conservative leaders, 214; chosen leader of the Home-Rule movement, 215, 217; did not make much use of his opportunities, 220; his p'acid leadership, 221; severs himself from the unpopular action of his fellow-members, 226; death of, 227, 235

Byrne, Miles, 48; a ready and daring colleague of Emmet, 70, 120

Byron, Lord, captivated by the story of Lord Edward Fitzgerald, 45

CAT

CALIFORNIA, 178

Campbell Bannerman, Mr. succeeds Mr. Trevelyan in the Irish Secretaryship, 344

Campbell, Thomas, Lord Randolph Churchill's stirring quotations from, 346

Canada, England threatened with loss of, 121; Fenian attempts on, 182-183, 190

Canning, George, 99

Capel, Lord, Viceroy of Ireland, 8; Parliament of, 8, 9

Captain Moonlight, 290; identified with a man named Connell, and arrested, *ib.*; turns informer, *ib.*

Carew, Shapland, his reply to Castlereagh's offer of a bribe, 59

Carey, James, arrest of, 315; turns informer, 318, 319; reveals the details of the Phœnix Park assassination, 319; his evidence, 319-320; his dramatically tragic fate, 322, 323

Carlyle, Thomas, his 'French Revolution' quoted, 293

Carnarvon, Lord, his South African Confederation Bill, 225; becomes Viceroy of Ireland, 344; known to have a strong Home-Rule-leaning, *ib.*; opens up negotiations with the Home-Rule leaders, 345

Cartouche, 189

Casanova, his escape from durance, 189

Cashel, rock of, its similarity to the Athenian Acropolis, 274

Castlereagh, 59, 64; death of, 69; his unpopularity, 254

Castor and Pollux, 324

Catholic disabilities, 6-13, 89

Catholic Emancipation, 68, 69, 75, 92, 94, 95; becomes law, 100

CAT

Catholic University in Ireland, proposed charter for, 205, 207
Catiline censuring Cethegus for treason, 285
Caulfield, James, Earl of Charlemont, 28, 30, 31, 40; gallant bearing of, 352
Cavendish, Lord Frederick, succeeds Mr. Forster as Irish Secretary, 300; arrival in Dublin, 301; assassination of, in Phœnix Park, 301–303, 317–318, 321–322
Cellini, Benvenuto, his escape from durance, 189
Cethegus and Catiline, 285
Chalmers, Dr., 99
Chamberlain, Mr., 230; his retirement from Mr. Gladstone's Cabinet, 346
Chanson de Roland, translation of, 57
Charlemont, Lord. *See* Caulfield, James
Charles I. and the Five Members, 266
Charles II., Court of, 2; reign of, 5, 7
Chartist movement in England, 112
Chatham, genius of, 27
Chatterton, at eighteen, 135
Chester Castle, capture of, planned by the Fenians, 190
Chesterfield, Lord, on landlords and Whiteboys, 15; his beneficent viceroyalty of Ireland, 20; his verses on Molly Lepell, 32; vision of, 352
Churchill, Lord Randolph, leader of the Conservative party in the House of Commons, 314; his crusade in the north of Ireland, 345
Cicero, 56, 99, 127
Clanricarde, Lord, his daughter married to Patrick Sarsfield, Earl of Lucan, and afterwards to the Duke of Berwick, 6
Clare election, the, 94–97
Clare, Lord, the basest of Pitt's tools against the Irish, 49, 59; death of, 69
Clontarf meeting, dispersal of, 115, 116
Cobden, Richard, death of, 156, 261
Coercion Bill, Mr. Forster's, 254, 255, 258–272; passed, 273
Cork Examiner, the most important paper in the south of Ireland, 198

DAV

Cornwallis, 58, 59
'Corrig-an-Aifrion,' or the Mass-stone, 13
Corry, a tool of the Castle, 62; his clumsy falsehoods, 63; his duel with Grattan, 64
Corydon, the informer, 190
Courtney, Mr. Leonard, 224, 225; his appointment as Under Secretary for the Home Department, 255
Cowen, Mr. Joseph, his strenuous attack at Newcastle on the Government policy of coercion, 281, 282, 287
Cowper, Lord, Viceroy of Ireland, 254; his resignation, 299, 300
Crawford, Mr. Sharman, his Bill to amend the law relating to landlord and tenant, 172; his Tenant-Right Bill, 172–173; his Bill to regulate the Ulster custom, 173
Crimean War, outbreak of, 151; end of, 152
Croke, Archbishop of Cashel, his approval of the Ladies' Land League, 274, 275; condemns the No-rent Manifesto, 288; on the invention and exaggeration of outrages, 291; induces Mr. Dillon to withdraw his intended resignation, 309
Cromwellian massacres in Drogheda, 2; atrocities, 47
Cromwell's Ironsides, 2
Curran, John Philpot, his heroic and desperate single-handed fight for the men of Ninety-eight, 54; his efforts for Wolfe Tone, 55; his poem of 'The Deserter,' 56; career of, *ib.*, 72; opposed to Emmet's love for his daughter, 73, 74; apparition of, 352
Curran, Richard, son of John Philpot Curran, 73
Curran, Sarah, daughter of John Philpot Curran, 6; the idol of Emmet's heart, 72–73; marries another, 74

DANTON, words of, 87
Daunt, Mr. O'Neill, his story of the Catholic and Protestant schoolfellows, 13
Davis, Thomas, his lyric on the grave of Wolfe Tone, 55; one of the

DAV

founders of the *Nation* newspaper, 118; the most genuine Irish poet since Moore, 125; death of, 129; soft-spoken lyric of, 337

Davitt, Michael, 228; his uncompromising opposition to all intimidation, 251, 257; arrest of, 267, 268; elected member of Parliament for Meath, 294; not allowed to take his seat, *ib.*; rumoured release of, 299; advocates the nationalisation of the land, 309; a large part of his life passed in prison, 312; imprisonment, *ib.*; release, *ib.*; content to act loyally with Mr. Parnell, 313; letter in the *Kerry Sentinel*, 331; released from prison, *ib.*

Dawson, Mr. Charles, M.P., a strong Nationalist, elected Lord Mayor of Dublin, 289, 292, 304; proclamations of, 306, 307

Deasy, Captain, a prominent Fenian, arrested, 191

Derby, Lord, 144

Desmoulins, Camille, 111

Devon Commission, 172, 173

Dickens, Charles, deeply affected by a speech of O'Connell, 92, 102

Dilke, Sir Charles, proclaims himself a Republican, 222, 224; in the South African debate, 224, 225

Dillon, John Blake, one of the founders of the *Nation* newspaper, 118; his personal appearance, 119; declines to censure the Phœnix Society, 155; in Parliament, 157; a great admirer of and implicit believer in John Bright, 157-158, 164, 167; sudden death of, 165; Mr. Bright's tribute to, 165-167, 246; his belief in the sympathies of English statesmen, 327

Dillon, John (son of the above), his singularly impressive appearance, 119; paternal inheritance, 235; his Kildare speech, 245, 246; his reply to Mr. Forster's attack, 246, 247; suspended, 268, 269; his series of speeches in Ireland supporting the Land League, 275; arrested and imprisoned, *ib.*; repudiates Mr. Gladstone's misstatements, and his compliments founded thereon, 286; arrested and imprisoned, *ib.*; in

EMM

Kilmainham, 288, 290, 292, 294; release, 299; freedom of the city of Dublin conferred upon him, 305; induced to withdraw or postpone his intended resignation, 309; resignation of his seat in Parliament, 326; his picturesque personal appearance, 326, 327; goes away to Italy and Colorado, 327

Dioscuri, the, 325

Disraeli, Mr., his keen political insight, 156, appeals to the country on the Irish Church question, 199; speech on Mr. Gladstone's Irish University Education Bill, 209, 210. *See also* Beaconsfield, Lord.

Doheny, Michael John, the companion in misfortune of James Stephens, 149; description of, in the *Hue and Cry*, *ib*; his fascinating story of the 'Felon's Track,' *ib*; goes to the United States, 151

Dopping, Bishop of Meath, his proclamation from the pulpit, 10

'Drapier's Letters,' the, 20

Drogheda, Cromwellian massacres in, 2; siege of, 4

Duffy, Edward, the life and soul of the Fenian movement west of the Shannon, 188

Duffy, Sir Charles Gavan, on Irish poverty, 110, 111; one of the founders of the *Nation* newspaper, 118; his description of Thomas Davis, *ib.*; and of the elder Dillon, 119; on John Pigot, 123; finds fame and fortune in Victoria, 133; a conspicuous champion of tenant-right, 144; account of M'Manus' escape from his Australasian prison, 171; 285

Dugald Dalgetty, 32

Dungannon, Convention at, 33

Dynamite explosions, 328-330

EMMET, Robert, his affianced bride, 46; at Dublin University, 66; his friendship with Thomas Moore, 67; his insurrection and its purpose, 70, 71; flight of, 72; his love for Sarah Curran, 72, 73; execution of, 73; his letter to Richard Curran, 73, 74; his dying

EMM

request, 74; his daring attempt and its failure, 75, 81, 88; traditions of, 129; scene of his execution, 179; apparition of, 352
Emmet, Thomas Addis, 46; banished, 51, 58
Eviction in full swing, 141

Feni, semi-mythic chivalry of the, 177
Fenian Brotherhood, the, origin of the title, 177, 178
Fenianism, rise of, 155
Finigan, Mr., member for Ennis, suspended, 270
Fionn, the son of Coul, 177
Fitzgerald, Lady Edward, 6, 45, 46
Fitzgerald, Lord Edward, 44; the ideal hero of romance, 45; his wife, 45, 46; death of, 50, 58; his grave, 73, 127, 179; house where he met his death, 179; apparition of, 352
Fitzgerald, Mr. Vesey, member for County Clare, his seat contested by O'Connell, 95
Fitzgibbon, Black Jack, 49, 59, 69
Fitzmaurice, Lord Edmond, 258
Fitzwilliam, Lord, his beneficent viceroyalty of Ireland, 20, 352
Flood, Henry, 21-25; accepts office, 28; his quarrel with Grattan, 28, 29, 34, 35; retires from the Irish and finds a seat in the English Parliament, 36; death of, 37; his far-seeing statesmanship, 62; apparition of, 352
Foley, Mr., his designs for O'Connell's statue, 304
Forster, Mr. W. E., 202; his appointment to the Irish Secretaryship, 236, 238, 239, 244, 245; his attack on Mr. Dillon, 245-247; receives the nickname of 'Buckshot,' 247; daily more unpopular, 254; his proposed revival of Coercion, 254-257; introduces his first Coercion measure, 258-260; sits doubled up, 265; moves third reading of Bill, 273; his incurable cecity to the signs of the times, 289; more unpopular than ever, 293; his journey of inspection into County Clare, ib.; abusive epithets levelled at him by transatlantic journalists,

GLA

297; resignation of Irish Chief Secretaryship, 299, 300; series of attempts to assassinate, 317; and their failure, 317, 319; his administration, however well-intended, unsuccessful, 322; his fondness for the Kilmainham-treaty topic, 325; his attack on Mr. Parnell, ib.; his defence of Mazzini, 325-326; his plea in answer to opponents, 341
Fottrell, Mr. George, Secretary to the Irish Land Commission, remarkable pamphlet of, published under the semblance of official authority, 296; resignation of his secretaryship, 297
Fox, Charles James, 38; genius of, 82; commanding influence of, 83; death and burial in Westminster Abbey, 83, 84; genius of, 352
Freeman's Journal, the, 21, 235, 296
French Revolution, the, 40, 46, 86, 87, 293
Froude, James Anthony, the most famous and the most unfair of anti-Irish historians, 52, 53
F's, the three, 276, 278

Galland, his 'Mille et Une Nuits,' 81
Gavelkind, law of, enforced on estates of Irish Catholics not having Protestant heirs, 11
General Election of 1865, 156
Genlis, Madame de, statements of, 45
George I., 10, 15
George II., his Irish Parliament, 25
George III., 10, 29, 52; stubborn folly of, 69, 75, 76, 84
George IV., the basest of the Georges, 90
George, Mr. Henry, arrested by mistake, 308
Geraldine, house of, 44, 45, 50, 127
Gibbon, Edward, irritating effect upon him of Pitt's unalterable composure, 81
Gibson, Mr., 324, 325
Gladstone, William Ewart, on the state of Ireland under Grattan's Parliament, 17-19, 38; on Wolfe Tone, 42; on the oratory of Richard Lalor Sheil, 99; becomes

GLA

a supporter of advanced Radical ideas, 156; his process of conversion, *ib.*; his Land Act of 1870, 175; the most advanced thinker and keen-sighted statesman in the House of Commons, 194; resolutions regarding the Established Church in Ireland, 199; in a mood for great legislation, 202, 203; his Irish University Education Bill, 204-207, 208-211; dislike and dread of, among Irish Protestants, 212, 223; acceptance of office in 1880, 239; his Midlothian speeches and Lord Beaconsfield, 255; defends the policy of the Government, 256; on the Irish question, 256-257; moves to declare urgency for the Coercive Bills, 260; justifies the introduction of Coercion and denounces Mr. Parnell and Mr. Biggar, 263, 264; his passionate oratory, 264, 268-272; accident to, 272; his 1881 Budget, 276; introduces the New Land Bill, *ib.*; his Leeds campaign against the Irish Parliamentary party, 284-285; his speech at Guildhall, 287, and announcement of Mr. Parnell's arrest, *ib.*; correspondence with Mr. Smythe of Westmeath, 295; conspicuous for his readiness to admit an error, 299; his return to power, 346; his views on the Irish question greatly widened, *ib.*; impressive scene in the House of Commons on the introduction of his measure for Home Rule in Ireland, 347-354; his oratorical capacity never more strikingly manifest, 348; the greatest speech of his life, 351

Gladstone, Mr. Herbert, speech at Leeds, 325

Goderich administration, temporary and trumpery, 95

Goldsmith, Oliver, 22, 31

Gordon, General, in Ireland, 252; proposal of, 253

Gorst, Mr., 324

Grammont, his 'Memoirs,' 2

Grattan's father, a fierce-tempered, narrow-minded man, 26

HAR

Grattan, Henry, 18; his speech on the triumph of Irish independence, 20, 21; the greatest Irish statesman of his age, 25-29; becomes leader of the Patriot party, 28; his quarrel with Flood, 28-29, 33-37; his great objects, 40; efforts for the removal of Catholic disabilities, 44; comes to the front again, 61-65; his speech in reply to Corry, 63; his duel with Corry in Phœnix Park, 64, 65-66; his first appearance in the English House of Commons, 82; commands of, 101; apparition of, 352

Grattan, Mr. Henry, son of the above, 170

Grattan's Parliament, 17-19, 66

Gray, Mr. E. D. (Home Ruler), proprietor of the *Freeman's Journal*, 235; committed by Justice Lawson for contempt of court, 305; released after two months' imprisonment, 306

Gray, Phil, a serviceable messenger, 138

Gray, Sir John, proprietor of the *Freeman's Journal*, 144

Greeley, Horace, 121

Greer, Mr., 144

Grenville, Lord, 82, 88

Griffin, Gerald, his novel of 'The Collegians' quoted, 142

Griffiths' (Sir Richard) valuation, 171, 248-249

Hafiz, 124

Hamilton, 2

Harcourt, Lord, 28

Harcourt, Sir William, 267, 268; introduces the Arms Bill in the Commons, 278; his Bill for amending the law relating to explosives, 328

Hardwicke, Lord, Lord-Lieutenantship of, 80; frees Ireland from his obnoxious presence, 83

Hardy, Mr. Francis, on Lord Charlemont, 31

Harman, Colonel King, regards a seat for Sligo as his personal property, 284

Harrington, Mr. Edward, editor of the *Kerry Sentinel*, imprisonment of, 331, 342

HAR

Harrington, Mr. Timothy, proprietor of the *Kerry Sentinel*, imprisonment of, 330, 342; rewarded by being elected to represent Westmeath in Parliament, 330

Hartington, Lord, attacks the obstructive policy of the Irish members, 258; his grimly erect attitude, 265, 272

Harvey, Bagenal, 51, 58, 352

Healy, Mr. (Home Ruler), career of, 234, 265; suspended, 273; his amendments to Mr. Gladstone's new Land Bill, 279; warrant for his arrest, 286; imprisonment of, and its result, 311-313; elected member for Monaghan County, one of the strongholds of Ulster, 331, 332; his mastery and consummate knowledge of the Land Act, 332

Hearts of Steel, 15

'Hedge-schools,' 13

Heliogabalus, court of, 32

Hennessy, Sir John Pope (Governor of the Mauritius), distinguished in parliamentary life for the skill and ability of his obstructive tactics, 223

Henry VIII., King, 45; act of, 109

Herbert, Mr. Auberon, proclaims himself a Republican, 222, 264

Heron, Mrs., her eating-house at Cork, 135-136, 138

Hervey, Frederick, Earl of Bristol, and Bishop of Derry, 31, 32; his later career and death, 37

Hervey, Lord, his Memoirs of the Reign of George II., 31; the 'Sporus' of Pope, 32

Hicks-Beach, Sir Michael, his proposal to suppress the Irish National League, 346

Higgins, Francis, editor of the *Freeman's Journal*, a traitor, 50

Hill, Sir George, recognises and betrays Wolfe Tone, 54

Hoche, General, 47

Hoffmann, weird stories of, 124

'Home Rule,' becomes the shibboleth of the new Irish party, 243

Home Rule Bill, Mr. Gladstone's, 346-354

Home-Rule movement, 215, *sqq.*; platform of, 215-216; demand

JOY

of the party not a very appalling one, 217, 345

Horsman, Mr., 173

Huddys, the, Lord Ardilaun's bailiffs, murder of, 291, 306

Hugo, Victor, on Ireland, 273; visited by Mr. Parnell, *ib.*

Humbert, General, 51

Hume, Mr., denounces the Ministry for their coercive policy towards Ireland, 171

Hurlingham, pigeon-shooting at, 252

Hutchinson, Hely, 16

Huy, 6

IDDESLEIGH, Lord, 345. See also Northcote, Sir Stafford

Inchiquin, Lord, brother of Mr. Smith O'Brien, 125, 153

Irish ballad literature, 2, 5

Irish Church disestablished, 202

Irish legend, 17

Irish National Land League formed, 228; declared an illegal body, 288

Irish National League established, 308; its programme and objects, *ib.*

Irish People newspaper, established by Stephens, 185; police descent on its offices, 186

Irish Republican Brotherhood(I.R.B.), 177

Irish World, the (New York journal), 297-298; 309

Ivanhoe, 260

JACKSON, Mr., an English clergyman, fate of, 43

James I., King, his creation of Irish boroughs, 16

James II., King, 1

Jason, legend of, 30, 62

Jenkins, Mr. Edward, his political tergiversation, 224, 225

Johnson, Dr., 23, 31

Johnson, Mr. William M., Solicitor-General for Ireland, returned for Mallow, 314

Jones, Paul, 29, 86

Joyce country, the, 291, 306

Joynes, Mr., assistant-master at Eton, arrested by mistake, 308; publishes a little book upon the Irish question, and resigns his post, *ib.*

KAV

KAVANAGH, Michael, car-driver, his evidence of the Phœnix Park murders, 318
Keats, John, at eighteen, 135
Kelly, Colonel Thomas, a conspicuous Fenian leader, arrested at Manchester, 191
Kenealy, Edward Vaughan, 118
Keogh, Mr. William, 145; made Irish Solicitor-General, 146; made a Judge, 147
Kerry Sentinel, case of the, 330, 331, 347
Kickham, Charles J., a follower of Stephens in the Fenian movement, 183; account of, *ib.*; speech at Mullinahone, *ib.*, 187; capture of, 188; his imprisonment and release, 307-308; death and funeral, 308
Killegrew, 2
'Kilmainham Treaty,' the supposititious, 299, 320, 324, 325, 326
Kilwarden, Lord, Chief Justice of the King's Bench, dragged from his carriage and killed, 72
Koran or death, 8
Kosciusko, 127

LABOUCHERE, Mr., 258, 287
Ladies' Land League, 274; members of, imprisoned, 288; declines to admit defeat, 293; abolished by Messrs. Parnell and Dillon, *ib.*
Lake, General, successor to Sir Ralph Abercrombie, 49
Lalor, Fintan, 129, 151
Land League, the, 228, 239 *sqq.*; declared an illegal body, 288; suppression of, 289, 290, 301
Land Question, the, 168-176
Landen, battle of, 6
Langrishe, Sir Hercules, a colleague of Flood, 25; Burke's eulogium on, 28
Law, Mr. Hugh, Irish Lord Chancellor, 332; death of, 334
Lawson, Mr. Justice, commits Sheriff Gray to prison for contempt of Court, 305, 306; attempt to assassinate, 310
Lecky, Mr., on the Irish borough system, 16; his essay on Grattan, 26; on Henry Flood, 36; on the Irish Penal Code, 40, 53; on the

MAC

eloquence of Meagher, 126, 127 on the Home Rule theory, 218
Ledru Rollin, declaration of, 121
Legion Club, the, 23
Lely, Sir Peter, his beauties, 2
Lepell, the beautiful Molly, married to Lord Hervey, 32
Limerick, siege of, 1-4; treaty of, 5-9
Lloyd, Major Clifford, extraordinary circular of, 296
Locke, John, 19
Louis XIV., 5
Louis XVI., execution of, 86
Lovelace, Richard, quoted, 189
Lowe, Robert, his fierce attack upon the Irish Church, 199; his hour of more than Roman triumph, 347
Luby, Thomas Clarke, accompanies James Stephens on his 'tour of personal inspection' in Ireland, 152; a conspicuous follower of his in the Fenian movement, 183-185; arrested, 187; sentenced to twenty years' penal servitude, 190
Lucan, Earl of. *See* Sarsfield, Patrick
Lucan, Lady, 6. *See also* Clanricarde
Lucas, Frederick, proprietor of the *Tablet*, 144; one of the most upright and pure-minded of politicians, 145
Lucas, Samuel, founder of the *Freeman's Journal*, 21, 23, 26; 352
Luxembourg, 6
Lytton, Edward Bulwer, Lord, his poem of 'St. Stephen's' quoted, 92

MACAULAY on Patrick Sarsfield, Earl of Lucan, 6; on Addison, 264
MacCarthy, Denis Florence, a contributor to the *Nation*, 123; death of, 126
Madrid, Gallery of, 119, 326
M'Manus, Terence Bellew, transported to Van Diemen's Land, 131; escapes to California, 178; closing years and death, 178, 179; funeral cortège through Dublin to Glasnevin, 179, 180
M'Namara, Major, declines to contest Clare, 96
MacNevin, 46; banished, 51; a contributor to the *Nation*, 123, 125

MAG

Maguire, Mr. John Francis, 145; leader of the Irish party, 174; strikes the first serious blow against the Established Church in Ireland, 198; withdraws his resolutions in favour of Mr. Gladstone's, 199

Mallow, one of the most peculiar constituencies in the south of Ireland, 314; election for, 314-315

Mangan, Clarence (a contributor to the *Nation*), his brilliant and unhappy genius, 123; described by Sir Charles Gavan Duffy, 124

Marseillaise, the, 48

Martin, John, 130; transported, 131; elected for Meath, 217; death of, 133, 221

'Mary of the *Nation*' and Joe Brenan, 135, 140

Mass-stone, the, 13

Mathew, Father, the inaugurator of the temperance movement, 112; makes common cause with O'Connell, 113

Maynooth Grant, increased, 84; again reduced, 85

Mayo, Lord, Irish Secretary, his occult phrase about 'levelling up,' 198

Mazzini and Mr. Forster, 325-326

M'Cabe, Archbishop of Dublin, denounces the participation of women in political strife, 274

MacCarthy, Mr. John George, a very moderate Home Ruler, member for Mallow, 314

Meagher, Thomas Francis, speech of, 50; his eloquence, 126; his speech against O'Connell's doctrine of passive resistance, 127; his speeches not studied as they deserve, 127-128; endeavour to raise an armed rebellion, 131; speech from the dock, *ib.*; transported, *ib.*; in the American civil war, 132, 182; curious and grimly inappropriate end of his brilliant career, 133; his description of Terence Bellew M'Manus, 178

'Memory of the Dead, The,' one of the best and bravest of Irish rebellious ballads, 48

'M'Grath, Terence,' his 'Pictures from Ireland' quoted, 335-336

M'Hale, John, Archbishop of Tuam, early training of, 13, 14

NAG

Milbank, Sir Frederick, and Mr. Biggar, 266

Mill, John Stuart, 156-157; his exertions to save the men of Manchester, 193; not re-elected for Westminster, 200; 208

Mirabeau, protest of, 46, 99; his shining sentences, 127; saying of, 155

Mitchel, John, fine words of, 5; replaces Thomas Davis on the *Nation*, 129; starts the *United Irishman*, *ib.*; arrested, tried, and transported, 130; no attempt to rescue him, *ib.*, 134; effects his escape while a prisoner on parole, 132; his return to Ireland and death, 133; unknown to the large bulk of the Irish peasantry, 139; saying of, 141; disqualified to sit in Parliament, 133, 295

Mitchell-Henry, Mr., 216-217

Moira, Lord, protest of, 49

Molyneux, William, his 'Case of Ireland.' 19, 20, 38, 352

Monteagle, Lord. *See* Spring Rice, Mr.

Moore, George Henry, leader of the Irish Parliamentary party, 174

Moore, Roger, 352

Moore, Thomas, on Sheridan's wife and Lord Edward Fitzgerald, 45; at Dublin University, 66; his friendship with Robert Emmet, 67; his song of 'The Irish Peasant to his Mistress,' 195; his Vale of Avoca, 220

Mountain (cobbler), a grimly appropriate name, 137

Moyers, Dr., Lord Mayor of Dublin, gives his casting-vote against conferring the freedom of the city upon Mr. Parnell and Mr. Dillon, 288-289; is refused the customary vote of thanks on his retirement from office, 292

Murger, Henri, 124

Murphy, Father John, 51, 352

Murphy, Father Michael, supposed to be invulnerable, 51

Musgrave, Sir Richard, his work on the Rebellion of Ninety-eight, 77, 78

Nagle, Pierce, the infamous informer, 180; betrays Stephens to the Government, 185

NAP

Napier, Mr., Irish Attorney-General, 174
Napoleon, Emmet's interviews with, 70; defeats the allied armies at Austerlitz, 82, 83
Nation, the, newspaper, 48, 114, 115, 119; publication of the first number, 120; motto of, *ib.*; contributors to, 121-125; filled a great want in Ireland, 122, 139; upholds its traditions of Nationalism through long years under disheartening conditions, 234
Newman, Cardinal, 99
Newton, Sir John, presides over a select committee to inquire into Irish agricultural distress, 169
Norbury, Judge, his brutal interruptions to Emmet's address at his trial, 73
No-rent Manifesto, the, 288; the clergy entirely against it, *ib.*; 292
Northcote, Sir Stafford, his appeal against obstruction, 266; his crusade into Ulster, 337. *See* also Iddesleigh, Lord.

OAKBOYS, 15
O'Brien, William, editor of *United Ireland*, 313; committed for trial, 314; returned by a large majority for Mallow, 315; his exposure of official corruption at Dublin Castle, 344
O'Brien, William Smith, comes forward as a prominent figure in Irish politics, 125, 126, 129; tries to raise an armed rebellion, 131; transported to Van Diemen's Land, *ib.*; receives his pardon, 133; death of, *ib.*; anecdote of, 138; 148, 149; allowed to return to Ireland, 153; his speech at Clonmel, 154; his appeal to the Irish people against the Phœnix conspiracy, 154-155
'Obstruction,' 223, 224
O'Callaghan, Mr., 6
O'Connell, Daniel, uncle of the liberator, romantic career of, 86
O'Connell, Daniel, declaration of, 42; his parentage and early career, 85-91; growing influence of, 89; unworthy passages in his life. 90, 101; his oratorical powers, 92;

O'KE

his duel with Mr. D'Esterre, 93; his first appearance in the English House of Commons, 93-95; re-elected and takes his seat, 101; portrait of, *ib.*; 109, and Father Mathew, 112, 113; his monster meetings, 114; never intended to use force, 115, 121; his dispersal of the Clontarf meeting, 116; imprisoned, *ib.*; waning influence, *ib.*; his hopeless passion for a young girl, 117; his death at Genoa, *ib.*; alarmed at the growing popularity of the *Nation* newspaper, 120, 121; and Smith O'Brien, 125-126; unveiling of his statue in Dublin, 304, 305; his societies for the promotion of Catholic Emancipation, 308
O'Connell, John, son of Daniel O'Connell, interrupts a speech of Meagher's, 128
O'Connell, Morgan, father of Daniel O'Connell, 85
O'Connell, Morris, eldest son of Daniel O'Connell's grandfather, 85
O'Connor, Arthur, 48, 51, 58, 120
O'Connor, Mr. T. P. (Home Ruler), his 'Life of Lord Beaconsfield,' 233
O'Doherty, Kevin Izod, 120; transported, 131; still living, 133
O'Donoghue, the, 165, 180; speech of, 261, 269
O'Donovan Rossa, Jeremiah, 152; sentenced to penal servitude for life, 190; disqualified to sit in Parliament, 294
O'Flaherty, Mr. Edmund, 145; made Commissioner of Income Tax, 146; his flight to Denmark and to America, 147
O'Gorman Mahon, Colonel, remarkable adventures of, 97; fifty years ago, 98; 235
O'Hagan, John, his impassioned poems in the *Nation* newspaper, 57, 123; his translation of the 'Chanson de Roland,' *ib.*; takes service under the English Government, *ib.*
O'Hagan, Thomas (afterwards Lord), his brilliant defence of Daniel O'Sullivan, 155
O'Kelly, Mr. James (Home Ruler), adventurous career of in foreign parts, 234, 235

O'Leary, John, a follower of Stephens in the Fenian movement, 183; character and career of, 184, 187; sentenced to twenty years' penal servitude, 190

O'Mahony, John, at Paris with James Stephens, 150-151; in America, 177; something of a Gaelic scholar and student, *ib.*

Omar, 8

Orange Society, the, origin of, 77; intolerable cruelties of, 88; revival of the feud, 334, *sqq.*

Ormond administration, 3

Ormond, last Duke of, his viceroyalty, 9

O'Sullivan, Daniel, defended by Mr. Thomas O'Hagan, 155; sentenced to ten years' penal servitude, *ib.*

Othman, 8

PALAFOX, 325

Pall Mall Gazette on Mr. Parnell, 343

Palmerston, Lord, death of, 156; his summary dismissal from office, 347, 349

Parnell, Charles Stuart, 90, 97; family and parentage, 220; elected member of parliament for Meath, 221; attracts no notice at first in the House, *ib.*; but gradually forces his way till his name begins to be talked about, *ib.*; not to be howled or shouted down, 222; opposition to the Prison Code and Army and Navy Mutiny Bills, 224; to the South African Confederation Bill, 225-226; his mission to America, 228; real leader of the Irish party, 229, 230; his popularity through Ireland, 232; his followers, 233-236, 245; motion of, 247; his pale, unmoved face, 264; 265; speech erroneously attributed to, 267; question on Mr. Michael Davitt's imprisonment, 267, 268; suspended, 269, 270; his visit to Paris and interviews with the Archbishop and with Victor Hugo and M. Rochefort, 273; explains his views to the Newcastle convention, 282; enthusiastic reception at Dublin, 283; entry into Cork with Father Sheehy, 284; Mr. Gladstone's censure of, 284-285; his attack at Wexford on Mr. Gladstone, 285-286; arrested and conveyed to Kilmainham, 286; signs the No-rent Manifesto, 287-288; his name removed from the Commission of the Peace for the County of Wicklow, 288; in Kilmainham, 290; 292, 294; release on parole and return to Kilmainham, 298; unconditional release, 299; freedom of the city of Dublin conferred upon him, 305; on the Irish National League, 308; his views on the land question, 309; 315; accompanies Mr. Healy on his Monaghan campaign, 332; a guest at the banquet to celebrate the opening of the Cork Industrial Exhibition, 333; banquet to, at Dublin, and presentation of the testimonial, 341; his speech on the occasion, 341-342; opinions of the Irish and English press, 342-343

Parnell, Miss Anna (sister of the above), President of the Ladies' Land League, 274, 293

Parnell, Sir Henry, the first Lord Congleton, 220

Parnell, Sir John, 59

Parnell, Thomas, the poet, 220

Parthenope, 33

Pascal, 147

Peel, Sir Robert, 95; opposes O'Connell's taking his seat under the new oaths, 100, 101; his contemptuous inquiry in Parliament, 120, 121, 172

Penal Laws, the, 1-14

Perceval, Spencer, 84

Persius, 147

Petrarch, Lord Charlemont's translations of, 31

Petronius, 24

Philippe Égalité, daughter of, 45, 46

Phœnix Conspiracy, the, 152, *sqq.*, 177

Phœnix-Park murders, 301, 302, 317, 318, 320-322

Pigot, John, 'the woman's ideal of a patriot,' 123

Pitt, William, his tools against the Irish, 49; his pledge to Ireland in

PLA

securing the Union, 68 ; his resignation, 69 ; return to office, 76, 77, 81, 82 ; death of, 83, 87
Playfair, Mr. (afterwards Sir) Lyon, 208 ; takes the Speaker's place, 265, 266
Plunket, Mr., 324, 325
Poe, Edgar Allan, 123, 124 ; his poem of 'The Raven' quoted, 123
Ponsonby, 18
Pope, Alexander, his satire on Lord Hervey, 32
Poyning's Act, repeal of, 2
Price, Mr. Bonamy, 277
Pulteney, his duel with Lord Hervey, 32 ; his secession from the House of Commons, 2:7
Punch, cartoon in, 332 ; severe in its condemnation of the Orange policy, 340

QUINN, Mr. J. P., Secretary of the Land League, arrested and conveyed to Kilmainham, 286 ; prosecution of, 311 ; released from prison, 331

READE, Charles, his novel of 'The Cloister and the Hearth,' 227
Redmond, Mr., elected member for Wexford, 332, 333
Repeal of the Union, 92, 113
Reynolds, Sir Joshua, 31
Reynolds, Thomas, spy, 49, 50
Ribbonmen, 88
Ribbon Society, the, 141-142
Richey, Mr., on the futility of certain clauses in the Irish Land Act of 1870, attempting to create a peasant proprietorship, 176
Richmond Commission, the, 277
Richter, Jean Paul, his 'Flower, Fruit, and Thorn Pieces,' 146
Robinson, Chief Justice, 10
Roche, Father Philip, 51
Rochefort, M., interview with Mr. Parnell, 273
Roe, Owen, 352
Rogers, Mr. Theo'o'd, 258
Rossmore, Lord, Orange proclamation and speech, 338, 339 ; removed from the commission of the peace, 339-340
Rouget de Lisle, 48

SHE

Rousseau, Jean Baptiste, his poem to posterity, 22
Rowan, Hamilton, his escape to America, 43 ; Curran's defence of, 56
Rowley's poems, 125
Russell, Lord John, carries the Repeal of the Test and Corporation Acts, 95 ; his suggestion to O'Connell, *ib.* ; settles the Irish Tithe Question, 108 ; his 'Durham letter,' 144 ; plan for kidnapping him, 150

SADLEIR, James, brother of John Sadleir, 145, 146 ; expelled from the House of Commons, 147
Sadleir, John, 115 ; his remarkable ability and audacity, *ib.* ; made a Lord of the Treasury, 146 ; his wholesale forgery and embezzlement, *ib.* ; supposed suicide, *ib.* ; and doubts respecting it, 146-147
Salisbury, Lord, 280, 281 ; on Mr. Gladstone's complaints of Mr. Parnell, 285 ; accepts office, 344, 345
Sarsfield, Patrick, Earl of Lucan, his defence of Limerick, 1-6 ; death of, 6-8 ; 352
Saturn, 87
Scævola, 130
Schiller, his immortal heroine, 196
Scullabogue, 52, 53
Secret Societies, 142 ; growth of, 289, 290, 301
Seward, William Henry, 121
Sexton, Mr. (Home Ruler), 233 ; a contributor to the *Nation* newspaper, 234 ; elected member of parliament for Sligo, in opposition to Colonel King Harman, 234 ; 275 ; arrested and conveyed to Kilmainham, 286
Shakespeare, quoted, 4, 5, 52, 61, 83, 90, 131, 189, 233
Shaw, Mr. ('sensible Shaw'), chosen leader of the Irish party in Mr. Butt's stead, 227 ; his leadership merely nominal, 229, 230, 232, 233, 236, 277
Sheares, the brothers John and Henry, 50, 51 ; present at the execution of Louis XVI., 86 ; in death as in life undivided, 352
Shee, Serjeant, his Tenant Compensation Bill, 174

SHE

Sheehy, Father Eugene, arrested and imprisoned, 275; set free, 283; commences a crusade against the Government, 284; his entry into Cork, *ib.*
Sheil, Richard Lalor, on Wolfe Tone, 44; his attack on the Duke of York, 79, 80; his description of the O'Gorman Mahon, 98; his eloquence and genius, 99; his brilliant and fascinating picture of the Clare contest, 100
Sheppard, Jack, prison-breaking feats of, 189
Shepstone, Sir Theophilus, his annexation of the Transvaal, 225
Sheridan, Richard Brinsley, 45
Sièyes, Abbé, 219
Sirr. Major, infamies of his gang, 48, 50, 72, 73, 88, 94; spectre of, 353
Skibbereen Literary Society, 152, 153
'Sliabh Cuilinn,' signature of Mr. O'Hagan, 57
Smith O'Brien. *See* O'Brien
Smith, Sydney, on the exactions of the Irish Church, 104
Smyrna Bay, 33
Smyth, Mr. P. J., an earnest and active Nationalist, effects the rescue of Irish political prisoners, 131; his later life only melancholy, 132; speech abounding in sneers against England, 180, 181; dies the placeman of an English Government, 181; 216-217
Smythe, Mrs. Henry, murder of, 295
Somerville, Sir William, Irish Secretary, 173
Spencer, Lord, succeeds Lord Cowper, as Lord-Lieutenant of Ireland, 300, 301; surveys a terrible scene from the windows of the Viceregal Lodge, 302; Mr. Biggar's attack on, 311, 342-343, 344
'Speranza,' *nom-de-guerre* of Lady Wilde in the *Nation*, 121
'Sporus,' Pope's nickname for Lord Hervey, 32
Spring Rice, Mr., afterwards Lord Monteagle, 170
Stephens, James, 148-150; at Paris, 150; returns to Ireland on 'a tour of personal inspection,' 151-152; finds ready confederates, 152; leader of the Phœnix Society, *ib.*; not disheartened by tempo-

TON

rary defeat, 177; establishes the *Irish People* newspaper, 185; betrayed by Pierce Nagle, *ib*; flight, 186-187; capture, 188; and escape, 189
Stepniak, the Russian Nihilist, his record of 'Russia under the Tzars,' 75
Stone, Primate, his base and profligate character, 24
Sullivan, Mr. A. M., on the varieties of Ribbonism, 143; on the funeral of Terence Bellow M'Manus, 179; his account of John O Leary, 184, and of Thomas Clarke Luby, 184-185; on the Parnellite opposition to the Prison Code and Army and Navy Mutiny Bills, 224, 269; defends the Ladies' Land League, 274; compelled by ill-health to resign his seat in Parliament, 294
Sullivan, Mr. T. D. (Home Ruler), touching poem by, 194; proprietor of the *Nation*, 234; a true poet of the people, *ib.*
Surrey, Earl of, 45
Swift, Jonathan, on the Irish bishops, 19; his services to Ireland, 20, 21, 24; his list of friends, 26, 33; his small fervid figure, 352
Swinburne, Algernon Charles, his 'Appeal to England' on behalf of the men of Manchester, 193
'Syndercombe, Letters of,' 25

Talbot, Richard, Duke of Tirconnel, 2, 3; death of, 4; his weary, haughty face, 352
Thackeray, W. M. on John Dillon the elder, 119; on the Eastern Counties' train, 258
Times newspaper, the, prophesies the gradual extinction of the Celtic Irishman, 141; its untimely and unseemly merriment over Mr. Smith O'Brien's speech at Clonmel, 154; on Mr. Parnell's speech at the Rotunda Banquet, 342
Tirconnel, Duke of. *See* Talbot, Richard
Tithe War, the, 102, *sqq.*
Tone, Theobald Wolfe, 41; his temporary exile in America, 43, 44;

TOU

his widow, 46; protests against the title of 'citizen,' *ib.*; in France, 47; his arrest and sentence, 54; his death in prison, 55; his grave, *ib.*, 58, 61, 179; 352
Toussaint, L'Ouverture, 96
Townshend, Lord, Viceroyalty of, 24–25, 29
Traill, Major, R.M., curious picture of his daily life, 295–296
Treaty of Limerick, 4–9
Trevelyan, Mr. G. O., appointed Chief Secretary for Ireland, 303; praise due to, 305; his great ambition, 342; gives up the Irish Secretaryship, 344; retirement from Mr. Gladstone's Cabinet, 346
Turk, the 'unspeakable,' 81
Tyrtæus, 48, 178

ULSTER tenant-right custom, 240, 243, 278
Union, the, 56
United Ireland, the most advanced of the National newspapers, proscribed, 288; suppressed and seized, but continues to appear surreptitiously, 297, 313–315
United Irishman newspaper, started by John Mitchel, 129
United Irishmen, Society of, founded by Wolfe Tone, 41–43, 55
'Usher Maillard, shifty,' 293

VELASQUEZ, 119, 326
Vergniaud, shining sentences of, 127
Vernon, Lieut.-Col., testimony of, 78
Victoria, Queen, visit to Dublin, 184
Volunteer movement in Ireland, 29–38

ZUL

WALLENSTEIN's horse, 280
Walpole, Horace, 31
Washington, George, 29, 33
Wellesley, his Lord-Lieutenantship, 88
Wellington, Duke of, 95
Whiteboys, 15
Wilde, Lady, a contributor to the *Nation* newspaper, 121
Wilkes, John, his answer to a threat of Luttrell's, 59
William III., King, 3, 6; no excuse for, 8, 9; his camp at Exeter, 77
Williams, poetry of, in the *Nation*, 125
Wingfield, Hon. Lewis, his powerful novel, 'My Lords of Strogue,' 52, 53
Wolfe, Rev. Mr., nephew of Lord Kilwarden, tragic fate of, 72
Wolfe Tone. *See* Tone
Wolseley, Sir Garnet, proposal to confer the freedom of the city of Dublin on, 309; withdrawn owing to a current rumour, contradicted by Sir Garnet, 310
Wood's copper money, 20
Wordsworth quoted, 96
Woulfe, Stephen, phrase of his in Parliament chosen as a motto for the *Nation* newspaper, 120

YORK, Duke of, his ostentatious patronage of the Orange Society, 78; *in articulo mortis*, 79, 80
Young, Arthur, on the condition of the Irish peasantry, 14
Young Ireland, 101

ZULULAND, policy of the Government in, 324

www.ingramcontent.com/pod-product-compliance
Lightning Source LLC
Chambersburg PA
CBHW022333230426
43664CB00040B/447